THE

POLITICAL AND MISCELLANEOUS

WRITINGS

OF

WILLIAM G. GODDARD.

EDITED BY HIS SON,
FRANCIS W. GODDARD.

VOL. II.

PROVIDENCE:
SIDNEY S. RIDER AND BROTHER.
1870.

HAMMOND, ANGELL & CO., PRINTERS.

CONTENTS OF VOL. II.

POLITICAL WRITINGS.

COMMEMORATIVE DISCOURSE.

POLITICAL WRITINGS.

POLITICAL WRITINGS.

PROVIDENCE JOURNAL, OCTOBER 10, 1835.

JOHN QUINCY ADAMS AND HIS LETTER.

WITH somewhat of epigrammatic point, an English Poet characterizes the illustrious Lord Bacon as "the wisest, brightest, meanest of mankind." Whether or not the Poet has, in this instance, sacrificed truth to point, it is not my purpose to inquire. One thing is certain—such were his vices as a statesman and a man, that Bacon suddenly and irretrievably fell from an eminence in public favor which it has been the fortune of few men to reach. He sunk, at once and forever, below the horizon along which he had traced for himself a track resplendent with glory. And it is a singular fact in the history of great men, that, while the vices and the fall of Bacon have cast deep shadows upon his character, as a statesman, his labors in the cause of philosophy and of truth challenge for him, as a sage, the tribute of unmingled and exhaustless veneration. But I must not be tempted further by this high theme. My business is not with Francis Bacon, but with John Quincy Adams—not with the Lord High Chancellor of England, but with the Ex-President of the United States—not with the Prince of Modern Philosophers, but with the correspondent—the volunteer, the friendly, the sympathetic correspondent of Dutee J. Pearce! Let me, then, Messrs. Editors, betrayed neither by the love of striking contrasts, nor by the observations of imperfect analogies, descend from this region of melancholy grandeur, to survey those depths of political degradation towards which John Quincy Adams seems, almost instinctively, to gravitate.

In regard to the true character of Mr. Adams as a public man, I was, Messrs. Editors, long since disabused. His treacherous desertion of the old federal party, in the year 1807, convinced me that no faith was to be resposed in his honesty; and his late signal, and, for himself, most disastrous obliquity, was not wanting to satisfy me how unprincipled is his ambition, and how inveterate his hate. After all, as an American citizen, I have felt somewhat of honest pride in the widely extended fame of Mr. Adams. I saw in his character redeeming traits which served to temper my indignation at conduct which I could not persuade myself was either patriotic or honorable. Indeed, who of the present generation of men has witnessed a more extraordinary personage than this same John Quincy Adams? How it will task "the Muse of History" to present to coming times even a graphic outline of the various forms of individual character under which he has exhibited himself! Where is the modern statesman who ever displayed such startling contrasts in character and in conduct? At one time, he would seem to be governed by the sternest principles of Christian rectitude—at another, he abandons himself to the sway of selfishness and of passion. Now, he walks in fellowship with pure men, and firmly plants himself in the defence of great constitutional principles; now, apparently without doing any violence to his natural sympathies, he leagues with "trading politicians," consorts even with the lowest of the court pimps—and, as if he had parted not only with the dignity of virtue, but with the sense of shame, he stands before his fellow citizens in the attitude of a hoary and reckless calumniator. Look at him again. At one time, in the solitude of his closet, he elaborates, with tranquil enthusiasm, a Report upon Weights and Measures, which, indicated a familiarity with some of the most recondite principles of mathematics, and extorted the admiration of European Savans. At another time, to amuse his leisure, he perpetrates a Poem which, happily for the fame of its author, few have had the courage to read; or, to show the versatility of his powers, he gives, at a public dinner, a toast, which, without explanation, no one can understand. Look at him again. The representative of his country at one of the most splendid Courts in Europe, see him retire from all the solemn plausibilities of such a scene to his own unambitious residence, and there address himself to the delightful task of inditing letters to his son, replete with paternal sensibility, and with the gravest lessons of religious truth. See him again. He now sinks the Secretary in the demagogue. In violation of the established decorums of official life, he mounts the rostrum on a fourth of July, and lets off a coarse and offensive tirade upon monarchy, almost within the hearing of its accredited representatives. Nay more, trampling not only upon the dictates of Christian benevolence, but upon the immunities of afflicted humanity, in this memorable attempt to please "the democracy" he spared not the awful calamity under which the aged monarch of England was then suffering. The number of these strange contrasts might be multiplied. I might ask the public to note how he grappled with Russell and with Smythe, men of no ordinary prowess in the field of controversy —and how, of late, he has gratified his belligerent propensities by becoming the champion in a paltry parish quarrel, and brandishing his controversial battle-axe over the luckless head of the Rev. William M. Cornell! But I forbear. Enough has been said, to show that Mr. Adams is not only exceedingly eccentric, but somewhat polemical. Indeed, his powers are never so fully developed as in controversy, and he seems to care as little what may be the strength of his foes, as what may be the character of his friends.

When it was currently reported in our political circles, that Mr. Adams had written a letter to Dutee J. Pearce, congratulating him upon his re-election, and lavishing upon the Whigs of Rhode Island the foulest abuse, the gentlemen of all parties were incredulous. They could not believe that Mr. Adams, who had hitherto maintained an elevated political and social rank, would so far degrade himself as to tender to such a man and to such a politician as Dutee J. Pearce the language of cordial congratulation upon any occasion, least of all upon the result of an election adverse to the success of those very principles which for years Mr. Adams had striven to uphold. Still less could they believe that upon the Whigs of Rhode Island, who nobly sustained him, even amid the wreck of his fortunes, this false-hearted man would pour out the rancid bitterness of his nature. The publication of the letter, however, terminated every doubt. The elective affinities between him and Mr. Pearce, it would seem, are quite strong—and the felicitous ease and copiousness with which he uses the stereotyped slang of a prostituted press are no equivocal indications of the new political connexions which he is about to form.

The temper and the language of the letter are decisive as to the estimation in which Mr. Adams is hereafter to be held. Every where it has excited a burst of honest indignation which speaks well for the unperverted sensibilities of the American people. Every where do the uncorrupt men of all parties lament that Mr. Adams should have broken down so near the end of his course. It is impossible that he should recover himself. The jockeys may gather around him, to console and to cheer him. But the jockeys, though they have much to do with the race for political honors, have, thank God, no voice in deciding what shall be the grave moral estimates of the present times, or in determining the permanent judgments of posterity.

Mr. Adams, I grieve to think, can never regain that respect which, in the indulgence of his passions, he has thus recklessly forfeited. He has lived too long for his own glory. An old age of bitterness and of desertion awaits him. Notwithstanding all his faults of temper and all the obliquities of his past political life, he was fast acquiring many titles to a species of prescriptive veneration. He might have enrolled his name high among those of the chiefs who flourished in the best days of the republic. As it is, however, I greatly mistake, if he does not pass off the stage of life, leaving the world to lament that the influence of his extraordinary powers was neutralized by the profligacy of his ambition and the misdirected energy of his passions.

A Rhode Island Whig.

PROVIDENCE JOURNAL, OCTOBER 15, 1835.

JOHN QUINCY ADAMS AND HIS LETTER.

I have not quite done with the Ex-President, and his last most exquisite manifestation of demagogism, treachery and meanness. He is indeed a moral phenomenon. So eccentric an orbit does he describe, and such opposite phases does he exhibit, that it would be no less difficult to paint him, as he really is, than to transfer to canvas the "goings of the serpent" and the shifting hues of the chameleon. Had he more honesty and less genius, he would present to observation a more simple and consistent character. He would be betrayed less frequently into incongruities which shock all notions of propriety, and he would sink less easily into vices which offend all sense of honor. The original elements of his moral and intellectual character were not happily mixed. A life of disastrous mistake and of transcendent meanness, has been the consequence. I admit that he has filled commanding stations in the republic—and that, in the main, he has filled them well. I cheerfully concede to him the praise of various learning—of indefatigable industry, and of extensive familiarity with public affairs—nay more, I rejoice to add my conviction of his unstained purity in the relations of domestic life. But, if it be asked, by what means he has acquired office, and to what purposes he has often devoted his industry and his learning, the answer, if impartial, would be most unwelcome. After all, have not his talents been overrated? Has not his success in life been assumed as the infallible test of his powers? In his case, has not fawning, rather than merit, been rewarded with thrift? Is he not lamentably deficient in that delicacy of tact, in that practical sagacity, and in that philosophical spirit, without which a statesman is unable to form well matured conclusions, or to pursue a wise policy? Can he, either in moral or in intellectual accomplishment, challenge a comparison with the political chiefs who maintained an undisputed ascendency in the best days of the Republic? The severe analysis and cogent argumentation of Madison—the unadulterated wisdom and chaste honor of Jay—the prophetic sagacity and prodigal splendor of Ames—the marvellous accuracy and comprehension of Hamilton! Does Mr. Adams possess any attributes which his parasites will venture to place in competition with these?

I have no disposition to disparage Mr. Adams's just claims to distinction; but, consistently with any veneration for the truth of history, I cannot join the tribe of his venal parasites in their efforts to exalt his name.

As a Rhetorician, I am not aware, that Mr. Adams's friends claim for him high renown. And yet, I know of none of his productions, which, upon the whole, are more creditable to him than the Lectures which he delivered within the walls of Harvard. While courting the muses, he seemed to have put aside his gladiatorial weapons, and to have given less free vent to the hoarded acrimony of his temper. His taste, after all, though less faulty than his temper, was never chastised by the models which it was his business to contemplate. As a writer, he is well supplied both with vigor and with venom; but in his pages we look in vain for the beautifully severe grace of the Grecian schools. We may find there the pomp and affluence of Asiatic ornament, but we do not find the simple grandeur and the chastened splendors of the Athenian intellect. Mr. Adams, without doubt, is rich in the spoils of ancient learning; but his taste has been imperfectly refined by his intercourse with the forms of classical beauty.

As a polemical writer, I acknowledge Mr. Adams to be without a rival. In this department of intellectual effort, he derives much aid from the counsels of selfishness and the impulses of passion. Like a skillful pugilist, he is animated by the shouts of the ring—or, to borrow a more classical comparison, like an ambitious gladiator, he gathers strength from the applauses of the amphitheatre. Never does he put forth such elephantine vigor, as when he seeks to trample an assailant in the dust—never is his genius more lively, than when his bad passions are stimulated—never is his imagination more prolific, than when he hunts its chambers of imagery, for a barbed metaphor—never is he so ardent as when he seeks to betray the people, in order to benefit himself!

A few words of the letter, Mr. Editor, and I have done. Mr. Adams abuses Mr. Burges, and compliments Mr. Sprague. The former may well be trusted with his own defence. Upon the latter I can waste no words. He is now honorable by courtesy. To use the language of Mr. Adams, "the people have repaired the injustice done by the Whig party to Mr. Sprague." With a generous ardor in behalf of neglected genius and persecuted patriotism, they have pursued him into his seclusion, taken him by the hand, and "led the blushing stranger into day!" What Representative ever had such constituents, and what constituents ever had such a Representative?

Several years since, Mr. Adams, while President of the United States, was feasted at Newport. Upon that occasion, in a most beautiful toast which, unlike that of "Ebony and Topaz" memory, every body could understand without a commentary, he complimented Rhode Island upon "the loftiness of her spirit." He was probably sincere then, for it was then his interest to be sincere. Let me tell him, that although Rhode Island has ceased to value the compliment, she is still true to the attribute. In the midst of a crooked generation, she still loves an erect and manly spirit—and while great men, the have-beens and the would-bes—are sinking in the mire of political prostitution—faithful to her ensign, she still "hopes in God"—trusting that in the order of His Providence, both good and bad men will ultimately find their level.

I mourn, Mr. Editor, over the fall of Mr. Adams. It would be a consolation to ascribe it to transient hallucination, or to an accidental explosion of his temper. But no such apology can be pleaded for him. I repeat it—it is impossible that he should restore himself to the respect and confidence of his fellow citizens. He has acted the part of an arch demagogue and most treacherous politician. He will die with the brand upon his forehead. His parasites, who pour into his ear their "leprous distillment," may talk as much and as loudly as they will of his merits—they may hail him as "the sage of Quincy"—but, Mr. Editor, not all their venal clamor can drown the voice ot his conscience—not all the shades of Quincy can hide from public scorn the inexpiable meanness of his conduct. To treachery he adds hypocrisy—for, while he prates of "sound principles and good morals," he signs himself, "with great regard, the friend and servant" of Dutee J. Pearce!

Ample justice will ultimately be done to the fame and character of John Quincy Adams. Upon this conviction, the Whigs of Rhode Island quietly repose. But can he anticipate, without emotion, the unfaltering record of History? Can he await, with an untroubled spirit, the impartial retributions of all succeeding time?

A Rhode Island Whig.

PROVIDENCE JOURNAL, APRIL 9, 1835

TO THE PEOPLE OF RHODE ISLAND.

Fellow Citizens:—Those who "lack preferment" sometimes attempt to soothe you by flattery or to beguile you by artifice. Will you listen, with candor, to the voice of a plain man, who has no interest in deceiving you—who has nearly travelled his course, without either seeking or receiving a solitary favor at your hands; and who now addresses you, because he feels that the great bulwarks of Popular Freedom are in peril? If the abuses and usurpations of power, which have marked the course of President Jackson's Administration do not find a corrective and a rebuke in the ballot box—if Mr. Van Buren and his organized corps of satellites are to carry out into more ample detail the current notions of Executive Power and Executive Responsibility—our Government, fellow citizens, will soon become "a machine" sufficiently "simple" for one man to conduct, without direction or control—in a word, the Constitution will be subverted, and a Monarchy, retaining the form, but not the spirit of a Republic, will overshadow this fair land. To this disastrous issue, affairs at Washington seem to be rapidly tending. There is yet hope, however, that it may be averted, and that, under the auspices of wise and upright men, the Constitution may be restored to somewhat of its original purity, and our Republican Institutions be rescued from the destruction with which they are threatened. Unless, however, the people, and by the people, I mean the thinking men of all parties, who want neither offices nor honors for themselves or their friends, and who ask only that they may repose under the shadow of the Constitution and the Laws, I repeat it, unless the people, such as I have described them to be, come to the rescue—all is lost. Your children and mine will lose the proud distinction of being Republican Freemen—and will become the unhappy subjects of a Monarchy, without balance, check or limitation! What, let me ask you, fellow citizens of Rhode Island, is your duty in a crisis like the present? If this be the issue which the people of the United States are to try, "what manner of men ought you to be," when you come to cast your votes for General Officers?

Keep in mind, fellow citizens, what is the issue which you are to try, at the approaching Election. It is, not so much whether John Brown Francis or Nehemiah R. Knight shall be your Governor, for the next political year. This is, in itself, a very subordinate question—and in ordinary times, every freeman might safely indulge his personal preference. I know and respect both of these gentlemen.

* * * * * * * *

It is in your power, by your votes on the 15th instant, to send to the American Senate, not only a gentleman, but an independent and fearless champion of the Constitution and the Laws. Elect a Van Buren Senator, and Rhode Island will soon become a mere province of the Empire State—into which will be introduced the abominably corrupt system of politics which threatens to make that State the great political cancer of the Republic. Let us, fellow citizens, beware how we thus commit suicide. For "the lowliness of her stature," Rhode Island will have no reason to blush, while she preserves "the loftiness of her spirit." Our territory we cannot enlarge—our numbers we cannot hope to swell greatly beyond their present amount—but we shall be false to ourselves and to our children, if we part with our erect and manly spirit—if we suffer the General Government to bribe us into a toleration of its encroachments—if we permit any noisy and unprincipled demagogue to betray and to disgrace us.

* * * * * * * *

Have you seen the Hon. Dutee J. Pearce's Letter to William Simons, Esq., the Editor of the *Republican Herald?* If you have not, obtain a sight of it, I beseech you, without delay; read it, again and again;

* * * * * * * *

Believing that there is truth in a familiar adage, I am always pleased to catch our Van Buren Representative in "black and white!" I wish to curtail none of his fair proportions—I wish to extenuate nothing, or to set down aught in malice. I will therefore give you his exact words, and his whole doctrine:—

"I now state, that so far as I can be instrumental in effecting it, every man in this State who holds an office under the State authorities, or those of the General Government, shall support the Administration which sustains them—this, in my opinion, all ought to do; this I have no doubt all will do, and none but a recreant traitor would hold an office under any Administration which he could not in conscience support. Support those who support you; this is my doctrine."

On this occasion, Mr. Pearce, I give you my confidence, believing that you are at least sincere. I believe that this is your doctrine—for I know it to be the doctrine of the kitchen (where "bread and butter" are wont to be spread) because I know that a similar doctrine was proclaimed, and, without a blush too! in the United States Senate, by Governor Marcy—because I know it is the doctrine upon which Martin Van Buren and his satellites avowedly act—and because, in short, it is the doctrine by which every needy and unprincipled demagogue in the country hopes to obtain possession of the "spoils." I thank you, Mr. Pearce, for the unwonted frankness of your declarations—but I greatly mistake, if you have not, even in this instance, proved too "leaky" for yourself and for your friends. Whenever I have to do with a Van Buren man, whether he be a Representative in Congress, a partisan Judge, a tide waiter, or, to descend to the root of the tail, a pitiful, office-hunting Anti-Mason, I am prepared for any thing but what is erect, open, manly—honest—I expect sinuosity—craft—paltry devices—I look for the instincts of a reptile—for the "goings" if not the venom "of the serpent." In this instance, however, Mr. Pearce's passions would seem to have got the better of his cunning. He is not true to the teachings of the Van Buren school—there is "no non-committal" policy here—there is "no joke" here!

What think you, fellow citizens, of Mr. Pearce's doctrine? Are you prepared to adopt it? If you are, let me tell you, boldly, you are prepared to become slaves! Will you submit to be told that every office holder, whether under the United States or State Government, shall support the Administration which sustains him? In the days of Washington, of Jefferson and of Madison, no man who was not demented, would have dared to promulgate such a doctrine. But the golden age of the Republic has been succeeded by a brazen age, when politicians do not care even to be thought honest, much less to be honest—when men, who once walked abroad in the freedom of independent thought and unfettered conscience, will now bend their necks to receive the collar, and suffer them to grow callous under the ignoble pressure.

How does Mr. Pearce's doctrine agree with the old-fashioned republican doctrine? How does it agree even with President Jackson's doctrine? In his Inaugural Message, he declared that "the public patronage ought not to be brought into conflict with the freedom of elections." This is the true doctrine. How far the President has exemplified it in practice, I leave you, fellow citizens, to decide. Mr. Pearce surely will not dispute Mr. Jefferson's claim to be considered the founder of the Republican party, and the ablest expositor of the principles of that party. And what says Mr. Jefferson, with reference to the interference of United States officers in popular elections? His sentiments on this subject, which are embodied in a Circular addressed to the subordinate officers of the United States Government, cannot be too often quoted. They are as follows:—

"The President of the United States has seen with dissatisfaction, officers of the General Government, taking, on various occasions, active parts in the elections of the public functionaries, whether of the General, or of State Governments. Freedom of election being essential to the mutual independence of Governments, and of the different branches of the same Government, so vitally cherished by most of our Constitutions, it is deemed improper for officers depending on the Executive of the Union, to attempt to control or influence, the free exercise of the elective right.

"This I am, therefore, instructed to notify to all officers within any department holding their appointment under the authority of the President, and to desire them to notify to all subordinate to them. The right of any officer to give his vote at elections, as a qualified citizen, is not meant to be restrained, nor, however given, shall it have effect to his prejudice; but it is expected that he will not attempt to influence the votes of others, nor to take any part in the business of electioneering,—that being deemed inconsistent with the spirit of the Constitution, and his duties to it."

The total and irreconcilable difference of opinion between Mr. Jefferson and Mr. Pearce, in this matter, is too obvious to require remark. Upon whose sleeve, republicans of Rhode Island, would you prefer to pin your political faith, upon Thomas Jefferson's or upon Dutee J. Pearce's? Upon the sleeve of him, who never turned his coat—or upon that of him who has both turned his coat and put it on wrong end foremost?

If Mr. Pearce's doctrine be the true one, what

become of the old-fashioned republican notions, that all offices are created for the benefit of the people—that they belong to the people—and that they are never to be perverted by the Government, in any way, to the injury of the people? Is that noble test—"is he honest—is he capable—is he faithful to the Constitution"—to be exchanged for a test, which would compel American citizens to part with the right of private judgment—to prove recreant to their consciences—to give up to party all that constitutes their proudest distinction not only as citizens, but as men? It is no longer deemed wise for the people to keep an eye upon the conduct of their rulers? Is perpetual vigilance no longer to be considered the price of freedom?

I have not yet done, fellow citizens, with Mr. Pearce's letter—but I am admonished not to extend my remarks, at the risk of exhausting your patience. Allow me, however, to say, before I close, one word to those who are so unfortunate as to be office holders at the present time. What think you, my fellow citizens, of Mr. Pearce's doctrine? Do you subscribe to it? Are you willing to submit to the test? Is there one among you who has an enlightened conscience and an independent intellect, who does not look with noble disdain upon this attempt to compel you to violate the injunctions of that conscience which God has been pleased to enlighten, and to trample upon the decisions of that intellect which He hath implanted within you? Again, I ask, is there one among you with the heart of a man beating in his bosom, who does not rise up in indignation at this infamous attempt to make him a slave?

* * * * * * * *

The honors of paternity cannot, however, in justice, be assigned to Mr. Pearce. He must be content with the humbler praise of being a faithful and affectionate dry nurse. Of this doctrine, Mr. Van Buren is the real father. For years, he has brought it to bear, with a most victorious energy, upon every department of political life in the State of New York. The consequences are such as might have been foreseen. The noble capacities of that noble State, are shamefully perverted. Men of property, and talent, and integrity, are driven into seclusion, and, with here and there an exception, men of desperate fortunes, of incompetent abilities and of profligate principles, occupy the high places once graced by the Jays, the Clintons, the Livingstons, the Lansings and the Kents. In her mighty metropolis, there prevails among the mob which governs it, a spirit of ferocity and of wild misrule which threatens, at no distant day, a repetition of the sanguinary atrocities of jacobin France.

To Mr. Van Buren also may be assigned the credit of introducing this doctrine into the politics of the General Government. On all sides, may be witnessed the evidence of its pestilent and potent sway. Connecticut, moral and enlightened as she has been reputed to be, has been unable to resist it. The standing army of office holders was too well disciplined and too intent on the "spoils," to be overcome by independent freemen who went into the battle, in the serene might of a righteous cause. Of all the New England States, Massachusetts and Vermont, alone, have escaped the contagion. They still tower in the pride of their original integrity—"among the faithless, faithful only they." Long may they be able to resist every effort to tear them down "from their pride of place."

Rhode Island, fellow citizens, is under the operation of this Van Buren poison. She is not, however, like New Hampshire, past all hope of cure. The poison has not yet reached her vitals—and it is not too late for you to administer an effectual antidote. Be not blind, I beseech you, to your danger. If, at every election, you are obliged to contend against a formidable and disciplined corps of office holders, who, that they may make a vigorous onset, are pulled by the collar and pricked in the flanks, by their drivers—your elective franchise will become a solemn mockery; you may retain the forms of freedom, but its spirit will have fled forever. All offices belong to the people—and any doctrine which goes to convert them into engines for corrupting or oppressing the people, goes to convert this republic into the worst species of monarchy,—a monarchy, without check, balance, or limitation. I exhort you, my fellow citizens, in the midst of this wide-spread corruption, to hold fast your integrity. Spurn the proffered bribes of the Van Buren emissaries, whether these bribes be coarse or delicate—be not intimidated by menace—quail not at angry denunciation—and concede no right even to open violence!

I do not despair of the republic. I am not without hope that the thinking men of the Jackson party will become alarmed at the tempest which they have invoked, before it is too late to allay its fury. I am not without hope, that such men as James Fenner and John Brown Francis, who delight in cultivating their patrimonial acres and in sitting under the shade of their patrimonial trees, will be aroused to a consideration of the public danger. If the war cry is to be raised against those who by their industry have acquired property, or who have had the felicity to inherit it, believe me, fellow citizens, those who raise the cry and hope to profit from it, will not be very discriminating in the selection of their victims or in the choice of their plunder. When this tug of war comes, and come it will, if Mr. Pearce's doctrines are to prevail, Farmer Francis with his "one thousand acres" will fare no better at the hands of the mob, than Farmer Knight with his "thirty-acre lot." The property of the humblest landholder or mechanic in the State, will be in peril—when the storm of revolution, which is now heard in the distance, shall break upon the land. Not only will this storm make a wreck of all the institutions of society—not only will it prostrate all the defences of property and of freedom—but it will end in a Baptism of Blood! It is not alone "the ruffle-shirt gentry," against whom the *Republican Herald*, with jacobin malignity, is wont to stimulate your prejudices—who, in such a fearful crisis, would be suspended from the lantern-post or expiate upon the scaffold the crime of being rich! No, indeed, all orders of society who have either property or character to lose, and none more than what is termed "the middling interest," would be exposed to the vengeance of the mob.

And who would profit from this wild commotion of the elements? I will tell you, fellow citizens, the no-shirt gentry, and the dirty-shirt gentry—men who are too lazy and too profligate to sustain themselves by honest labor—men who would level to the dust all the established institutions of society—who would check the progress of the human race in the arts of civilization, and who, in the blindness of their fury, would fain banish the Deity himself from the Universe which he hath created. These, fellow citizens, are not the dreams of a morbid visionary. They are the sober lessons of history—they are the genuine sentiments of every reflecting American citizen, who allows himself to survey the prospect before us. I repeat it, however, I do not despair of the republic. The North, save one bright spot, is mantled in gloom. But light beams from the South. Virginia, consistent Virginia, is still true to her first love—she still maintains her integrity. Let us, my fellow citizens, one and all, go to the polls, on Wednesday next, and put forth all our strength for the complete regeneration of Rhode Island. Let us do our duty as becometh freemen—and, in no event, shall we lose our reward. If we succeed, and unless we suffer the ministers of corruption to drug us with their opiates, we certainly shall succeed—glorious will be the fruits of victory. If we fail, we shall still have in reserve the proud consolation, of which the chivalric Francis I. availed himself, after his defeat at Pavia—"all is lost, but honor!"

A Rhode Island Man.

PROVIDENCE COURIER, JANUARY 24, 1838.

STATE POLITICS.

NO. I.

To the People of Rhode Island:—

A Whig Convention has nominated the Hon. William Sprague as a candidate for the office of Governor of Rhode Island. This nomination may bind the consciences of the Convention; it remains, however, to be seen whether it will obtain the sanction of the people. The collar men, for alas! there are collar men in more parties than one, will feel themselves obliged to vote for Mr. Sprague, however opposed they may be to his election. But I greatly mistake, if there be not found a large number of independent freemen who will withhold their suffrages from a candidate who presents so very equivocal claims to their support. One of your number, fellow citizens, who has no interest in deceiving you, begs leave to offer to your candid consideration sundry reasons why Mr. Sprague should not be our Governor. With his private character I have no concern; I have never heard that it is other than respectable—and his deserts as a politician are so very humble that I could not have the heart to detract from his merits as a man. It is with his political character only that I wish to deal, and that I shall not hesitate to discuss, with all the freedom which the importance of the occasion demands, and with that candor which, in judging of an opponent, we should be specially careful to exercise.

A French philosopher, D'Alembert I think it was, once remarked, that the apex of the social pyramid is reached only by eagles and by reptiles—the one, in his imperial flight, seizing upon the proud eminence—the other, creeping up to it! This remark of the French philosopher illustrates two distinct classes of character. To which of them the Hon. William Sprague belongs, it is perhaps unnecessary to intimate. His tortuous course, as a public man, is far more aptly illustrated by the "goings of the serpent," amid the dirt to which the primeval curse has doomed him than by the fearless range of the bird of Jove amid the depths of æther. In plain language, Mr. Sprague is to be deemed rather as a man of temporary and ingenious expedients than of fixed and elevated principle—rather as a politician of a secondary order, who is not fastidious about the means of gratifying his ambition, than as a Statesman of large capacities and generous purposes, who is embarked in defence of well defined principles, and resolved, come what may, to stand upon them to the last.

What opinion of his fitness for the commanding station of Chief Magistrate of Rhode Island, does Mr. Sprague's whole political course oblige his fellow citizens to entertain? He entered the General Assembly, an anti-mason, I believe—for, in describing the hues of the chameleon, it is wise not to deal in confident assertion. At all events, he soon made himself conspicuous as the leader in the House of Representatives of the anti-masonic party—and, in and out of the House, as one of the fiercest assailants of the masonic fraternity. I am no mason—I have no sympathy for masons, as such,—I have no partiality for the principles and the rites of their order. But, even to this day, my Rhode Island blood boils in my veins, when I revert to the crusade which was preached up against them, here and elsewhere, by apostles of agitation, and by aspirants for office,—by knaves who practised upon the simplicity of dupes—by little men who saw that their only chance to become great ones, was to fan the flame of social discord, and to unfurl the banner of a distinct and organized party.

How the experiment succeeded is now a matter of history. In Rhode Island, Mr. Sprague and his adherents, powerful neither in numbers nor in character, soon came to hold the balance of power. Through their instrumentality, the election of Governor Arnold was defeated; and had it not been for the exercise of a conservative power by the General Assembly, the State would have been left without any Government. To the same sort of instrumentality is to be ascribed the election of Mr. Francis in opposition to Governor Arnold, and the defeat of General Greene, when a candidate for the office of United States Senator, in opposition to Mr. Potter. Strange titles these to the approbation and support of the Rhode Island Whigs!

The Jackson and the Anti-Masonic parties ultimately coalesced; though ostensibly their action was independent. The leading anti-masons were hungry for office, and those with whom they had leagued dared not withhold whatever was demanded. These soldiers of fortune were, in most cases, well provided for—and the Jackson party, the most numerous and far the best principled, were obliged virtually to succumb to the allies by whose aid they had conquered.

This was the case in Rhode Island. Other States may furnish some parallel. In Massachusetts, I have reason to know, that one of Mr. Sprague's coadjutors in the blessed work of prostrating Free Masonry, the Rev. Moses Thacher, was elected to the Massachusetts Senate, in consequence of his disinterested zeal in the good cause. Of late, he has rendered himself worthy of a different kind of elevation! I allude to him, in connexion with Mr. Sprague, to show what sort of men are concerned in organizing third parties—and that however loud may be their profession of principle, self-aggrandizement is their fixed and unceasing aim. Every man who values the quiet of the State ought to vote against Mr. Sprague, for this, if for no other reason, that he got up and that he kept up a third party, for the purpose of securing to himself and his friends a measure of influence to which he and they had no just claim. For one, I would rather hazard the ascendency of Whig principles in Rhode Island, than reward with the highest office in the gift of the people, a man who can plead no better title to their favor than a series of factious and selfish movements. Much should I prefer the re-election of Governor Francis, who, whatever may be his political sins, is always moderate, and sometimes magnanimous.

A few words more, fellow citizens, and I have done for the present. I have alluded to the Masons of

Rhode Island. Do you not share in my indignation at the treatment which they have received? Have they not been virtually disfranchised? A few years ago, when Mr. Sprague's party was in full blast, what mason could be proposed as a candidate for any office of emolument or of honor? So stern was the sentence of proscription, that some of our best citizens were banished from the counsels of the State, merely because they would not renounce an order to which they were attached by many endearing ties and consecrated associations. I felt then, and I feel now, that they were persecuted men, in a land which boasts its exemption from the spirit of persecution. I felt then, and I feel now, that the great principles of personal and social freedom were outraged in their persons—that they were trampled upon by men whom they would not have "set with the dogs of their flock!" This unmanly and bitter persecution has ceased, I trust never to be renewed. But one of the aiders and abettors of this persecution, a man who mounted the ladder of ambition amid the incense of an unholy sacrifice, now wants to be your Governor. Give him, my fellow citizens, a practical illustration that you at least will not prove recreant to your principles.

A PROVIDENCE MAN.

PROVIDENCE COURIER, JANUARY 26, 1838.

STATE POLITICS.

NO. II.

TO THE PEOPLE OF RHODE ISLAND:—

I allege nothing, my fellow citizens, in disparagement of the private character of the Hon. William Sprague. Relying on the testimony of those who know him familiarly, I am happy to believe that, in the relations of domestic and of social life, he is not without strong claims to confidence and respect. He is said, moreover, to be wealthy, enterprising, and industrious;—sagacious in the transactions of business, and friendly to the great interests of Rhode Island. All this may be true, and I am not disposed to raise any question in the premises; but it does not satisfy my mind, and I cannot think it will satisfy yours, that Mr. Sprague is, therefore, fit to be your Governor. Recollect, fellow citizens, that wealth is a very doubtful test of a man's capacity to preside with wisdom, and dignity, and success, over the concerns of a political commonwealth;—that the shrewdness which is acquired by the collisions of pecuniary interest is far remote from the far reaching sagacity of the statesman; in fine, that the habits of thought and of action, which fasten themselves upon a man amid the ceaseless din of a cotton factory, are not precisely those which enable him to guide, with discretion, the counsels of a state. Are there not hundreds of men to be found in the Whig ranks, in whose favor, similar if not stronger reasons might be urged—men, moreover, who, through all the changes of the fight, have stood firm in the ranks—and who never deserted to the enemy, when victory was about to perch upon his banner?

Mr. Sprague was, for several years, a member of the legislature of Rhode Island. As a legislator, what service did he render to the State—what evidence of talent or of high moral purpose, did he give? By the aid of Jackson votes, he was elected Speaker of the House in opposition to Mr. Tillinghast; and, as the champion if not the chief of the anti-masonic party, he distracted the counsels of the State, and helped to scatter, far and wide, the seeds of personal and social animosity. If he was conspicuous for any thing else, let his supporters show the fact, and I will cheerfully admit it. The course of action which Mr. Sprague, as a politician, has pursued, under circumstances too, attaching some suspicion to his motives, indicates, in my view, none of those qualities of mind or those tempers of heart which ought to be found in the Chief Magistrate of Rhode Island.

I cannot pretend, fellow citizens, to describe, with accuracy, or with much regard to connexion, Mr. Sprague's political course. He must have a keener and a steadier eye than I have, who can follow the movements of a snake in the grass—who, with a new skin upon his back, is either darting towards his prey, or, with instinctive sagacity, is escaping from the bruise which menaces his head. In process of time, Mr. Sprague was dyed a Jackson man. As the result has proved, he was not dyed in the wool, nor was he dipped in a very fast color! He was nominated and elected to Congress by the Jackson party, in opposition to the Hon. Tristam Burges, once the idol—the magnus Apollo—of a large majority of the Rhode Island Whigs. Whether Mr. Sprague succeeded by the force of unaided talent, or by means of skillful party tactics, I leave you, fellow citizens, to decide. When he reached Washington he soon found, as all such men under similar circumstances must find, that it is one thing to be a manœuvring demagogue in the General Assembly of Rhode Island, and quite another thing to be an accomplished statesman in the halls of Congress. May those who, with pretensions equally humble, are now courting, at any sacrifice, a similar distinction, take warning from the fate upon which Mr. Sprague precipitated himself. In his praise, however, it ought to be admitted that he had the wisdom to be silent, and that he burst his collar when he found that the measures of the administration threatened to lighten his pocket.

Nearly up to the time of the last August Election, Mr. Sprague was deemed by all parties to be a Van Buren man. As such, he was again nominated a candidate for Congress, in connexion with Mr. Pearce. It is even said that this nomination was pressed upon him by the Van Buren party, after they knew that he was opposed to them upon very important questions of public policy. All this I fully believe; they were in straits for an available candidate, they knew their man—they knew that if they could put the right brand upon him, he would pass inspection—that ultimately, when the conscience of his pocket should have become somewhat less sensitive, he could be re-dipped in a good strong Van Buren dye, which would make his new coat appear just like the old one.

Seeing, however, that the tide was turning, Mr Sprague determined to come out as a Whig, and as such to support the Whig candidates for Congress. Mr. Sprague's conversion was sudden, and is therefore exposed to the suspicion which never fails to attach to all sudden conversions. For one, in view of his course as a public man, I cannot feel much confidence in the stability of any political opinions which he may from time to time chance to entertain, and still less confidence can I feel in the permanent triumphs of any political party who may court his alliance. I shall vote for the Whig candidates for Lieutenant Governor and Senators, unless a more acceptable ticket should be offered to my choice, because I am friendly to those principles of public policy which the great Whig party throughout the Union are endeavoring to re-establish.

Thus far, fellow citizens, I ask you to go with me—and if you think of Mr. Sprague as I do, go with me a step farther—withhold, from him your suffrages, at least till the gristle of his Whig principles has hardened into bone. Hereafter, he may establish some claim to your confidence. At present it would seem wise to distrust him. Act independently in this matter, fellow citizens, and be not alarmed for the result. Despise menace, and heed not the voice of melancholy vaticination. All will come out right in the end—if you only stand on your principles rather than by your men;—if in fine you do not suffer Mr. Sprague and his party to conjure up apparitions to fright you from an honest purpose.

A PROVIDENCE MAN.

PROVIDENCE COURIER, JANUARY 30, 1838.

STATE POLITICS.

NO. III.

TO THE PEOPLE OF RHODE ISLAND:—

WHEN I commenced these numbers, fellow citizens, I expected to encounter misrepresentations and abuse. In this expectation, I have not been disappointed. Before the sheet which contained my first number was fairly dry, sundry grave offences were laid to my charge. I was accused of calumniating the Hon. William Sprague and the whole anti-masonic party; of indicating an unqualified opposition to all third parties; and worse than all, of betraying the spirit of aristocracy. In order to sustain these charges, my words have not only been severed from their original connexion, but they have been perverted, by a jesuitical commentary, from their true and obvious meaning. My accuser has not only tortured my language to answer his puposes; but, in violation of every principle of honorable controversy, he has ascribed to me language which I have never used! I have had too much knowledge of hackney politicians, to be at all surprised that in this matter, I should be met by what Lord Bacon calls the expedients of "a crooked wisdom;" and I have had too much experience of life, to suffer such annoyances to disturb my repose. With men, whose moral instincts have become depraved by a sordid and exclusive devotion to politics, I do not care to find favor. They need not expect, however, to tempt me aside from my main object to the discussion of irrelevant and unimportant points. I shall make with them no extraneous and subordinate issue.

Postponing, for the present, all further examination of the qualifications of the Hon. William Sprague, as a candidate for the office of Governor, I invite your attention, fellow citizens, to a topic connected with the organization of the late Whig Convention.

The Convention, it is said, was unusually "numerous," and, for aught I know to the contrary, it may have been unusually weighty. One thing is evident—the moral power of all such Conventions—or in other words, their influence over the minds of the people, depends, not only upon the character of the individuals who compose them, but upon the fact that these individuals owe the trust confided to them to the free and unbiassed choice of large and intelligent masses. I do not say that, in this respect, the late Convention is obnoxious to very serious objection. The manner in which the delegates from this city were elected, may however be thought to deserve some animadversion, inasmuch as it may be deemed a significant commentary upon a system of management which has disgusted no inconsiderable number of the Whig party in this city, and which, if not abandoned, will ultimately repel them from the connexion, and drive some of them perchance into the ranks of the adversary. The facts of the case, so far as I have been able to ascertain them, for it was never thought worth while to publish them in the newspapers, are briefly these.

A meeting was held in the Town House, at an unusual hour in the evening, for the purpose of electing Delegates to the Whig Convention. Out of more than one thousand Whig freemen, only nine, it is said, were present! Mr. * * was appointed Chairman of the meeting. According to the modest and truly republican usage, which seems to be adopted by the Whig managers in this city, some gentleman pulls from his breeches pocket, and, with all imaginable gravity, presents to the Chairman, a list containing the names of eight gentlemen who are thus nominated to take care of the interests of the party in the approaching Convention. The Chairman looks at the list; now pauses, with affected surprise, over this name and over that; and now startles, with a mixture of surprise and modesty, to behold his own! Recovering, however, his self-possession, he puts the question, and with united voice the breeches pocket nominees are elected! The meeting is then dissolved, and the nine patriots retire to their homes, with the proud consciousness that they have rendered to the city a most disinterested service. I do not assert that the late farce went off exactly after this fashion—but my description will not, it is believed, vary substantially from the truth. To resume, however, what, after all, is intended to be a sober discussion and a plain statement of facts. At the late primary meeting in this city, our four Representatives, and Messrs. James G. Anthony, William R. Watson, George W. Jackson, and Martin Robinson were elected Delegates to the Whig Convention. Whether all of these gentlemen are entitled to the distinction of being selected from the one thousand Whig voters, for the purpose of exercising a most responsible political function, I leave you my fellow citizens of Providence, to determine for yourselves.

I have introduced this local topic into a discussion upon State politics, because I believe that Whig management in this city, will endanger, at no distant day, the ascendency of the Whig party in Rhode Island. It is notorious that the great body of the intelligent and substantial men of that party, in this city, men who neither hold office nor want office—are as much strangers to its counsels, as if they were deemed traitors to its principles. Indeed, it would not be too much to say, that all influences, except those of a certain sort, are systematically excluded. Understand me, fellow citizens, I claim for wealth, and talent, and moral character, no extraordinary distinctions—no exclusive privileges. I contend only for equal rights—for the principle that no man ought to be virtually disfranchised, because he happens to have more wealth, or more principle, or more brains than his neighbor. I go against all oppressive monopolies. I go for the true republican doctrine that, in this country, the Constitution and the laws recognize no distinctions—that, as citizens, the rich and the poor—the learned and the unlearned—the intelligent and the dull, are and ought to be upon terms of the most perfect equality.

I desire, fellow citizens, to see a different state of things in this city. I desire to behold, in our Whig primary assemblies, the merchant, who, by a course of honest industry, has come to own a stake in the community, be that stake great or small; the lawyer, whose studies have familiarized and endeared to his mind the great principles of constitutional freedom and popular right; the intelligent and unobtrusive mechanic who contributes so largely to the prosperity and to the moral power of the city; and the manufacturer whose business is so closely indentified with the wealth and the population of the whole State. Why are not such men as I have described found in our Whig assemblies? It is because they are not welcome there!

Is it not time, my Whig fellow citizens of Providence, that there was a reform in this matter? I invoke your aid for that purpose. I exhort you to devote more of your time to the politics of the State and city, and to watch with increased jealousy the movements of selfish politicians. Attend, habitually, our ward and other primary meetings. Suffer yourselves neither to be brushed aside, nor to be elbowed out of your place, by a few noisy and obtrusive men. Believe me, they can be made to surrender their usurped control. Apply, in the first place, the "searching operation" to your city government. Reform, as soon as may be, and as much as need be, your Common Council. Next, take care that you select, with a wise deliberation, your Representatives in the General Assembly; and see that they always be men who will never balance between principle and popularity; and who can have no temptation to sacrifice your interests to promote their own. If you make a vigorous and timely effort to correct the abuses which have crept into the management of the Whig party in this city, you may preserve the integrity of that party, and consolidate its strength. Thus will you do good service to yourselves, to Rhode Island, and to the whole country. If, on the other hand, you leave things as they now are, depend upon it, the Whig party in Providence and, by almost inevitable consequence, the Whig party in Rhode Island, will, ere long find themselves in a hopeless minority. For one, I should rejoice to avert this catastrophe. I have therefore, spoken to you with great plainness of speech. I have probed the wound deeply—because I saw no other means of effecting a cure. I have sounded the alarm. It is for you to come to the rescue.

A PROVIDENCE MAN.

P. S. Since writing the above, I have learnt that no meeting was held at the Town House; but that a few of the faithful assembled in what is called the Committee Room, (those who wish to know where that is may inquire at the Journal Office) and elected the delegates to the Convention! These eight delegates have recommended to their fellow citizens of Providence, a Prox which gives to this city, with nearly one fifth of the population of the whole State, neither the Governor, nor the Lieutenant Governor, nor a single Senator! In one branch of the Legislature, Providence has only four Representatives—in the other, according to present arrangements, she is to have none!

PROVIDENCE COURIER, FEBRUARY 13, 1838.

STATE POLITICS.

NO. IV.

To the People of Rhode Island:—

The Whig Convention, it seems, has nominated a candidate for the office of General Treasurer, in opposition to Mr. Sterne, the present incumbent. I am not alone, fellow citizens, in regretting this movement, nor am I alone in believing that it will prove, in the end, injurious to the Whig cause. Mr. Sterne, it is admitted on all sides, is a capable officer, and an honest man. He may be decided in his politics, but I do not learn that he is an intemperate partisan. He has been, for several years, our General Treasurer, and you need not be told, fellow citizens, that the benefits of experience, especially in matters of finance, ought not to be lightly regarded. He has no vote in the General Assembly;

no political influence growing out of the business or the emoluments of his office; no extraordinary means of any sort for making converts to his political opinions. Such being the case, does it comport with the avowed principles, and with the loud professions of the Whig party, to displace a faithful public servant, merely because his politics are not in accordance with their own? Shall we who have felt the terrors of proscription—shall we who have defended, with so much indignation, the rights of opinion against the assaults of our adversaries—shall we, even before our triumph is assured, commence the work of ferocious retaliation? I trust not, my fellow citizens. I trust that however false the Convention may be to Whig principles, that you will resolve to maintain them, through evil report and through good report.

In this matter, however, fellow citizens, I assume other if not stronger ground. The late dominant party in this State, thanks to the interposition, the intrepid and magnanimous interposition, of Governor Francis, have never formally opposed the re-election of the Whig Secretary of State, and the Whig Attorney General. They may have sought to do it; but they have not done it. They yielded their desires, nay, in one instance it is believed, their fixed purpose, to the wise and moderate counsels of our present Governor. Thus, not only have these excellent officers been suffered to remain undisturbed amid the strife of opposing parties; but, what I deem of vastly more importance, strength has been given to the sentiment that there ought to be, at least, three offices which, the trading politicians of our State, are not to include in their account of stock.

So long as action is irreproachable, it is not wise too nicely to scrutinize motive. In preventing opposition to Mr. Bowen, and to General Greene, it is well known that Governor Francis hazarded the displeasure of many of his political friends; and I am persuaded that he acted, in the premises, from an honest desire to promote the welfare of the State. Let the Whigs of Rhode Island now reciprocate these tokens of magnanimous forbearance, or, if they are resolved to quarrel with motives, let them imitate the sagacious policy of their opponents. Let them leave honest Mr. Sterne to smoke his pipe, undisturbed within the precincts of the Treasury office. If he take good care of our money, let us not seek to "punish" him for his opinions. Let us, above all, look well to the distant future. It is proclaimed by our trumpeters, that we are on the eve of a brilliant triumph. How this may be, I know not. But this I do know, that the hour of triumph is often the hour of the greatest danger; and that for parties as well as for individuals, the truest policy is an uncompromising adherence to principle.

Lest I should greatly transcend the limits which I had prescribed for this address, one other, and what seems to me an equally well founded objection to the Whig Prox, must be deferred till a more convenient season. Meantime, fellow citizens, allow me to offer to your consideration a few general remarks.

The more I reflect upon the nomination of Mr. Sprague, the stronger becomes my hostility to the new dynasty, which the Johnston and Providence Regency is attempting to fasten upon us. For several years past, the people of Rhode Island have elected for their

Governor, a gentleman whose good sense, unblemished private morals, conciliatory manners, and patriotic intentions have commanded, even from his adversaries, confidence and respect. Governor Francis, moreover, from his peculiar position, is better fitted to be our Governor than almost any other man in Rhode Island. His occupations, as a practical farmer, leave him sufficient leisure, not only to discharge with fidelity, the duties of his office, but to acquire and to put forth, for the benefit of the State, a powerful and conservative influence. That he is identified with the agricultural interest, and that he enjoys the special favor of that interest, is, with me, in the present situation of our State politics, a decided reason for preferring him to Mr. Sprague. To be more explicit. In these times of political and social agitation, I look chiefly to the farmers to protect the State against crude and dangerous projects of reform; against legislative encroachment upon the rights of private property; against philanthropic disorganizers of all sorts; against genteel demagogues, trading politicians, and hobby-horsical legislators;—in fine, against the animating spirit of all political mischief—that spirit which seeks to fasten upon Rhode Island the curse of universal suffrage! I believe, fellow citizens, with one of the illustrious statesmen of the school of Washington, that "those who own the country ought to govern the country." In this sentiment, I rejoice to think, that an immense majority of my fellow citizens most cordially concur. I beseech them however, to beware, how they peril the distinctive glory of Rhode Island—the grand conservative principle of her tranquillity, her prosperity, and her honor! Let them have a care, how they elect a man to be their Governor, who is supported by the odds and ends of all parties; and who, whatever may be his avowed principles or his secret wishes, can hardly be expected, with the Regency at his elbow, and the Radicals at his heels, to stand firmly upon the good old Rhode Island platform!

I do not know, fellow citizens, that Governor Francis will consent to be a candidate for re-election. I am not in his confidence, and I am a stranger to the counsels of his party. I repeat it, however, that I should be reluctant to exchange him for Mr. Sprague. I believe, moreover, that such an exchange would ultimately be fatal to the Whig party in Rhode Island. Thus far they have contended for principle, and they have deserved success. Betrayed by their leaders, into the support of a man in whose political principles they can feel no confidence, they may chance to come off victorious in the approaching contest. But such a victory will be worse to them than a defeat. If they succeed in electing Mr. Sprague, the Whig party will not only put in jeopardy their distinctive principles—but they will lose their proud name. They will come to be denominated "The Sprague Party." They will be named after their Chief; and by him, under the supervision of the Regency, will they be ruled. What may we expect will be the policy of the new Regency? Their cardinal purpose—their overruling consideration—their inflexible aim—my fellow citizens, will be to maintain themselves in power and place! And for what purpose? That such men as John Whipple, John Pitman, Tristam Burges, Benjamin Hazard, and Joseph L. Tillinghast may be chosen to do you both good service and high honor in the Halls of Congress?

No, my fellow citizens, they seek power and place, for no such end. The whole matter is well understood. When Mr. Robbins's term of service expires, Governor Sprague is to be his successor! If Mr. Knight should resign, "the gentleman from Johnston" is to be transferred from our General Assembly to a wider theatre of ambition and renown. In due season, the other members of the Regency are to come in for their share of the spoils. If those who are in the way will neither resign nor die, to accommodate the expectants, why, in the last resort, they can be pushed aside! This operation the Regency well understand.

A PROVIDENCE MAN.

PROVIDENCE COURIER, MARCH 23, 1838.

STATE POLITICS.

NO. V.

TO THE PEOPLE OF RHODE ISLAND:—

I HAVE no fears, fellow citizens, for the success of Whig principles, at the approaching election. These principles, unless my wishes strangely mislead my judgment, will be sustained by a triumphant majority.

Whether or not Mr. Sprague will be elected your Governor, is quite another matter. For one, I should rejoice at his defeat. He has no title to the confidence of the people, and no hold upon their affections. He commenced his political career as a disorganizer, and he followed his trade, so long as he found it profitable. For years, he was conspicuous only for his ability to work confusion in the counsels of the State, and for his skill in thwarting Whig measures. For his agency in producing the downfall of the Whig party, he was ultimately rewarded with a seat in Congress. Recollecting these things, I cannot cease to wonder that the Johnston and Providence Regency, should have caused such a man to be placed at the head of the Whig Prox—a man who has been true to no political connexion, now leaguing with this party, and now with that,—now joining the anti-masons that he might use them as tools; and now allying himself with the Van Burenites, that he might make them his dupes;—now persecuting the Freemasons, and now exulting over the fall of the Whigs. Would the Regency have us believe that policy is better than principle—that victory is before honor—that the sagacity of practised Jesuitism is more available in politics than the decisions of an unsophisticated conscience.

It is declared by one of his supporters that, at a particular crisis in the affairs of the State, "the Jackson party came over to Mr. Sprague!" This declaration is made to illustrate the political influence of Mr. Sprague. Those of you, my fellow citizens, who are familiar with English history, have heard of the Earl of Warwick, whom Shakspeare terms the "proud setter up and puller down of kings." The illustrious poet makes this formidable political manager exclaim as follows:—

> "Neither the king, nor he that loves him best,
> The proudest he that holds up Lancaster,
> Dare stir a wing, if Warwick shake his bells,
> I'll plant Plantagenet—root him up who dares."

The tone of "our sweet Warwick," is somewhat more subdued. He is not a man to deal in boasts or to resort to intimidation. That business he has wisely left to his supporters; and they have been faithful to their trust. Again and again, have they told us of the power and the influence of this modern Earl of Warwick, who has signalized himself as the "setter up and the puller down," not of kings but of parties. First, he set up the anti-masonic party;—next, he set up the Jackson party; he is now employed in setting up the Whig party, which once he pulled down! It remains to be seen whether aid so liable to be found treacherous in the end will be accepted or rejected by the majority of the Whigs. In past times, they have had a bitter taste of Mr. Sprague's quality. Let them beware of him, for the future. I hope and believe they will prefer a more consistent and upright politician. The Whig party may be a free horse—but is that a reason why any jockey should be free to mount him?

I come, now, fellow citizens, to another well founded objection to which, in my judgment, the Whig Prox is liable. In my third number, a brief reference was made to this objection. It will not now require a prolonged examination.

I was conversant, my fellow citizens, with the

politics of Rhode Island, when the gentlemen of the Regency were studying their political hornbook. If my memory be not in fault, during the last thirty or forty years, the preceding year excepted, Providence has been represented in our State Senate. For nearly the whole of that portion of time, our Governor was a citizen of Providence. If our Governor was, in any case, selected from another town, our Lieutenant Governor was selected from Providence. But this is not all. A Senator, has almost always been assigned to Providence. Year after year, have such men as John Innes Clarke, Henry Smith, Moses Lippitt, Nicholas Brown, Jeremiah B. Howell, Philip Martin, &c., all Providence men, occupied the post of first Senator, and guarded, in a co-ordinate branch of our Legislature, the interests and the rights of their fellow citizens. It is now some time, since Providence has been without a single Representative in the Senate. With nearly one fifth of the population of the State, with various and important interests to be affected by almost every act of legislation—and with only four Representatives in the House, it would seem to be no more than right, that Providence should have at least one voice in the Senate. Understand me, fellow citizens, I claim for my town, no accumulation—no monopoly of political honors—I ask for her simply a fair participation in the sovereign power of the State. I supplicate no favors for Providence, but, in her behalf, I demand justice.

In the Whig Convention, this city was represented by eight delegates, chosen, it is believed, by less than twenty freemen! These delegates may have been true to their numerous constituents, but I cannot see that they were true to the interests of the city. Did any one of them remonstrate against the injustice of thus leaving Providence, with no other political distinction than that of bearing a large share of the public burthens, and of being the head quarters of the Regency? Representing, in theory, more than a thousand Whig freemen, they might, without risking the imputation of arrogance, have insisted that at least one of the ten Senators should be selected from Providence. To Warwick, they consented to give not only the Governor, but a Senator—for Providence they obtained nothing but the privilege of bearing burthens, without sharing in benefits. Our antagonists were more just and more sagacious. They have nominated Richmond Bullock, one of our oldest and most substantial citizens, as a candidate for the office of first Senator. So much confidence is felt in his good sense, and so exempt is he known to be from a feverish thirst for promotion, that many Whigs will no doubt vote for him. They will support him, for another reason. Extraordinary as the assertion may seem, our four Representatives are not always the free and deliberate choice of a majority of the freemen. He must be a stranger to our city politics, who does not know that individuals are elected Representatives from this city, sometimes upon the nomination of packed conventions, and sometimes by the influence of artificial combinations. For these and other reasons, therefore, it is desirable that Providence should have an intelligent, disinterested and intrepid Representative in the Senate. This city has important interests to be guarded, and to be fostered—interests liable, as the history of our State Legislation will show—sometimes to be bargained away, and sometimes to be trampled upon. As "A Providence Man," I covet for my fellow citizens, and for myself, some additional protection. We need such protection. Our right to it we have neither surrendered nor forfeited. In justice, it ought no longer to be withheld.

A PROVIDENCE MAN,

PROVIDENCE COURIER, APRIL 6, 1838.

STATE POLITICS.

NO. VI.

TO THE PEOPLE OF RHODE ISLAND:—

IN addressing you, my fellow citizens, on the subject of State Politics, I have been swayed neither by personal enmity, nor by factious impulse. Dissenting from the nomination of the Hon. William Sprague for the office of Governor, I have assigned various reasons for such dissent. To what weight these reasons may be entitled, is left for you to determine. Dissatisfied, in common with a large number of my Whig brethren, with the cabal who are permitted to shape the destinies of the Whig party, I have expressed, let me hope with no unwarranted severity, their dissatisfaction and my own. My task is done. Having no taste for gladiatorial strife, I leave the arena to those who love the fight most when it becomes the hottest.

In the progress of this discussion, I have paused to retaliate no blows. Thickly, if not heavily, have they fallen upon me; but I have survived them all, in unbroken strength, and what is better still, in perfect good humor. One opponent, who signs himself "A True Whig," has denounced me as an aristocrat. This is a genuine Loco Foco argument. Had I been disposed to carry the war into the enemy's country, it would not have been difficult to have convinced you that the worst aristocrats are the demagogues who flatter the people in order to betray them, and that there are collar men and spoils men in more parties than one.

Again, another newspaper opponent has made the notable discovery that I have lost my popularity, and that I "want to be Governor!" Fellow citizens, it matters little who or what I am, but allow me to tell you, at parting, that I belong to the rank and file of the Whig party in Rhode Island; and that my highest ambition is to follow the lead, not of versatile, trading politicians, but of consistent, wise and patriotic men—of men who, through evil and through good report, will stand by their PRINCIPLES, leaving their POPULARITY to take care of itself.

A PROVIDENCE MAN.

PROVIDENCE JOURNAL, OCTOBER 9, 1841.

TO THE PEOPLE OF RHODE ISLAND.

THE SUFFRAGE MOVEMENT.—NO. I.

A BODY of men is now in session, in this city, for the purpose of framing a written Constitution for the State of Rhode Island. If the Masonic Hall be used by these men as a theatre, in which Messrs. Dorr, Atwell & Co., are permitted to rehearse their speeches which they are to "bring out" at the November Convention, who so churlish as to object to an effort to contribute to the innocent amusement of this dull town? If, moreover, this same hall be used either for the manufacture of political capital which is to go to the benefit of the Loco Focos, or as an arena on which Messrs. Dorr and Pearce shall engage in a generous strife, in order to show which of them is the truer democrat and the more disinterested patriot, why, even then, there would be no cause for the language of indignant reprobation. If, again, the Masonic Hall be used on this occasion, as a sort of safety valve, through which superabundant steam is to be allowed to escape, the friends of peace and of order will not be slow to applaud the ingenious contrivance. If, however, this suffrage Convention, a body deriving its origin from no law and acting under the sanctions of no law, mean to impose the constitution which they may adopt upon the people of this State, why, then the matter is to be received in a very different light. It parts at once with its innocent theatrical attributes; and with its shrewd political ends and aims, it loses, even, the poor merit of being allied to the "peaceable remedy of nullification!!" It becomes revolutionary in its character, and treasonable in its designs.

Men belonging to this Convention, have formally proclaimed over and over again, "that a Constitution, adopted by a majority of the male citizens of the State over twenty one years of age, will be, and of right ought to be, the supreme law of the land!! Attempt to carry out this principle, and we should at once be in the midst of scenes which would require Messrs. Dorr, Pearce, Atwell, and their deluded followers, to wield some other weapons than their tongues and their pens. Do these gentlemen suppose that the people of Rhode Island, the legal people, the people proper, will tamely suffer the best. State government now existing in the United States to be trampled in the dust, by men whom, if they are true to their principles, it would be most unsafe to entrust with power? In a solemn address to the People of this State, adopted at Newport, in June last, and signed by Charles Collins, Dutee J. Pearce, and by others, who, in the language of Doctor Johnson, "have made themselves public, without making themselves known," we find the following significant declarations:

"The friends of the reform must depend on their own active energies. The laws of the State are against them. The legislative authority is against them. The custom of more than half a century is against them. And no doubt the opinions, interests, political aspirations, and the prejudices and prepossessions of a majority of the landed interest, are against them. To the timid mind, and to the mind that has not investigated the subject, all these may present a powerful, hostile array.

"However forbidding the obstacles that may present themselves—however dark and frowning the aspect of the opposition—however threatening the arm of power suspended over us—they are mere shadowy and unsubstantial forms; and a single act of the majority of the whole people of Rhode Island, will be found sufficient to sweep them all away. The people—the "numerical force," have but to proclaim their will, to resume their orginal powers, and assert their original rights."

If, fellow citizens, these declarations do not imply a determination to resort to the "revolutionary power," for the redress of grievances, I am at a loss to comprehend what they do mean. In harmony with the spirit of these declarations, were several of the mottoes which decorated the banners of the grand Suffrage Parade, in this city. In harmony with the spirit of these declarations, also, is the language of "the New Age"—the language of Resolutions adopted, and of speeches made in public meetings—and the street talk of some of the most violent of the party. Alluding to the suspension of work at the cotton mills, when the delegates to the Suffrage Convention were chosen, the "New Age" remarked thus—"this shows that the people had learned that they have rights, and are determined to take them, come what will!" Such language evinces what spirit these Suffrage men are of. If they be such in the green tree, what will they not be in the dry?

"The Laws of the State," say the Suffrage men, "are against us; and the legislative authority is against us." But what of all that? What do we care for the laws, or for the legislative authority,—so long as the "numerical force," is with us! to numerical force we mean to appeal—and the numerical force will adjust, in a summary manner, all vexatious questions concerning such antiquated matters as law and authority!

Think not, fellow citizens, that I am betrayed by the violence of misguided men, into the belief, that we are about to be precipitated into the midst of a Revolution! I have no fears that the tyranny of the land holders, of which such grievous complaints have been uttered, is in danger of being exchanged for what, if King Numbers, is to lord it over our heritage, according to his own pleasure, would be little better than the tyranny of the mob. At a crisis like the present, I place my hopes, not in the numerical force—but in the moral power of the State; in the wisdom and good sense of citizens of every order—but more especially in the sober and conscientious judgments of the farmers of Rhode Island—too intrepid to be overawed by menace; too patriotic to remain inert, when the institutions of the State are thus sought to be overthrown. I repeat it, fellow citizens, I have no fears for the issue. Desperate politicians, who "lack preferment,"—may rush madly into the strife—timid politicians, who cannot dismiss their apprehension that fidelity to principle may, some time or other, cost them a vote, may shrink,—I had almost said, skulk, from the strife; but enough of stout hearts and stout hands will yet remain, to defend the laws against violation—to protect the legislative authority from usurpation—to maintain the legal people in the possession of their legal rights—to rescue the State not only from anarchy—but from disgrace.

A Rhode Island Man.

PROVIDENCE JOURNAL, OCTOBER 29, 1841.

TO THE PEOPLE OF RHODE ISLAND.

THE SUFFRAGE MOVEMENT.—NO. II.

Fellow Citizens:—I believe, with John Jay, that those who own the country ought to govern the country. That illustrious republican statesman knew something about the nature of man, the science of government, the dangers to which the liberties of the people are exposed. In all these high matters, he was, it is not too much to say, quite as well versed as any of the men who, in the late Free Suffrage Convention, spouted loud and long in the support of principles which they had neither the honesty nor the courage to carry out. During every stage of this agitation, theories, the most wild and impracticable, have been paraded in the speeches and documents of the Rhode Island Suffrage Association. All this, it would now seem, was intended only for the purposes of parade,—to captivate the unthinking, to dupe the ignorant—to exasperate the discontented. The men who have broached these theories never meant to reduce them to practice. In the prosecution of their design to win to the support of their cause all sorts of men, by all sorts of means, they have dealt largely in prosy disquisitions about natural right,—freedom and equality—the largest liberty, &c.; and have lavished the most eloquent vituperation upon the aristocracy usurpation, despotism, &c., under which the people of Rhode Island have groaned, for two hundred years, and from which multiform tyranny they affect to believe that God has given them a mission to deliver the oppressed. The secret of all this agitation about Free Suffrage in Rhode Island, is coming to be pretty well understood. An air of suspicion has been thrown around the whole movement, by the extremely active participation therein of certain gentlemen, who have never been remarkable for taking very good care of the people, except when they expected the people to take very good care of them. These gentlemen, in the late Convention, trampled upon some of their favorite theories, with an audacity so calm and collected that, under circumstances less grave, there would arise in the public mind, a struggle between admiration and merriment. As things are, however, the predominant sentiment is indignation—indignation, that those who have preached up, till they were hoarse, the doctrines of undiluted democratic equality, should not hesitate, for the sake of expediency, to turn their backs upon their own principles! The zeal of the apostle is however a more easy virtue than the courage of the martyr; and bankrupt politicians, and third rate lawyers, and little men, rebelling against the destiny which nature has assigned to them, are, after all, not the most disinterested patriots; or the most suitable persons to lay broad and deep the foundations of civil government.

To recur, however, to the maxim of John Jay—those who own the country ought to govern the country—or, accommodating the maxim more precisely to our purpose, those who own the State of Rhode Island ought to govern the State of Rhode Island. Woe be to us, my fellow citizens, if we ever adopt a Constitution, by whomsoever framed, which does not embody this principle, and, which does not at the same time protect it, as far as practicable, against the machinations of the demagogue, and the temporary excitements to which the popular mind is exposed. For one, I object to no extension of the right of suffrage which will leave unimpaired the principle of a landed qualification. I am, however, free to confess my fears that any change would ultimately be perverted to the destruction of that great conservative principle of our government.

Is not the maxim of Jay—those who own the country ought to govern the country—fortified by the dictates of common sense and of universal experience? It is admitted, on all hands, that the right of voting should be subjected to some restriction, with a view to secure, as far as may be, the discreet exercise of that right. Hence, the qualifications, as to sex, age, residence, and sometimes even color, which are prescribed by the constitutions or the laws of different communities. These laws all proceed upon the general principle that no one should be permitted to exercise the elective franchise, who does not furnish some evidence of his fitness for the discharge of that important function. These loose and inadequate regulations are better than none—though they are next to none. They do not furnish the best evidence of capacity for a faithful, independent, and patriotic exercise of the right of suffrage. The least fallacious standard of such capacity is the possession of property; and the safest standard for any community to adopt is property in the soil. In Rhode Island, be it remembered, no man is disfranchised. Every man may vote, who is qualified by law to vote; and the rate of qualification is not so high as to operate as a virtual disfranchisement. Be it likewise remembered, that, in requiring a landed qualification, no privilege is conferred upon any man, merely because he owns land, be it much or little. Ownership of the soil is deemed to be evidence of interest in the stability and wise administration of that government which must protect the soil; and, moreover, it is deemed to be evidence that the voter, in the hour of danger, will not join the floating masses in flying from the post of danger. Again: The possession of property in land implies, generally speaking, those habits of industry, sobriety and economy, in a word, those mental and moral characteristics—without which no man is fitted to discharge the right of suffrage. Under our Rhode Island system, a few worthy men may find it inconvenient to become voters; but let them reflect how large would be the number of worthless men who would make themselves felt at our elections, if ever our Rhode Island system should be discarded. When oppression exists, or when any danger of oppression is apprehended, it will be time enough to resort to the revolutionary power. At present, is it not the part of virtue and of wisdom to remain tranquil under what, in individual cases, may seem to be the harsh operation of a most excellent general rule?

The evils of universal suffrage are illustrated, my fellow citizens, by the experience of every State in this Union. In some States rather than in others, these evils, for obvious reasons, are less conspicuously exhibited. Where the territory of a political community is large, and the interests of the people of that community are alike; and, especially, where the landed interest is predominant, universal suffrage cannot do its work of unmitigated mischief. It helps no State to advance in the career of wealth, honor, or happiness; though, thanks to the elastic energies of freedom, and other counteracting agencies, States prosper in spite of it!

For two hundred years and more, we, the people of Rhode Island, have lived happily under our present form of government, enjoying the richest blessings of civil and religious freedom—increasing constantly in wealth and population—oppressed by no taxes—cursed by no expensive establishments—disturbed by no rancorous factions. Throughout all this time, the political power of the State has been in the hands of the landholders. In other words, those who own the State have governed the State. Who so deeply interested in her prosperity as the proprietors of her soil? Who so exempt from the malign influences of the demagogue? Who so discreet in exercising the power of taxation? Who so economical in the expenditure of the public money? We are now exhorted, by the apostles of reform, to change this government; to part with that which, when once gone, can never be recalled—to discard our long tried and safe institutions, for institutions which are recommended by no practical excellence, and for which even the poor merit of theoretical perfection cannot be claimed. Let us pause, my fellow citizens, before we make this bold experiment. Let us not advance a single step, till we know whither that step will carry us. Is there no cause for regarding with jealousy the counsels of the men who have placed themselves at the head of this movement? Is this the first experiment of these men in the science of hobby horseism? Do you think that they or the pack who obey their whistle can make a better government for us than the one under which we have so long lived in peace and prosperity?

The wisdom of retaining the principle of a landed qualification is recommended to the special favor of the people of Rhode Island, by the peculiar circumstances under which they are placed, and by the evils which universal suffrage would fasten upon them and their children. To the consideration of some of these topics, I purpose, on a future occasion, to invite your attention.

A RHODE ISLAND MAN.

PROVIDENCE JOURNAL, NOVEMBER 2, 1841.

TO THE PEOPLE OF RHODE ISLAND.

THE SUFFRAGE MOVEMENT.—NO. III.

Fellow Citizens:—It is gratifying to perceive that those Rhode Island politicians whose trade is agitation, have thus far, in the matter of Free Suffrage, driven their trade without much success. If I mistake not the signs of the times, these politicians, with all their industry and eloquence, have utterly failed to persuade you that any radical changes in the government of this State are necessary;—least of all, such change as they would give us. They have, to be sure, made bold experiments upon your credulity. They have endeavored to convince you, that you are living under an aristocracy, a usurpation, a despotism! They have appealed to bad passions in support of a bad cause. They have prated about the rich and the poor, with a view to array popular prejudices against the one class, and with the hope of getting the votes of the other. All this is pure demagogism—the resort of desperate politicians who, while professing to love only the people, care only for themselves. They have mistaken their men. The people of Rhode Island are not to be swayed by appeals which should be addressed only to those trained bands of loafers, who, under the blessed influences of universal suffrage, hold in their hands the political destinies of the empire city and the empire State.

I rejoice, likewise, my fellow citizens, to perceive the generous indignation which has been excited in your breasts, by the attempts which have been made, more than once, to bring your judgment, concerning the Suffrage question, under an influence foreign to Rhode Island. We want no foreign sympathy;—we need no foreign aid. We are competent to reform our institutions if they require reform—without the assistance of other States, or of men from other States, who have no ties in our own. Above all, we may be pardoned for repelling, with disdain, the insolent interference of New York politicians, who would fain spread over our little commonwealth the same political and moral corruption which has made their metropolis the great ulcer of the body politic.

A Convention of the Representatives of the people of Rhode Island is now in session in this city, called, according to law, for the purpose of proposing such alterations in our political institutions as may seem to be necessary.

What may be the nature and extent of the alterations which this Convention may propose, remains to be known. Quite sure, I am, they will not suffer the agitators, great or small, from within or from without, to exert upon their deliberations or their acts, any undue influence. They will, it is confidently believed, proceed to their great work, resolved to make no change, which justice does not imperatively demand.

The people of Rhode Island are not ripe for great organic changes in their system of government—which, whatever may be its defects, is unsurpassed by any other, for economy, and for a just administration of the laws—for the alacrity with which it responds to popular sentiment; and, yet more, for the securities which it provides for popular liberty and social order. The people of Rhode Island do not wish to see this venerated system of government either sacrificed to the spirit of reckless innovation—or stripped of its most conservative element, in order to benefit men who hope to gain more by agitation than by an honest calling. In words more explicit, the people of Rhode Island are not prepared to adopt any Constitution, which, in establishing the qualifications for the exercise of the right of suffrage, shall abandon the principle of a landed qualification. This is the distinctive excellence of our government. Abandon this principle—and that of which we have most reason to be proud, and on which we can the most securely repose, would be gone—and, let it never be forgotten, gone forever.

The Convention, such are the elements which compose its majority, will go to their work, with direct and fearless aims. God forbid that they should resort to any clap-traps—any pitiful expedients to win a few votes here, or to save a few there—to conciliate the country at the expense of the town—to stifle opposition in one county, by doing injustice to another. In all these matters, there is a model before them, which they will in vain essay to equal.

Not much difficulty, it is apprehended, will be experienced in adjusting the portions of representative power to which the several towns shall be entitled. Nothing more than an approximation towards equality will be attempted; and nothing more is needed. As, however, the city of Providence is represented in the Convention by six men, who have elsewhere committed themselves to a project for giving her twelve Representatives, to be chosen in districts, I may be excused for saying, that this project is not only unjust, but, so far as the mode of choice is concerned, insulting to the city of Providence. The people of Providence do not want twelve Representatives. They would be more than satisfied with eight; especially when they recollect that it is not always easy to select four who go to the General Assembly, with no other view than to take care of the interests of their constituents. Whatever number of Representatives may be assigned to Providence, she has a right to demand, that in the mode of electing them, she shall be left equally free with her sister towns—trammelled by no restrictions, at once injurious to her political interests, and offensive to her self-respect. The majority of her people are quiet and industrious, indisposed to faction—caring not who rules the State, so long as the State is well ruled. Under such circumstances, it is not fair, or manly, or honest, that her permanent interests and rights should be sacrificed, in order that demagogues may make a little capital for themselves. In reference to this matter, however, I have no apprehensions. The rights and interests of this city may safely be intrusted to the majority of the freeholder's Convention. The men whom she has chosen to represent her in that Convention, have, in advance, taken sides against her. She looks, therefore, to the members, from other towns for justice; and she will not look in vain.

A RHODE ISLAND MAN.

PROVIDENCE JOURNAL, NOVEMBER 10, 1841.

TO THE PEOPLE OF RHODE ISLAND.

THE SUFFRAGE MOVEMENT.—NO. IV.

FELLOW CITIZENS:—The Convention now sitting in Providence appears to be guided by a truly conservative spirit. This is as it should be. This, too, is what might reasonably be expected. The Convention, such is its composition, can have no sympathy with disappointed politicians, who hope to profit from confusion; or with speculative statesmen who, in establishing the foundations of government, consult theory rather than experience. Governments owe their stability, not so much to any theoretic excellence, as to their adaptation to the wants of the people, and their hold upon the sympathies and the affections of the people. For one, I rejoice that the Convention is disposed to make no changes in our present constitution of government, except what extraordinary alterations in the circumstances of the State may seem to demand. In the matter of representation, one of our most respectable country towns has asked for a change; and, from present indications, a change will be made upon principles satisfactory to all and safe for all.

The Suffrage Question is, after all, the great question. The highly respectable committee to whom that subject was referred, have, with only one dissenting voice, reported in favor of embodying in a constitutional provision the present landed qualification. It remains to be seen whether or not the Report of the Committee will be adopted in its present shape, or whether it will be so modified as that, while it maintains unimpaired the principle of a landed qualification, it shall extend the right of suffrage to a class of citizens well fitted to exercise it with a sound discretion. Owing to the licentious and disorganizing opinions which have been so industriously propagated, in reference to this matter, there is an intrinsic difficulty in making, at the present crisis, any change. The people of Rhode Island, I hope and believe, will never adopt any constitution which shall abandon the principle of a landed qualification, or which might reasonably be thought to endanger that principle.

Universal suffrage is the radical vice of our popular institutions. It pervades, for all practical purposes, every State in this Union, except that in which we have the honor and the happiness to dwell. Wherever it prevails, it works mischief; though, in States having extensive territories, a scattered population, and homogeneous interests, its vicious tendencies are, in various ways counteracted. In New York, Pennsylvania, and the great agricultural States of the West, the landed interest is the predominant interest. In these, therefore, universal suffrage, though it is felt to be a great and an increasing evil, exerts upon the public welfare comparatively few of those disastrous influences which, under different circumstances, are sure to indicate its presence. If, my fellow citizens, you would seek to know what evils universal suffrage would entail upon Rhode Island—if you would see this idol of the demagogues of the day, in all its rich bloom and naked beauty, direct your eyes to the metropolis of the Empire State. There universal suffrage has free course. There it works, almost without check or counteraction, its legitimate mischiefs. Is there, in this land, a city where social disorders prevail to so frightful an extent? Is there, in this land, a city where crimes the most atrocious are so frequently committed, and, what is worse, pass undetected, or, if detected, unpunished? Where is there a selecter field for the operations of the demagogue? Where is there congregated, within the same space, a larger number of the ignorant, the profligate, and the venal? And who doubts that, under ordinary circumstances, the balance of power in the great city of New York is held by the ignorant, the profligate, and the venal? Think not, my fellow citizens, that I am dealing in extravagant assertions, or am terrified by apparitions. A New York paper more than insinuates that the "rowdies" of that city can control elections, and that public officers, mindful of such base influence, are afraid to do their duty, and to bring these miscreants to justice, even when they commit flagrant outrages against the laws! Who doubts that this horrible state of things is owing to universal suffrage, which places the political power of the city, not in the aristocracy of intellect, or morals, or property, but in the aristocracy of the dram shop, the brothel, and the gutter; not in the "ruffle-shirt gentry," but in the gentry who have no shirts at all! This may be the largest liberty—but it surely works not the greatest good of the greatest number! The evil is manifestly and confessedly great, and, more than this, it is irretrievable. Let us, the people of Rhode Island, heed the voice of warning that comes to us from the city of New York. Let us take good care, that the political power of this State is perpetuated in safe hands—in the hands of those whose home is among us; who have an interest in the soil; who have never abused their power, and are without temptation to abuse it.

The city of Providence already contains more than one fifth of the population of the whole State. There is reason to believe that her "numerical force" will continue to increase; and that time will not diminish her relative importance. Need you be told, my fellow citizens, that Universal Suffrage would prove a curse to the city, and make the city, at the same time, a curse to the State? Again, Rhode Island is destined to be a manufacturing State—employing, in her factory villages, and in her principal towns, a numerous class of individuals, many of them foreigners, and a large proportion of them bound to the State by ties which may, at any moment, be severed. Shall the political power of our little commonwealth be withdrawn from the proprietors of the soil, and be confided to men, of whose fitness to exercise, discreetly, the right of suffrage, we have no evidence? Shall the right of suffrage be vested in men who, if all history be not false, will be sure to pervert that right to their own injury and to the injury of others?

Again—a naval depot, it is confidently expected, will ere long be established in Narragansett Bay. This establishment will attract to itself hundreds of irresponsible men from abroad. They will all do the bidding of the agents of the federal government, for to the federal government they will all owe their bread. Shall such men be suffered to vote at our elections? The demagogue answers, yes! The patriotic Rhode Islander, who loves the soil, and who desires good government, responds in a voice of thunder—No!

It would be easy to show, my fellow citizens, that the landed qualification is better fitted than any other qualification, to ascertain the true state of popular sentiment, and to give effect to the genuine popular will. But, for the present, I forbear. The materials of which the Convention is composed, and the calm wisdom which has marked their proceedings, forbid all apprehension concerning the decision of the Suffrage Question. Unawed by threats of revolution, they will place the right of suffrage where alone it can with safety be placed—in the proprietors of the soil. And the people, believing that those who own the country ought to govern the country, will say Amen.

A Rhode Island Man.

PROVIDENCE JOURNAL, DECEMBER 17, 1841.

TO THE FARMERS OF RHODE ISLAND.

THE CRISIS.—NO. I.

Fellow Citizens:—You are too watchful observers of the signs of the times, not to know that the political affairs of Rhode Island are in a most extraordinary condition. The history of civil society may be challenged to furnish a parallel to the scenes which are now passing before us—scenes at which it is sad to think that multitudes idly gaze, as if they were but the painted and fantastic exhibitions of the drama, got up for amusement, and doomed to perish in a night! You, I am persuaded, do not thus lightly regard the onward movement of the political revolution into which the demagogues speculative, and the demagogues practical, threaten to precipitate us. It is easy to see why the city of Providence reposes, in such unbroken apathy, amid agitations from which some of her citizens, and, for aught that appears to the contrary, the majority hope to derive, in the end, some paltry political advantage. Providence wants to govern the State, and if we are to be cursed with universal suffrage, she will govern the State. She will govern the State, too, not by means of her intelligent, industrious, and moral citizens, having a permanent interest in her welfare, but by means of those floating masses, often turbulent and always irresponsible, which make great cities great sores. Between these masses and the genteel demagogue of the day, there comes to exist a warm sympathy and a strong alliance. He knows how to flatter their prejudices and to inflame their passions. If he be rich, he is sure to desert his order, to abuse rich men, to declaim against monopolies and the money power—to pour into the popular ear all those "leprous distillments" which are fitted to poison the popular mind! He wants preferment—and if he can but obtain preferment, he cares not how he obtains it. He has no idea of being a nice casuist, when political emoluments and honors are in one scale, and the requisitions of a scrupulous conscience are in another. Hardly is there a State in this Union, where these monstrous and dangerous alliances are not to be found. They are the spawn of universal suffrage; and wherever universal suffrage prevails, they may be expected to prevail. Need you be told how hostile are such alliances to the just political importance of the great middle classes, who, in all countries, are the most virtuous and industrious and quiet; the most truly conservative in their notions of government and legislation—the safest depositories of political power?

Another reason may be assigned for the treacherous apathy which is manifested by the city of Providence, in reference to the revolutionary movements of the day; for the strong delusion which seems to have overpowered her better reason. She demands a more equal distribution of representative power. She is promised twelve Representatives in the General Assembly! With open mouth, she stands ready to swallow this bait; and when she has once swallowed it, she will discover, when it will be too late, that she has swallowed, along with it, the barbed steel! Yet another reason may be assigned for the apathy, with which this city seems to regard the movements of the agitators. Her masses, like all masses in populous towns, are accustomed to follow the lead of the politicians. And where, at this momentous crisis in the history of Rhode Island,—where are the politicians? Where are the men who, when a comparatively unimportant election is at hand, or some minor question of public policy is under discussion, boil over with love for the people, and with passionate devotion to patriotism, law, liberty, and order, where are they now?

Are they wielding their pens or raising their voices, now, when their pens and their voices might be of immense service—in sounding in the ears of the people the tocsin of alarm; in giving the note of warning; in rebuking the spirit of faction; in upholding the rights and liberties of the people against all attempts to destroy them, either by fraud or by force? This conduct, on the part of the politicians does not surprise me. The elements are in conflict—and, with all the instinctive sagacity which marks the race, they are watching the winds and the tides—not to discover how they may best save the State—but, how they may best serve themselves. So be it. I have no fears that we shall not be able, without the aid of the politicians, to rescue the State from anarchy and from disgrace. And, moreover, I have no doubt that, after we shall have come victoriously out of the fight, they will be among the foremost to encumber us with their help —help which they withheld, in the hour of danger, but which they would not be ashamed to proffer in the hour of triumph. Such being the condition of things in the city of Providence, at a crisis like the present, I turn to you, my fellow citizens, the farmers of Rhode Island, with undoubting confidence that you will not prove recreant to your own interests; and to your commanding obligations as citizens and as men.

The disorganizers have greatly underrated your understanding, if they persuade themselves that you do not comprehend fully the causes, character and consequences of the movement now in progress to overthrow the government of this State. The controversy is mainly between you, the farmers of Rhode Island, and the masses who congregate in the cities and factory villages of Rhode Island. If you believe it to be for the greatest good of the greatest number, that the farming interest should abandon the political power which it has so long and beneficially exerted, why then you will fall into the motley ranks which the Suffrage Association is training for the work of revolution. If, on the other hand, you are of opinion, that, at a period of great plenty and in the absence of all practical grievances, the exercise of the reserved right of revolution is not demanded, you will gird yourselves for the conflict in behalf of the constitution and the laws. Your calm, concentrated might would, in such a conflict, be irresistible. As to the issue, I have never allowed myself to entertain a fear. The people of Rhode Island will never suffer any body of men, by whatsoever spirit animated, or by whomsoever led, to trample down with impunity, the muniments of law and of order. For the motives and character of many of the persons engaged in this factious movement, I have great respect. These persons sin not without excuse. Some of them are misled by erroneous notions concerning their rights. Others are the dupes of artful leaders. These leaders deserve no such charitable construction of their conduct. Perverting their talents to the purposes of mischief, they sin without excuse; and when the day of reckoning comes, as come it will, they should not be suffered to escape without punishment. They should be taught that disappointed politicians are not to be permitted to solace their griefs, by becoming disorganizers; and that ambitious politicians, however they may barter their consciences for the sake of promotion, must be careful not to become disturbers of the public peace.

COUNTRY BORN.

PROVIDENCE JOURNAL, DECEMBER 18, 1841.

TO THE FARMERS OF RHODE ISLAND.

THE CRISIS.—NO. II.

FELLOW CITIZENS:—In my yesterday's number, I remarked to you that the history of civil society might be challenged to furnish a parallel to the scenes now passing before us. Is the remark obnoxious to the charge of extravagance? Let us see, for a moment, what are the facts of the case. In the year of our Lord, 1841, the government of Rhode Island, the noblest, the freest, and the most truly democratic, on the face of the earth, is, by certain persons, some of them natives, some interlopers from other States, and some emigrants from foreign countries, all at once discovered to be a despotism, or usurpation, or oligarchy, or aristocracy, so insupportably oppressive, as to demand a resort to the Revolutionary Power! These persons have banded themselves, under the direction of leaders, some of them honest enthusiasts, others reckless demagogues, with the professed design to overthrow this government, and to overthrow it by force! They do not pretend that it is inadequate to the protection of life, liberty, and property, or that it, in any way, interferes with the pursuit of happiness. Deluding themselves with abstractions, which, in matters of government, can never be fully reduced to practice, they contend that every white man, (why, upon their own principles, exclude black men?) twenty one years of age and over, shall be allowed to exercise the right of suffrage. They contend, not only that the landed qualification shall be discarded, but, practically, that no property qualification shall be required. I am not now about to discuss this grave question. If the people of this State, to whom alone, under the present constitution and laws of this State, the decision of this question belongs, choose to discard the landed qualification, and even all property qualification, so be it. I understand too well the duty of a good citizen, not to submit, without a murmur, to any organic changes in our government, however much I may deplore them, which may be made in conformity to the laws and constitution under which we now live. The question to which I now wish to invite your attention, is this:—Shall we tamely suffer this government to be overthrown by force? What an extraordinary spectacle do we now exhibit to ourselves, and to the world! The trained bands, who are preparing for the work of revolution, meet, day after day, week after week, and month after month, in edifices belonging to the city or the State; and there brood over schemes to embroil the city and to destroy the State! They invite ministers of that Gospel, which is so full of peace, and love, and submission to legal authority, to offer their prayers for the work in which they are engaged! They proclaim their unalterable resolve to push matters to extremes; and their proceedings are in perfect harmony with their resolves. They send abroad lecturers, to impart to you, the farmers of Rhode Island, new light concerning your rights and your duties. They assemble in the Town House, with, perhaps, even more regularity than they are accustomed to assemble in the house of God, to listen to prosy dissertations about natural rights; to manufacture public opinion, in behalf of free suffrage; and, under the inspiration of thrilling eloquence, to recruit their courage for the day of battle. All these scenes are passing before us; and yet no general and concerted effort is made to awaken a righteous popular indignation against the conspirators, or to make them feel that their revolutionary phrenzy will never compel the people of Rhode Island to acknowledge any despot but the law. I have no faith in the politicians at this crisis. They are always cautious and timid, because they are always selfish. It requires not an army with banners to cover them with affright. If but a Corporal's guard appear in the field, they, at once, post themselves on neutral ground, or they shelter themselves behind an intrenchment. You, my fellow citizens, the farmers of Rhode Island, are of a different order of men. Having no vaulting ambition to gratify, and living independently upon your farms, you are not affected by the gales of popular applause or of popular displeasure. What you most want, is not the votes of the multitude, but a quiet life, under the reign of equal laws. When your mettle is once aroused, and aroused in behalf of the principles of social order, woe be to the man, and woe be to the party, who, in a contest of any sort, shall seek to trample upon you!

What, my fellow citizens, farmers of Rhode Island, is the plan devised by the advocates of free suffrage for the purpose of obtaining a majority for the Constitution which they have framed? Look at it, and then say whether it does not carry fraud upon its very face! The Constitution, framed by the Suffrage Convention, which body, be it remembered, was elected without law, and proceeded from first to last, without law, is to be submitted to "the people" for adoption or rejection, on the 27th inst., and the two following days. In a week, then, from Monday next, the Rhode Island Revolution of three days is to begin! Three days did I say! The half is not told; six days, I should add, are to be set apart for the complete doing up of the glorious work! The provisions made by the Suffrage Convention, in relation to the mode of adopting their Constitution, are so familiar to you, that I need not particularize them. The meetings are to be held according to no law. The moderators and clerks will act under no legal responsibilities. No efficient checks are provided against the introduction of votes by minors, paupers, felons, transient persons or foreigners. In the most sharply contested elections, experience has proved that, in most of our towns, six hours, or even less, is a sufficient time for keeping the polls open. It seems, however, that, on this occasion, they are to be kept open three days, for what purpose, it needs no wizard to divine.

The great object in view is to obtain a majority; and, according to this patent mode of voting, it would be strange, indeed, if a majority were not obtained. The state of the poll will be ascertained every night; and you, fellow citizens, need not be told how many plans may be devised to produce, on the third day, the right result. And after all, if a majority is found wanting, at the close of the poll on the third day,—why, then mark the abundant provision made to cheat you! any person, who, from sickness, or other causes, failed to vote on the day assigned, is allowed three more days wherein he may vote! The votes are to be sealed up and kept by the Free Suffrage Moderator and Clerks; and, last of all, they are to be counted by the Free Suffrage Convention! This scheme ought to immortalize its author—whoever he may be. The palm of superior ingenuity can no longer be claimed by the practised artists of West Greenwich.

Farmers of Rhode Island:—You are not thus to be cheated. You know, that, in the ordinary manner of conducting town meeting, as to time, &c., the free suffrage men would be unable to command a majority in favor of their constitution. Watch them narrowly, but, I pray you, shun all alliance with them. If they obtain a majority, it will be a majority obtained by fraud. And the resort to fraud is only to prepare the way for a resort to force.

Farmers of Rhode Island:—The General Assembly will convene in this city, in a few weeks, when its interposition will doubtless be invoked to uphold the supremacy of the laws; to protect the people in the enjoyment of their rights; to maintain the government in the exercise of its powers. The shameful neutrality of leading politicians on both sides, and the sinister counsels of a few ultra suffrage men, who are too far committed to retreat, have given to this whole movement an artificial importance. It is time that quiet was restored to the State. It is time that the dangerous precedent of attempting to subvert a good government, by force, was withdrawn from the public observation. Let the General Assembly do its duty; and, my word for it, the people will do theirs. The farmers, who compose a majority of the people, are, as I believe, sound to the core. They are not to be circumvented by fraud—they are not to be overawed by threats; and, without a struggle, they will yield nothing to force.

COUNTRY BORN.

PROVIDENCE JOURNAL, DECEMBER 22, 1841.

TO THE FARMERS OF RHODE ISLAND.

THE CRISIS.—NO. III.

FELLOW CITIZENS:—The present crisis in the political affairs of Rhode Island demands that the wisdom, and the firmness, and the courage of all good citizens, should be put forth in defence of law and of order. For the first time in her long and not inglorious history, a faction, not only without reason, but without shame, arrays itself against the laws and the government established by the people for the preservation of social order. Nay, more—this very faction, not ascertained, and not believed to be even a majority of the people, according to any definition of that term which may be adopted, has the matchless assurance to plead, in defence of its treasonable designs, the authority ot illustrious statesmen and jurists. It seeks to find a shelter for its dark designs in the well settled and imperishable principles of popular right. Mr. Justice Story, one of the most accomplished constitutional lawyers of the present age, and others not inferior to him, in juridical learning and in an extensive acquaintance with civil polity, have been quoted, for the purpose of sanctioning the plan now in agitation to overthrow, by force, the existing government of this State. You and I, my fellow citizens, may know little about law—but we claim to have some portion of common sense—and it is by no dextrous special pleading, that we can be made to distrust the conclusions of our common sense. If our laws and our government need reform, who denies the right of the people to reform them; and who would not cheerfully submit to any reform which might be thus lawfully made? Even before the free suffrage men put in motion their ball of revolution, legal provision was made for the assembling of a Convention of the representatives of the people of this State, in order to revise our present system of government, and to make such changes as time and the altered condition of things have shown to be necessary. That Convention has held one sitting, and has agreed upon some important changes—including, among others, an extension of suffrage. That Convention is still in existence, and is again to assemble, for the purpose of completing the work intrusted by the people to its hands. But the faction which claims to be the people, and the majority of the people, has become so intoxicated by the fumes of vanity or of passion, that it cannot wait the tardy-gaited proceedings of a Convention called according to law, and acting according to law. It is determined to rush madly into extremes—hoping to accomplish something, either by intimidation or by force. The leaders of this faction—I say faction, for it is now time to call men and things by their right names—greatly mistake themselves, and they greatly mistake you, the farmers of Rhode Island, if, for a moment, they believe that, in a controversy with you, they can gain aught, either by intimidation or by force. You will surrender nothing at the bidding of these men. If reforms are to be made, you know who, and who alone, are authorized to make them. On this point, they need not hope to throw dust in your eyes.

Farmers of Rhode Island:—Let us inquire, in our plain common sense fashion, who are the people of Rhode Island. Who, under a lawful government, have a right to reform or to change that government? Can it be any other than those, and those only, who have the right of suffrage, or who, in other words, hold the political power under such government? Have those who, by the laws of Rhode Island, cannot vote in the enactment of a single law, or in the choice of a single magistrate, have they a right to vote in the enactment of all laws, and in the choice of all magistrates? Men who have come into Rhode Island, under her existing laws, and who, by this very act, put themselves under these laws, and owe obedience to these laws, and allegiance to the government, now claim a right to set up their will against these laws! Nay, more. They claim the right to put in motion a system of measures, unauthorized by any laws, and intended to destroy the government to which they owe allegiance!! Can this be law? Can any judge or civilian, out of the ranks of the Free Suffrage Convention, be found to sanction a doctrine so subversive of all regular government?

Where there is no government, all stand upon an equality of right; and, from the necessity of the case, there being no law to regulate the action of any, the majority of all have a right to form a government for themselves. After, however, such government has been established, the voice of the government is the voice of the people. Such government can be reformed legally, only in two ways. Where there is a written Constitution, it must be reformed, according to the mode provided by that Constitution. Where there is no written Constitution, it belongs to the legislative power, and to that alone, by a solemn act, to originate, in behalf of their constituents, the process of reform. The officers of the established government must so preside over such measures of reform, as to determine whether the Constitutions or the laws, providing for, and regulating such reform, have been complied with, that all frauds may be prevented, and that the voice of the people may be legally ascertained and declared. Under any other mode of conducting the business of reform, a set of men, by usurping all the functions of government, would be able to legalize their own usurpations; to take advantage of their own wrong; and, under the forms of a Constitution, to save themselves from the punishment which is due to rebels and to traitors. When did Mr. Justice Story ever countenance any such doctrine? and, if the authority of Mr. Madison can be fairly alleged in its favor, I have read the "Federalist" in vain.

COUNTRY BORN.

PROVIDENCE JOURNAL, DECEMBER 23, 1841.

TO THE FARMERS OF RHODE ISLAND.

THE CRISIS.—NO. IV.

FELLOW CITIZENS:—The demand, at this time, upon the columns of the *Journal*, admonishes me to be brief. I have many things to say to you about the revolution which is in progress to overturn, by force, the government of the State. This is, now, the paramount concern. Let no false issue be raised. The question, now, is not whether we shall have Universal Suffrage, or an extension of Suffrage—but whether we shall have a government or no government—whether the law or the mob shall rule. The movements of the suffrage party cannot be disguised, and if they are not arrested, must end in the exertion of that "numerical force" of which that party has often boasted, and to which it now threatens an appeal. The existing government, it can hardly be supposed, will remain passive, and suffer any unlawful combination of men to usurp its legitimate powers. I do not think so humbly of the understandings of the suffrage party as to believe that they really suppose themselves to be now pursuing legal and constitutional measures for the redress of their alleged grievances. In this matter, they have practised no deception upon themselves. Have a care, Farmers of Rhode Island, that they practise no deception upon you. Have a care, that they do not divert your attention from the inevitable consequences of their treasonable designs to the consideration of incidental and subordinate questions. For however important it may be, in the end, to prevent the irretrievable injury which would be done to the interests of all classes, if the evil of universal suffrage should be entailed on Rhode Island—yet the great question, and the question first to be decided, is, shall the reformers be suffered to accomplish their object by force—not only without law, but against law?

To this grave question, all good citizens, I am persuaded, will give a united and indignant response. In a voice of thunder, they will answer No! and, if need be, they will vindicate, at all hazards, the supremacy of the constitution and the laws.

The question, shall the existing government of Rhode Island be sustained, or shall it be put down by force, far transcends, in importance, the question, who shall be our next President, or our next Governor—or even the question whether we are to have a protective tariff, or a "judicious," or a "horizontal" tariff. We could live, peacefully and happily, nay, perchance, prosperously, under the rule of Mr. Van Buren. We should not lose our political existence, even if we exchanged our King under the Royal Charter, for either of the ambitious Warwicks, who may seek to pull him down! Nay, more—we are, in some sort, independent even of the Tariff. Our one hundred and thirty four dollar aristocrats know how to make the land yield, and we shall not starve so long as we enjoy the right of going to the shore! But to live without a government, or under a usurpation, would be a very different matter. We do not want to make any such "experiment in living." We, and our fathers before us, have known as much of true democratic freedom as any people under the sun, and we do not want to see, and we do not mean to see, the ark of that freedom fall before such hands as are now raised for its destruction.

Farmers of Rhode Island:—Be true to yourselves, and all will be well. On Monday next, the revolutionary drama will begin. How it will end, is known only to Him who seeth all things. One thing is clear, He has no attribute which can take side with the crafty or the violent. The Suffrage Convention have contrived a scheme to obtain a majority for their Constitution, which can hardly fail of its design. This scheme leaves us in a doubt which most to admire, the ingenuity with which it is contrived to answer the purposes of fraud, or the cool impudence with which it is proclaimed in a community of honest men! See that this majority is obtained without the aid of a single vote from the farmers of Rhode Island! Do not so far recognize the Free Suffrage Convention, as to vote even against the speckled, ring-streaked bantling, which they have christened by the name of "Constitution." Come not, I beseech you, into their secret;—to their assemblies be not your honor united!

COUNTRY BORN.

PROVIDENCE JOURNAL, DECEMBER 24, 1841.

TO THE FARMERS OF RHODE ISLAND.

THE CRISIS.—NO. V.

FELLOW CITIZENS:—If the free suffrage men were striving to obtain, by honest means, a majority for their Constitution, in order to make political capital for ulterior "peaceful remedies," they would be left to go on, without let or hindrance. If they sought only to obtain the means of courting successfully the embrace of some subordinate faction, or of driving a shrewd bargain with some trading politician, they would transgress no law, except perhaps the law which binds a scrupulous conscience. For such transgression, they would be accountable, not to us—but to a tribunal whose judgments no mortal may escape. But, when these men leave their own manor, to trespass upon yours—when they boldly proclaim their determination to prosecute their treasonable designs, "in defiance of all opposing force," you cannot misunderstand, either their language, or their aims. They leave you no alternative, which you can embrace without dishonor. You must suffer the existing laws and government of the State to be trampled in the dust, by a faction, or you must oppose to the assaults of that faction the most determined resistance. These men, who are constantly threatening force, and who are doing what they can to provoke a resort to force, now have the assurance to reproach us for standing upon our rights, under the broad shield of the laws of Rhode Island, and of the Constitution of the United States. They begin to talk, too, about carrying the question at issue, to "the constitutional tribunal of the nation, to be there tried and decided." What constitutional tribunal is vested with the power to decide this question,—in other words,—to determine for the people of Rhode Island, how their domestic affairs shall be managed—and in what hands the political power of the State shall reside, we are not told. This notion is suggested by the free suffrage men, merely for effect; for no other purpose than to deceive the unwary; to beget, in the minds of the credulous, the belief that the suffrage party is pursuing naught but legal ends by legal means. By no such shallow artifices can the farmers of Rhode Island be deluded. You, my fellow citizens, ignorant though you may be of the subtle distinctions which lawyers either make or find, you know, in the first place, that no practical grievance exists under our present form of government; and that, theoretic imperfections may easily be corrected, without a resort to force. You know, too, quite as well as any lawyer knows, that the present movement, on the part of the suffrage party, can plead no example in history;—no sanction in the opinions of statesmen, or of jurists;—no justification in any law or Constitution, human or divine. In its whole aspect, and in its whole character and purpose, it is naked REVOLUTION, and it is nothing less!

Farmers of Rhode Island:—Are you prepared for revolution? Do you think that the inhabitants of this State are groaning under oppressions so insupportably grievous, that they would be justified in resorting, without further delay, to those reserved rights which are the last refuge of the oppressed? Do you think that, at a crisis like the present, a more mild, and conciliatory, and constitutional course is not greatly to be preferred? Would it not be well for some of these bellicose gentlemen, who are so impatient for the fight, to wait till the Convention of the people, about to re-assemble in this city, has completed the work which the people gave it to do? The revolution, at any rate, ought to be postponed till after the General Assembly has had a session; for, in the exercise of its ample powers, it will interpose for the relief of all cases of intolerable oppression! Fellow citizens, if the doctrines advanced by the suffrage men were not so utterly subversive of all law and order, it would be difficult to repress the merriment which their reasons for rebellion would excite.

These reasons may be comprehended in a nut shell. Certain people want to change the centre of political power from the country to the town; from the farm to the workshop; from the plough to the spinning-jenny,—in other words, the existing government of Rhode Island is to be trampled down, in order that the political power may be wrested forever from you, the farmers, who have earned it and never abused it, and be placed in the hands of men who have no interest in the soil—no permanent ties to bind them to the discharge of their duties as citizens; men who will raise a conflagration within your borders, and then, swinging their pack, will leave you to extinguish it. In other words, the political power of the State is to be wrested from the farmers, and confided to the hands of the foreign population, already numerous and now rapidly accumulating in our cities and manufacturing villages—and to the hands of that lazy and profligate class of our native citizens, who are the pest of great cities. These people, strangers to our interests—slaves to their own passions—and ever ready to become the tools of crafty politicians, will govern the State. The intelligent, and frugal, and industrious foreigners among us, and the no less intelligent, and frugal, and industrious of our own people, who have unthinkingly embarked in this revolution, can, by no antidote within their power to administer, neutralize the poison which they will have introduced into the body politic. They, as well as you, will, in the progress of events, be trampled down, by the demagogues of the day, who, under the new order of things, will never want instruments wherewith to depress others and to exalt themselves.

Farmers of Rhode Island:—You have now the political power of Rhode Island—and long may you have it! You can retain it, if you will to retain it. Your destinies are in your own hands—and, let me tell you, that, if you fall in this contest for your dearest rights, it will be your choice, and not your fate, to fall!

COUNTRY BORN.

PROVIDENCE JOURNAL, DECEMBER 27, 1841.

TO THE FARMERS OF RHODE ISLAND.

THE CRISIS.—NO. VI.

FELLOW CITIZENS:—THIS DAY, will commence, in the State of Rhode Island, one of the most extraordinary proceedings which has ever signalized the history of popular governments. So out of the line of all precedents is this whole proceeding, that the political philosopher, in after times, will hesitate in what class of moral phenomena to place it; and yet more, when he comes to scrutinize the motives of the authors, not less will he hesitate whether to trace them to the folly which cannot anticipate consequences, or to the cunning which overreaches itself, in its efforts to overreach others. Was there ever such an exhibition before; men preaching up rebellion, incessantly and lustily,—and yet insisting, all the while, that they are, and that they mean to keep themselves within the pale of the law! How would you regard the man, who, in order to extort a compliance with unlawful demands, should threaten to commit arson or burglary in your premises,—and who should, at the same time, have the assurance to tell you, that he was going according to law; that if you will let him quietly steal your horse, he will not burn your barn; that if you will throw into his hat the leathern wallet, in which you keep your gold and your silver, he, like a peaceable citizen, will forbear to break into your house! Is not this something like free suffrage logic? Would you, under the circumstances supposed, be convinced by such logic? Would you, without struggle, give up your horse, to save your barn? Would you "down with your dollars," that the house breaker might not wrench open your doors?

You are invited, fellow citizens, nay, you are exhorted and implored, by the Free Suffrage men, to vote, in all this week, for a document which they call a Constitution. This Constitution they have manufactured to suit themselves, and, if there be any virtue in a resort to physical force, they are determined to make it suit you. Six days are set apart by these men for the purpose of beginning in fraud a revolution, which is to be consummated in force. Farmers of Rhode Island—let me ask you to read, again and again, this so called Constitution. Mark, more especially, the provisions which regulate the mode of receiving and counting the votes, and, then, judge ye, whether or not these men mean to deal fairly by you in this controversy. They will have the voting and the counting, all to themselves, for six days and for six nights! You are not so simple as to require to be told, how the vote will stand at the close of the poll! These provisions to which I have alluded, need no extended comment. I dismiss them with a single remark. The time has been, when the political man, or the political party who would contrive such a scheme, to effect a favorite purpose, would be covered with infamy and with defeat. Unless morality, as well as laws and Constitutions, is to be trampled under foot, in Rhode Island, the authors of this scheme will yet discover, to their cost, what a blunder they have committed in not taking more pains to appear honest. They mistake their men, if they think that they can thus come over you by a juggle. As well might they attempt to overawe you by threats, or to put you down by force.

John Jay, of illustrious memory, once said—"I have known many demagogues—but I have never known one honest man among them." Were Jay now living among us, would he have any reason to retract this assertion? Would he not rather be tempted to think that demagogues have parted not only with the essence, but with the form of common honesty; that they have lost not only all regard to conscience, but all sensibility to shame.

Farmers of Rhode Island:—I pity the simplicity of the man, who hopes to delude you into the belief, that the Revolution which begins to-day, has in store a single benefit for you. And yet more,—I marvel at the intrepidity of any class of men who may attempt to wrest from you your legal and constitutional rights. In the days which tried men's souls, you feared not the

King and Parliament of Great Britain. You will not now grow pale, because the Free Suffrage Convention is collecting its might to overthrow you.

With genuine satisfaction, do I hear that you are not indifferent to the present crisis, that you mean to stand firmly upon your rights,—that, come what may, you will be true to yourselves and to your government. Duty to yourselves and to your government demands that you take no part in the work of mischief that is to be commenced this day. Vote neither for nor against the so called Constitution. Exert your influence to keep others from voting. Your antagonists are arrayed in opposition to the laws; their moral force is therefore not to be dreaded. Do what you can to show that they have greatly overrated the numerical force by which they threaten ultimately to put you down.

Farmers of Rhode Island:—Be moderate, but be firm. Do nothing to inflame animosities; admonish the unwary; reclaim the wandering; rebuke, with calmness, the noisy and the presumptuous; but, amid all these tokens of conciliation and good will, be prepared for decisive and courageous action. Let your thunder sleep in the cloud, while it may—but let it fall upon any man or any set of men who come to trample you in the dust!

COUNTRY BORN.

PROVIDENCE JOURNAL, DECEMBER 29, 1841.

TO THE FARMERS OF RHODE ISLAND.

THE CRISIS.—NO. VII.

WITH this day, closes the first act of the revolutionary drama, got up under the auspices of the Rhode Island Free Suffrage Convention ! How the vote will stand, at the close of the poll, does any reasonable man doubt ? A majority of persons, of all colors, twenty one years of age and over, will be found arrayed in favor of the instrument, which was framed by the anarchists, and which is contrived, most ingeniously, to perpetuate a usurped dominion over the people, the Legislature, the laws, and the Constitution of Rhode Island.

Suppose, however, that, by some mischance, either the misgivings of tender consciences, or the hesitation of coward neutrality, a majority should not be found arrayed in favor of the misnamed " People's Constitution ? " Why then, three days more are, very considerately, allowed, not only that the whole of the antecedent process may be revised and corrected,—but, likewise, that all persons who, " from sickness or other causes," failed to vote on either of the first three days, may have a chance to aid in this work of mischief and misrule. "Sickness and other causes!" Mark, the generous comprehension of the terms! Within these notable three days, "other causes," and not sickness will be the prevailing epidemic!

Farmers of Rhode Island:—Look, once more, at this patent scheme, by which it is attempted to cheat you out of your rights and liberties. These votes, thus given in, under no sanctions of law; in the night time, as well as in the day; in secret corners, as well as in public assembly; with no jealous minority to shame unscrupulous men, even into the appearance of honesty; these votes, thus tendered and thus received,—are to be counted by the Rhode Island Free Suffrage Convention—by the very men who devised, and put into operation, the revolutionary movement; and who know, full well, what momentous issues hang upon the final success of this movement. What have they not perilled on these issues? the hopes of those whose ambitious fingers are impatient to clutch the highest honors of the State; and the hopes of a yet larger number, who will be "fierce as the evening wolves" to seize upon the "spoils!" If the thirty one moderators, in six days and in six nights, cannot make the vote come out right, why then the men who contrived the scheme, will see that the scheme does not prove a failure! At the critical hour, they will take good care that their skill in political midwifery shall suffer no reproach. They will take good care that the child is born. To hide, if possible, their own shame, they will stamp on its bastard forehead, the mark of legitimacy. In insolent contempt of all your rights, they will seek to palm it off upon you, as the true heir to the inheritance bequeathed to you by your fathers.

Farmers of Rhode Island, it is now no longer a matter of doubt, what these men mean, by their words and by their acts. Within a few days, emboldened by dreams of success, they have thrown off the mask, and come out, openly and fearlessly, as Revolutionists —"proceeding not only without law, but against law." I thank them for abandoning the policy of Jesuits for the intrepid zeal of open revolutionists. "Show your colors, if you are an Algerine," is yet remembered among the caustic sayings of the famous Judge Parsons—a man no less witty than wise. Right glad am I, that the Free Suffrage men have, at last, shown their true colors. A writer, in yesterday's *Journal*, who signs himself "a Revolutionary soldier of 1841"—exhorts "every friend of order and peace to vote for the people's Constitution, and to insure its adoption by a triumphant majority." Mark the language which this writer uses. "Nothing," says he, "short of such a result, will prevent a scene of anarchy and confusion in this State, such as never has been witnessed in any republican country!!" Again, he says, "should the Free Suffrage party fail to succeed in their present peaceable operations, all the laws of the State may be set at defiance! and we have reason to fear that physical force will reign over all law and order!!" This is plain language. The writer has shown his colors, though he does not appear to know that they are the colors of "an Algerine!"

Farmers of Rhode Island—if, without a sentiment

of honest indignation, you can listen to such language, I have sadly mistaken your real character. If you can be terrified by such threats, your ancient spirit has, indeed, departed. If you can tamely suffer the men who use such language to ride over you rough shod, why, then, the breed of noble bloods, is extinct among you. If such threats are to be put in execution, force and not right; faction and not government;—the mob and not the law, is to begin its disastrous reign in the land of Roger Williams! Mark the words of this apostle of Revolution. "Nothing short of this result," aye, nothing short, will prevent all the multiform horrors which follow in the train of social revolutions. In other words, unless you and those who think with you, adopt on compulsion, this Constitution, which you had no agency in making,—and which will be fatal to your influence in the government,—why, then, anarchy and confusion are to reign throughout our hitherto peaceful boders! This instrument, called a Constitution, it would seem, is to be forced down our throats. We are to take the Free Suffrage prescription for the diseases of the body politic, whether we like it or not. I am as much for peace as any other man, if peace can be maintained without abandoning that which is dearer than peace. I would address to you, even now, the counsels of peace. You and I ask nothing from society but its protection. We want to live and to die under the reign of the laws—and we want nothing more. The reign of the laws, however, it seems, is to end, if, without deliberation and upon compulsion, you will not adopt the Free Suffrage Constitution as your Constitution!

My fellow citizens, how disastrous would prove the triumphs which these men seek—how fearful the precedent which they are striving to establish!

Farmers of Rhode Island, my confidence in you and in the General Assembly is still unshaken. The laws are not to be prostrated without an effort to vindicate them. Faction, as I believe, is destined to meet with a scorching rebuke. Neither threats nor violence will move you to surrender one iota of your rights. Be ready, at a proper time, and under proper circumstances, to make all reasonable concessions for the preservation of fraternal concord; but rather beat your ploughshares into swords, wherewith to repel the invaders, than suffer these invaders, be they few or be they many, to triumph over you—"without law and against law."

COUNTRY BORN.

PROVIDENCE JOURNAL, JANUARY 1, 1842.

TO THE FARMERS OF RHODE ISLAND.

THE CRISIS.—NO. VIII.

FELLOW CITIZENS:—The work of anarchy is in progress. King numbers has advanced another step, in the march of usurpation. He now claims to be the sovereign people, and he denounces his vengeance upon all who may dare to oppose his will. Mark, how bright upon his cheek is the flush of triumph, and with what proud disdain he surveys the antagonists of his power! The authority of the legal people, composed, mainly, of farmers, mechanics, merchants, and manufacturers, is to be trampled under foot; and a faction which has recruited its ranks, by enlisting minors, non-residents, colored people, and foreigners not naturalized; nay more, which has raked even our jails for materials wherewith to increase its strength—such a faction has now the unblushing effrontery to call itself the Majority of the People of Rhode Island! In this censure, I mean not to include every single man. "In all lead," says the chemist, "there is silver, and in all copper, there is gold. But mingled masses are justly denominated by the greater quantity; and when the precious particles are not worth extracting, a faction and a pigment must be melted down together in the forms and offices that chance allots them."

Farmers of Rhode Island:—The scheme devised by the Free Suffrage Convention to ensure the adoption of their Constitution, worked to admiration. The result so confidently predicted by friends and by foes, was obtained. The sum came out exactly right! The majority is declared to be in favor of the Constitution; and how, it is now asked, can the majority be guilty of tyranny, or be resisted with success? This may be free suffrage doctrine, but it is not your doctrine. You believe that majorities are often capricious and oppressive; and that no worse form of despotism can exist, than the despotism of a majority, goaded on by unprincipled leaders to aggressions upon the rights of the minority. The axe or the bow string may rid an abused people of a single despot, who in the wanton excesses of his might, has trampled them in the dust; but when King numbers turns despot, and perpetrates his enormities under the forms of law—perchance " without law and against law," the abuse may be insufferable, but the remedy is not always easy. The King can do no wrong, says the courtly sycophant. The majority can do no wrong, says the pliant demagogue. This doctrine may suit the times;—it is, nevertheless, the doctrine of tyrants, whenever, and by whomsoever it may be preached. God forbid that it should find favor in Rhode Island!

The anarchists seem to be experimenting upon public forbearance, already taxed somewhat heavily, by boasting that they are now the majority; and as the majority, by challenging the quiet submission of all good citizens to the new government. What law authorized them to put any question to the people? Under the sanction of what law were the votes given in and counted? The provisions in favor of fraud were abundant. What single effective provision was made against fraud? What a series of paltry expedients was resorted to, in advance of the final movement, to hoodwink the public judgment! Respectable clergymen were urged to pray over scenes of anarchy, that the religious public might be duped into the belief that men who thus called to their aid the offices of piety could meditate no mischief to the State. The lessons of history have, indeed, been read in vain, if by so bald an imposture, the most simple can be deceived. Again, it was proclaimed, without the shadow of truth, that the Governor of this State meant to vote for the Suffrage Constitution; and it was more than intimated, that one of our Courts of Justice looked, with complacency, upon this revolutionary movement. Throughout the whole affair, the suffrage men seemed to be oppressed with a secret consciousness that they were perpetrating a grievous public wrong. Something, therefore, must be done to pacify their consciences. And, yet more, something must be done to win honest but unreflecting men to the support of their cause.

You are, fellow citizens, to some extent informed by what means that majority, to which your obedience is now demanded, was obtained. The half, however, is not told. The leaders may laugh over the success of their juggle; and, in their secret council chamber, they may begin to make a division of the spoils. But the end is not yet. If the people of Rhode Island have not come to consider the principles of honor and fair dealing as pedantic and superannuated rules of morality, not applicable to public bodies, they will place on this whole scheme to defraud them, in a matter of the gravest concern, a seal of reprobation which shall make its infamy imperishable. When all the facts connected with this scheme shall have been developed, they will kindle within you all your ancient fires. Enough is already known to arouse you to an indignant sense of your wrongs, and to a timely perception of your danger.

The Suffrage men boast of the large number of freeholders who voted for their constitution. If you have examined the manner in which the "People's Ticket" is printed, you will feel surprised that the number of freeholders was not greater. Here is this People's Ticket, word for word, letter for letter, blank for blank. Examine it carefully, and then cease to wonder that so many freeholders voted for the people's constitution!

"1776. 1841.

"ADOPTION OF THE CONSTITUTION OF RHODE ISLAND.

"PEOPLE'S TICKET.

"I am an American citizen, of the age of twenty one years, and have my permanent residence or home in this State.

"I am qualified to vote under the existing laws of this State.

"I vote for the Constitution formed by the Convention of the People, assembled at Providence, and which was proposed to the People by said Convention, on the 18th day of November, 1841."

Let me remind you that this was the only ticket prepared for the occasion; that all who went to the meetings, went burning with zeal to vote for the constitution; that many of the votes were polled at night, and that most people are unused to these delicate typographical contrivances which make this ticket to surpass, in ingenuity, many counterfeited bank notes! How many, do you think, paused to read the ticket, before they voted it? How many perceived that there was any blank at all? How many left it unfilled—some with a design to defraud—but more, from ignorance, or carelessness, or haste?

Farmers of Rhode Island:—Let me again recall your attention to the true question which now demands your decision. Whether or not suffrage shall be extended, you are not now to determine. A much graver question must first be settled. Shall your government be put down by a faction—shall the mob and not the laws reign; shall a combination of men be permitted, in defiance of all law, to proclaim themselves a majority of the people, and, in the exercise of a despotic power, obtained by fraud, shall they be suffered to force us into submission? This is the true question. Can there be more than one answer?

Farmers of Rhode Island:—Examine the elements of this faction; mark the spirit which animates it; look at the men who are destined to be immortal as its leaders. Are you prepared to surrender your political power into such hands? Do you think that it would conduce to the greatest good of the whole, that the large towns and the factory villages should govern the State? Do you think that Providence, with such a mass of voters which she will have at command, will long be content with twelve representatives? Will she not insist that the abstract principle on which the whole battle has been fought by the suffrage men, shall be carried out in her favor? Will she not demand, that, as numbers govern at the polls—numbers shall govern in the Legislature? and will she not have the power to make her demands effectual? If she cannot bring you to terms, in a legal and constitutional manner, will she not form alliances, get up a faction, and availing herself of the precedent now before you, go behind the laws and the Constitution? She has now a population of nearly twenty five thousand people. That population is rapidly increasing, and in a few years may be expected to embrace, at least, one third of the population of the whole State.

Think not that the present race of demagogues is the last. Demagogues enjoy perpetual succession. Our soil yields them in profusion. The present individuals will die off, in time, and there is mercy in the provision, but the race is immortal. Large cities are the field of operations for a demagogue, for, in large cities, is to be found the materials best fitted for his use. Beware, then, ere it be too late, how you inflict upon this city and upon the State, a curse, which, when once inflicted, is irremediable.

Farmers of Rhode Island:—I appeal to you once more. Do you think that men, who seek an alliance with all sorts of persons in all sorts of ways, are fit to be trusted with the life, liberty, and property of honest men?

Farmers of Rhode Island:—I was born among you, and I lived among you, long enough to know the stuff whereof you are made. These men cannot, by an array of numbers, make you flinch a hair's breadth from any position which you may take in the defence of your rights. Their threats of force, in case you do not meekly surrender your political power into their hands, will not fright you from your settled purpose—to stand firm in defence of yourselves, and of the government which protects you. Be as mild and conciliatory, as may be, in your language and conduct towards these men; but let them not suppose, for a single moment, that, by any thing which they have said or done, or by any thing which they can say or do, they can make the slightest impression upon your fears. The laws, and not faction, must reign in the land of Roger Williams!

COUNTRY BORN.

PROVIDENCE JOURNAL, JANUARY 4, 1842,

TO THE FARMERS OF RHODE ISLAND.

THE CRISIS.—NO. IX.

Fellow Citizens:—Those who seem to resent all opposition to the suffrage movement in this State, have been at the pains to tell the public, that "Country Born" is "a city man," and, moreover, that he is an obscure man. Pleading guilty to both of these charges, I "put myself on the country." Why should not a city man deprecate a movement, which, if successful, will, in his judgment, increase the power of the city for evil, rather than for good; which will fasten upon us a government, without any effective checks or balances; which will transfer the political power of the State from the hands of the farmers into the hands of the demagogues. Is it not in cities that demagogues most do congregate? And, in the event of an unlimited extension of suffrage, can there be a doubt that masses in this city, and kindred masses in the factory villages, acting under impulses communicated by demagogues, will govern the State?

Again—why should not a quiet and obscure man be allowed to take some interest in a question, which is to fix, perhaps for many years, the destinies of this State? Are none but those who hold office, or who are in pursuit of office, interested in the discussion of grave public questions, or in the establishment of a government upon sound principles? Are you to welcome only the testimony and the counsels of those who may have some interest in deceiving you, and who are liable to be themselves deceived? Are you to listen to him who pants for office, and turn a deaf ear to him who seeks nothing but quiet, and freedom from oppression? At some future day, I may take occasion to "define the position" of some of those gentlemen who are so impatient to retrieve their forfeited popularity, that they stop neither to save from destruction your interests, nor to calculate the cost to their own honor. The present is no time to pursue such game!

Farmers of Rhode Island:—I commend the subjoined extracts from Burke's Reflections on the French Revolution, to your sober attention. They are not altogether inapplicable to the state of things in Rhode Island. You well know how to run the parallel. Since the experience of last week, the free suffrage men will be slow to reproach me for appearing "by proxy."

"What signifies the empty compliment paid to the country, by giving it perhaps more than its share in the theory of your representation. The whole of the power obtained by this revolution will settle in the towns, among the burghers and the monied directors who lead them. The landed gentlemen, the yeoman and the peasant have none of those habits or inclinations, or experience which can lead them to any share in the sole source of power now left in France. The very nature of a country life, the very nature of a landed property, in all the occupations they afford, render combination and arrangement (the sole way of procuring and exerting influence) in a manner impossible among country people. Combine them by all the art you can, and all the industry, they are always dissolving into individuality. Any thing in the nature of incorporation is almost impracticable among them. Hope, fear, alarm, jealousy, the ephemerous tale that does its business and dies in a day, all these things which are the reins and spurs by which leaders check or urge the minds of followers, are not easily employed, or hardly at all, among scattered people. They assemble, they arm, they act with the utmost difficulty, and at the greatest charge. Their efforts, if ever they can be commenced, cannot be sustained. They cannot proceed systematically. The country gentleman, therefore, the officer by sea and by land, the man of liberal views and habits, attached to no profession, will be as completely excluded from the government of the State, as if they were legislatively proscribed. It is obvious that, in the towns, the things which conspire against the country gentlemen, combine in favor of the money manager and director. In towns combination is natural. The habits of burghers, their occupations, their diversion, their business, their idleness, continually bring them into mutual contact. Their virtues and their vices are sociable; they are always in garrison, [in caucus] and they come embodied and disciplined into the hands of those who mean to form them for civil or military action.

"All these considerations leave no doubt on my mind, that, if this monster of a constitution can continue, France will be wholly governed by societies in the towns formed of directors in assignats, and trustees for the sale of church lands, attornies, agents, money jobbers, speculators, and adventurers, composing an ignoble oligarchy, founded on the destruction of the crown, the church, the nobility and the people. Here end all the deceitful dreams and visions of the equality and rights of man. In the 'Serbonian bog of this base oligarchy,' they are all absorbed, sunk, and lost forever.

"Though human eyes cannot trace them, one would be tempted to think some great offences in France must cry to heaven, which has thought fit to punish it with a subjection to a vile and inglorious domination, in which no comfort or compensation is to be found in any, even of those false splendors which, playing about other tyrannies, prevent mankind from feeling themselves dishonored while they are oppressed. I must confess, I am touched with a sorrow, mixed with some indignation, at the conduct of a few men, once of great rank and still of great character, who, deluded with specious names, have engaged in a business too deep for their understanding to fathom; who have lent their fair reputation and the authority of their high sounding names to the designs of men with whom they could not be acquainted, and have made their very virtues operate to the ruin of their country."

Farmers of Rhode Island:—Should the suffrage men ultimately prevail, whom may you not expect to see representing you in Congress? While you are "oppressed" at home, may you not be "dishonored" at Washington?

Country Born.

PROVIDENCE JOURNAL, JANUARY 5, 1842.

TO THE FARMERS OF RHODE ISLAND.

THE CRISIS.—NO. X.

Fellow Citizens:—Since the time when Arthur Fenner wielded, for seventeen successive years, the democracy of Rhode Island, a great change has been wrought in the social condition of our people. The population of the State has doubled, and the population of this city has more than doubled. In respect to their political power, the commercial interest, and the agricultural interest, have both suffered, in the progress of events, a decline never to be retrieved. The extension of suffrage to every male inhabitant twenty one years of age, will leave them utterly powerless. The foreign population in this city, and the manufacturing population out of it, composed, to a considerable extent, of persons having no permanent interest in the State, will be invested with the power to elect its officers, and to determine what shall be its laws. Whether or not such a concentration of all the political power of the State in such hands, will be for the greatest good of the whole, I leave you to determine.

Farmers of Rhode Island:—It is said, and such is the voice, not only of "Providence," but it is the voice of every man conversant with the principles of our government,—that "the majority must rule, and the minority must submit." Who questions this doctrine, that it should be thus authoritatively proclaimed? "The majority," it is true, "must rule." But the majority to which submission is demanded, must be a legal majority, legally ascertained. It must be a majority speaking through the regular channels, the constitution, laws and ordinances of the government. It must be a real, and not a fictitious majority. It must be a majority, not obtained by fraud, and not intended to be followed out by acts of force. To such a majority, and to none other, ought the minority to submit.

Farmers of Rhode Island:—When a majority of the people of this State, legally ascertained to be such, shall think proper, in a legal and constitutional mode, to put aside the old Charter—the present system of representation—the present suffrage law, &c.,—it will be found that those who are most hostile to the change, will submit, with a very good grace, to the regular operation of popular power. For one, I cling, with unwavering fidelity, to the principle, embodied in the following declaration made by the delegates of the people of this State, when, in the year 1790, they ratified the Constitution of the United States. They then solemnly declared, "That all men having sufficient evidence of permanent common interest with, and attachment to the community, ought to have the right to vote!" The practical question, for I reject all theories of natural right in this matter, is, what shall be adopted as the evidence of such "permanent common interest with, and attachment to, the community." The ownership of land, would seem to be the least doubtful and the safest rule by which to settle this question. The Freeholders' Convention, as it is called, however, have decided otherwise. They will soon meet again "fresh from the people;" and from their decisions, if sanctioned by a majority of the people, there can be no appeal. The principle of an exclusive landed qualification, I lament to say, has been surrendered already. You and I will have great reason to rejoice, if any principle shall be finally adopted, which shall extend the right of suffrage to those, and to those only, who have "sufficient evidence of permanent common interest with, and attachment to the community."

A writer, under the signature of "Providence," in the *Journal* of yesterday, seems to be quite enamored with the late proceedings of the suffrage party. Listen to the voice of "Providence":—

"The proceedings I have referred to, have been denominated, and that too by well meaning men, revolutionary, illegal, treasonable. Revolutionary they may be, for our principles admit of those peaceable revolutions which are determined at the ballot box; but illegal or treasonable they cannot be. No body of men have ever proceeded more quietly, more in perfect submission to the laws, more in strict observance of the peace of the good people of this State, than have the friends of free Suffrage."

Does this writer mean to be understood as likening the proceedings of the last week to those peaceable revolutions which are accomplished by the people, when acting under the authority of the laws of the land? Would he institute any comparison between "the ballot box" of the free suffrage party and the legal and constitutional ballot box, which determined the great political revolution in 1801, or the no less memorable political revolution in 1840? Does he mean to say that if the free suffrage constitution should, without further proceeding, go into operation as the supreme law of this State, such a result would be a legal result, determined at the legal "ballot box?" Was this the way in which the people of Connecticut determined, a few years since, to put aside their charter for a written constitution of government? Had the recent proceedings of the suffrage party any sanction from law? Had they even the appearance of being intended to give a fair expression of public opinion? Nay more, is there a lawyer in the suffrage party or out of the suffrage party, who, having any reputation as a lawyer, could be found to risk that reputation, upon an opinion in favor of the legality of the present suffrage movement?

"What is revolution?" once asked Daniel Webster, perhaps the ablest constitutional lawyer of the age. Let Daniel Webster answer. "That is revolution which overturns, or controls, or successfully resists the existing public authority; that which arrests the exercise of the supreme power; that which introduces a new paramount authority into the rule of the State." Now, I ask, is not this the precise object of the free suffrage party? What is their language? "This constitution [see Article 14, section 5,] shall, if adopted, go into operation on the first Tuesday of May, in the year one thousand eight hundred and forty two." And then follows sundry provisions, relative to the time and mode of electing State officers in the Spring, and of effecting a complete organization of the new government. They even proceed so far as to legalize the existing government, by providing, in the most condescending manner, for its temporary continuance! Look at the 17th section. It reads thus:

"The present government shall exercise all the powers with which it is now clothed, until the said first Tuesday of May, one thousand eight hundred and forty two, and until their successors under this constitution shall be duly elected and qualified."

Now, fellow citizens, all this seems to me to smell somewhat strong of Revolution, not a peaceable Revolution, but a Revolution, in the last resort, to be accomplished by force. It is contended by the Free Suffrage party that their constitution is adopted by a majority of the people, and that at the appointed time it will become the supreme law of the State. Suppose, however, that the existing government does not care to surrender, either to fraud or to force, its rightful authorities. Suppose it should consider the result of the six days' balloting as not conclusive evidence of the will of the majority. Suppose, moreover, that the Convention of the people of this State, acting under the authority of law, should form another constitution, differing, essentially, in its provisions, from the instrument voted for, during the whole of last week, by all sorts of men, and in all sorts of ways. Suppose such constitution should be adopted by the people, in a legal manner. Should we not, then, have two governments, each claiming paramount authority?

Would there be no danger of collision, of angry collision, between the two governments? If force should be used, who would be morally and legally responsible for the consequences?

Farmers of Rhode Island:—An appeal has been made by "Providence" to the Whigs of Rhode Island. On this topic I have a few words to say. What matters it to us, quiet and obscure citizens, which of the two great political parties has the ascendency in this State? Let me tell you, and let me tell "Providence," the men of the city, and the writer who adopts that signature, that the little finger of free suffrage, will be found heavier than the loins of locofocoism! Though not a trading politician, there is one bargain which I would make. I most cheerfully would surrender to the locofocos, as they are called, the whole political power of this State, for the term of twenty years, provided you and I could be permitted to live securely under a government of laws and not of men;—under a government which would represent "the sober second thoughts of the people," who have some permanent interest in the State, rather than the passions of an irresponsible and unreflecting floating mass—a government which should have within itself some elements of stability, and some principles adverse to the principles of the demagogue and the disorganizer; a government, in fine, which, in its practical operations, would neither invade the rights of the minority, nor dishonor the wisdom of the people.

Country Born.

PROVIDENCE JOURNAL, JANUARY 11, 1842.

TO THE FARMERS OF RHODE ISLAND.

THE CRISIS.—NO. XI.

Fellow Citizens:—"I am the State," once said a despotic prince of the House of Bourbon. "We are the people," now says the despotic faction which has, again and again, proclaimed its determination to fasten upon us a Constitution—"without law and against law!" The boast of the Bourbon was not an empty one. He had a mind capacious of magnificent designs, and he was sustained by the consciousness of unlimited power. By what authority does the faction, which aims to overthrow, by violence, the existing government of this State, proclaim itself to be the majority of the people? When and how did it become the majority of the people? When it began the work of mischief, it confessedly was not the majority. Is there a tittle of evidence to convince any man of common sense and common honesty, that it is the majority, now? What legal or paliamentary tribunal would not reject, on the instant, as utterly inadmissible, the sort of proof by which the suffrage men now attempt to convince the public, that the numerical force is now theirs? And, what if the numerical force be theirs? Though I concede not to them even this poor advantage, yet I would ask, is an appeal to be made to the numerical force, in a matter involving, for many years to come, the dearest constitutional rights of thousands? Is a body of men representing only one class of people in the State, the suffrage men, and bent, after all, only on establishing one principle, the principle of universal suffrage—is a body, thus constituted, and thus under the dominion of a single idea, fit to be trusted with the grave and delicate task of modelling a system of government? Is such a body fit to regulate nice adjustments, to interpose checks and balances, where checks and balances are needed; in fine, to accommodate such a system of government to the temper, genius, habits, and peculiar conditions of the people? Nay more, may not the whole history of popular governments be challenged to produce an example of a Constitution formed, not only amid clamor, and passion, and almost fanatical fervors—but without undergoing the deliberate and searching scrutiny of a jealous minority? The Free Suffrage Convention was got up by party acclamation; the Constitution was adopted in that Convention, by party acclamation; and the same Convention, will, in a day or two, end this solemn farce, by proclaiming that Constitution, so framed and so adopted, to be, in Rhode Island, the supreme law of the land! In other words, these men got together, in their own fashion—all by themselves—and made a Constitution to suit themselves; they voted for the instrument, after their own fashion; and they are about to proclaim the result, after their own fashion! Are such men to be deemed the people, and upon such evidence? Is a Constitution, thus adopted, to become the supreme law of the State? Is this the majority which, with an intrepid impudence truly inimitable, the General Assembly is now gravely summoned to obey? These men, I repeat it, do not deceive themselves in this matter; but they mean to deceive others. They know, as well as you, that if the votes given in for their Constitution could be properly sifted, all cause for boasting would, upon their own principles, be excluded. They would be found in a minority; and that, after all their bluster, is now their true position. Thousands voted for the Suffrage Constitution, with no other view than to express their opinion in favor of a liberal extension of the right of suffrage. They were told by those who had an interest in deceiving them, that such, and such only, would be the effect of their votes. These men are not less hostile to revolutionary schemes than you are. They would disdain the fellowship of any man, or set of men, who preach up doctrines subversive of all government; and who engage in licentious schemes, to endow faction with the attributes of law. Like thousands of you, they believe that the time has arrived for a liberal extension of the right of suffrage. They are willing to be counted as the friends of such liberal extension; but they would repudiate,—indignantly repudiate—the revolutionary doctrines which the leaders of the suffrage party now openly avow. They are willing to wait for the regular and peaceful expression of the popular will. They are not in such a hurry to exercise the right of suffrage, that they are disposed to trample down every principle and institution which can give dignity, or value, or security to that right.

On the revolutionary question, the numerical force, as I firmly believe, is against the suffrage party; the moral power of the State is against them; the principles of constitutional law are against them, the unadulterated conclusions of common sense are against them. They need not hope, by means of noise, or menace, or compact organization, to effect an easy triumph over the government and the people of Rhode Island.

Farmers of Rhode Island:—Our little State will come out of these fierce trials, with untarnished honor. The reforms which our institutions may seem to require will be accomplished, with deliberate wisdom, and in a spirit of magnanimous compromise. Inequalities in the representation will be corrected; and the right of suffrage will be extended to all those persons who have "sufficient evidence of a permanent common interest with, and attachment to, the community." It ought to be extended to none beside; unless it be designed that the demagogues and the floating population of the State shall govern the State. Clamor and menace and fraud have had their day. It is now time for sober counsels, and patriotic purposes, and unflinching courage to have theirs. The government, I am persuaded, will be true to itself; and the vital question, whether faction or the laws shall triumph, will not long be left undecided. I have no fears for the issue, come when and how it may.

Upon the men who for months have turned our little State upside down, some discountenancing mark should be placed. They have violated, in several instances, and in the most shameful manner, the liberty of speech. The Anti-Slavery men found that they could discuss, without interruption, all subjects, save one. Whenever they assailed what they deemed to be an objectionable provision relative to suffrage, in the so called "People's Constitution," king mob kindled into fury. Again and again were these people interrupted and grossly insulted; confounded sometimes by rude clamors, and, in one case at least, pelted by missiles: and all this, simply because in Newport, Providence, and elsewhere, they took the liberty to speak freely of the Suffrage Constitution! I have no special sympathies for anti-slavery men or anti-slavery women, as such; but I cannot conceive how any man whose veins are coursed by Rhode Island blood, can repress his honest indignation, whenever the right of free discussion is thus trampled upon by a mob! No matter how uncongenial the theme; no matter how profitless the debate; no matter how obscure the speakers—the right of free discussion should be held sacred: and be maintained, at whatever cost, against any man or any set of men who may dare to invade it!

Farmers of Rhode Island:—Would you wish to be ruled by men who have bullied and blustered so long, that vanity and passion have betrayed them into false judgments and rash measures? Would you confide to such men the task of forming for yourselves and for your children a constitution of government—a fundamental law which is to determine what shall be the securities of life, liberty, and property?

COUNTRY BORN.

PROVIDENCE JOURNAL, JANUARY 11, 1842.

TO THE FARMERS OF RHODE ISLAND.

THE CRISIS.—NO. XII.

FELLOW CITIZENS:—It has, again and again, been intimated, that we do not behold upon the stage, all the chief actors in this revolutionary drama. It has been said, that for some of the chief actors and managers, we must look behind the scenes. To discard all metaphor—it has been said, that certain influential political gentlemen are in favor of this scheme of the Free Suffrage party to overthrow the existing government, and to establish, "without law and against law," another government upon its ruins! These gentlemen, it is alleged, have not only countenanced this scheme, by their ostensible neutrality, but, in secret, and by various means, no less powerful for being indirect, they have administered "aid and comfort" to the apostles of anarchy. In proof of these assertions, it is stated that large bands of men, over whom, at every insignificant contested election, these gentlemen have been accustomed to exert a controlling influence, marched to the polls, in solid columns, and voted for the Free Suffrage Constitution! And, moreover, it is predicted, that the developments at the present session of the General Assembly, the arrangements for the April election, and the result of that election, will furnish very significant indications that these gentlemen have, indeed, lent themselves to this work of confusion.

Fellow Citizens:—I warn you not to listen to these vague and uncharitable rumors—allied as they are, in character and in design, to the political gossip and "loose libels," with which the scene shifters and the candle snuffers in the revolutionary drama have amused their leisure hours. This is not the first time that the authority of distinguished men, has, for a sinister purpose, been indecorously pressed into the service of the revolutionary faction. The device is almost too plain to be effectual. It discredits the practised ingenuity of its inventors; it will fail to increase the number either of proselytes or of dupes.

Fellow Citizens:—Do you require to be told that the prominent political gentlemen to whom I have alluded, would be among the last to embark in a piratical bottom, under a piratical flag—fitted out by desperate men, for desperate purposes? Would they peril their commanding influence by joining in this unlicensed enterprise against the peace and welfare of the State? Would they turn their backs upon their own principles, and for a consideration too paltry, to seduce the veriest political drudge from the path of honesty? Would they dishonor the memory of their forefathers, by an alliance with men, who are seeking to trample in the dust the doctrines and institutions, which those forefathers would have maintained against fraud and violence,—and maintained even unto blood?

For these gentlemen, thus sought to be dishonored by imputations intended to give an artificial dignity to this factious movement, I have no special political, or personal sympathies. Their lines of motion are not coincident with mine. Their objects of pursuit and of enjoyment are not mine. They move, thanks to God for my safe mediocrity, in regions far above that in which I am destined to live and to die. "I have no vulgar admiration, nor any vulgar antipathy, towards them. I hold their order in cold and decent respect."* As an humble citizen of Rhode Island, I cannot, however, help feeling some concern in the characters of her public men, because the characters of her public men are, in some sort, public property. They cover a free State with glory, or they cover it with shame!

Fellow Citizens:—While I put forth this effort, however feeble, to rescue the reputation of these distinguished gentlemen from undeserved reproach, I ought, in justice, to add, that to their neutrality on a question of such vital importance, these vague and disreputable rumors owe all their power to work mischief. Whether the people of Rhode Island are to live longer under the old charter or not; whether the landed qualification shall be preserved or not; whether suffrage shall be universal or restricted;—these are all subordinate questions, about which differences of opinion may be honestly entertained. These, too, are questions, in reference to which public men may be at liberty to reserve their opinions. These are questions,

* The beautiful language of Edmund Burke, when speaking of the British Peers, and defending himself against the charge of being "a man of aristocratic principles."

upon which neutrality can be maintained, without suspicion and without reproach. But the question, whether or not the established government shall be overthrown by a faction; whether force or the laws shall triumph; whether king numbers or the people shall rule—these are questions which abhor all neutrality. These are radical and momentous questions, in the discussion and settlement of which there ought to be no timid reserve—no equivocal disguises; nothing, in short, which wears the semblance of compromise or of fear. "There are times and circumstances," says that great political philosopher, Edmund Burke, "in which not to speak out is at least to connive." Surely, it is not enough, that dangerous doctrines are not owned; they should be indignantly and openly rejected. It is not enough that turbulent men are not aided; they should meet with the most determined and unfaltering resistance. A combination of persons, acting under the direction of a political society, has filled our little State with confusion. Has this combination been openly condemned and opposed by the influential gentlemen who are now subjected to the mortifying suspicion of belonging to the brotherhood? I lament, in all sincerity, that, in this great controversy of right against might,—in this noble struggle, nobler far than the triumph of any man or of any party, we have been unable either to muster them in our ranks or to see them doing battle, in their natural position, at the head of our columns!

Fellow Citizens:—These gentlemen ought to be admonished of their high responsibilities to the State which protects, and which has delighted to honor them. Their social position; their talents; their wealth; their wide personal popularity; all serve to give great weight to their opinions, and great strength to whatever cause they may seem to support. As citizens and as public men, they ought to remember, that the peace, prosperity, and honor of Rhode Island are now in peril; and that if confusion and disaster, and disgrace, are to be her destiny, neither they nor their children can hope to escape the common lot. The storms of revolution make no discrimination. They cast the whales as well as the periwinkles upon the strand! I will not draw into question the moral courage of these gentlemen, by the intimation that they are frightened by the clamor which now disturbs the public repose. They know, full well, the difference between the clamor which is caused by abuse and which aims at redress, and the clamor intended to produce discontent, and to gratify personal ambition. Such a clamor, in the language of Mr. Burke, "is indeed one of the worst acts of sedition." Such a clamor they ought to be the last men to fear.

COUNTRY BORN.

PROVIDENCE JOURNAL, JANUARY 13, 1842.

TO THE FARMERS OF RHODE ISLAND.

THE CRISIS.—NO. XIII.

Fellow Citizens:—Have you read the "Address to the members of the General Assembly," which was published in this city, last week? This Address, spread over a pamphlet of twenty four pages, embodies facts and principles, which, at the present extraordinary crisis, in our State affairs, commend themselves, with peculiar force, to the attention of every citizen of Rhode Island. It is understood to be from the pen of one of our most eminent citizens and ablest constitutional lawyers; a man whose independent position, elevated personal character, and exemption from party influences are ample pledges for the wisdom and the sincerity of his counsels. If, my fellow citizens, you have not read this address, let me advise you to read it, without delay. Read it and ponder it! Though specially intended for the present crisis, it contains facts and principles which cannot lose their value with time; facts and principles which ought to form a part of the intellectual furniture of every man in Rhode Island; facts and principles, which, had they been familiar to the public mind, would have saved thousands from rushing madly into the present scenes of confusion and dishonor. For one, I feel largely indebted to this gentleman, for the able and efficient service, which, stepping aside from his quiet and dignified pursuits, he has felt himself, in duty bound, to render to his fellow citizens. I welcome the aid of so distinguished a champion in the good cause of law, and order, and popular right!

I bear my humble testimony to the value of his labors, and to the generous ardor which has impelled him, not to enter the political arena, as a political gladiator, but to work, with his might, in the vineyard of the people,—to save that vineyard from being trampled by lawless feet! The politicians of the day are sadly puzzled to understand the motives which should induce citizens, habitually quiet and unobtrusive, to come out and show their colors, at the present crisis. They seem to think that the field of discussion and of action, on all occasions, belongs exclusively to them. When they are engaged in shrewd contrivances to frustrate the intentions of nature, and to vote little men to be great men; when they seek to make men governors of the people, who have never yet learnt to govern themselves; when they are contriving to make men Senators, to whom God has refused wisdom;—why, in all such manufacturing processes,—in all such paltry manipulations,—I am content that they should do all the work. I, for one, prefer to keep out of the mill! But when they attempt to manufacture a constitution of government, and, especially, when they attempt to force a constitution of government upon the people, as one of the people, I claim the right to be heard. No array of numbers, however formidable, no political combinations, however strongly cemented, no proscriptive frenzy, however epidemic,—no factious domination, however insolent, should ever fright an honest man, humble though he may be, from the intrepid maintenance of his great legal, and constitutional rights. I have thought it not improper to say these things; because living as I do, near the crater of the belching volcano, I may be presumed to know something of the materials which cause the mountain to burn, and the sky to flash with tempest.

Fellow citizens:—It has been found convenient to ascribe the "Address" of which I have above spoken, to the individual who now addresses you. Proud should I be, of the honors of such paternity; but after what I have said, you will, of course, infer that such honors are not mine. A plain man, without pretensions to learning, either scholastic or professional, I never venture upon trains of profound consecutive reasoning; I put forth only those simple elementary truths, which are familiar to the common mind; I circulate the current coin, leaving abler men to deal with ingots of gold.

Fellow Citizens:—It seems to be conceded, on all sides, that we must have a written Constitution of government for this State; and that that Constitution must embody provisions for a large extension of the right of suffrage. So be it. Whenever the people, the whole people, shall declare, in an authentic and legal manner, such to be their will, the whole question will be settled. The MAJORITY MUST, in that event GOVERN; and the MINORITY MUST SUBMIT! Thus far, we are without any evidence, deserving the name of evidence, that such is the will of the people. No popular clamor; no array of numbers; no vote of the General Assembly, can ever impart to the Free Suffrage Convention, a single attribute of legality. That Convention was bottomed on usurpation; it proceeded in the spirit of usurpation; and it threatens to finish its work, by an act of usurpation. I have, after all, no fears for the issue. We shall not escape an extended suffrage; but that is, now, a subordinate matter; but we shall escape the disgrace, the deep, the imperishable disgrace, of submitting to a government, established over us by fraud and by force. We, who are contending for the supremacy of law, may be a scattered host; we may not meet together to inflame each other's zeal, or to strengthen each other's hands; but we are, nevertheless, strong in numbers, and still stronger in spirit. We are not to be put down so easily as some seem to think. We are on the side of law, and order, and right, and truth. Who can show a broader basis whereon to stand, and to do battle? With such allies, I fear not the issue. With such allies, we can shiver their corrupt combinations into atoms. With such allies, we can save the State from confusion and from reproach. The judgment of the people is with us; the verdict of uncorrupted consciences is with us; the verdict of impartial history will be with us!

Farmers of Rhode Island:—My task, extended already far beyond my original design, is well nigh finished. In my next, I shall take my leave of you. The distinguished gentleman who has addressed the General Assembly, has reaped the field. There is no need of my raking after his cart!

COUNTRY BORN.

PROVIDENCE JOURNAL, JANUARY 25, 1842.

TO THE FARMERS OF RHODE ISLAND.

THE CRISIS.—NO. XIV.

Fellow Citizens :—Many topics press upon me for notice, at this closing scene of my humble labors. To a few only of these topics, I now purpose briefly to allude. With each other, they may be somewhat slightly connected, but they all stand in relation, more or less intimate, to the present crisis.

Again and again, have I expressed my decided convictions, that Rhode Island would come out of this fierce strife, with untarnished honor; that the government would not yield a hair's breadth to threats; that the people, of all political parties, would rally around the government, in the defence of the laws and institutions of the State. These convictions remain unchanged. Nay more, they have been fortified by the firmness, spirit and dignity, thus far manifested by the General Assembly, in relation to the matters of commanding interest, which await their decision. The vote in the House of Representatives, on Mr. Atwell's motion to refer the Free Suffrage Constitution to a Committee, who should be instructed to ascertain how many freemen voted for it, is a pretty decided indication that this "paramount law of the land!"—is not in the best odor with those who represent the bone and the muscle of the State. Only eleven members out of seventy two could be found to vote in favor of touching the unclean thing. The majority against the motion was truly overwhelming; and, what is better still, this majority was the result of no political drill; it was the spontaneous, emphatic, and solemn testimony of men of all parties against the attempt which is now maturing to establish, by force, a government in opposition to the existing government of this State! The majority of those who voted for Mr. Atwell's motion, were whigs—three of them, Messrs. John H. Clarke, William Sprague, and Amasa Sprague, but yesterday, active and efficient leaders of the whig party. Among those who helped to swell the majority against the motion, it was especially gratifying to note those veteran democrats, the venerable Elisha Mathewson, of Scituate, and Colonel Barber, of Hopkinton. In mentioning these facts, I seek not to manufacture capital for any political man or political party. I disdain the business. It belongs exclusively to politicians, and I should be among the last to interfere with their monopoly. I state these facts, simply to show, that because the paramount interests of the State are in peril, men of both parties, without any abandonment of their political principles, have come to the rescue. In this connexion, it may not be amiss to add, that, unless present appearances are deceptive, the next political campaign in Rhode Island will be conducted solely with reference to Rhode Island interests, and Rhode Island institutions. The contest will not be between whigs and democrats—or between Clay men and Tyler men—but between those who are for establishing a Constitution "without law and against law;" and those who, by "all necessary means," are resolved to resist this desperate scheme of anarchy.

Fellow Citizens:—I have often asserted, with confidence, the belief, that the Suffrage Constitution, never obtained, in any sense, the votes of a majority of the people; that a majority of the freemen never voted for it; that a majority of all male citizens, twenty one years old and over, never voted for it. This my belief, remains unshaken. It is not denied, that non-residents, and minors, and foreigners not naturalized, aided this movement to fasten a Constitution upon us; and it is more than intimated that support was sought for this paramount law of the land, even among the felons in our jails! Thousands voted for it, under an entire misapprehension of the true issue. They meant to indicate their opinions in favor of an extension of the right of suffrage; and they meant nothing more. The statements made in the House, by Mr. Whipple, of Coventry, Mr. Robinson, of Cumberland, and by other members, were not necessary to convince any candid man, that the alleged majority for the Suffrage Constitution, was the result of frauds perpetrated in almost every town, and under every form which fraud could be made to assume.

Fellow Citizens:—In the course of this controversy, doctrines of the most licentious character and dangerous tendency, have been broached; not only by the spouters in our town house; but by a grave legislator, who has some reputation to lose. These doctrines, if carried out, would be fatal, not only to the rights of individuals and of minorities; but to all the securities of social order. If the people, in the exercise of their transcendent powers, can be permitted to trample upon all the forms of law; if majorities are to act without checks; if minorities have no rights, and no duty but that of submission, popular freedom, losing its grand conservative principles, would become extinct, or exist but in name. The sternest oriental despotism would be more welcome than the despotism of King numbers. It would be far easier to propitiate the one than the other—and far easier to get rid of the one than of the other. Besides, the one might sometimes redeem itself, by acts of magnificence, and by freaks of generosity. The other, amid all its caprices, never forgets its nature; it is always inquisitorial, always malignant, and always mean. The legislator to whom I have alluded, seems not to consider that while he is putting forth these crude and lax notions, he is furnishing texts which, in times to come, may be quoted by the apostles of anarchy; that he is teaching to future agitators, the great potency of revolutionary movements; that he is proclaiming doctrines which may make our State the theatre of revolution for every discontented faction.

Fellow citizens:—We have heard much of "the aristocracy of sand and gravel." Who, let me ask, compose this aristocracy, so odious to the champions of the largest liberty? Are they large proprietors, living upon their patrimonial acres, in a style of baronial splendor and baronial independence? You smile at the question, knowing as you do know, that this formidable and oppressive aristocracy is made up, almost to a man, of plain farmers, mechanics, traders, and merchants, who work hard for their living; and who are among the people, and of the people! Of such materials is the aristocracy of sand and gravel composed! Now let me ask, by what sort of an aristocracy is it about to be succeeded? Should it be the will of the people to introduce universal suffrage, will those who own the State govern the State? Will those who are interested in the public welfare, be intrusted with the care of the public welfare? Who will govern the city of Providence? Providence county will govern the State. Who will govern Providence county? Under what sort of rule will Smithfield, Cumberland, North Providence, Warwick, &c., be placed? Will quiet Portsmouth be swayed by the men who were born upon her soil, and who love the homestead, or by the laborers who come thither, to-day, to delve in her coal mines, and are gone elsewhere, to-morrow? And what is to become of Newport, amid this wreck of our old institutions? Newport, always conservative, and standing, even in the darkest hour, by her ancient principles, is destined to be ruled, in part by foreigners, and, in part by dependants on the national establishments within her limits. And as to Tiverton, the calico and spinning-jenny aristocracy of Fall River, Massachusetts, will take good care of her! Questions of a similar import might be put in reference to almost every town in the State. I have asked these questions. It cannot be necessary to answer them.

Fellow citizens:—The history of the present revolutionary movement ought to be written for the instruction of posterity. In distant times, those who may examine the political annals of our State, for the years

1841–2, will be interested to know something of the true causes which, in the absence of all practical grievances, and at a season of general prosperity, have driven a hitherto orderly and contented people into a fierce and turbulent combination against the established authority, and the public peace. They will be inclined to doubt the fact that no practical grievance existed to justify even a complaint of oppression. They will ask, did not a scarcity of bread, the result of vicious legislation, fill these people with madness? Did they not rebel against the laws, to save themselves from perishing with hunger? Again, they will ask, was there no attempt of associated wealth to trample on the rights of the poor, or no attempt of associated poverty to plunder the possessions of the rich? Were not some of the great muniments of popular freedom and equal rights assailed and broken down? Was not the liberty of the press or the liberty of speech invaded by legislative enactments? Were not the writ of habeas corpus and the trial by jury denied to the people by a tyrannical government? And, lastly, they will ask, did not the government, or some ambitious sect, controlling the action of the government, seek to trample on those great principles of religious freedom which the illustrious founder of the State established, and which successive generations, with almost idolatrous veneration, preserved inviolate? When the diligent inquirer into our historical records discovers that none of these things were so, will he not be at fault? When he is told that there was no famine in the land; that "Jeshurun kicked," not so much because he hungered, as because he "waxed fat;" and that all men of every age, condition, and color lived, in ease, and comfort, and freedom, under the protection of mild and equal laws, he will be apt to conclude that the Rhode Island rebellion is a sort of phenomenon in political history, which must forever puzzle the brains of political philosophers to explain. Such, as I verily believe, will be the interrogations which will hereafter be put, when these scenes of revolutionary violence shall come to be calmly reviewed.

We, my fellow citizens, are embarrassed by no doubts as to the true causes of this revolution. We are familiar with these doings; with the plot of the drama, with the subalterns who have crowded the stage, and with the chiefs who have kept themselves behind the scenes. What phenomena do we see which are not capable of easy explanation, upon well known principles in the constitution of man? In the ranks of the suffrage party honest and well intentioned men, are to be found. They have been misled as to their rights and their duties, by prostitute politicians—by politicians who care not what becomes of the government or of people, if they can either creep or vault into place and power. Pursuing their selfish ends, these politicians have labored, by artful perversions of the great elementary principles of constitutional liberty and natural law, to seduce masses of men in this State into the belief that their sacred and inalienable rights were withheld from them; that forbearance in them had ceased to be a virtue; that resistance was justifiable; that triumph was inevitable. For months have they sought not only to mislead but to exasperate the minds of the people. In the impassioned language of Fisher Ames, "they have addressed something persuasive to every prejudice; they have put something combustible to every passion; to the mean they have whispered suspicion; to the rapacious they have offered plunder; to the violent revenge; to the envious the abasement of all that is venerable; to innovators the transmutation of all that is established." Need you be told how proscriptive and furious have been some of the leaders of this faction towards every man who has dared to oppose it? Do you require to be told that, transcending all the licensed violences of political controversy, they have assailed the personal character, and dragged into public notice the private relations of private citizens? Nay more, not content with vilifying the living, they have trampled even upon the immunities of the grave. In the excesses of their revolutionary fervor, they have spared not even the memory of the venerated dead. The dupes and the victims of this faction deserve our pity; but the men who have infused into it all its vigor, and all its venom, have placed themselves beyond the pale of compassionate forbearance. What, says Pope, must the priest be, when a monkey is the God; what must the drudges of a party be of which such men as I might name—are the leaders? These men have mingled, again and again, in the jacobin clubs at our Town House. By their harangues, they have goaded masses of people almost into acts of violence. The power of these men, God be thanked! is not equal to their malevolence. They differ from each other in character and in pursuit. Some of them are vivacious and noisy. Others are moved by a sedate malice; "and when they smile, I feel an involuntary emotion to guard myself from mischief." *

Fellow Citizens:—If the politicians, the tribe of the has-beens and the tribe of the would-bes, had done their duty in this matter, there would have been no trouble. They connived at the free suffrage movement; they supplied the vital fluid, which has nourished the monster; and they now hope to make political capital for themselves, by magnifying his strength, and spreading abroad reports of his fearful prowess. They might have put a spear into the hide, or a hook into his nose of the leviathan; but they preferred to follow in his wake, or to nestle themselves by his side. In the language of Job, "They made a covenant with him!" He was to lash the elements into fury; he was to "make the deep boil like a pot;" and they were to ride the storm, and to bring in halcyon days after the tempest!

Farmers of Rhode Island:—This is probably the last time, that any political writer will address you. The sceptre is about to depart from you, and to depart from you, forever. Those of you who have lent yourselves to your enemies, will repent, when it is too late, your fatal error. Those of you who have stood by your principles, will console yourselves by the reflection that you did what you could to breast the storm; and that, although you could not avert defeat, you have escaped without dishonor.

COUNTRY BORN.

* Junius.

PROVIDENCE JOURNAL, JANUARY 13, 1842.

THE VOICE OF "PROVIDENCE."

MR. EDITOR:—If the doctrines maintained by your correspondent "Providence" are to be received as orthodox, God save both the city and the State! They are, in my judgment, not only unsound, but dangerous. This it would be easy to show. But I am spared the task. The dispassionate and most able "Address to the members of the General Assembly," which is now before the public, and which should be read by every man in Rhode Island, goes fully into the consideration of some of the worst heresies broached by "Providence." To that pamphlet, I beg leave to direct the general attention—and, more especially, the attention of those of your readers who may be beguiled into error, by the bland and winning voice of your correspondent.

Mr. Editor:—I take exceptions, not only to the doctrines, but to the facts, reasonings, and suggestions of your correspondent. I differ from him, entirely, with reference to the character, and conduct, and aims of the free suffrage party. From first to last, that party has threatened force; and it is well known that some of its proceedings have not been marked by extraordinary reverence for the freedom of speech and the press, and the rights of private property.

Your correspondent, somewhat triumphantly, appeals to the practical operation of an extended suffrage in the States of Massachusetts and New York; and asks, "what have we to dread" from a suffrage equally extended? Is there any parallel between Rhode Island and New York and Massachusetts? Are not the landholders in both of those large States the predominant interest; and, under any system of suffrage, political power may be safely intrusted to the land owners. Are not the malignant influences of universal suffrage in the city of New York, counteracted by the votes and moral influence of the agricultural portions of that immense State? Is there the same danger that Boston and Lowell will rule Massachusetts, by means of their floating masses, as that Providence and Natick will rule Rhode Island by means of their floating masses? Is there, in fine, a State in the whole Union, where the experiment of universal suffrage would be so dangerous to public peace, and to the rights of property, as in the State of Rhode Island? We have political gamesters and hucksters enough, in all conscience, even under our present system. Once extend the right of suffrage to every man, twenty one years of age and over, and these political gamesters and hucksters will be spread over the State as plenty as blackberries; they will constitute the majority, to which, if the pliant doctrines of the times are to prevail, "the minority must submit"—no matter how that majority is obtained, or of what materials composed.

Mr. Editor:—I am sorry not to be able to agree with your correspondent in any thing. He suggests to the Whigs of Rhode Island the propriety of assembling and urging upon the Legislature the adoption of further measures in relation to a written Constitution. We have had disorder and agitation enough already; and any meeting, got up for the purpose intended by your correspondent, would inflame rather than allay excitement. For one, I have no idea of backing up the General Assembly, in this irregular manner. If they have not the spirit and the firmness to protect their own honor and authority from violation, it is quite time that they abdicated their places, in conformity to the summons which they have received from those who assume to be their masters!

As a Whig, I wish well to the Whig party, but I would concede nothing to the threats of these suffrage men, in order to save that party from utter prostration. As a citizen and as a man, I love quiet, and am for healing counsels; but I protest against the sacrifice of the dignity of the State and of the securities of public freedom, in order to propitiate a turbulent faction, or to evade that "responsibility" which every legislator, worthy of the name, ought to be willing, in a crisis like this, to "take." In fine, I would take my stand upon the great principles of constitutional freedom. Relying on those principles, I would scorn to calculate the chances of failure or of success—more proud to fail with such principles, than, by meanly surrendering them, to win a deceitful and dishonorable triumph.

A Rhode Island Man.

PROVIDENCE JOURNAL, JANUARY 15, 1842,

THE TRUE ISSUE MADE AT LAST!

THE delegates to the Free Suffrage Convention have proclaimed, with formal pomp and ceremony, the Free Suffrage Constitution, to be the paramount law and Constitution of the State of Rhode Island and Providence Plantations! They have, also, resolved and declared, that they "will establish said Constitution, and sustain and defend the same by all necessary means!" In other words, if force be necessary, force will be used!

The delegates to this same Free Suffrage Convention have, also, directed that a certified copy of the Report of the Committee appointed to count the votes upon the Constitution; of the Resolutions which pledge its friends to sustain and defend it by all necessary means; and, likewise, of the Constitution itself, be communicated to his Excellency, Governor King, with a request that he communicate the same to the General Assembly. With that request, the Governor, as a matter of course, has complied.

The whole matter is now before the Legislature. What will the Legislature do; what ought the Legislature to do; are now the current and absorbing questions. These questions, are more easily asked than answered. If the transient interests of party could be postponed for the lasting interests and priceless honor of the State; if certain influential gentlemen would forget themselves, and stand forth, with the old fashioned indomitable spirit of their Rhode Island forefathers, this most extraordinary attempt to overawe and to dragoon the highest legislative authority in this State, would signally fail of its intended effect. What may be the tactics of party, and what the course of politicians, in reference to this matter, must be left to time to disclose. "In God, we Hope." Parties and politicians will, it is to be feared, take exclusive care of themselves! To offices, and influence, and honors, at home and at Washington, they are welcome. But, let them not, in order, either to save or to make themselves—let them not touch that patrimony of civic renown—bequeathed to us by noble ancestors; that patrimony in which every Rhode Island man is proud to share—that patrimony which parties and politicians never accumulated; and which, God forbid, that parties and politicians should now recklessly squander!

The true issue is now fairly made by the Suffrage Convention. A new government is to be organized, in opposition to the existing government; and to be "sustained and defended, by all necessary means!" How will the members of the Legislature meet this issue? Will they abdicate their places, in obedience to the notice which has been served upon them? Can they abdicate their places, without abdicating their own honor, as legislators—without staining, with everlasting reproach, the fair and bright escutcheon of Rhode Island? Will they legalize or gloss over the doings of the Suffrage Convention? Will they decline "the responsibility" which, as men and as statesmen, they are bound to "take?" Will they evade the issue which has been thrust in their faces; or will they meet it as it deserves to be met, with that courage, and calmness, and determination which belong to Right, and Law and Order, and which, if exhibited on this occasion, will secure the ultimate triumph of Right, and Law and Order? I have little or no confidence in parties or in politicians, as such; but the times, bad as they are, have not taught me a universal distrust of men. I see, in our General Assembly, fearless and honorable men, who, on an occasion like the present, will do what they can to save the State from confusion and from dishonor! Such men will not be awed by menace; they will not be terrified by an array of numbers; they will scorn the expedients of pimping politicians.

The people look to the General Assembly to assert, by some solemn act or resolutions, the authority of the laws of the State. A convention of their delegates is soon about to re-assemble, for the purpose of finishing the important work confided to them, under the most solemn legal sanctions. The people ask, that this Convention may be protected in the exercise of its legitimate powers. They ask, in fine, their Government to stand by them, and to stand by itself. In the hour of need, they will not be wanting; they will sustain and defend their government, and themselves, "by all necessary means."

We have, indeed, fallen on evil times, if the outrage meditated by the Free Suffrage Convention, can be quietly consummated. I am about to adopt, as my signature, a name, without fear and without reproach. Were John Brown and the patriots of his time now alive, with what mingled shame and indignation, would they look upon the scenes now passing in review before us! But that noble race of men has perished from off our land! "Those suns are set! Oh rise some other such!"

JOHN BROWN.

PROVIDENCE JOURNAL, JANUARY 17, 1842.

TO THE PEOPLE OF RHODE ISLAND.

THE FREE SUFFRAGE CONSTITUTION.

FELLOW CITIZENS:—The constitution of a State is the fundamental law of a State. It regulates the action of the government organized under its provisions, and it regulates also the action of the people, by whom, in their sovereign capacity, it is established. Acts of ordinary legislation, which affect large interests and numerous individuals, are required to pass through many cautious forms, and to be debated, day after day, and, sometimes, week after week, in assemblies composed of men representing opposite sentiments and conflicting interests. This is all right and proper. Truth is elicited by discussion; jarring opinions are harmonized, and the greatest good of the whole is, in the end, presumed to be accomplished. The minority, in all such cases, are present; the minority are heard in defence of their rights and interests; and, whatever the result, the minority abide by it—because it is a result fairly obtained, in the regular constitutional exercise of the legislative power.

If grave acts of ordinary legislation require so much deliberation, and form, and discussion; if they demand the presence and scrutiny of a jealous minority; what shall be said of the manner in which a constitution, the fundamental, the paramount law, should be formed and established? Ought a constitution, which is intended to last, perhaps, for centuries; which cannot be repealed or amended, like an ordinary statute; which operates on all interests and on all individuals—ought a constitution, I ask, endowed, as it must be, with vast power, either for good or for evil, to be formed and established in any other than the most grave, deliberate, and solemn manner? Ought not all its principles and provisions to be scanned by the best men in the State—men animated by the best spirit, and intending the best ends? Ought it not to be made by the people, and for the people, and according to forms which secure to the minority the right to be heard?

When a constitution is once formed, according to regular and safe precedents, ought it not to be submitted to the people, in the mode best fitted to ascertain the opinions and the will of the people; and at a time, too, when reason, and not passion, governs the public mind? Above all, if, in the election of the humblest officer in the State, the most cautious provisions are made against fraud, ought a constitution to be voted for in a mode, which, if not contrived to facilitate fraud, is most happily adapted to the purposes of fraud?

Fellow Citizens:—Under what circumstances was the free suffrage constitution formed and adopted by the Convention? By whom and for whom was it made? In what manner was it submitted to the people, for their sanction? I do not purpose to review all of the extraordinary proceedings of this extraordinary movement. Some of these proceedings, however lightly they may now be regarded, are of a character to live in history—perpetual memorials of the shame and dishonor of profligate politicians. Do these men never pause, in their mad career, to think how their conduct will appear to future times? Have they forgotten the indignant reproach which Washington applied to the people of Rhode Island, in consequence of their conduct relative to the adoption of the present national Constitution? The exact words of Washington I will quote. In a letter to General Lincoln, he thus vents his almost impassioned reprobation of the course into which political leaders had betrayed the people of this State:

"No doubt is entertained of North Carolina; nor would there be any of Rhode Island, had not the majority of those people bid adieu, long since, to every principle of honor, common sense, and honesty."

Let the political leaders of the present day have a care how they act in reference to the free suffrage constitution! Let them neither do, nor suffer to be done, aught which shall stamp a whole people with disgrace on the records of history!

At the present time, I invite public attention to only one of the unprecedented circumstances, under which this Free Suffrage Constitution was formed and adopted by the Convention. A party and not the people, was represented in that Convention. A party and not the people made the Constitution—made it, too, in a single week, and what is worse, for a single purpose! Was the like ever known before? Since the declaration of American Independence, perhaps forty Conventions have assembled, at different times for the purpose of making or altering State Constitutions. Among all these Conventions, where can the Free Suffrage Convention find its model? Was there ever before a Convention, claiming to be a People's Convention; and assembled for the express purpose of making a People's Constitution, which was so constituted that the great body of the people felt, and not without reason, that they had neither lot nor part in the matter? Was there ever before a Convention, which was composed only of one class of men, representing one political interest—and bent only upon carrying out one favorite theory? And yet this is the Convention which dubs itself the People's Convention! This is the Constitution, which is heralded forth as the People's Constitution!

Fellow Citizens:—In a question of right, I would cavil for the ninth part of a hair. In a question of right, I would make no compromises. In a question of right, I would take no counsel of fear. This Free Suffrage Constitution had a bad origin, and it deserves a bad end. It is the offspring of unhallowed political ambition; it is tainted with the grossest frauds; it cannot be established, unless the people of Rhode Island are prepared to submit to usurpation, and are willing to be covered with disgrace. There is now but one issue before the public. It is conceded, on all hands, that the distribution of representative power must be made more equal; and that the right of suffrage must, under proper regulations to protect it against abuse, be largely extended. The great question, the only question, now is—shall a Constitution be forced upon the people which they had no agency in making; in other words, shall an array of men, acting under the influence of designing leaders, and fortifying themselves by political combinations, be permitted to organize a government, in opposition to the existing government of the State? This, I repeat, is now the question. The issue has at last been fairly made. Let it, both by government and by people, be fearlessly met!

A CONSERVATIVE.

PROVIDENCE JOURNAL, MARCH 8, 1842.

RESOLUTIONS

PASSED AT A "LAW AND ORDER MEETING," HELD IN THE OLD TOWN HOUSE.

WHEREAS, a Convention of the Delegates of the people of this State, legally assembled, has framed a Constitution of government, and has submitted the same to the people for their ratification or rejection; and whereas, in the judgment of this meeting, the time has at length arrived for abandoning the frame of government under which Rhode Island has so long enjoyed the blessings of civil and religious liberty; and whereas, the important changes which the whole social condition of the people of this State has undergone, demand that the foundations of our political society should be laid anew; therefore,

1. Resolved, That we entertain a profound sense of the solemn issues which hang upon the decision of the present hour; and that we are impressed with a deep conviction, that it is both the duty and the interest of the people of Rhode Island to put forth, one and all, their most strenuous efforts, in order to ordain and establish the proposed Constitution as the supreme law of the land.

2. Resolved, That, as Rhode Island men, attached to Rhode Island institutions, and proud of the rich patrimony of civic renown bequeathed to us by our forefathers, we rejoice to perceive embodied in the proposed Constitution, those grand seminal principles of religious and civil liberty, which were set forth at the settlement of the State; which have been fearlessly maintained, through the most trying vicissitudes in her political history; which can be fettered by no territorial limits, however narrow; and which, unless, at the present crisis we prove recreant to ourselves, are destined to constitute the most precious birthright of our children.

3. Resolved, That we deem the provisions of the proposed Constitution, in relation to the right of suffrage, to be eminently liberal and conservative; because these provisions extend that essential right to all persons who "have sufficient evidence of a common interest with, and attachment to, the State;" and because, while they peremptorily exclude no man from the right to vote, they so qualify the exercise of it, in certain cases, that the whole political power of the State is not placed in the hands of persons, who, however meritorious as individuals they may be, are neither familiar with the practical working of democratic institutions; nor identified with our interests; nor, perhaps, even severed from sympathies and associations formed in foreign lands, and under monarchical governments.

4. Resolved, That while we perceive, in the organization of the Senate, no principle or provision which, in practice, will be found inconsistent with the legitimate operation of the popular will, we recognize, in

the organization of that branch of the Legislature, provisions which, while they are conservative of the rights and interests of the whole people, are wisely intended to guard from aggression the rights of minorities; and to protect from oppression the agricultural interest, no longer able, by the power of numbers, to protect itself.

5. Resolved, farther, That the organization of the Senate, as provided for in the legal Constitution, is eminently favorable to a stable and economical administration of the affairs of the State, and that, at the same time, it is adapted to operate as a salutary check upon precipitate, partial, and excessive legislation.

6. Resolved, That the provision in the proposed Constitution, relative to the mode of amending the same, allows ample facility for making such alterations as time, experience, and the sober judgment of the people shall indicate to be necessary; and that it, at the same time, interposes a barrier against the efforts of faction to alter the Constitution during those temporary inflammations of the popular mind, which are so perilous to the rights of minorities, and so hostile to a wise decision of fundamental questions in constitutional law.

7. Resolved, That, inasmuch as the proposed Constitution was framed in a spirit of compromise, it ought to be adopted in a spirit of compromise; and that, in a matter involving the highest interests of the State, its peace at home, and its reputation abroad, it is the solemn duty of all good citizens, waiving every objection, and surrendering every prepossession, to go for the proposed Constitution, heart and hand.

8. Resolved, That, in the opinion of this meeting, should this Constitution be rejected, the State could not fall quietly back upon the old Charter; but that she would inevitably be exposed to all the evils of anarchy, or sink, with tarnished honor, and with dejected hopes, under a dominion established "without law and against law."

9. Resolved, That the Honorable General Assembly of Rhode Island is entitled to the respect and confidence of every friend to the supremacy of the laws, for the calm and yet fearless manner in which, at its late session, it maintained "the rights of the existing government, and the rights of the people at large."

10. Resolved, farther, That should any crisis occur to demand our aid, we will support the General Assembly in its efforts to "maintain its own proper authority, and to protect and defend the legal and Constitutional rights of the people."

11. Resolved, That, inasmuch as the law is the highest and most authoritative expression of the popular will; and that, when the law is trampled upon, minorities are left without protection, and freedom without security, we will never tamely submit to usurpation, and that we will resist all attempts, by whomsoever made, to establish over us, a Constitution which the Legislature and Judicial departments of our Government have, in the most formal and solemn manner, proclaimed to be of "no binding force whatever."

12. Resolved, That, we shall hail the adoption of the proposed Constitution, as a signal for the termination of the unhappy strife, which has too long agitated the State, and for the return of all good men

and true to those feelings of confidence and good will, from which fellow citizens, having a common interest in the common weal, ought never to be estranged.

13. Resolved, That, while we entertain the strongest confidence that the proposed Constitution will be adopted, by an overwhelming majority, we are admonished, by the unparalleled efforts which are making to defeat it, not to repose in inaction; but to labor, in season and out of season, until this great work is accomplished, and our little State true to herself, and still hoping in her God, shall stand, with unforfeited honor, before her sister States, victorious in her noble struggle to preserve inviolate the securities of individual right, and of social order.

14. Resolved, That since the adoption of the Constitution of the United States by this State, more than fifty years ago, no crisis in her history has occurred, so big with peril to her peace, and to her character; and that it is the paramount duty of all good citizens, postponing every minor consideration, to come to the rescue of the State in this season of her trial; and to put forth their best energies to carry her triumphantly through this strife of opinions and of passions; and to anchor her safely in the grand and imperishable principles of POPULAR RIGHT AND CONSTITUTIONAL FREEDOM.

PROVIDENCE JOURNAL, APRIL 7, 1842.

THE CRISIS.

ITS PERILS AND ITS DUTIES.

THE people of Rhode Island do not require to be told that the peace of the State is in imminent danger! At such a crisis, it becomes every man, of every party, to pause and to consider, what ought to be done to avert an issue, which every man of every party must deprecate; an issue which would jeopard property, stain the public honor, for all time, and perhaps carry desolation and anguish to many a happy fireside. These are fearful hazards, which, amid the madness of passion and the shock of contending parties, men are prone to overlook. I counsel my fellow citizens to no pusillanimous compromise of principle; to no timid desertion of that which is dearer even than property or life; to no abstinence from the use of all such means as a calm prudence shall enjoin to be essential to the preservation of the public peace, the maintenance of the authority of law, the defence of the existing government of the State. I approve of all that the General Assembly* has done to save the State from anarchy, to uphold its own legitimate powers, to protect the legal and constitutional rights of the people.

I say these things, not because my individual opinion is of any moment, but because I am not willing that my counsels, at the present crisis, should be deemed to be the counsels of an enemy in disguise. I go for the laws and for the constitution of the State; and I go for them come what may. But I wish to rescue them, if not at the least possible cost, yet without provoking, by any intemperance of speech or rashness of conduct, a conflict, a tumultuous, nay, perhaps a sanguinary conflict between those who, however widely they may now be sundered, have a common interest in the State, and, come what may, be it evil or be it good, must have a common destiny. I appeal to every good citizen, whether he be friend or foe to the existing government, to exert his influence, in every way, to allay the intense excitement which now agitates the public mind. Abstain, I pray you, from all hard speeches—from all which wears the appearance of taunt, or menace, or triumph. Be as firm and as courageous as may be, in defence of your rights, but never forget that moderation, and forbearance, and magnanimity are the truest ornaments both of patriotism and of valor.

The whole question now at issue between the two parties, I yet hope, may be settled by a resort to the

* The General Assembly had recently passed "an Act in relation to offences against the Sovereign Power of the State," and had also decided upon stringent measures for the protection of the Government. This Act was called by the Dorrites "the Algerine Act."—*Ed.*

ballot box. Who would recklessly refer this grave and agitating controversy to the cartridge box? I trust there is not a man in Rhode Island who would not, if possible, avoid so fearful an alternative.

The duty of moderation and of forbearance is more especially imperative upon the friends of the existing government. The law is on their side—and the law's name, in a free government, is a tower of strength. Besides, if the exigency should require it, the friends of the existing government may look to the Executive Power of the Union, for protection against "domestic violence." According to the letter and the spirit of the Constitution, this protection must be extended, whenever it is demanded. It belongs to the Legislature of Rhode Island, or to the Governor, if the Legislature cannot be convened, and not to the President, to decide when the necessity exists for requiring the interposition of the national arm. These things are referred to, not for the purpose of intimidating the suffrage party, but to remind the friends of the State government that, with such ample resources at their command, they ought now to combine exemplary moderation with whatever energy they may be compelled to put forth in defence of the laws.

The People's Constitution is not, and never will be, the paramount law of the land. No Legislature will ever be found to legalize it. Submit it to the people, to-morrow, and they would reject it, even by a larger majority, than that which was lately arrayed against the legal constitution. It was made by a convention representing, confessedly, a minority of the people; and there is not a tittle of evidence, which would stand a moment in a court of law, to show that it has ever been adopted by a majority of the votes of the people. Mr. Atwell has publicly confessed his doubts, in relation to this matter; doubts which the result of the late contest has only served to strengthen in every mind not blinded by ignorance or by passion.

The moderate and shrewd men of the suffrage party ought, by this time, to begin to suspect that every thing which they have been told by their leaders is not true. Among other things, they have been told, that the legal constitution would be rejected by a majority of four or five thousand votes! It was rejected by a majority of six hundred and seventy six! Abstract from the whole number, the anti-slavery men, the charter men, &c., and the pure suffrage party would be left in a clear minority! They were told that if the legal constitution should be voted down, the People's Constitution would become the paramount law of the land. Does any man in his senses believe that this will be the case? They were told that the General Assembly would not dare to adjourn without legalizing the People's Constitution. The General Assembly, it is needless to say, did no such thing. They were told that all they had gained thus far, they had gained by intimidation, and that they must rely on intimidation for all they hope for. Is there not some evidence before the world, that the game of intimidation is up? Is it not time for the honest and thinking men of the suffrage party to consider what they have gained by following the counsels of men who have betrayed them to the verge of civil war? I entreat these men to pause, in their career, ere it be too late. All for which they contend, every principle involved in the controversy, can be secured, without rushing, with exasperated passions, into a conflict, of which no man can tell the issue.

Finally, fellow citizens of both parties, let me tell you that the courage which you most need is the courage to do right; and the only fear with which I seek to move you is the fear of doing wrong.

PACIFICATOR.

PROVIDENCE JOURNAL, APRIL 11, 1842.

THE CRISIS.

ITS PERILS AND ITS DUTIES.

TIME and reflection are fast bringing multitudes of our fellow citizens to the belief that the present crisis, although it will not leave us unharmed, is destined to pass by, without either tumult or bloodshed. When great interests are at stake, and strong passions are aroused, it is not strange that the bounds of temperate deliberation are sometimes transcended; and that men feel almost irresistibly impelled to dart into the arena of civil strife. In our case, I trust, this will prove but a momentary impulse. Passion will subside, and reason and law will regain their rightful ascendency.

A numerous portion of our fellow citizens have, as I believe, misconceived both their rights and their duties, in the matter which now threatens the peace of this State. I am unwilling, however, to think that any considerable number of these men are either resolved or disposed to proceed to extremities. I think so, because I believe that they must be satisfied that, even should temporary and partial success attend their efforts, the existing government and those who sustain it, will, in the end, be found in the ascendant. It is, after all, a ticklish matter even for a decided majority of the people, to subvert, in an irregular mode, the regular government of a sovereign State. And it is especially a ticklish matter, for a body of citizens, who can furnish to the world no satisfactory evidence that they are not, upon their own principles, a decided minority, to organize an opposition government, and to maintain it, come what may. When, in any case affecting the public safety, and individual and social rights, there exists a doubt, the law is entitled to the benefit of the doubt.

The law which the General Assembly felt themselves compelled to enact, in order to preserve the existing government from the meditated overthrow, and to save the people from the fearful evils of civil strife, has been stigmatized by epithets most opprobrious. What other course was left to the General Assembly, unless they abdicated the government? and even Mr. Atwell voted not to do that. The members of the General Assembly owed allegiance to the State; and, clothed as they are with all the power of the State, they would have been recreant to their trusts, if they had done nothing to arrest the threatened aggression. Justice to the people did not require them to do more. Common prudence would not permit them to do less.

No opportunity, I trust, will be given for enforcing any of the provisions of the law. So far from being vindictive, or arbitrary, or sanguinary, it is intended, by explaining the provisions of the common law, to operate rather as a paternal warning to those who might, otherwise, ignorantly incur the penalties of the common law. All States have similar laws, and with penalties, too, in some instances, much more severe.

I repeat my conviction, that if the friends of the government continue both firm and conciliatory, our little ship of State will ride out this storm in safety. Her cordage may be strained, and her sails may be torn, but her masts will remain strong, and her hull tight and buoyant. Her crew, after some hard words, will come to the very wise conclusion, that, as they are embarked in the same bottom, the interest of one is the interest of all—and the safety of one the safety of all.

On one topic, there ought to be no misconception and no disguise. There is, now, no party in this State opposed to the adoption of a written constitution, which shall extend, liberally, the right of suffrage, equalize, as far as practicable, representation in the Legislature, and define and limit the powers of the Legislature. Here, at least, we are all agreed; and if we are agreed as to the main questions, why should we quarrel about what violates no man's rights, insults no man's feelings, wounds no man's conscience. The existing government and the friends of the existing government, through every stage of this agitating controversy, have shown a spirit of moderation and forbearance which, it seems to me, is entitled to be met by a corresponding spirit. Let the tempers of men once come right, and I will answer for it, that their notions of constitutional law will come right. All parties are tired of this strife. All parties need repose, and sigh for repose. The sooner quiet is restored to the State; the sooner that the laws regain their undisputed ascendency, the sooner shall we have a written constitution—extending the right of suffrage, and redressing whatever other evils have been made a topic of complaint. For one, I shall go, heart and hand, for a constitution, deliberately framed and deliberately adopted, which shall secure the rights of all. The work of framing such a constitution ought to be delayed, only till all parties have so far cooled, that it can be the work of reason, and not of passion. In the mean time, the existing government and its friends should, calmly and resolutely, proceed in the adoption of such measures as may be necessary to preserve the public peace, and to maintain the authority of law. The interposition of the General Government has been invoked; and there is good reason to believe that it will not be refused. There is good reason to believe that the General Government, either by some emphatic declaration of its opinion or its will, or by some significant exertion of its power, will step forward, and promptly step forward, to terminate this unhappy controversy. The danger of the precedent which is attempted to be established in Rhode Island cannot be overrated at Washington, and it will not be overlooked. Should the lawful government of this State be overthrown by "the Revolution Power," without a single practical grievance to warrant the exertion of that power, who will say that any where, in this country, either individuals or minorities, or State constitutions can, for a single moment be deemed safe? Nay, more; should the principles of regulated freedom be trampled down in Rhode Island; should her gallant people be conquered by brute force; should a gloomy and malignant usurpation be suffered to overshadow them, who will answer for the stability of this glorious Union?

Whatever deluded men may think about this matter, they cannot change the true relations of things; they may deplore, but they cannot avert the consequences, the calamitous consequences, of their own acts. This Union cannot be preserved, if their creed, in respect to popular sovereignty, and the right of Revolution, is to become the orthodox creed. The true theory of democracy is eminently conservative—it is in harmony with law—it is friendly to the elevation and safety of the individual—it is regardful of the equal rights of all—but if the bastard notions of democracy which are current among us should ever find favor beyond our limits, this whole land will grow pale at the excesses which will be committed in the sacred name of liberty. Scenes of anarchy and bloodshed, not unlike those of revolutionary France, will be beheld by affrighted and oppressed millions, till they flee for refuge to a stern and relentless military despotism. Within the awful shade of such a despotism, popular freedom would perish from among us. The land which was its cradle would become its grave. And yet more—our afflicted race, in all lands, who have looked to popular freedom as the pioneer of modern revolution, and as, next to Christianity, the great hope of man, would feel in bitterness of soul, that the shadows of a long night were about to settle upon all nations.

PACIFICATOR.

PROVIDENCE JOURNAL, ARIL 8, 1842.

TO EDITORS ABROAD.

THE RIGHT.

FROM the tone of many of the papers in other States, it is presumed the true question at issue in Rhode Island, between the government of the State and a portion of the people on one hand, and another portion of the people on the other hand, is not clearly and distinctly understood. The papers to which we allude, treat the matter as though the present existing controversy was between those who demand an extension of suffrage, and a written constitution, and those who oppose both, and determine to maintain the old charter form of government through all time, and at all hazards. Such is not the case. The very men who oppose the party which wage war against the government—the very men who stood by the government for its support—have just voted for a constitution which, had it been adopted, would have extended the right of suffrage to every native born citizen of the United States, resident in this State for two years, and being twenty one years of age and upwards; and that, even without so much as a tax qualification. Had the other party accepted that constitution, which the aristocrats, as its friends are so significantly called by others, labored so earnestly and zealously to have done, it would, at the approaching election, have thrown the entire political and civil power of the State, and the city of Providence, at once into the hands of those who have rejected it. And why was it rejected? It was a constitution prepared and given out by a convention duly called under the sanction of the legal authorities of the State. It conceded more than the advocates of an extended suffrage had ever demanded. Not only so, but the convention that framed it had been called, though not formed, before the call had gone out for the, so called, People's Convention. To contravene the doings of the General Assembly, and to render nugatory the doings of the legal convention, the call for the People's Convention was issued after the call for the other, and the delegates to it chosen before the election of delegates to the other. And the People's Constitution was given out, and pretendedly adopted, before the legal constitution had closed its labors, and before it was known, or would be known, what the result of those labors would be.

The true issue between the parties is, not whether the non-freeholder shall or shall not, have the elective franchise. That he shall, has already been decided by the vote on the constitution; because those who voted against the constitution, and those who voted for it, are alike in favor of an extended suffrage; and the measure will be carried out. The true reason why the late proposed constitution was rejected is, not the demerits of the instrument itself, but the fact of its not being the offspring of the party that rejected it; for they have frequently avowed that they would vote against it, even were it word for word like that they had already sanctioned. This declaration, and the principle it contains is well known to have pervaded the body of our opponents at large, sets the matter in its true light. They will abide by no constitution, but one of their own creation, unless compelled by circumstances beyond their control. And, while the government of the State, and the voters under the laws of the State, have held out the offer of concession on legal grounds, the opposing party have spurned those conditions, laughed at the laws, treated the proposed concession with scorn and contempt, planted themselves firmly on revolutionary ground, boldly declared that they will accept no compromise, and that, by physical force, if necessary to their object, they will overthrow the existing government, and erect their own on its ruins. This is the true state of the case as it actually exists; and it does appear extraordinary, if people in other States are acquainted with the facts, that they should, for a moment, deem it expedient or right to encourage a spirit that not only spurns the restraints of existing laws, but seeks to rend, and trample on, the social bonds which constitute the only ground of law and safety to any community.

One of the People.

PROVIDENCE JOURNAL, MAY 24, 1842.

THE CHIEF OF THE INSURGENTS.

THOMAS W. DORR, late the commander in chief of the Rhode Island Insurgents, has proved to the world that he is no hero. He ran away once—he ran away twice! Let his accomplices in guilt seek to wrap it up as they may, this is the naked fact. There is no mistake. He ran away, neither to seek temporary repose for himself, nor to allow temporary repose to others, but for the express purpose of shielding his mortal body from harm. He left both his cloak and his sword behind him! That well known cloak, of revolutionary memory, which the veteran constitution builder never laid aside, till, having exhausted the argument, he stood before the world, in Hidden's barouche, a warrior in arms, and with a warrior by his side! that venerable and venerated cloak, ah! what a tale it might unfold! That sword, too, which, when danger was at a distance, the Insurgent Chief brandished so fiercely,—who is to inherit that precious relic? Who more worthy to inherit it, than his gallant Secretary of State, who shared with him the pomp and

* On the night of the 17th of May, the insurgent forces, led by Dorr in person, made a demonstration against the State's Arsenal.—*Ed.*

circumstance of glorious war—who helped him fire off a Proclamation daring the whole Union to take the field against him—who, more glorious service still! picked up the nosegays thrown by the girls into the barouche which bore the Governor and his valiant Secretary along the streets of Providence in triumphal progress; and who, it is related, ever and anon coolly smelt of the senosegays, even while the commander in chief was flourishing his sword aloft in air, and threatening to baptize it in blood!

Prolific as this whole drama is in topics for ridicule and for withering sarcasm, we are disposed to leave the weapons of ridicule and of sarcasm to be wielded by other hands. The wrongs which have been done the State, the awful perils from which we have been most mercifully delivered, and the developments of dark passion and of evil purpose, which have been witnessed through every stage of this revolutionary strife, incline us, far more strongly, to the sad than to the mirthful mood. We owe it, under God, to the stout hearts and to the strong arms of those citizens of Rhode Island, who perilled their lives upon the issue, that this fair city did not, on the night of the 17th, become the prey of terrific ruffianism. Woonsocket and Pawtucket, and the myrmidons of the insurgent chief in this city, did what they dared to do, to bring about a result so fearful. Let the damning fact be remembered, and remembered for all time. The men of Newport, and Warren, and Bristol, and East Greenwich came to the rescue; and, in alliance with our own brave spirits, they won a bloodless triumph over the ferocious bands collected by Dorr for the purpose of establishing, by military force, his usurped authority.

Let this fact, too, be preserved in imperishable and grateful remembrance. These men, these "aristocrats," as they have been reproachfully termed, stood, foot to foot, and shoulder to shoulder, in defence of the supremacy of the laws; in defence of the rights of the majority, sought to be trampled upon by a factious minority; in defence of the great principle of the sovereignty of the people, which, had the insurgents triumphed, would have received its death blow; in defence of the blessings of regulated liberty, against the assaults of an armed mob. The scenes to which we have alluded will not soon be forgotten. When they come to be faithfully recorded, none but the insurgent chief and those whom he and the men like him have instigated to acts of treason, need blush to look upon the record.

How full of instruction for all, more especially for young and aspiring politicians, is the fate of Thomas W. Dorr! He is now a wretched wanderer; the object of vulgar curiosity abroad; the theme of deep execration at home; a fugitive from justice; a companionless exile from his native State; an alien from the blessed sympathies of the fireside; a victim to perverted ambition; carrying about, whithersoever he goes, the brand of treason and of cowardice stamped upon his forehead! Such is his fate. A far nobler destiny he might have achieved. He is endowed with intellectual powers which, had they been properly directed, would have always secured him a commanding influence. Those powers, too, were disciplined by an education more accomplished perhaps than any man of his age in Rhode Island has been privileged to obtain. As a man of science or of letters, he might have attained honorable distinction, had he chosen to dedicate his time either to science or to letters. As a statesman, but for his impracticable temper and his utter destitution of moral principle, he might have rendered his native State substantial service. Had he proved true to her, she would not have been slow to confer upon him her highest honors. At any rate, he might have been a true hearted private gentleman, and what station we ask, is higher than that, enjoying the affections of home; honored by the respect and confidence of the community in which he resided; and sustained, through life, by the noble consciousness that he had sought to live in all good conscience, before man and before God. All these distinctions, so worthy of a generous ambition, he chose to forego, that he might work with dark and dirty men, in the dark and dirty mine of Rhode Island politics! Had he held fast to his integrity, he would have acquired the weight which belongs to a well formed character, and won the applause which follows upon a life of consistent virtue. His star might have shone in the ascendant, with benignant splendor. Naught but folly and wickedness have caused it to set, thus prematurely, behind clouds which can never pass away!

PROVIDENCE JOURNAL, NOVEMBER 29, 1842.

THE CRISIS.

THE people of Rhode Island have, at last, succeeded in establishing a new constitution of government. Our ancient constitution, familiarly called the old Charter, had, in some respects, become unsuited to our condition. Long had we lived under it, in freedom and in peace. The time for a change had, however, come, and a change has been effected, which, if it render more permanent the blessings so long enjoyed under the Charter, will leave us nothing to regret and little to desire. This important result has been accomplished under the sanctions of law. The convention which framed the constitution, assembled agreeably to the provisions of law. In all their doings, they proceeded according to law. The people voted for the constitution, according to the forms of law, without frenzy, or force, or fraud. Under the circumstances of the case, the vote in favor of the constitution may be considered as a commanding expression of the popular will. Had "the insurgents," as President Tyler very aptly denominated them, attempted to array their forces, on this occasion, they would have met with a most signal overthrow. No influence of the family of "Squirts," or of any of their numerous relatives, would have averted the catastrophe. All this they very well knew. Hence, they declined the arbitration of the ballot box. Hence, they attempt to break their fall, by talking about the interposition of a democratic Congress, or of the Supreme Court, or of the great democratic family, rendered, by recent elections, so powerful in numbers, and so full of the confidence which numbers inspire. If they can find either amusement or solace, by this sort of talk, why let them have it to their heart's content. All we desire is, that the friends of law and order, the Rhode Island party—the only party which true Rhode Island men ought now to acknowledge—will not suffer their tranquillity to be disturbed by the impotent menaces of desperate men. Having established a constitution, let us, disregarding clamor or threat, stand by our work—let us keep ourselves prepared to resist, and to resist "by all necessary means," every attempt, by whomsoever and whensoever made, to overthrow that constitution, which has now become the supreme law of the State. We have nothing to fear from any quarter, so long as we are true to ourselves. The friends of State Rights, in a democratic Congress, will never consent to the establishment of a principle, which would leave every State constitution in the Union at the mercy of the party which happens to be paramount in the national Congress. This would be consolidation with a witness. This would establish at Washington a great centralized despotism, which would be fatal alike to the rights of the States and the liberties of the people. As to any judgment which the Supreme

Court might give, should resort be had to that tribunal, we have no fears. A question, in its nature exclusively political, that Court would not consider as within its province to decide; and any decision which, in the exercise of its rightful jurisdiction, it might give, in reference to the Rhode Island question, would only serve to settle that question still more unequivocally in favor of the great principles for which we have contended. As to the great democratic party, it is not too much to say that it will be slow to interfere in our domestic concerns. "Governor Dorr" once made a strong appeal to them; but they refused to come to the rescue. The George Bancrofts and the Bradford Sumners, of Boston; and the Cambrelengs and the Vanderpoels, of New York, were, it is true, so far forgetful of themselves as good citizens and as gentlemen, as to pass resolutions expressive of profound sympathy in the most unjustifiable attempt which was ever made in any civilized community to prostrate the great bulwarks of social order. This was all they ever did, and all that they dared to do. So will it be again—and in all time to come. If unprincipled politicians can make any political capital for themselves, by taking some of the Dorr stock, they will resolve and re-resolve that Mr. Dorr is the Governor, and that the "People's Constitution" is the constitution of Rhode Island. This they may do, and this is all that they will do.

We have heard an occasional expression of alarm at the prospect of Marcus Morton's election to the chief magistracy of Massachusetts. This seems to us altogether a needless alarm. What if Marcus Morton is elected Governor of Massachusetts? What shall we lose by the change? What have we to fear from the change? How has Governor Davis helped us? How can Governor Morton harm us? Should he be elected, he will find too many troubles in Massachusetts, to leave him any disposition to seek troubles in Rhode Island. During the canvass, he made good use of the Rhode Island question; but the canvass is now over, and the season of clam-bake gatherings and of clam-bake letters is, likewise, over. We shall have no more of either. Should Marcus Morton become Governor of Massachusetts, he will kick away, in disdain, the ladder upon which he mounted into place.

We repeat it, if true to ourselves, we have nothing to fear from the enemy which lurks within, or from the enemy which may bluster from without. We have established a constitution, and we must maintain it. More than all, we have vindicated, and triumphantly vindicated, the true doctrines of popular sovereignty, and the essential principles of genuine democracy. Here, in little Rhode Island, without the aid of the general government, and with no might but that which slumbered in our own right arms, we have won a bloodless triumph in the cause of regulated freedom throughout the length and breadth of this whole land. Let not the season of triumph become the season of repose. Let us keep our armor on, ready to do and to dare, for the right, even unto the end, whatever Rhode Island may ask at our hands.

PROVIDENCE JOURNAL, DECEMBER 12, 1842.

THE CRISIS.

ITS DANGERS AND ITS DUTIES.—NO. I.

To the Members of the Rhode Island Party:—

Fellow Citizens:—Will you allow one of your number to address to your candid judgment a few considerations, in relation to the duties and the dangers of the present crisis in the affairs of Rhode Island. We have reached, at last, a stage in our progress, at which it may be well to pause, and to ask ourselves what dangers yet menace us in the distance, and in what fresh conflicts we should prepare ourselves to engage. Disdaining the wretched sophistries which thorough paced politicians, by a sort of instinct peculiar to themselves, so unwisely prefer to the simple truth, and believing that, even in politics, an upright and a manly course of action, is, in the end, the course of action most successful, I am at no loss what motives to address—what counsels to give—what measures to recommend. In one line, pregnant with meaning, your whole duty is comprehended. Persevere as you have begun, and persevere unto the end! Dismissing all personal considerations, and assigning to all party connexions a subordinate place in your regards, you combined your efforts for the vindication of a great principle. You came to the rescue of the State, when lawless violence threatened the safety of the State—you stood up for the "sovereign law, the State's collected will," when a band of "insurgents"—some of them bent on plunder, and all of them frantic with revolutionary impulses—sought to prostrate all law, except the law of force. Standing foot to foot and shoulder to shoulder, in the might of a holy cause, you presented an array of physical force and an exhibition of moral power, on which every true son of Rhode Island looked with a sentiment of exultation too profound for utterance. This array of physical force, which caused the armed bands of the insurgents to quail and to fly, was the result of a spontaneous impulse moving to their very depths the hearts of a brave and a patriotic people. No force could have summoned it into being—no force could have been the parent of that inflexible purpose and of that sustained enthusiasm which marked every look and action of these soldiers for the laws. Of what avail, in such a controversy with such men, was all the jacobin frenzy into which Dorr and Parmenter, and Stiness and Luther, had lashed their followers and their dupes? Of what avail, in such a controversy with such men, was the distempered vigor of the whole band of Rhode Island Revolutionists? I allude to these scenes, not for the purpose of recalling to memory the fearful anarchy into which these Revolutionists sought to plunge us, but to yield a tribute of honest praise to deeds which, whenever the history of Rhode Island shall come to be written, will constitute its brightest page.

Fellow Citizens of the Rhode Island party:—Thus far, all is well. You have scattered the armed forces of the insurgents. But the men who went to Acote's hill, let it not be forgotten, are the same men still. They have forsworn none of their errors—they have parted with none of their bitterness—they have renounced no scheme of mischief which you may give them an opportunity to execute with impunity. Be it, also, remembered, that the men who patronized, throughout, the doctrines which betrayed the Acote chivalry into such deep disgrace, and who waxed valiant rather in speech than in fight, are the same men still; counselling others to acts of treason, and, under whatever specious name they may seek to mask themselves, still seeking to break down the existing government of the State,—still the acknowledged champions of Thomas W. Dorr, and of that constitution which he and his adherents sought, by force, to fasten upon the people of this State. These are undeniable facts. They admonish the Rhode Island party that they ought not, in the least, to relax their vigilance, or to suffer any considerations, personal or political, to weaken the bonds of that union which is essential to the final triumph of the cause in which they have embarked. In the season of adversity, we stood by each other with a constancy which no perils could shake. Let not the season of prosperity, which now dawns upon us, be a signal for dissension—a prelude to disasters, which, if the fruit of our own doings, would doom us, after all we have suffered and achieved,

23

not only to defeat, but to dishonor. Let us not forget that, although much has been done, much yet remains to be done. We have scattered the rebel force, but we have not subdued the rebel spirit—we have taught jacobinism a lesson of caution, but we have left it full of undying hate—its powers, but not its appetite for mischief, impaired. We have established a constitution of government. It behooves us now to maintain it—to carry out its provisions with wisdom, and moderation, and firmness. To this end, the most vigorous measures ought, at once, to be adopted to effect a complete organization of the Rhode Island party; for, upon the unbroken union, and the efficient organization of that party, its success at the April election will depend.

Be assured, my fellow citizens, that your antagonists will not forget the work of organization. Not a man of them will neglect to qualify himself to vote at the election in April. Not a man of them will then fail to meet you at the ballot box. They will contend with desperate energy for political power under the constitution which has just been adopted. Need you be admonished that their success would be trumpeted by themselves, and would be hailed by their sympathizers throughout the land, as a triumph of the cause in which they have so long contended, and which, if their own words are to be credited, they are yet resolved to maintain. Can you doubt what use such men as Dutee J. Pearce, and Burrington Anthony, and John S. Harris, would make of political power? Are you willing that these men, and that men like them, should carry out the constitution which you have established? Will you give these men a chance to thrust that constitution aside, for that which they still say "has been adopted by a majority of the people, and of right ought to be the supreme law?" Do you desire that Thomas Wilson Dorr, whom these men have, in a formal manner, recently recognized as "the rightful Governor of this State," should come to rule over you? Do you wish that the Judges of the Supreme Court should become victims to the vengeance of men who have so often stigmatized and denounced them? Shall a Bench, learned and incorruptible, be sacrificed, to accommodate any three of "the nine learned lawyers," who, by their opinions on constitutional law, won for themselves so unenviable a celebrity?

If, fellow citizens, you covet none of these blessings, which our reformers are quite ready to give you, you have but to put forth your strength, and you will escape them. Remember, however, that the time for preparation is short. Whatever is done to keep Rhode Island from falling into the hands of men who will betray and dishonor her, must be done at once—in the true Rhode Island spirit—with a fixed determination, one and all, to adhere to the Rhode Island party, till every object for which that party was formed, shall be fully and triumphantly accomplished.

OLD NARRAGANSETT.

P. S. Since the above was written, I have read, in the Providence Daily Express of Saturday evening, the resolutions passed by the Suffrage Association on Friday evening. These resolutions unequivocally make known the determination of "the Insurgents" to register their names, agreeably to the provisions of the legal constitution. Let it, however, not be inferred, that, in so doing, they mean to acknowledge the validity of that constitution, or to repudiate the "people's constitution." Far otherwise. The resolutions, taken in connexion with the emphatic and very significant commentary upon them, by the editor of the "Express," remove all doubt in relation to this matter. "Governor" Dorr has been consulted, and "Governor" Dorr advises and consents to the measure which is about to be adopted, and adopted too with the distinct avowal that the legal government of the State is to be prostrated, in order that his constitution may be erected upon its ruins! It is well that these men have thus clearly defined their position. The issue is fairly made up; and by the friends of law and order, it will be fearlessly met. The Insurgents have abandoned not an inch of their original ground. They have only changed their system of tactics. Bluster, and menace, and force they have tried, and tried in vain. They are now about to try the ballot box, not for a legitimate purpose, but in the desperate hope of gaining power to sanctify, by some plausible procedure, their enterprise of anarchy and misrule. I rejoice that they have so seasonably apprised us of the profligate scheme which they have planned, and which they will endeavor to execute. The true Rhode Island men will again rally in defence of the laws. More than once, they have withstood force—they are not destined to fall before cunning. The constitution which they have just established, they will, "by all necessary means," maintain; and the reckless disorganizers, who are again plotting mischief to the State, will reap a fresh harvest of disappointment and disgrace.

PROVIDENCE JOURNAL, DECEMBER 14, 1842.

THE CRISIS.

ITS DANGERS AND ITS DUTIES.—NO. II.

To the Members of the Rhode Island Party:—

Fellow Citizens:—Never were the obligations to union and energy in support of the cause of law and order, more imperative upon you than at the present crisis. By union and energy, you have thus far, successfully resisted a most profligate attempt, and the only attempt that has been made in the history of our country, to overthrow, by force, a government founded upon the broad principles of civil and religious freedom, and administered, at all times, "for the protection, safety and happiness of the people." You have abundant reason to congratulate yourselves, not only upon the great moral triumph which you have won in the defence of regulated freedom, but upon the multiplied calamities which you have escaped. You have given to the enemies of popular institutions abroad, a renewed evidence of the capacity of the people for self government, and, at the same time, you have exhibited to the friends of such institutions at home, "an example of change without revolution, and a redress of grievances without force or violence."* All this you have done, and more than this you have done. By defeating the operation of the misnamed "people's constitution," you prevented the erection, in Rhode Island, of a popular despotism, which though, in words, it savored strongly of liberty and equality, would in its practical operation, have been fatal to both. A system better adapted to perpetuate political power in the hands of a few demagogues, and to leave both minorities and individuals, without protection against the oppression of majorities, was never devised. It was a system without checks and balances, providing for a representation of numbers in both branches of the Legislature, and making no provision, in either, for a representation of interests.

The floating population of Providence, and of every factory village in the State, was permitted to vote, without other qualifications than those of age and residence. This would have worked the complete destruction of the political power of the agricultural interest, and of all other conservative interests. The floating masses of Providence, Woonsocket, Chepachet, &c., would have ruled the State. Need you be told, fellow citizens, who and how many would have ruled these masses? Such are the provisions of the constitution recently adopted, that the farmers are not left utterly without the power of protecting themselves. They have saved something valuable to themselves and to the State, from the wreck of the old Charter. In the Senate, they can still make themselves to be felt—and their rights to be respected. Constituted

* The language of John Tyler, the President of the United States, in his first letter to Governor King.

most wisely upon principles different from those upon which the House is constituted, the Senate, it is to be hoped, will prove an efficient check upon those irregular impulses, to which the House may be temporarily liable. All experience has shown the wisdom of making, in one branch of the legislative department, some provision by which "the sober second thoughts of the people," and not their rash impulses, shall be allowed to obtain the ascendant. No such provision can be found in the "people's constitution"—for the men who made it, very well knew that it is through the passions, and not through the reason of the people, that demagogues seek to compass their ends.

There is rare truth and wisdom in the following remark by one of the ablest statesmen which it has ever been the fortune of a free country to give to the world: "Legislative assemblages are swayed by the fears and passions of individuals; when unchecked, they are tyrannical and unjust; nay more, the most unjust and tyrannical measures are the most popular." Were the "people's constitution" now in operation, what effectual barrier for the preservation of the rights of individuals and of the minority would exist? Under pretence of the public advantage, burthens, unequal and oppressive, would be imposed upon the holders of property. The evil would not stop here. Such is the malignant spirit which seems to animate the Insurgents, that they would be found to exercise political power, not only for the purposes of injustice, but to satisfy a sharpened appetite for revenge. Mr. Charles J. Ingersoll, one of the ablest of the leading democratic statesmen of the present day, declares, with as much truth as point, that "free government depends on constitutional checks; otherwise, democracy is despotism." This is sound, old fashioned democractic doctrine, which ought never, for any transient purpose, to be repudiated. The absence of all efficient checks and balances in the so called "people's constitution," and the admission of foreigners as well as of native citizens to a participation, upon equal terms, in the elective franchise, invest that instrument with the worst characteristics of a popular despotism.

I have here adverted to some of the radical defects of this "people's constitution," because the insurgents have avowed their determination to "restore its suspended animation." They persist in declaring that it is "the supreme law," and that "Thomas W. Dorr is the rightful Governor of Rhode Island." They have determined to register their names according to the provisions of the legal constitution, only that they may the more effectually consummate the work of treason and insure the triumph of jacobinism. They prate, to be sure, about carrying out in a peaceable manner the rights and doctrines heretofore advanced by the suffrage association. The whole drift of their present movement is, however artfully they may attempt to disguise it, towards another and more fearful conflict of arms. The friends of the legal constitution do not believe in a peaceable submission to despotism, and they will never tamely permit any set of men, under any pretence, to force upon them either "Governor" Dorr, or the people's constitution.

Men of the Rhode Island party—prepare yourselves for the strife which awaits you. Organize your forces at once. See that every friend to the supremacy of the laws, qualifies himself to vote at the April election.

Our success is certain, if we but preserve our union, and put forth our energies. To borrow the eloquent language of the prince of modern political philosophers, "in a cause like this, and in a time like the present, there is no neutrality. They who are not actively, and with decision and energy, against jacobinism, are its partisans. They who do not dread it, love it."

OLD NARRAGANSETT.

PROVIDENCE JOURNAL, DECEMBER 15, 1842.

THE CRISIS.

ITS DANGERS AND ITS DUTIES.—NO. III.

TO THE MEMBERS OF THE RHODE ISLAND PARTY:—

FELLOW CITIZENS:—Till we have settled the Rhode Island question, let us agitate no other question. Till we have ascertained, whether or not we are to live under a government of law, or in a state of revolutionary anarchy, let us waste no time in profitless debate about measures of public policy, affecting either the State or the nation. Till we have settled the great principles now involved in the issue before us, let us defer, till a more fitting season, all differences of opinion about men. Our dearest rights and our most valued blessings are again to be put in peril, by a band of traitors who have more than once disturbed our peace, and menaced the destruction of our whole social order. Concession and clemency and conciliation have all been thrown away upon these people, who, at the call of their leader, are again gathering their forces for the work of mischief. Let it be our main business, as it is our imperative duty, to meet this rebel power at the threshold, and to crush it forever. Our fate is in our own hands. We are strong in numbers, and our cause was never more worthy of our best endeavors to maintain it. Let us then come up, without delay, to the work of preparation for the great and the final conflict. Whether Mr. Tyler, or Mr. Calhoun, Mr. Clay, or Mr. Van Buren, shall be the next President; whether the tariff shall be revised or shall be left untouched; whether the Exchequer or the Sub-Treasury shall be adopted, are questions, which, however they might, under ordinary circumstances, excite our attention, and divide our opinions, shrink, at the present crisis, into comparative insignificance. Matters of far graver inport to us and to our children—matters that come home to our business and to our bosoms now await our decision. They demand all our thoughts, and before they are settled, they may require all our courage.

The Rhode Island Question does not require to be stated with logical precision. In November last, the people of Rhode Island established, under all the sanctions of law, a constitution of government, which was framed by their delegates assembled in convention according to the forms of law. Shall this constitution, thus established, be maintained, or shall it be overthrown? and overthrown, too, by the violent men who are steeped, to the very eyelids, in rebellion and treason against the laws and the government of the State? Shall the legal constitution, at once eminently liberal and conservative, be sheltered against the acts of usurpation by which it is attempted to be destroyed; or shall it be trodden under foot by men who avow it to be their "express purpose" to overthrow it, in order to establish the "people's constitution" upon its ruins? This is the Rhode Island Question, which every man among us well understands, and one side or other every man must take.

Men of the Rhode Island Party:—Hereafter I may have occasion to call your attention, more particularly, to some of the wise and liberal provisions of the Constitution which you have just adopted, and which you are pledged, by every consideration of attachment to the principles of temperate freedom, to maintain. At present, my chief aim is to arouse you to immediate and to strenuous efforts; to apprise you of the fresh dangers with which you are menaced; and to remind you that it is only by vigilance and activity, and constancy and courage, that those dangers can be averted. I fear nothing for the Rhode Island question, or for the Rhode Island party, but the perilous fallacy that effort is not, in the present case, needed to insure success; that our cause is safe, and that every man may now take good care of his farm, or his merchandise, his workshop, or his spindles. Let me tell you, that if you think thus, you are cherishing a delusion which may entail shame and disaster upon yourselves and upon your children. God forbid, that the fate of irresolute virtue should be yours. God forbid, that "the men of poinards" should triumph in Rhode Island, as they triumphed in Revolutionary France, over "the men of principles."

In closing this address, permit me again to appropriate the language and the sentiments of the celebrated political philosopher, whom I yesterday had occasion to quote: "In all that we have to do, whether in the struggle or after it, it is necessary that we should constantly have in our eye, the nature and character of the enemy we have to contend with. The jacobin revolution is carried on by men full of levity, arrogance, and presumption, without morals, without probity, without prudence. What have they then, to supply their innumerable defects, and to make them terrible even to the firmest minds? One thing, and one thing only—but that one thing is worth a thousand—they have energy." The jacobinism which Mr. Burke, in such emphatic terms describes, is not limited to the age of the French Revolution. No obscure traces of its footprints may be found in Rhode Island.

OLD NARRAGANSETT.

PROVIDENCE JOURNAL, DECEMBER 16, 1842.

THE CRISIS.

ITS DANGERS AND ITS DUTIES.—NO. IV.

To the Members of the Rhode Island Party:—

Fellow Citizens:—Mr. Dorr, in his recent answer to the New Hampshire sympathizers, claims that his constitution has been adopted "by the free votes of the great majority of the whole people." With that cool effrontery, for which he is somewhat remarkable, he alludes to this alleged fact, as if it had never been either denied or disproved. He likewise seems to take it for granted, that a majority of the whole people, without reference to any existing laws regulating the right of voting, have a right to change the government, at any time and in any manner they may choose. Both of these points are examined with great ability and candor, by the Hon. Elisha R. Potter, now a member of the Senate of this State, in a pamphlet entitled "Considerations on the Rhode Island Question." I am happy to avail myself of this opportunity to invite the attention of men of all parties to this pamphlet, which, together with a clear and faithful narrative of all the important facts, embodies an elaborate discussion of the great elementary principles applicable to the question in controversy. Mr. Potter does not, of course, deny the right of revolution—a right, belonging to minorities as well as to majorities, to redress their grievances by force, when grievances have become intolerable, and when they can, in no other way, be redressed. The doctrine of a peaceable, legal revolution, he very properly classes among the discoveries reserved for this enlightened age and people! After showing, very conclusively, that even a majority of the whole people have not the right to change the government of a State, at any time and in any manner, without consulting either the government or the minority, he examines, somewhat at length, the alleged fact of the majority claimed for the People's Constitution. To this part of Mr. Potter's pamphlet, which is here subjoined, without alteration or abridgment, I ask the special attention of every man of the Rhode Island party. Thus far, the insurgents have tried both fraud and force, without avail. They are now about to try the former alone, in order to consummate by fraud an act begun in fraud. The extracts from Mr. Potter's pamphlet, given below, show how they managed matters at the outset. What good thing have we a right to hope from these desperate men, hereafter?

"EXAMINATION OF THE FACT OF THE MAJORITY CLAIMED FOR THE PEOPLE'S CONSTITUTION.

"Its advocates claim that the people's constitution received the votes of a majority of American citizens in the State, over twenty one years of age, and also a majority of the legally qualified freemen. In proof of this, they appeal, first, to the return and canvass of the votes by their own convention in January; and, secondly, to their having succeeded in defeating the landholders', or legal constitution, as it was called, in March, 1842. Let us examine both these assertions.

"The circumstances, under which the vote was given for the people's constitution, in December, 1841, have already been stated. The party was supposed to have for its object, extension of suffrage alone, and few, at least, in the country part of the State, except its leaders, suspected any ulterior design. A great number, therefore, who were sincerely in favor of extension of suffrage, gave their votes for it as a mere expression of their opinion, never thinking that the constitution could go into effect. That this was the case with a great number, we think will appear from the reasons we shall offer presently.

"But it has, also, been charged, that there were great frauds committed in taking the vote; and it certainly offered great facilities for fraud. There was no challenging of votes, because the opposite party refused to take any part in it. The voting was, for the first three days, in open town meeting, and then, for the three following days, all the active friends of the cause exerted themselves in going around and procuring the signatures of as many as they could, and sending in their names to the moderators. Between four and five thousand were obtained in this way, in the last three days.

"The census of 1840 makes the number of free white males in the State, over twenty one years of age, as near as can be computed, twenty five thousand six hundred and seventy four; free colored males, over twenty four years of age, six hundred and sixty eight.

In calculating the number necessary to make a majority, a deduction of three thousand has generally been made from this, for foreigners not naturalized, paupers, &c.

"The greatest number of freemen who ever voted at any election, was eight thousand six hundred and twenty two, at the presidential election, in November, 1840. But, in the country towns especially, the population is scattered, and there is seldom a full attendance, and, by calculating the number of voters and of absentees in several towns, and applying the same ratio to the State, the number of legally qualified voters, under the old laws, has been variously estimated at from eleven to twelve thousand. The number of freemen, claimed to have voted for the people's constitution, is four thousand nine hundred and sixty. On the tickets, which they voted, were printed the following words: 'I am ——— qualified to vote according to the existing laws of the State.' And it has been said, that a great many of the non freeholders forgot to insert the not.

"In the town of Newport, they have long been charged with committing the greatest frauds, and the reason they have never attempted to disprove these charges is, probably, because they could not be refuted. They claimed to have obtained one thousand two hundred and seven votes for the people's constitution, of whom they say three hundred and seventeen were freemen.

"In making up the whole number of one thousand two hundred and seven, they took the names of the soldiers at the United States fort, of the people at work for the government at Fort Adams, of people who had been, for a long time, gone to sea, or absent from the State. And, from an actual and careful examination of the list of their voters, it is estimated by a person, who is probably better qualified to judge than any other man in that town, that not more than seven hundred and fifty, at most, out of the one thousand two hundred and seven, were qualified to vote even upon the very liberal terms of the people's constitution, which admitted foreigners to vote for it, and required no specific period of residence. And when, only three months aferwards, in March, 1842, the vote was taken upon the legal constitution, and every person who had resided in the State two years, was admitted to vote, and only foreigners and the transient population excluded, the people's party, notwithstanding they brought every man to the polls, could only obtain three hundred and sixty one votes against it. Here is a falling off from one thousand two hundred and seven, when they took the vote their own way, to three hundred and sixty one, when it was taken in legal town meeting, where the votes were challenged, and the transient population excluded. And both parties together, at this same town meeting, could only obtain one thousand and ninety one votes, while the people's party claimed to have obtained for theirs, one thousand two hundred and seven votes.

"Again; they claim to have obtained, in Newport, three hundred and seventeen freemen for the people's constitution. The same gentlemen, before referred to, who personally knows almost every freeman in the town, estimates that, at least, ninety of these were no freemen at all. And, of the others, a great number voted merely as an expression of opinion, and some for party purposes. How else, if there was no fraud, can it be accounted for, that, in the legal town meeting, where the very same freemen voted, subject, however, to a legal scrutiny, that this vote fell off from three hundred and seventeen to one hundred and two, and that both parties together could only obtain four hundred and seventy five. The town meeting of December, the people's party had all their own way. The other was conducted according to law, although the same people voted, and every offort was made on both sides.

"Such frauds as these would be most likely to be committed in the cities and large manufacturing towns, such as Newport, Providence, Smithfield, Cumberland, Warwick, &c. In a great many of the country towns, the vote was probably very fairly conducted.

"The convention, on counting their votes, declared the whole number, freeholders and non freeholders, to be thirteen thousand nine hundred and forty four; and that their constitution was adopted by a majority of the American citizens over twenty one.

"The people's party did, indeed, offer all their votes to the examination of the General Assembly, and it has been triumphantly proclaimed abroad, that the Assembly, by refusing to receive or examine them, had waived all right to dispute the fact of a majority. But it is to be recollected, that the General Assembly considered all the proceedings illegal, and they could not receive the votes without giving up the principle they contended for. The fact of there being a majority, has always been denied by the other party.

"The People's Convention, at their meeting, January 13, 1842, by resolution, authorized the secretaries to copy any part of the registry of the votes, or of the votes themselves, upon the application of any person. Several individuals, accordingly, obtained lists of those who had voted in their own towns, and commenced examining them. But a stop was soon put to this, and, at a meeting of some of the suffrage party in Providence, they actually undertook to overrule the orders of the convention of the sovereign people; countermanded this authority, and prohibited any more copies being given. How they can justify this, even upon their own loose principles of government, remains to be seen.

"Thus the General Assembly cannot examine the votes without yielding the principle contended for; and private individuals are not permitted to. They are thus effectually secured against examination.

"The next vote which has been appealed to as a test, is the vote on the landholders' constitution in March, and it is contended, that the defeat of this constitution, amounted to a reaffirmance of the vote on the people's constitution.

"Soon after the vote on the people's constitution, the legal convention completed theirs. It extended suffrage to all native American citizens, upon two years' residence, without any property or tax qualification. Foreign born citizens were required to possess a freehold. All who could vote under the constitution, were authorized to vote for or against its adoption.

"The "people's" party resolved to attempt the defeat of the legal constitution. The contest was of the most exciting character. The like of it has not been in Rhode Island within the writer's recollection. The result was, for the constitution, eight thousand and thirteen; against it, eight thousand six hundred and eighty nine; total, sixteen thousand seven hundred and two. Majority against it, six hundred and seventy six.

"Now, let us examine of what materials this number of eight thousand six hundred and eighty nine, was composed. A large number of the freeholders voted against the constitution, because they were opposed to so great an extension, and some, because they were opposed to any constitution at all. A large number of people in the northern part of the State opposed it, because too much strength in the Senate was given to the southern counties. Still more were influenced by the misrepresentations circulated, in relation to the right of fishery. They were told, that the legal constitution abridged, or took away their rights on the shore, and their rights of fishery. There was no part of the constitution that was not fully discussed, and every possible objection urged to suit different localities and prejudices. In allowing one thousand five hundred to have voted from all these considerations, we think we are very reasonable. There would then remain, seven thousand one hundred and eighty nine. What a falling off from the thirteen thousand nine hundred and forty four, who are said to have voted for the people's constitution, in December, 1841, only three months previous!

"But, even all of these seven thousand one hundred and sixty nine, did not vote against the legal constitution, because they wished the people's constitution to become the law of the land. It cannot be denied, for it was industriously circulated, and the impression was generally produced, that, as the whigs had a majority in the freemen's convention, the legal constitution was so framed, that its adoption would secure the power of the State to the whigs, or the aristocracy. It was considered as a whig measure, and great numbers of democrats voted against it for no other reason. And a report was circulated in the south part of the State, that Governor Fenner and Governor Francis, men who stood high in the confidence of the democratic party, had voted for the people's constitution. It is almost needless to say, the report was false; but numbers were influenced by it.

"But even if no deductions are to be made at all, if the whole eight thousand six hundred and eighty nine, were supporters of the people's constitution, where were the rest of the thirteen thousand nine hundred and forty four? No exertion was spared to bring every one of their men to the polls, every argument was used, and every passion appealed to, as the files of the suffrage newspaper will show, and the people, in all parts of the State, were aroused and excited by means of paid lecturers, for several weeks preceding the election. The prejudices of the poor against the rich, were openly appealed to. The falling off can only be accounted for in another way. We have said, that, at the voting for the people's constitution, there was no challenging of votes, for there was no officer who had the authority to administer an oath, and no means of preventing fraud, and also that a considerable number put in votes for it, merely as an expression of opinion in favor of free suffrage, and not meaning that it should ever be the supreme law of the land. But in voting for the legal constitution, both parties were present, the votes were challenged, the closest scrutiny applied, and the foreign population, and transient persons, (of whom there is a very great number, manufacturing being the leading business of the north part of the State, and the government works employing a great many at Newport,) were excluded. All these had probably voted for the people's constitution. Besides, all those who had voted for the people's constitution merely as an expression of an opinion, now came forward and voted for the legal constitution, because it provided a very liberal extension.

"Here, then, even taking the whole number, the friends of the people's constitution, in March, in a town meeting, conducted according to law, and where the voting was confined to the permanent population, could only muster eight thousand six hundred and eighty nine votes, just about one third of the male population over twenty one. So much for this second test of their majority.

"The number of freemen claimed to have voted for the people's constitution, in December, was four thousand nine hundred and sixty. The number of freemen who voted against the legal constitution, in March, was about two thousand six hundred and eighty, from examinations of the records made by the town clerks of the several towns. Here, too, is a large falling off, which can only be accounted for in a similar manner.

"The vote for State officers, in April, 1842, was no test of anything. On the charter election day, Governor King and his ticket, received four thousand nine hundred and sixteen votes from both political parties. General Carpenter was voted for by the qualified voters of the suffrage party, and by a considerable number of democrats, and received two thousand three hundred and ninety two votes. As these elections were under the old law, none but freeholders voted. There was no serious opposition, and the strength of neither party brought out. On their election day, the people's party put in over six thousand five hundred for Mr. Dorr, as governor. There was no opposition, of course, but yet considerable exertion was made to get their voters out, in order to make a show of numbers.

"We will close this examination of the question of the majority, by observing, that the famous nine lawyers, in their Statement of Reasons, in defence of their course, do not assert that they ever obtained a majority. They contend for the right of the majority to make a constitution, and, although the whole document is so worded as to produce the impression that they believed the constitution had been adopted by a majority; yet they did not dare to risk their reputation upon a positive assertion of it as a fact. The document is thus, though perhaps unintentionally, deceptive. One of the number, an able and distinguished advocate, has since, repeatedly and publicly, expressed his doubts of the people's constitution ever having obtained such a majority."

In connexion with the significant facts which Mr. Potter has embodied in the preceding extract, it should, also, be remembered, that the convention which formed the people's constitution owes its origin to a committee appointed by a mass meeting of the suffrage party, at which a majority neither of that party nor of the people was present. It should, also, be remembered, that even according to the showing of the insurgents, not more than seven thousand persons, freeholders and non freeholders, took any part in electing their delegates, "and to make up this number, it has been said that spectators and people of all sorts were included."* And yet more; the constitution, framed by a convention thus authorized and thus chosen, was adopted, if the fraudulent votes be excluded, by less than a majority even of those persons, whom the sovereigns permitted to vote upon the question. During all that memorable struggle, in what Mr. Dorr, with inimitable gravity and self complacency, designates "the cause of constitutional freedom and equal rights," the discussion and the voting were all on one side! In the midst of the new born fervor for equal rights, it seemed to be forgotten, that individuals and minorities had any rights to be acknowledged and protected. The spirit of the mob seemed to rule in every thing; and these men disposed of the gravest matters, according to their own crude notions of "constitutional freedom," and with the same temper of insolent domination which marked the Parisian jacobin clubs in the days of revolutionary France. The constitution which they had denominated "the people's," they could not, either by menace or by the exercise of actual force, compel the people to accept.

This is the constitution, thus framed, thus adopted, and thus attempted to be forced upon us, which the insurgents now avow their determination, by an act of most flagitious usurpation, to establish—by an act of usurpation which must provoke the sternest resistance of every Rhode Island man who is not prepared to become a slave. This is the constitution for which a man

* Mr. Potter's pamphlet.

of education, and, at one time, of gentlemanly associations, consented to become the chief of "a robber brood," and threatened, with blood and rapine, the fair city which now blushes for her degenerate son. This is the constitution for which the legal constitution is to be thrust aside, if, by any means, the insurgents can obtain political power. This is the constitution, for the purpose of establishing which, unprincipled men now seek to betray the ignorant into the crimes of rebellion and treason, and to plunge the State into all the horrors of anarchy! No man complains, nor has any right to complain of those who, for any legal purpose, may choose to qualify themselves to exercise the right of suffrage under the new constitution, at the elections in April. No man would have a right to complain, whatever might be his regrets in the matter, should the insurgents gain the political power in April, and use it according to the plain provisions of the new constitution. But every man has a right to complain, and to feel alarmed and indignant, when these men avow their intention to acquire political power, through the instrumentality of that constitution, and then, "without law and against law," to establish the people's constitution upon its ruins!

Men of the Rhode Island Party:—The act which your opponents, in plain language, declare that they mean to do, would be without a parallel in the annals of political profligacy. It would involve you and the State in fresh and complicated troubles—it would be destructive to all constitutional freedom in Rhode Island—it would be hailed by despots throughout the world as the most fatal blow which has yet been given to the great cause of democratic liberty. It remains for you to decide whether these men shall have the power to do this great mischief. You have the physical power and you have the moral power. You have both the might and the right—and naught but activity and energy are wanting to insure your final triumph. Remember that the time is short. After the 30th day of this month, no name can be registered. Let me counsel you, then, to imitate, in one respect, the conduct of your opponents. Divide and subdivide every town into such districts as will enable you to ascertain, with perfect accuracy, how many of the friends of legal government remain to be registered. If you do your duty in this matter, the State will be saved from the rule of men who would dishonor her character by acts of usurpation and revenge, which would leave us naught of freedom but its name.

OLD NARRAGANSETT.

PROVIDENCE JOURNAL, DECEMBER 20, 1842.

THE CRISIS.

ITS DANGERS AND ITS DUTIES.—NO. V.

TO THE MEMBERS OF THE RHODE ISLAND PARTY:—

FELLOW CITIZENS:—The shameless doctrines which are avowed, and the no less shameless plans which are meditated, by the Insurgents, ought to convince every thinking man that the Rhode Island Question is the great question of the day—not only for the State, but for the Nation. These doctrines and these plans ought, likewise, to arouse every man who carries a Rhode Island heart in his bosom, to put forth, at once, all his might to defeat the desperate enterprise which Dorr and his accomplices are now seeking to accomplish. The Presidential Question, however important it may be to the country at large, is not vitally important to us. However the people may decide it, our essential rights and our essential interests will be left unimpaired. Nothing disastrous to the great cause of constitutional freedom have we to apprehend, either from Mr. Tyler, Mr. Calhoun, or Mr. Clay. Differ they may about measures of administrative policy, yet, they are all conservative Statesmen—all friends to a government of checks and balances—all hostile to the revolutionary principles of Dorr and his party. In asserting the transcendent importance of the Rhode Island question, I am betrayed into no exaggeration. It is a domestic question of the gravest character. It should be treated in a grave mood, and settled by every man among us under a sense of the most solemn responsibility. It touches, in innumerable points, our dearest rights and our most important interests—not only affecting our own present peace, and security, and good name—but extending its influence, for good or for evil, to the generations who are to come after us.

While the general government provides for the common defence and the general welfare, it is exclusively the province of the State government to exercise its powers on that large mass of rights and interests which most deeply concern life, liberty and property. It becomes us, then, to look well to our State government; it becomes us to take good care that it is established upon right foundations, and is administered by the right men, and in the right spirit. The laws which come home the most nearly to our business and our bosoms, emanate from our own Legislature. The magistrates, executive and judicial, who are charged with the administration of those laws, derive all their authority from the same source. Whether those laws shall be enacted and executed by wise and well principled men, and in a spirit of justice and moderation, or whether they shall become, in the hands of profligate rulers, the instruments of oppression, depends upon the intelligence and virtue and moral courage of the people. Your fate, my fellow citizens, is in your own hands. If you do but comprehend the issue which is now made, I have no fears that you will not manfully meet it. Still less do I fear that you will fail, by another and yet more emphatic declaration of your will, to convince the disturbers of your peace that it is quite as hard to circumvent as to frighten you.

Men of the Rhode Island Party:—Is not the Rhode Island question the great question of the day, not only for the State, but for the nation? If the licentious doctrines now broached by the insurgents, and which they will endeavor to reduce to practice, should ever come to be sanctioned as American constitutional law, what, I ask you, will be the fate of American constitutional freedom? Of what avail will be those checks and balances, without which a democracy is a despotism, if the majority may, at any time and in any manner, destroy them? If a constitution framed by a convention, assembled according to law, and adopted by a vote of the people according to law, can be thrust aside for a constitution framed and adopted "without law and against law," the people of this country will soon come to feel little reverence either for laws or for constitutions. If Mr. Dorr's revolutionary dogmas are to find favor in this State, Revolutions, but not always peaceable revolutions, will become the food, rather than the extreme medicine, of the body politic. If great fundamental laws can be thus unceremoniously changed, how long will the American constitution escape a formidable assault? How long will the friends of "equal rights" in "the empire State" be satisfied that one hundred and eight thousand Rhode Islanders should possess as much political power in the Senate of the United States, as nearly three millions of New Yorkers? Finding other modes of redress unavailable, how long will the sovereign people of the United States forbear to touch, in their "primary capacity," some of the organic provisions of this Constitution now deemed to be unjust? Should they unite their strength, what difficulty would the "sovereignty" of the great States find in carrying out their doctrines of "equal rights?" Not only do Mr. Dorr's doctrines bring into peril the Constitution of the Union, which, by the by, the people, in their primary capacity, never adopted, and to which a majority of them, as is well known, were decidedly opposed, but it endangers the stability of every State Constitution in the land. Connecticut and New Hampshire may yet come to taste of the poisoned chalice which they have commended to our lips. Their Constitutions may be thought to demand reform, and some illustrious tribune of the people, emulous of Dorr's fame, may yet rise up to begin the work.

Fellow Citizens:—Settle the Rhode Island Question according to the principles maintained by the Rhode Island Party, and this tide of revolutionary frenzy, which threatens to roll over the land, will be turned back. Visit, once more, with your scathing rebuke, the man and the party, who twice made an abortive effort to subdue you by means of an armed mob. Let him and them be made to feel that all sorts of crimes are not to be perpetrated, with impunity, in the name of "democracy and equal rights." Teach him and them, once and for all, the lesson which they seem so slow to learn, that no man and no party can ultimately triumph, who, in their choice of means, and in their estimates of success, make no account of the moral sense which God has implanted in the heart of man. Mr. Dorr may brandish once more that sword, in tragic fury; he may issue valiant proclamations; he may write letters to the faithful at home; he may recruit, by his harangues, the declining sympathy of friends abroad—yet, for his darling purpose, all this will be of no avail. He has outraged too deeply the moral sensibilities of the people of Rhode Island—he has animated them with too much righteous indignation against himself and his principles, ever to regain their forfeited confidence and favor. Instead of making penitence the companion of that banishment which his friends are pleased to dignify with the name of exile, he is now engaged in maturing fresh plans of mischief. In a letter addressed to his partisans, under date of December 15, and written at Concord, he counsels them to register their names, under the legal Constitution, for the purpose of effecting the great object which they have in view, viz.: "The establishment in fact as well as in right, of the People's Constitution." In the same letter, he likewise, with his characteristic modesty, speaks of the existing government as "the military despotism which now controls the State." Shame upon the man who thus defames the State which he has done so much to injure! Shame upon the man who, while boasting that he has both the right and the might, does not oppose to this "military despotism" the most heroic resistance; but runs away to New Hampshire, there to concoct, in communion with her dirty politicians, a dirty scheme, for compassing, by fraud, what he has not the courage to attempt by force!

Men of the Rhode Island party! We engage, under the most cheering auspices, in this fresh strife to sustain the laws and the constitution of the State. Our ranks are unbroken, and are animated by a spirit worthy of our cause, and prophetic of the victory which awaits us. One struggle more with the disturbers of our peace, and the principles of a rational and temperate freedom, for which we have so long contended, will be finally and triumphantly vindicated. Let us then go, one and all, for Rhode Island, and for nothing but Rhode Island! Preserve to us our old Rhode Island ANCHOR, which has clung through many a storm, the noble patrimony of liberty and law inherited from our fathers—and we will rest in HOPE—confident of our ability to ride out in safety whatever tempests may chance to gather in the distant sky.

OLD NARRAGANSETT.

PROVIDENCE JOURNAL, DECEMBER 24, 1842.

THE CRISIS.

ITS DANGERS AND ITS DUTIES.—NO. VI.

To the Members of the Rhode Island Party :—

Fellow Citizens :—A stranger to our political history would infer, from the reproachful epithets lavished by the Dorrites upon the old Charter, that, for the last two hundred years, the people of Rhode Island had been subject to an insolent and overbearing aristocracy. They have railed, in such good set terms, against the royal Charter, and against the "sand and gravel aristocracy," that numbers have been betrayed into opinions not very creditable to their reputation for good sense, or for their knowledge of the subject upon which they have undertaken to pronounce. Let us then turn aside, for a moment, from all this eloquent vituperation, with which Rhode Island institutions have, for the year past, been loaded, to a single historical fact, which, though lying upon the surface, the insurgents have found it convenient to overlook.

I do not purpose to travel farther back into the records of the past, than the year 1789, when the

American Constitution went into operation, and when were formed the two great political parties, the federal and the democratic, which, for so many years, divided the people of this country. In 1789, Arthur Fenner was the Governor of Rhode Island, and he continued to be annually elected Governor, and without opposition, till, in the year 1805, death terminated his long career of influence and honor. Here were sixteen years of unbroken democratic rule, for I assume the fact that no one will be found hardy enough to draw into question the democracy of Arthur Fenner. In the days of Arthur Fenner, the farmers governed the State. Would to God they could always govern it; for the farmers, by whatever political name they may be distinguished, are, especially in our State, the chief conservative interest. In the days of Arthur Fenner, the city of Providence did not threaten to overshadow the State; and the population in our manufacturing districts was then too scanty to contend with the farmers for political power. Had it not been for the growth of manufactures among us, which has attracted within our borders a population, from its nature and position, peculiarly exposed to the malign influences of the demagogue, Dorr and his accomplices in rebellion and treason, would never have found a base whereon to build their schemes of revolution and anarchy. With marvellous ingratitude, these men now denounce the passage of a tariff, which gives moderate protection to American labor. They term it a tariff "of abominations." Had they termed it and preceding tariffs the parent of "abominations," the justice of the denunciation would not be disputed by those who feel what a deep wound Dorr and his doings have inflicted upon the State—by those who know that along the valley of the Blackstone, the chief seats of his power and influence are to be found.

It is only a very few years ago, that the democratic party in this State were alarmed, and not without reason, lest the political power of the State should be wrested from the hands of the farmers. I have now before me a pamphlet, written with much ability, and addressed "To the Freemen of the Agricultural and Manufacturing Interests of Rhode Island." This pamphlet, which was printed in 1829, at the office of the Republican Herald, then the organ of the democratic party, alludes, in pointed terms, to "the efforts of certain political adventurers" to deprive the agricultural towns of the predominant influence they had so long exercised in the public counsels of the State. It is somewhat curious to remark the contrast between the Herald of 1842, and the Herald's pamphlet of 1829. Read the following extracts from this pamphlet, and be thankful that the constitution which the insurgents are endeavoring to overthrow, by acts of usurpation which, if carried out, must end in acts of force, leaves to the farmers a valued relic of their ancient power. In the House of Representatives, they will be overborne by numbers. In the Senate, however, if they are faithful to themselves, they may be able to interpose a check upon that precipitate or oppressive legislation, into which the representatives of mere numbers are liable to be betrayed:

"What, then, was to be done? What? Why, call a convention, and establish a constitution which would give them representatives according to their population of all sorts. The population of the manufacturing towns was increasing, that of the agricultural towns was diminishing, and would, they well knew, be still further diminished when the contemplated prohibitory system of protection was carried completely into effect. This measure they understood would secure eventually, if not at once, a majority to them in the House of Representatives. In an evil hour the General Assembly consented, that a convention should be held for the purpose of forming a constitution, but they wisely provided that the country towns should send the same number of delegates to the convention, that they were entitled to of representatives in the General Assembly. The convention was held, but from the organization of that body, the scheme of stripping the landed interest of all political power, was even then partially defeated, and was finally completely overthrown when the constitution proposed was submitted to the people."

So late as 1829, as will be seen by the above extract, the legal people, the qualified voters under the existing laws, were deemed, even by the democracy of Rhode Island, as the only people to whom the right pertained to "alter or abolish the government."

The General Assembly was then blamed for consenting to the call of a convention, for the purpose of forming a constitution. They have since been denounced as despots, because they would not recognize a convention, called for the same purpose, by a small minority, acting "without law and against law!" They were then commended for their wisdom, in providing that each town should have the same number of delegates in the convention, as it had representatives in the General Assembly. They have since been censured for injustice, in not providing that to the representatives of numbers, and numbers alone, should be confided the momentous duty of framing a constitution for the government of our small State. They have since been blamed for not overlooking the fact that a State which has one populous city, several populous towns, and a large and constantly increasing transient population, concentrated in factory villages, requires, for its safety, a government under which numbers alone, and such numbers too, as are to be found in the county of Providence, should not be allowed to exercise, without check or balance, the political power of the State. As to all these matters, the opinions of the larger and the more influential portion of the old democratic party have undergone no essential change. That party still believes that, without checks, a democracy is a despotism; that the agricultural interest in Rhode Island ought, for obvious reasons, to be clothed with some power to protect itself;—that the farmers, spread over a great extent of territory and seldom interchanging political opinions with each other, are not liable to form factious combinations; and that their interest in the soil, is one of the best pledges of their attachment to the permanent welfare of the State.

Should the misnamed friends of "Equal Rights" succeed in their profligate efforts to overthrow the legal constitution, and to establish the "People's Constitution" on its ruins, farewell, a long farewell to the power of the farmers! This city and every factory village in the State would teem with demagogues, who would make it their vocation to mislead and to inflame the masses. Every ward in Providence, would be cursed with "lots" of them, and along the valley of the Blackstone, these pests of a popular government would be found "thick as the leaves which strew the brook in Vallambrosa's vale!" To transfer the political power of Rhode Island to demagogues and to arch demagogues, is now the prime object of Thomas W. Dorr, Dutee J. Pearce & Co. Will the old fashioned democracy of Rhode Island suffer these men to triumph in such a cause, and by the use of means which call up on the cheek of every honest man the blush of shame, for those who have transgressed beyond the reach of shame? Quite sure I am, they will not be frightened from their propriety, by the denunciations of a convention, which has usurped a popular name, in order to mask its meditated aggression upon the great cause of popular rights. The convention lately assembled in this city, by a resolution introduced by Doctor Ballou, and unanimously adopted, proscribed certain leading and influential democrats as having forfeited, by their alliance with "the foes of popular liberty, all claim to democratic principles, and to the confidence of that party in this State and of the Union!" Heaven help the body politic, when it becomes the patient of such political Doctors! Does Doctor Ballou think it necessary to "be particular"—and that "none are genuine, unless marked" T. W. D.? If he thinks thus, why had he not the manliness to say so? If he knows who these recreant democrats are, why did he not "take the responsibility" of naming them? The answer is obvious. Neither he nor the convention dared to name the distinguished men whom they have thus indirectly proscribed.

To return, however, from this long digression, to the

single historical fact to which at the outset I wished more particularly to direct your attention. From the death of Arthur Fenner in 1805, till 1839, a period of thirty four years, the democratic party have been in the ascendant twenty six years. Thus has the reign of quiet, old fashioned democracy in Rhode Island exceeded the term of forty years, since the organization of the government under the constitution in 1789. This is the historical fact to which your attention is invited; and all this has happened notwithstanding the old Charter, which, in the slang of the day, is so flippantly denounced as royal, aristocratic, anti-democractic!

The late convention and their doings furnish abundant topics for animadversion. They will not in the end find me forgetful of the notice with which they have honored me and my unpretending efforts to do some service to my native State. At present, when great interests are at stake, I cannot be tempted to step aside from my course, to retort personalities. My purpose, in these essays, and my only purpose, is to arouse my fellow citizens to a just consideration of the duties and the dangers of the present crisis. Dorr and his ruffians fled before the forces which Old Narragansett poured forth in defence of liberty and law. True to the name, which I have adopted, I shall not be found to quail before the denunciations of any convention which has assembled, or which may hereafter assemble, to uphold the TRAITOR and HIS CAUSE.

OLD NARRAGANSETT.

PROVIDENCE JOURNAL, DECEMBER 29, 1842.

THE CRISIS.

ITS DANGERS AND ITS DUTIES.—NO. VII.

THE DORRITE CONVENTION AND ITS DOINGS.

TO THE MEMBERS OF THE RHODE ISLAND PARTY:—

FELLOW CITIZENS:—Let us examine, briefly, the composition and the doings of the late convention, held in this city, for the ostensible purpose of "re-organizing the democratic party of Rhode Island." The real purpose of that convention you can be at no loss to understand. It was neither more nor less than the establishment, by means allied to FRAUD, and which, if pursued, must end in FORCE, of the misnamed "People's Constitution," and the triumphant return to this State of that man who had well nigh fastened upon her a DESPOTISM, and drenched her soil in the blood of her noblest sons! Wrap them up as they may in a phraseology fitted to ensnare the unthinking, these are the darling objects which this convention sought, by its deliberations and its votes, to accomplish. These are the objects, for which men, dishonoring the name and the principles of democracy, matured, amid the silence and the gloom of midnight hours, their dark conspiracy against the peace of the State, and the rights of the people. Every thing was in excellent keeping. The men were suited to the work, and the work was suited to the hour. It abhorred the light of day—it shrunk from the gaze of honest men. The most rabid Dorrites to be found in Rhode Island were the ruling spirits of the convention. The accomplices of Dorr, throughout the various stages of his treason, were there. Delegates to the convention which framed the so called People's Constitution, were there. Members of the foundry legislature, were there. More than one of the never-to-be-forgotten "nine learned lawyers," was there. Men whom no sad experiences can teach wisdom, and whom no lenity on the part of the government can soften into contrition for their offences, were there, ready to begin anew the work of mischief, perchance of violence, which nothing, it seems, but their pusillanimity caused them to suspend.

Were this inquiry into the composition of the late convention to be pushed, it would not be difficult to show that some men were there, who, though they now proclaim themselves as democrats, are fresh from the ranks of the Whig party. The log cabin lyrics have hardly died away upon their lips, before they take it upon themselves to launch the thunderbolt of proscription at the heads of veteran champions in the cause of democracy. A convention thus constituted, usurps the name of democratic, in the hope of giving the sanction of a powerful and respectable party to principles which the best men of that party indignantly reprobate, and to plans of revolutionary violence which they are resolved at every hazard to oppose. The device, however, is too clumsy to succeed. It may, in some cases, seduce weak understandings into error, and, in others, it may furnish a convenient refuge for pliant consciences. After all, it will, in the end, deceive few beside those who, when caught in such company, must inevitably become dupes, and those who seek not so much a knowledge of the right, as a plausible excuse to do wrong.

Since the members of the late Dorrite convention have assumed to themselves the captivating title of "Democrats and friends of Equal Rights," it may not be amiss to look beyond names to things, and to inquire whether the ardent and ostentatious professions of the men who composed that convention, are illustrated by a consistent practice. Let us appeal to such portions of the record of their proceedings as they have permitted to see the light. By their fruits ye shall know them. Do men gather grapes from thorns, or figs of thistles?

During the sittings of this convention, assembled for the alleged purpose of "re-organizing the democratic party," the following were among the Resolutions which were adopted:

"Resolved, That in Thomas Wilson Dorr, the rightful Governor of this State, we recognize the incorruptible patriot, sound Democrat and unwavering friend of Equal Rights.

"Resolved, That in recommending this course, (the registry of names) and in order to avoid all doubt or misconstruction of our purposes, we explicitly avow our object to be, to accomplish in a satisfactory manner, and with the least delay, the establishment in fact, as well as in right, of the 'people's constitution.'"

Here at least, is plain language. This is "going the whole figure" for Dorr, and for Dorr's constitution. This is an endorsement of all the measures, whether of fraud or force, which were connected with his rebellion and treason. This is virtually a declaration that Governor King is a usurper, and that the existing government, in the defence of which you have poured out your treasure, and were ready to pour out your blood, is in fact, what the fugitive rebel, with characteristic insolence, has pronounced it to be, "a military despotism."

All this, to my mind, savors more of Dorrism, than of democracy. The language of the resolutions above quoted, leaves no doubt as to the object which the men who adopted them mean to accomplish. "Governor" Dorr and the "people's constitution," they have selected as watchwords to animate the revolutionary forces in the coming strife. All who may refuse to embark in the new crusade, to which the revolutionary chief has summoned his vassals, must expect to be denounced, in the language of Doctor Ariel Ballou's famous resolution, as "foes to popular liberty." How the establishment of the "people's constitution" is to be effected, we are not permitted to know. The work, it seems, is to be done, "in a satisfactory manner, and with the least delay!" What does this language import? What scheme of jesuitism or of usurpation is here dimly shadowed forth, in phraseology so vague, that none but the faithful, whose gifts and graces enable them to look beyond the letter to the hidden meaning, are able to understand it? In what manner, I ask again, do these people design to establish, "in fact," the "people's constitution?" How can they work their end, without "delay," and in a manner which shall be "satisfactory" to the friends of liberty and law? Do they seek to gain political power under the legal constitution, in order to overthrow it? Would they proceed to trample that constitution in the dust, with the oath of fidelity which it requires them to take, yet warm upon their lips? Under ordinary circumstances, to put such questions would convey an insult which I should be among the last to offer to any man or to any set of men. But the language of Dorr and of his followers, though it deals in obscure hints as to the precise means to be employed, is sufficiently explicit as to the foul end to be accomplished. A great public mischief is meditated by these men. This we know. The means will, in all repects, be such as unscrupulous men can use with the best effect in the prosecution of a foul end. Of one thing, they may rest assured. No Rhode Island man, with a Rhode Island heart throbbing in his bosom, would remain, under the circumstances supposed, a passive spectator of an act of political turpitude, which would cover him with eternal dishonor, and strip him of all security for life, liberty and property.

The legal constitution provides a mode in which it can be amended—a mode wisely requiring deliberation and delay. All attempts to amend or to change it, in any other mode, would be an exercise of the Revolutionary Power—the substitution of the ferocious energy of jacobinism for the wholesome vigor of constitutional freedom. If these men really intend, and their language justifies the worst suspicions, ultimately to resort to the revolutionary power, in order to fasten their constitution and their Governor upon us, let them lay aside their deceptive talk about accomplishing their iniquitous schemes "in a satisfactory manner." Let them, like bold, bad men, declare, in words not to be misunderstood, by what means they are resolved to consummate the work of treason. Let them not skulk behind constitutional forms, in order to gather strength to violate great constitutional principles. Whenever the people of this State may exercise their sovereign power, in amending the legal constitution, according to the mode which they themselves have prescribed in that constitution, they will find not a man of the Rhode Island party disposed to thwart their will. But woe be to the man, and woe be to the party, who may attempt, either by chicane, or by force, the establishment of a constitution, which the majority of the people have never adopted, and to which, if the blood of heroic sires yet flows in their veins, they will never tamely submit!

Fellow Citizens:—Ponder these resolutions, on which it is impossible to comment without indignation, and then judge for yourselves, whether they are animated by the spirit of democracy or by the spirit of Dorrism. Judge ye, likewise, for yourselves, whether the men who guided the counsels of that convention are concerned to re-organize the democratic party upon old fashioned democratic principles, and under old fashioned leaders, or whether they have sought the alliance of a desperate faction, and have pledged themselves to sustain the fortunes of a desperate man.

Hereafter, I may again call your attention to this Convention and its doings. For the present, however, let me exhort you to attend to the duties of the present. Take good care that, before to-morrow's sun has set, every friend to law and order, within the limits of Rhode Island, who is entitled, by the provisions of the Constitution, to vote, shall have qualified himself to vote! This is the paramount duty of the present hour! If you neglect to do it now, remember that your neglect will be without remedy. Towards the future, I look with a strong and cheerful confidence. It can never be, that the people of Rhode Island, who have perilled and who have endured so much in the cause of constitutional freedom, will fail to win for that cause a final triumph. It can never be, that a patriotic and a gallant people are doomed to pass under the domination of men whose principles are revolutionary, and whose rule would not only oppress, but dishonor us.

OLD NARRAGANSETT.

PROVIDENCE JOURNAL, JANUARY 5, 1843.

THE CRISIS.

ITS DANGERS AND ITS DUTIES.—NO. VIII.

THE DORRITE CONVENTION AND ITS DOINGS.

TO THE MEMBERS OF THE RHODE ISLAND PARTY:—

FELLOW CITIZENS:—The extraordinary pains which the Revolutionists take, in order to convince the people of Rhode Island that they, and that they alone, are "democrats and friends of equal rights," ought to awaken your suspicions. Men who deserve a good name, never ostentatiously proclaim their own merits, nor do they seek to derogate, in a censorious or proscriptive spirit, from the merits of others. Men who are the acknowledged representatives of great principles do not find it necessary to "define their position," or to enter into an elaborate vindication of their fidelity to great principles. Those, however, who occupy a doubtful position, are apt to be full of nervous agitation, lest the pompous claims which they set up should not obtain general acknowledgment. These remarks, the truth of which is obvious to every observer of character and manners, are signally illustrated by the doings of the Dorrite Convention, lately assembled in this city, for the purpose of trampling down the laws and the constitution of Rhode Island. These men, admonished by that conscience which even guilt cannot bribe into silence, that they were about to engage in a nefarious scheme, took counsel of their cunning. They voted themselves, by acclamation, to be "democrats and friends of equal rights," and, in beautiful consistency with the tolerant spirit of true democracy, they voted that all those who would not go with them to the death for Dorr and for Dorr's constitution, were no democrats, but were whigs, "foes to popular liberty," aristocrats, "Algerines!"

Mark, fellow citizens, with what practised skill these pure and gentle democrats use the language of obloquy and proscription! When they calumniate, how rapturous are their hyperboles—when they denounce, with what vehemence do they mount into climax! All this, to my mind, savors very little of democracy or of equal rights. It looks vastly more like the reorganization of the rebel forces of Thomas W. Dorr, than of the reorganization of the old fashioned democratic party of Rhode Island, upon democratic principles, and under democratic leaders. This convention, in order still further to mask their evil designs, go into a sort of post mortem examination of the men and measures of the old federal party, which have long since become matters of history. In an address adopted by the convention, which measures many feet, if not yards, in length, and which, in one of these short days, no man ought to be expected to read, Dexter Randall comes forth, "with his bow and arrow," to slay the giants of other days! Most unfortunate is his attack upon the giants of other days! Most unfortunate is his attack upon the fame of the elder Adams, the chairman of the committee who reported the Declaration of the American Independence! now tortured by Dorr and his accomplices into a plausible defence of rebellion and treason; the elder Adams, whom Mr. Jefferson, speaking of the Declaration of Independence, pronounced "the pillar of its support on the floor of Congress; its ablest advocate and defender against the multifarious assaults it encountered!"

Hardly more fortunate is Mr. Randall in his attempt to fasten upon the character of Hamilton, one of the ablest champions of constitutional freedom which the world has yet seen, the reproach of preferring either monarchy or aristocracy to republicanism. "The essential criteria of a government purely republican, are that the principal organs of the executive and legislative departments shall be elected by the people, and hold their offices by a responsible and temporary or defeasible tenure." Hamilton never favored any plan of government inconsistent with this truly republican theory; and if he sinned against republicanism in the proposition which he submitted to the General Convention, touching the constitution of the executive department of the government, James Madison was not less guilty, for, on this question, he voted on the same side with Hamilton! Not even Dexter Randall will dare to draw into question the republicanism of James Madison, the illustrious associate of Hamilton and Jay, in the work of expounding and defending that constitution which binds these States together! On the past, however, I can no longer dwell. Our interests are with the present—our business is with the present. Let us, then, look a little further into the doings of this self styled democratic convention, for the purpose of seeing how well these doings square with the theory of democracy.

This convention, it will be recollected, sat with closed doors, and they brooded, at midnight hours, over their schemes of disorganization and anarchy. They claimed to defend the rights and to be endowed with the power of the people, and yet they excluded the people from their sittings, with that jealous vigilance which distinguishes the rule of despots. And yet more. Not only did they bar their doors against the intrusions of the "sovereignty," but they appointed a select committee (John S. Harris being chairman) "TO DECIDE WHAT PART OF THEIR PROCEEDINGS SHOULD BE PUBLISHED!" If this be democracy, it is democracy of a new school. It may bear the image of Cæsar, but it derives naught of its form or pressure from the people. It may shelter itself under an imposing name, but it is without even a particle of that inspiration which springs from an attachment to popular freedom, and which cannot exist without it.

This convention has permitted the following resolution to see the light. And a most extraordinary resolution it must be deemed by all who are not instructed in the new doctrines of "equal rights!"

"Resolved, That this convention reprobate and condemn the course pursued by the Post Master and Collector of the city of Providence, the Marshal of the district of Rhode Island, and all other officers under the Government of the United States in this State, who armed themselves and searched the houses of the free citizens of this State, and in contravention of the Constitution of the United States, taking from peaceable citizens their arms; and generally in lending their personal aid to crush and stifle the doings of a majority of the people of this State as expressed in the adoption of the People's Constitution."

We are told by one of the organs of the revolutionary faction, that, "after some evidence produced by members of the convention to substantiate the correctness of its allegations, this resolution passed unanimously." We are likewise told, that a copy of the same, signed by the President and Secretaries, was ordered to be transmitted to the President of the United States! If this resolution does not savor more of jacobinism than of democracy, I have yet to learn what is jacobinism and what is democracy.

Fellow Citizens:—Weigh well the import and the bearings of this resolution. Mark the spirit which animates it; look at the flagrant violation of all legal and constitutional principles which it involves. A body of men take it upon themselves to accuse, to try and to condemn, in a secret session, and under the shades of night, a number of their fellow citizens, for grave offences affecting both their official and their personal characters. The alleged culprits are allowed no opportunities of defending themselves; they are not even permitted to know, in advance, that they have provoked the vengeance of jacobinism; their trial is conducted in a manner so summary, and according to forms so unusual, as hardly to be reconciled with any well established principle of "equal rights." Those who accuse, and those who witness against them, are both jurors and judges. Imitating, somewhat closely, the jacobin clubs of revolutionary memory in Paris, our Rhode Island revolutionists are determined to be embarrassed by no legal forms, either when they attempt to trample down constitutions or to blast private and official characters. Why was this resolution sent to the President of the United States? The people of these United States have confided the power of removal from office to the President, and to the President alone; and the whole theory of our government supposes him to exercise that important power, heedless alike of the clamors and the denunciations of any body of men who, by such means, may seek to influence him.

What, my fellow citizens, are to become of the rights of individuals, or of minorities, if this Dorrite convention is to become a pattern convention? It has rushed madly from its sphere, and it threatens to light up, within our borders, another conflagration. Professing the most ardent attachment to democracy, and to equal rights, it seeks to bring in, by the exercise of the revolutionary power, the reign of anarchy, which endangers all rights. We have had quite enough of these men, and more than enough of their leader—quite enough of the doctrines which they preach, and of the spirit which they breathe. Let us, then, continue firm in our purpose to maintain the laws and the constitution of Rhode Island. Let us stand firmly upon our "equal rights." Let us illustrate our democracy, by a consistent regard for the principle of democracy; by an exemplary respect for the rights of individuals and of minorities; by efforts to accomplish the greatest good of the whole; by appeals to the reason, and not to the passions of the people. In the end, we cannot fail to succeed. Already, I seem to hear, in the distance, those shouts of triumph which, on the first Wednesday of April next, the true champions of constitutional freedom will send forth from every hill top in the land of Roger Williams, to meet responsive echoes from the shores of our emerald Isle, and from every farm house and hamlet in the domain of

OLD NARRAGANSETT.

PROVIDENCE JOURNAL, JANUARY 9, 1843.

THE CRISIS.

ITS DANGERS AND ITS DUTIES.—NO. IX.

THE DORRITE CONVENTION AND ITS DOINGS.

To the Members of the Rhode Island Party:—

Fellow Citizens:—The persons who composed the Revolutionary Convention, which lately held its secret midnight sessions in this city, are never weary of proclaiming themselves as "the friends of democracy and of equal rights!" The very imperfect examination to which I have subjected such of their doings as they graciously permitted to be published for the information of the sovereignty, must have satisfied every candid mind, that these men have violated, over and over again, and in the grossest manner, the very principles of which they claim to be the exclusive champions. Not satisfied with denouncing as "foes to popular liberty," such men as James Fenner, John Brown Francis, Elisha Mathewson, Nathan Brown, Nathaniel Bullock, Judge Westcott, Judge Howard, Judge Branch, Elisha R. Potter, Colonel Barber, and other old fashioned democrats, they hurled at "Old Narragansett" a bolt of vengeance, in the shape of the following resolution, which is here subjoined, stripped of none of those typographical embellishments, which graced its first appearance in the columns of the "Providence Express:"

"Resolved, That we hold the late exposition of the whig policy, as indicated in the polluted columns of the Journal, over the signature of "Narragansett," denouncing the friends of Democracy and Equal Rights, as "Insurgents and French Jacobins," because they have resolved to redress their grievances and assert their rights, by complying peaceably with the steps prescribed by the government itself—as the phrenzied essays of an alarmed Aristocrat—ensconced in "Leisure and Education," by an accidental acquisition of wealth—as insurrectionary in their tendency, and unworthy of imitation."

I advert to this resolution, my fellow citizens, for the purpose of asking you to mark its spirit, and to observe under what adroit forms of expression the convention attempt to shelter from the indignation of the people their meditated revolutionary aggression upon the most sacred rights of the people. Mark, I say, the spirit of this resolution. How oddly it contrasts with the doctrine of "equal rights!" How it smacks of the fanatical fervor and the vengeful hate of the jacobin clubs of Paris, who vociferated aristocrat to-day, and a la lanterne to-morrow! If these men think that injustice is done them by a comparison which I have more than once insinuated, let them look into the first two volumes of Alison's History of Europe, and they will be amazed to discover in how many points they resemble the jacobins of revolutionary France. In courage, I admit, they fall far behind their Gallic prototype; but in falsehood, vindictiveness, and cunning; in the skill with which they address the worst passions, and in their power of attracting to their standard the worst men, the revolutionists of Rhode Island are not greatly surpassed by the revolutionists of France. They have shown themselves to be moved by the same spirit which ultimately proved fatal to the liberties of France—the same spirit, which, in the name of democracy and equal rights, brought upon her the fearful evils of anarchy, and forced her, at the last, to seek repose in despotism. These men must not act like jacobins, and then affect to be indignant, because they are called by their right name. They are termed "Insurgents," and they are likened to "French Jacobins," not because they "have resolved to redress their grievances, and assert their rights, by complying peaceably with the steps prescribed by the government itself," but because they still uphold the fortunes of that man who, on two occasions, arrayed an armed mob against his fellow citizens, and who is resolved that Rhode Island shall have no rest till, by force or by fraud, his constitution is established! They are termed "Insurgents," and they are likened unto "French Jacobins," because they avow their determination to obtain political power under the legal constitution, for the express purpose of trampling it under foot,—thus plunging the State into all the evils of anarchy, and perchance into all the horrors of a revolution! They comply peaceably with the steps prescribed by the government itself! What honied words are these! Can it be that under the tongue of these men there lurks the poison of asps?

When, let me ask them, did the government of

Rhode Island ever prescribe any steps by which its own destruction should become inevitable? These men have, again and again, in the most formal manner, avowed their determination to establish the people's constitution—not by the slow and cautious "steps" which the legal constitution, in its chapter on amendments "prescribes," but by some summary process, which they cunningly forbear to explain. If, however, any one has a tittle of doubt what sort of "steps" these men mean to take, in order to accomplish their purpose, let him appeal not only to the records of the late convention, but to the records of every primary meeting which has echoed the voice of that convention, and he will doubt no longer! They talk about democracy—about the redress of grievances —and the assertion of their rights—but, after all, the work which they are pledged to do is the work of revolution—the spirit which they invoke is the spirit of revolution—the instruments which they employ are the instruments of revolution—the calamities which they would bring upon us are the calamities of revolution!

At a crisis like the present, when the very frame work of our social edifice is threatened with destruction, I cannot be induced to turn aside from my purpose, to retort the personalities in which this convention has seen fit to indulge. On one point, however, it may not be amiss for me to say a word. These humble essays have no claim whatsoever to be considered as "an exposition of the whig policy." They are written without concert with any man or with any set of men—and by one too, who, though enjoying no political distinction and aspiring to none—is not disposed to yield a hair's breadth of those "equal rights" which can be secure only under the protection of liberty and law. Belonging to the mass of the people, and sympathizing with them, I have felt both indignant and "alarmed" at the sort of instrumentality which a few selfish politicians in this State are employing to effect their purposes. They thirst for political power, and they employ in their service those whose rapacity they have stimulated with the hopes of plunder, and those whose passions they have exasperated for the work of vengeance.

They unblushingly declare, too, that they mean to use the forms of the constitution, in order to perpetrate their meditated outrage upon the great principles of constitutional freedom. I take comfort, however, in the prospect before us. I rejoice in the cheering evidences presented on every side that the people of Rhode Island are resolved to administer a scorching rebuke to the revolutionary faction; and to maintain, at every hazard, the legal constitution, "till it is changed by an explicit and authentic act of the whole people."

Fellow Citizens:—I have now done with this Revolutionary Convention and its doings, and I shall gladly pass to other themes. The men who composed that Convention knew very well what they were about; and they knew very well that the publication of all their proceedings would revolt the moral sense of those whom they are trying to deceive. They have become somewhat alarmed at the issue which they have made. Hence, their recent efforts to wrap it up, and to represent the pending controversy as an ordinary controversy between political parties—as a simple question whether a Whig or a Democrat shall be our next Governor; whether this or that political party shall manage the affairs of the State. Were this, in fact, the true issue which these men have made up, for one, I should be little concerned how it should be decided. Let these men stand to their original words. Let them not seek to shelter themselves behind ambiguities of language, now that they have discovered that ambiguities of language are needed to conceal a desperate purpose. Let them not hope to come over the people of Rhode Island, by soft talk about "democracy and equal rights." They dare to talk of democracy and equal rights, when they are bent on establishing principles which would soon convert democracy into despotism, and leave the people without the slightest legal protection for any Right! They complain of proscription when they denounce and proscribe every man, be he distinguished or be he humble, who will not consent to dance to their revolutionary pipe!

The true issue between us and our opponents cannot be too often presented. It admits of no compromise; it disdains all neutrality; it involves whatever is dear to us as free citizens and as free men. Let this momentous issue never be absent from your thoughts. The coming strife is not for political power, to be exercised in an ordinary manner, under the ordinary legal and constitutional forms. Far otherwise. It is a strife between antagonist principles lying at the very foundation of all regularly organized political society; a strife between ANARCHY and GOVERNMENT; between REVOLUTION and LAW; between DEMOCRACY and JACOBINISM; between the PEOPLE and the MOB! Never, for one moment, have I desponded concerning the future; and I have now no solicitude except that we should vindicate our cause, by a majority so commanding as forever to terminate a conflict which has so fearfully agitated the State—which has injured her best interests, and sullied her bright name.

OLD NARRAGANSETT.

PROVIDENCE JOURNAL, JANUARY 11, 1843.

THE CRISIS.

ITS DANGERS AND ITS DUTIES.—NO. X.

TO THE MEMBERS OF THE RHODE ISLAND PARTY:—

FELLOW CITIZENS:—One of the organs of the revolutionary party in this State, with an effrontery almost amusing, stoutly affirms that the legal constitution "was artfully contrived in such a manner, that the large manufacturers should control all elections!" This complaint comes with an exceeding ill grace from those who, all along, have sought to fasten upon the people of Rhode Island a constitution, which would have forever destroyed the political importance of the agricultural interest; from those who used the term landholder as a term of reproach, and who so contrived their constitution as to erect a sort of cog wheel aristocracy upon the ruins of what they courteously denounced as "the aristocracy of sand and gravel!" During every stage of the controversy in this State, respecting the extension of suffrage, the Rhode Island party struggled, with all their might, to preserve to the farmers, justly deemed to be a conservative interest, a substantial control in the direction of our public affairs. In this matter, the Rhode Island party did what they could do, under the strong conviction, that political power can be safely intrusted to such hands.

It is not the fault of that party that they did not do more to give the agricultural interest the means not only of defending itself, but of infusing into the legislation of the State, that spirit of equity, moderation and economy, which, in an especial manner, characterizes those who own the soil and live by the soil. Were the revolutionists sincere in deprecating the ascendency of the manufacturing interest in the politics of Rhode Island, they would be grateful to those who framed and to those who adopted the legal constitution, for doing all that they could do to prevent either "large manufacturers" or, what is no better, small manufacturers, from controlling all elections. Let us, briefly, examine some of the provisions of the so called "people's constitution," for the purpose of ascertaining whether or not it erected any barriers against the predominant influence of the manufacturers, great or small, and whether it provided the farmers with any effective power to defend themselves.

In the first place, fellow citizens, examine the article in the "people's constitution" respecting "Electors and the Right of Suffrage," and after comparing it with the article on the same subject in the legal constitution, judge for yourselves, which constitution furnishes the most security against the irregular exercise of power, on the part of the great manufacturers, and against the no less dangerous ascendency of that floating population which is to be found in our large towns and factory villages.

The "people's constitution" declares that "Every white male citizen of the United States, of the age of twenty one years, who has resided in this State for one year, and in any town, city or district of the same for six months next preceding the election at which he offers to vote, shall be an elector of all officers who are elected, or may hereafter be made eligible by the people." This provision would entail universal suffrage, or what is next to universal suffrage, upon a State which, owing to the nature of its population, a large majority being concentrated in manufacturing towns and districts, could ill bear the effects of a system of suffrage so widely extended. This provision would admit foreigners of all sorts to vote upon the same terms as native citizens; and when the facilities of naturalization, provided by our laws, are taken into account, it would virtually place the whole political power of the State in the hands of men, who are comparatively strangers to the working of popular institutions;—who are governed more by passion than by reason, and who, in an especial manner, are liable to come under the "malign influences" of the demagogue. With a suffrage thus extended, what would become of the farmers of North Providence, Cumberland and Warwick? Who would wield, now and in all future time, the political power of this city, already too great for its own good and the good of the State? How, under such auspices, would fare the quiet farmers of Rhode Island, Conanicut and Prudence, and the no less quiet farmers who feed turkeys and hoe corn in old Narragansett? It is sufficient to put these questions. They admit of but one answer; and that answer is too obvious to be given. It may be said that, in all these respects, the legal constitution is not much better than the "people's." Examine it, and decide for yourselves. If the former be not, in this respect, what the conservative party in this State could wish, it is not too much to say that it is the best which, under existing circumstances, could be obtained. Immensely superior to the "people's constitution," it must be deemed by every man who deprecates the concentration of all political power in a few manufacturing towns—which towns would, in the end, inevitably be swayed by the worst demagogues in the State.

Examine, in the next place, my fellow citizens, the "people's constitution" and the legal constitution, in respect to the organization of the legislative department. The construction of the House of Representatives being substantially the same under both constitutions, let us look at the construction of the Senate under both; for, here, lies the distinctive excellence of the legal constitution; here, and in its chapter relating to amendments, is to be found its decided superiority to that instrument which the revolutionists are now seeking to fasten upon you. According to the "people's constitution," the Senate consists of twelve, chosen annually in twelve senatorial districts, fixed by the constitution, and so fixed that the manufacturers would always be next to certain to obtain a majority. According to the legal constitution, the Senate consists of the Lieutenant Governor and of one Senator from each town or city in the State. The advantages of this organization are too apparent to require more than a cursory notice.

In the first place, the Senate, from its increased size, will become a deliberative body, in which the merits of questions, affecting the public welfare, will undergo the ordeal of able and searching debate. Owing to the same cause, and to the fact that it is founded on different principles from the House, it will feel itself to be, and in fact, it will be, a more effective check upon the House, which is constituted on the basis of population. In the second place, in a Senate thus elected, the minority, under ordinary circumstances, will always be represented; and that minority may be large. In the third place, a Senate composed of over thirty members, representing different interests, is most too large, and would probably be found most too impracticable, to be hovered by the Governor of the State, whoever the Governor might be. The Senate might rule the one man. The one man could hardly hope to rule the Senate! In the fourth place, the Senate, under the legal constitution, is so organized, that the agricultural towns and districts, if they are true to themselves, will have the power of protecting themselves.

If a majority of the House, representing the masses in Providence, Smithfield, Cumberland, North Providence, Warwick, &c., are disposed, in the exercise of their power, to forget right, they will find that the whole people have so constituted the Senate, that it will be both willing and able to resist oppression, and to maintain, against all encroachments, the rights of the whole people.

Fellow Citizens:—At present, I have not leisure to go more at length into an examination of this important subject. Enough, however, I trust, has been said to expose the inconsistency of those who complain that our constitution gives to the manufacturers too much power; and, likewise, to make us feel grateful that, from the wreck of our old institutions, we have rescued an ANCHOR which will enable our good ship Rhode Island to ride out many a storm in safety, long after the revolutionary surges, which now beat upon her sides, shall have raved themselves to rest.

OLD NARRAGANSETT.

PROVIDENCE JOURNAL, JANUARY 14, 1843.

THE CRISIS.

ITS DANGERS AND ITS DUTIES.—NO. XI.

TO THE MEMBERS OF THE RHODE ISLAND PARTY:—

FELLOW CITIZENS:—The framers of the people's constitution, in their hot haste to grasp political power, and to perpetuate it in the hands of a few, overlooked entirely the actual condition of things in Rhode Island. They contrived their machine according to certain speculative notions, without seeming to consider that it was to operate, not upon pure abstractions, but upon living men, moved by various passions, existing under different circumstances, and perchance divided by conflicting interests. They overlooked the obvious and important facts, that Rhode Island is a small State, having a very large proportion of its population interested, directly or indirectly, in a single pursuit, and concentrated in a single county, not to say in a single city. They overlooked, likewise, a fact, hardly less important, that owing to the vast amount of capital invested in manufacturing establishments, the population thus concentrated would, under ordinary circumstances, embrace, for all time, a great number of persons born both out of the State and out of the country; and that such persons, from their character and condition, could hardly be deemed safe depositaries of political power. Hence, in utter disregard of all the lessons of history and of all the peculiarities of our actual condition, they framed a constitution of government entirely without any efficient checks and balances—a constitution of government which, though it ostensibly placed the political power in the hands of the many, would practically confine it to the hands of the few. That these assertions are not without warrant, may be seen by a reference to the following considerations:

The people's constitution, abandoning not only the landed qualification, but property qualification of every sort, extended the right of suffrage to every white male citizen of the United States of the age of twenty one years, who has resided one year in the State and six months in the town where he offers to vote. This is universal suffrage with a vengeance! This presents the bitter draught undiluted! This menaces us with a calamity which would shake the very foundations of our peace, prosperity, and freedom, and which no effort short of revolution would enable us to retrieve! In a large State, where the agricultural interest happens to predominate, or in a small State, where the character and pursuits of the people are homogeneous, a suffrage thus widely extended might fail to produce the amount of evil which, under other circumstances, it never fails to produce. Universal suffrage, whenever, and under what circumstances soever it is adopted, whether the agricultural interest be the predominant or the subordinate interest, demands in the constitution of the legislative, executive, and judicial department of the government, some efficient check, which will prevent or correct its evils.

The "people's constitution" provides no such check. It constitutes both branches of the legislative department upon principles substantially the same. Hence, if the House should be precipitate or oppressive in its legislation, no corrective would be found in the Senate. It withholds from the Executive any participation in the legislative power, which would be found of practical value in restraining the excesses of the legislative power. It establishes the judiciary with a tenure of office so precarious as to render that important branch of the government a comparatively feeble check upon the unconstitutional exercise of power, either by the executive or by the Legislature. In some of these respects, candor obliges me to acknowledge that the legal constitution is hardly less defective. It should, however, be recollected that that constitution gives us less of the bane, and that, consequently, we need less of the antidote. While it is not without defects which are to be regretted, but which may hereafter be remedied, it has large compensating advantages which give it, as a system of government, a vast superiority over the so called people's constitution.

In respect to the qualifications of electors, and in respect to the organization of the Senate, the legal constitution leaves us so much for which to be grateful, that any complaint would seem to be captious. So long as we can maintain that constitution, those who may be presumed to understand the interests and to be attached to the institutions of Rhode Island, can hope to exert some influence in the government of Rhode Island. But should the provisions relative to suffrage in the people's constitution ever come to be adopted, the political power of this city and of this State will inevitably pass, and pass forever, into the hands of a floating population who are comparative strangers to our interests—and who will on all occasions be found to maintain with the demagogues of the hour a most sympathetic and unbroken fellowship. To the dangers to be apprehended from universal suffrage, even Mr. Dorr, no longer ago than the year 1837, was not insensible. This fact is established by the following resolution, draughted, as it is believed, by his own hand, and adopted by a formal convention of which he was a leading member:

"Resolved, That in the opinion of this Convention, in addition to the voters qualified by the present law, all white male citizens of the United States over twenty one years of age, (excepting paupers and persons under guardianship,) who have resided within this State for a period not less than two years preceding their claim to vote, and within the town where they shall offer to vote, for the term of not less than three months preceding their claim to vote, should be entitled to the right of suffrage, upon producing a certificate that they have during the year previous been assessed to pay taxes in said town, and have actually paid the same: and that no person born out of the jurisdiction of the United States should be allowed to vote, unless he have first been naturalized according to the Acts of Congress; be possessed of a freehold estate according to the provisions of the present law, and have resided, previously to voting, two whole years in this State, and three months in a town as aforesaid; and that there should be a strict registration of all the qualified voters; and for the protection of the voter a vote by Ballot."

So thought and so voted Thomas W. Dorr, in the year 1837! What a change came over him in 1841, when he draughted and voted for the people's constitution, which goes to establish what Martin Van Buren called, in the New York Convention, "a wholly unrestricted suffrage!" Mr. Van Buren remonstrated against "the precipitate and unexpected prostration of all qualifications." Among the many evils which would flow from this unrestricted suffrage, he deprecated the increased number of voters which would be given to the city of New York. He added, with great truth and emphasis, "that the character of the increased number of voters would be such as would render their elections rather a curse than a blessing;

which would drive from the polls all sober minded people!" So spake Martin Van Buren, when debating the question of universal suffrage, only a few years ago, in the New York Convention. This is the language of genuine conservative democracy. This is a picture of what would be the inevitable condition of this city and of this State, should the revolutionary party ever succeed in prostrating the legal constitution, and in erecting their own upon its ruins.

Fellow Citizens of the Rhode Island Party:—Remember, the revolutionists stand pledged to establish the people's constitution! Mr. Dorr counsels his confederates in the work of revolution, not to "abate either heart or hope, or remit their exertions, till the people's constitution shall become in fact, as in right, the paramount law of the State!" The voice from the granite hills of New Hampshire, meets a devout response from all the faithful throughout the length and breadth of Rhode Island. A meeting of revolutionists in Warwick, over which John R. Waterman presided, declared that they "acknowledge no allegiance to the provisions" of the legal constitution, "or that it has any moral binding force upon their consciences!" The revolutionary convention which recently held its secret midnight sessions in Providence, is no less explicit in declaring its settled purpose to go ahead in the work of anarchy. "In order," says this convention, "to avoid all doubt or misconstruction of our purposes, we explicitly avow our object to be, to accomplish, in a satisfactory manner, and with the least delay, the establishment in fact, as well as in right, of the people's constitution!" These declarations indicate the course which the revolutionists intend to pursue. Our duty in this matter, fellow citizens, is thus made not only imperative, but it is exalted, by the magnitude of the crisis, into an obligation of the most sacred character—binding upon our consciences as men, and demanding of us as citizens to put forth our vigorous, united and sustained efforts to save the State from those who are plotting to ruin her prosperity, and to lay her honor in the dust. The revolutionists permit you neither to doubt nor to misconstrue their object. Let us keep their words constantly before our minds. Let us meet the issue which they have made; and let us meet it, too, in that spirit of patriotism, disinterestedness, and courage, which a crisis so solemn demands.

Fellow Citizens:—Who would not scorn the man, be he Whig or be he Democrat, who, at a crisis like the present, can find it in his heart to sit down and calculate the temporary losses or gains of temporary parties! I rejoice to think that no such man is to be found in our ranks. I rejoice to think that the Rhode Island party continue to be animated by the Rhode Island spirit; and that merging all minor differences of opinion in an enlarged sentiment of public duty, they are resolved, standing foot to foot and shoulder to shoulder, to maintain to the last, and through every peril, the sacred principles which they originally combined to defend.

Fellow Citizens:—I am admonished by the space which I have already occupied in the columns of the Journal, to suspend these remarks. I cannot, however, close them, without again invoking you, in the exercise of a thoughtful and magnanimous spirit, to consider well the present crisis—its duties and its dangers. Your opponents are active and energetic. They are stimulated to effort by the most operative motives which can address the hopes and the fears of men who have perilled every thing upon a desperate issue. They have in vain attempted to conquer you by force of arms. Beware, that they do not come over you by the wiles of treachery. Keep constantly in mind the disgrace and the disaster which the people's constitution would bring upon yourselves, and entail upon your children. A conflagration which should sweep through the State, laying low the pride of your forests, and desolating your fruitful fields, and your vallies rejoicing in verdure, would be a calamity far less to be deprecated than the establishment, by the revolutionary party, of their revolutionary government. Nature, in her exhaustless energy, would restore to your forests their primeval beauty; again would she cover your fields with plenty, and your valleys with verdure. But if you once suffer these revolutionists to lay their hands upon the sacred ark of constitutional freedom, you would find that a most grievous and irretrievable calamity had come upon you. You would find that, under the forms of a popular constitution, you would be subjected to a most oppressive and degrading rule—to a rule, marked by all the meanness and all the rapacity of despotism, but without a solitary exhibition of that taste or splendor which sometimes decorates the reign of despotism in other lands.

OLD NARRAGANSETT.

PROVIDENCE JOURNAL, JANUARY 19, 1843.

THE CRISIS.

ITS DANGERS AND ITS DUTIES.—NO. XII.

To the Members of the Rhode Island Party:—

Fellow Citizens:—The men who are now striving to plunge Rhode Island into scenes of fearful anarchy, seem not only to have abandoned all principle, but to be lost to all shame. Last summer, they sought, by menace, to intimidate us into submission. That expedient failing, they resorted to force. They invoked the spirit of our revolutionary fathers; they affected to be moved by a sanctified frenzy in the cause of liberty; they put themselves before the country and before the world, as a band of worthies, prepared to do and to dare whatsoever the cause of equal rights might ask at their hands—ready, in fact, if need be, to die upon the field of glory, and half impatient to win for heroic brows the crown of heroic martyrdom. What they dared, and what they did, we all very well know. They collected, from Pawtucket, Woonsocket, Providence and other places, a band of rowdies, and marched, with deadly weapons in their hands, under the command of a rebel chief, to attack the State's arsenal in this city. The result of that affair has become a matter of history; and the assailants have cause to blush at the record. Without firing a gun, the rowdies retreated; and before another sun had set, they and their chief all fled to escape the just vengeance of the law. But this is not all. After recruiting his courage at the Pewter Mug, Dorr again rallied all his chivalry at Acote's hill, resolved to strike, for the "people's constitution" and for liberty, a blow which should render his name immortal. The result of this second demonstration has also become a matter of history. He struck no blow for liberty—but he and most of his band again ran away! Thus has he become immortal as the hero of two flights—and this, surely, is glory enough for one summer, and for one man!

Mark, fellow citizens, the meanness of the men who have all along claimed to be animated by the most elevated and heroic principles! We all know what they said and what they did, when they made the experiment of force. Let us now inquire, under what conditions, they are about to make the experiment of fraud. Abandoning all their sanctified frenzy in the cause of liberty—doffing all their martial plumes, and putting aside all the weapons of war, alas! shall that sword rest in its scabbard! these men now assume the gentleness of doves! With an air of inimitable gravity, they declare that "they are opposed to the use of physical power to enforce their rights!" Who can look, without scorn, upon men who can thus consent to put upon their own foreheads the seal of infamy! Not enforce their rights by the use of physical power! This new article in the creed of our Rhode

Island Revolutionists, ill comports with their impassioned appeals to the great principles and to the generous spirit of the American Revolution. Our fathers, when they resolved to vindicate their rights, after exhausting all peaceable means to avert the fearful issue, trusted to the power of their own right arms. They counted no cost, when their rights were in peril; they appealed, like true hearted men, to the God of Battles; and the God of Battles succored the cause of freedom with his might.

And how do these dove like professions of the revolutionists harmonize with their military preparations to capture the Arsenal; and with their cool malignity in collecting at Acote's hill a band of desperadoes, who were fierce for plunder as the evening wolves, and who would have stained the streets of Providence with blood, and covered her habitations with mourning? I allude to these things, for no purposes of exasperation. They ought never to die out of your memories. Especially ought they to be recalled to your remembrance, when the very men who counselled such evil things against you are, at this very moment, under another guise, plotting to bring disaster and disgrace upon you. They have tried force, and tried it in vain. By their own shameless confessions, they are now about to try fraud. The arbitrament of arms they have abandoned. To the arbitrament of the ballot box they now mean to resort. All this would be fair, and just, and constitutional, if these men did not tell you, over and over again, and in the most formal manner, that they resort to the ballot box, for the express purpose, not of establishing our government upon constitutional principles, but for the purpose of overthrowing it by some summary act of usurpation! They have confessed, in advance, that they mean to perpetrate, under the forms of law, a fraud, which, if you suffer them to prevail, will bring upon you not only irretrievable ruin, but irretrievable dishonor. What confidence, fellow citizens, can you place in men who thus violate, not only all principle, but outrage all decency! Beware, true democrats of Rhode Island, beware, how you contaminate yourselves by an alliance, or suffer yourselves to be disgraced by the suspicion of an alliance, with politicians so utterly prostitute, as not to perceive that they have proclaimed, with their own lips, their own infamy.

Fellow Citizens:—The revolutionists have become alarmed without becoming penitent. They now perceive that the fraud which they have, again and again, pledged themselves to perpetrate, needs some disguise; that the moral sense of those whom they are seeking to ensnare, will not tolerate quite so bald an exhibition of political and moral turpitude. Hence, they are changing, as fast as they can, their front, without changing, however, either their purposes or their principles. Their oracles, the Express and the Herald, are silent as the grave about putting down the legal constitution, in order to establish the people's constitution upon its ruins. No second voice breaks upon the faithful from the shades of Westmoreland, bidding them onward to the work of revolutionary license and anarchy. The subordinates in the work of mischief, likewise, see that they have gone too far. Hence they are endeavoring to explain away their own declarations, and to put upon them a gloss which may deceive the unwary. They now say, aye, and say it too with an unblushing front, that the resolutions passed by the Dorrite convention, and responded to by John R. Waterman and others in every town in the State mean nothing—that nothing is sought for but the peaceful triumph of democracy; that the men who have raised the tempest, and who must sink into oblivion whenever the tempest may subside, are only putting forth their serene might to bring back to Rhode Island her halcyon days of peace, prosperity and honor! This is the new system of tactics. It will, in the end, be found unavailing. It will deceive none, beside those who are wishing for a plausible excuse to trample upon every principle which binds the consciences of honorable men.

Fellow Citizens:—The present crisis in the affairs of Rhode Island must be met in the right spirit. It demands, on the part of those who compose the Rhode Island Party, a magnanimous, fearless, self sacrificing, and uncompromising adherence to the principles and to the policy of that party. If either be now abandoned, the most precious interests of the State will be put in peril. This is no time for politicians, whether Whig or democratic, to mouse over petty schemes of personal or political aggrandizement. Rhode Island is in danger of being plunged into anarchy! She has a right, therefore, to look for succor to all her true sons; to the great mass whom she has protected by her mild and equal laws; and to the distinguished few whom she has been proud to honor. She disdains, on an occasion like the present, all timid neutrality, and all pusillanimous reserve. She needs, and she demands, intrepid, unambiguous, unfaltering allegiance to the principles and to the policy of the Rhode Island

Party—till the vital interests which that party was formed to protect against revolutionary violence, shall be placed under the securities of a constitution, administered by the men who made it—and not by the men who stand pledged to overthrow it.

OLD NARRAGANSETT.

PROVIDENCE JOURNAL, FEBRUARY 8, 1843.

THE CRISIS.

ITS DANGERS AND ITS DUTIES.—NO. XIII.

TO THE PEOPLE OF RHODE ISLAND:—

FELLOW CITIZENS:—It would now seem to be the purpose of the revolutionary party to muse, by "expressive silence," the praise of "the rightful Governor" and of "the people's constitution." Once, these were the themes on which primary assemblies and august conventions delighted to dwell. Every speech and every resolution were instinct with the spirit of devoted loyalty to the "people's constitution" and to the people's governor. Equally fervid was the exhibition of this spirit of loyalty on the part of the Herald and the Express. Once, their columns were loaded with panegyrics upon his Excellency, and upon his Excellency's constitution, as if he were "democracy and equal rights" embodied, and as if Divine Providence had chosen that instrument to preserve from extinction the vital flame of popular freedom! This was the fact once. What is the fact now? Speeches are made, and resolutions are passed, but they bear no tribute of homage to the "rightful Governor," and to the "people's constitution!" The "Express," in contempt of its own name, now only implies that its ancient loyalty hath not departed; and the Herald no longer blows the hoarse trumpet of Revolution, but breathes only the soft piano notes of democracy! One exception, going to show that the age of chivalry is not left entirely without a witness, deserves to be noted. At a recent meeting of the Suffrage Association, the gallant Colonel Wales narrated, in fit phrase, the incidents of his rambles in Westmoreland. He had seen his Excellency—had conversed and had counselled with him; and, by the relation, as is surmised, of minute events, which, however they may sink below the dignity of history, are peculiarly fitted to warm the heart of friendship, he woke the Association to some portion of its primitive enthusiasm in behalf of the fortunes of its leader. At the mention of his name, the faithful men thundered forth applause; the faithful women smiled applause! All this was very decorous, perhaps very touching to those more immediately concerned. But mere applause, be it loud or be it gentle, will not prove a substitute, in the work of establishing the "people's constitution," for unalterable resolve and for energetic and persevering effort.

Fellow Citizens:—I have adverted to these signs of the times, because they are deemed to be somewhat significant of a change, at least an ostensible change, in the policy of the revolutionary party. This opinion is not without warrant. The leaders of that party have given the signal, and are preparing, with what grace they can, to take the back track! They have discovered that the people of Rhode Island are not ready to sanction perjury, treachery, and usurpation. They have discovered that the texts of sedition from which they have so long preached, must be preached from no longer. They have discovered that the people's constitution and "the rightful Governor" must be abandoned to their fate! Hence the marvellous silence, in respect to these once fruitful topics of declamation, which now pervades the ranks of the party. Hence the convulsive efforts which are now making to represent the antagonist parties in Rhode Island as identical with the whig and democratic parties in the other States of the Union. Hence the laborious diligence with which the pending controversy in this State is put forth as a mere controversy about the matters which divide whigs and democrats from each other, in other States—and not as a controversy between Revolution and Law—between Riot and Order—between Government and Anarchy. Hence, too, the deceptive means which are adopted to persuade the democracy abroad that the Whigs of Rhode Island, under a new name, are struggling to preserve their ascendency, and likewise to persuade the democracy at home, that Mr. Dorr, his revolutionary party, and his revolutionary doctrines are sustained, by a deep and pervading sympathy throughout this Union.

Hence, too, the effrontery, almost amusing, with which the organs of the revolutionary party stigmatize James Fenner as a "renegade democrat!"

Fellow Citizens:—The political principles of James Fenner, and his unwavering attachment to them, through evil and through good report, are too well known, in Rhode Island, to stand in need of vindication. A few unprincipled men, most of whom were puling in their nurses' arms, when he was active in the field of political controversy, now seek to draw into question his democracy, and to cast reproach upon his motives. It is not necessary that any man should step forth, either to endorse the one or to defend the other. In accepting the nomination of the Rhode Island party for the office of Governor, he has neither surrendered nor compromised a single principle of his long and eventful political life. Where he was to be found forty years ago, he is to be found now. He was nominated by the convention with cordial unanimity; his nomination has been hailed with equal cordiality by the friends of the constitution throughout the State; and, if the present indications are not deceptive, he will be elected the first Governor under the constitution, by a triumphant majority of the whole people. Nothing but a strong sense of duty to his native State, at this extraordinary crisis in her affairs, could have induced James Fenner again to become a candidate for the high and responsible office for which he has been nominated. Advanced in life, though with his natural force unabated, he desires the repose of private life rather than the unavoidable excitements of a commanding public station. He has passed through various stages of civic honor. He has been elevated to the highest posts within the gift of his native State. He has been distinguished by marks of respectful consideration on the part of the general government. He is known and recognized throughout the country as a veteran adherent to that party with which, from his very boyhood, he has been connected. Now, when life is far spent, and when the dreams of ambition are over, he has consented, with unaffected reluctance, again to become a candidate for the chief magistracy of Rhode Island. No other candidate could have been selected with more commanding claims to the confidence of the people. No other candidate could have been proposed, who, under existing circumstances, would obtain a more cordial and efficient support.

Fellow Citizens:—Hereafter, I shall endeavor to show you, that the democracy of this country has not espoused the cause of Mr. Dorr, or the doctrines of his party. At present, allow me to direct your special attention to the doings of the second revolutionary convention which is to assemble in this city, to-day. Mark well, the elements of which it is composed; the spirit which may animate it; the language which it may adopt; the purposes which it may avow. Experience must have taught you a salutary distrust in the professions of the men who have sought by turns to intimidate and by turns to beguile you. Continue to be on your guard against their cunning. They already assert, in private, that their solemn and oft repeated declarations in favor of "the rightful Governor" and the people's constitution, mean nothing! They may have the effrontery to put forth, at this late hour, some public and formal declarations intended to deceive you into the belief that you may safely trust them with political power. This intimation would, under ordinary circumstances, be withheld, as uncharitable, if not insulting. But, what confidence, fellow citizens, can be reposed, either in the honor or the consciences of men, who are so profligate as to tell you, without blushing, that neither honor nor oaths shall be suffered to intercept their purposes of revolutionary ambition?

OLD NARRAGANSETT.

PROVIDENCE JOURNAL, FEBRUARY 13, 1843.

THE CRISIS.

ITS DANGERS AND ITS DUTIES.—NO. XIV.

THE SECOND DORRITE CONVENTION AND ITS DOINGS.

TO THE PEOPLE OF RHODE ISLAND:—

FELLOW CITIZENS:—The doings of the Dorrite Convention number two are before you. How marvellously unlike they are to the doings of its illustrious predecessor! What a curious development of character do they exhibit! How inimitable the gravity, with which these political harlequins ask you to applaud every new costume which they put on, and every bold summerset which they find it necessary to turn! To drop the metaphor, with what felicitous ease do these men renounce their principles and violate their solemn pledges! With what indecent haste do they leave "the rightful Governor" alone in his glory, and betake themselves to the shelter of that "military despotism" which both he and they once so eloquently denounced! With what matchless effrontery do they, on the 9th of February, give in their adhesion to that Algerine constitution, against which, on the 29th of November, they solemnly protested as formed "in contravention to the sovereign power," and as "intended to be imposed upon the people without their consent!" Finally, with what cold blooded indifference do they trample upon the people's constitution, and deny to it even the rites of Christian burial! A more exquisite specimen of political coquetry, the annals of the loves and hatreds of politics cannot supply. It recalls to my memory the following lines, which, in the days long gone by, I found in a captivating romance, and which I commend to the careful consideration of the self styled Democratic Convention:

"It is good to be honest and true,
It is good to be off with the old love,
Before you are on with the new."

Fellow Citizens:—I mean to treat, with becoming seriousness, this second Dorrite Convention and its doings. In the first place, the composition of that convention demands inquiry. In the second place, a "searching operation" needs to be applied to the address and to the resolutions which it has put forth. In the third place, the merits of the candidates whom the convention has recommended to your confidence and support, require to be fearlessly and impartially canvassed. All this will prove no easy task. It is no light labor to subject to a rigorous examination elements which seem to know no law but that of change. It is no light labor to extricate from studied ambiguities of language palpable evidences of a dishonest purpose. It is hazardous to pronounce upon the hues of the chameleon. It is difficult to trace "the goings of the serpent." As a knowledge of the character of the workmen will help us to discover the excellence or the defects of the workmanship, let us inquire at the outset, who composed the Dorrite Convention. Were the ruling spirits of the first convention the ruling spirits of the second?

This preliminary inquiry may be readily answered by an appeal to the record. You need not be reminded that the most rabid Dorrites in Rhode Island were members of the Convention of the 29th of November. You need not be reminded that they gave to that Convention its "form and pressure." They infused into it the spirit which animated themselves; they shaped its proceedings into a correspondence with their own purposes of revolutionary ambition. If you deem these imputations to be harsh, do me the justice to read, once more, the resolutions which that convention deliberately adopted, and no less deliberately published to the world.

Read, too, in the same connexion, the various resolutions passed in this city and elsewhere, which uttered the same voice; and then say whether they do not sustain every charge which has been brought against these men, and every inference which has been drawn in respect to their motives and designs. Let us see, then, who were the ruling spirits of the Dorrite Convention number two. Benjamin Cowell, one of "the nine learned lawyers," and the author of a letter to "the Hon. Samuel King, late Governor of Rhode Island," a privy counsellor of the arch traitor, and for months an exile from the city which joint treasons had well nigh covered with infamy and with mourning, was very appropriately selected to call to order this Dorrite convention in disguise. Burrington Anthony, Governor Dorr's sheriff, and Governor Dorr's companion and friend, then nominated, for the office of President, Fenner Brown, of Cumberland. A more artful and persevering fomenter of the troubles through which we have passed, could not probably be found; and had Fenner Brown's intrepidity been equal to his cunning, the State would not, in the hour of her trial, have contained a more dangerous man. His titles to the confidence of the convention were felt to be unequivocal, and he was unanimously elected. Five Vice Presidents and three Secretaries were then appointed—some of them known to fame, and some of them not. To preclude, as far as practicable, all doubt, that the genuine sympathies and attachments of the convention were, in spite of every profession to the contrary, for "the rightful Governor," one of the secretaries was selected from the office of the Republican Herald, and another from the office of the Providence Express! This latter print, it may be well to inform you, endorsed, no longer ago than the 28th of January, all the revolutionary doctrines set forth in the resolutions, which the Dorrite faction, in primary assemblies and in State conventions, has from time to time adopted. No longer ago than the 28th of January, the Express pronounced those resolutions to be "patriotic," and declared, with emphasis, that it sought not to "avoid a trial on that issue!"

Who were the rank and file of the late convention, it is not important to inquire. It is sufficient for the purpose which I have in view, to ascertain the names, and characters, and political and personal sympathies of those men who trained the rank and file into unquestioning obedience to the commands of their superiors. It is sufficient to know that members of the convention which formed the people's convention were there; that senators and representatives in the foundry legislature were there; that three or four of the "nine learned lawyers" were there; that one man who has been tried for treason, and that others who have been charged with treason, were there. Besides the worthies whom I have already named, Dutee J. Pearce, who, says Mr. Dorr, "meant no fraud" in the matter of the Newport votes, and who in his letter to Mr. Dorr, apologized "for encroaching a little upon the Sabbath!" was there. John R. Waterman, who, in December last, declared that the legal constitution had "no moral binding force upon his conscience," was there. William H. Smith, Dorr's Secretary of State, Jonah Titus, Dorr's Attorney General, and John A. Brown, Dorr's Missionary to Washington, were there. Last of all, Doctor Ariel Ballou, of insurrectionary memory, was there, again to try his healing art upon the body politic! Can any man doubt that it is the sacred mission of these men, and of men like these, to uphold the sound, old fashioned conservative democracy of Rhode Island? Did they not, on the 29th of November, denounce "certain leading and influential" democrats as "foes to popular liberty," and as "aiding materially in establishing despotic power in this State?" Did they not, on the 29th of November, pass the following truly democratic resolutions?

"Resolved, That, in Thomas Wilson Dorr, the rightful Governor of Rhode Island, we recognize the incorruptible patriot, sound democrat, and unwavering friend of equal rights.

"Resolved, That, in recommending this course, [the registry of names] and in order to avoid all doubt or misconstruction of our purposes, we explicitly avow our object to be, to accomplish in a satisfactory manner, and with the least delay, the establishment in fact, as well as in right, of the people's constitution."

Such was the democracy of these men on the 29th of November last; and, as democracy is both unchangeable and eternal, it cannot be supposed to have altered since!

Fellow Citizens:—Having briefly examined the composition of the late Convention, let us now proceed to an examination of the address and resolutions which have been addressed to you as a genuine exposition of the unchangeable democracy of the State of Rhode Island and Providence Plantations! This address is, verily, a most precious document. It occupies only four columns of the Express. Its predecessor, but not its archetype, occupied more than twelve columns of the same paper! There is mercy here. Our patience and our credulity are not both taxed at once. The comparative brevity of the address, I should be wanting in magnanimity not to acknowledge—for that is its only merit. Its whole drift and purpose is deception. By declarations, in which, after what has passed, you can place no confidence, and by the use of words and phrases, so equivocal in their meaning, that they will warrant not only different but directly opposite interpretations, the men who have put forth this address, would fain persuade you that they are the fast friends of law and order—that they seek to carry out the legal constitution, in good faith, and, more than this, that they are already struggling to rescue it from acts of Algerine usurpation!

Really, fellow citizens, this is one of the boldest experiments which unprincipled men ever made upon the credulity of any people! The address proceeds, throughout, as it would seem, upon a false basis. It presumes that the people of Rhode Island have very short memories; and likewise that, in a matter affecting their rights and interests, they will fail to exercise the good sound common sense with which they are so largely endowed. It presumes, moreover, that the people can look, without disdain, upon men, who now underrate their discernment, as much as they once underrated their courage—and who, while claiming to be men of principle, seemingly repudiate, at one convention, principles which they had avowed, and issues which they had made at another. This conversion is somewhat too sudden to be sincere, and, if not sincere, it cannot be lasting.

Hardly six weeks ago, and these men were rampant in behalf of "the rightful Governor" and the people's constitution. Before the ink was dry, with which they recorded their professions of attachment to the champion of the people, and to the paramount law, which, as they contended, the people by a large majority had established, they turn all at once quite round, not even pausing to compliment Governor Dorr with a solitary adieu. With unsurpassed effrontery they declare themselves to be the friends and supporters of the Algerine constitution—adopted, as they say, by a "minority only," and "in contravention of the sovereign power!"—that constitution which so recently had "no binding moral force upon their consciences," and which, "with the least delay" they had pledged themselves to overthrow! Surely these men ought to be the last to complain of me or of others for charging them, upon evidence furnished by their own records, with "revolutionary purposes and insurrectionary designs." From time to time, they have defined their own position. I have described that position just as they have defined it—"nothing extenuating or setting down aught in malice." They have been wrong from the beginning—and they ought to take shame to themselves for the injuries they have done to their fellow citizens, and for the lasting discredit they have brought upon their own characters. They will, I am persuaded, "take nothing by their last motion." To superadd meanness to wickedness is but a poor expedient to win the public favor, and, after having been "engaged in the same tontine of infamy" with Dorr, it is quite too late for these men to retrieve their own fortunes by pretending to thrust him aside.

Fellow citizens:—The address and resolutions in question I beg you to read and to ponder. They will, hereafter, furnish abundant topics for animadversion.

At present, I must leave them to your keen judgment of men and of things—convinced that you will do them impartial justice; that you will visit with scorn and with indignation those hollow professions and that systematic duplicity to which desperate men have, at last, resorted, for the purpose of accomplishing a desperate end.

OLD NARRAGANSETT.

PROVIDENCE JOURNAL, FEBRUARY 15, 1843.

THE CRISIS.

ITS DANGERS AND ITS DUTIES.—NO. XV.

THE SECOND DORRITE CONVENTION AND ITS DOINGS.

TO THE PEOPLE OF RHODE ISLAND:—

FELLOW CITIZENS:—In my thirteenth number, I intimated my intention to show you that the democratic party in this country has not espoused the cause of Mr. Dorr, or the revolutionary doctrines of his faction. In this matter, great pains have been taken to deceive you. Again and again, have Mr. Dorr, his partisan State Conventions, his partisan primary assemblies, and his partisan presses, appealed to the great and now triumphant democratic party, throughout the Union, for sympathy and for support. The true issue between the contending parties in this State has been systematically misrepresented. Calumny, in all its varieties, has been resorted to, in order to excite popular indignation, at home and abroad, against those who have stood forth manfully to protect Rhode Island from the disasters and the disgrace of anarchy. Reiterated and most impassioned appeals have been made, with a view to enlist the active sympathy of the democratic party in favor of a set of men who have been most leniently treated by the government which they sought, by violence, to overthrow—a set of men, who have put on the garb of democracy for the purpose of masking principles and designs abhorrent to the nature and hostile to the very existence of democracy.

In the absence of any well devised plan to counteract its influence, the system of calumny and deception, pursued by the anarchists, has, to some extent, succeeded. Portions of the democratic party in Massachusetts, Connecticut, Maine, New Hampshire, and New York, have been deceived into the belief that Mr. Dorr and his followers were perilling their lives and fortunes, at one time, for free suffrage, and, at another, for the vital doctrine of the sovereignty of the people. Thousands of that party have yet to learn that there is not a man in Rhode Island who has ever denied the doctrine of the sovereignty of the people. Thousands of that party have yet to learn, that suffrage in Rhode Island was made almost as free as water, some time before Mr. Dorr and his followers took up arms to conquer their "equal rights." The peculiar condition of the antagonist parties, in some of these States, likewise favored misconception in regard to the Rhode Island question. The democrats of Connecticut had just won a triumph over their opponents. The democrats of Massachusetts felt themselves to be on the eve of a triumph over theirs. "Can't we," says Dutee J. Pearce, in his Sunday letter to Mr. Dorr, "can't we make something out of the Bemis case?" Dutee, though he may have no parallel at home, is not without brethren of the same principle abroad—skillful tacticians, who said within themselves, the moment the Rhode Island question began to be agitated, "can't we make something out of this Rhode Island Question?" They did make something out of it in Massachusetts, but nothing out of it, elsewhere. Listen, fellow citizens, to the conclusion of the whole matter. The democratic Governor of New Hampshire has sheltered the "rightful Governor" of Rhode Island. The democratic Governor of Maine has recommended to the Legislature of that State, to sustain him by "resolutions or otherwise." Has Maine, since that recommendation, done the one thing or the other? Has she passed resolutions, or has she done "otherwise?" The democratic Governor of Connecticut was prepared to surrender Mr. Dorr to the Governor of Rhode Island, when he took refuge in New Hampshire! The democratic Governor in New York countenances the late insurrection in this State, only by a cautious and oblique allusion, which occupies about two lines of his Inaugural Message. Lastly, the democratic Governor of Massachusetts is silent as the grave about the people's constitution and "the rightful Governor." How unlike, in this instance, are the candidate and the Governor! The voice which woke the echoes of Medbury Grove, in behalf of the cause of the people, how it dies away in frigid silence, within the walls of the Capitol!

Fellow Citizens:—In this attempt to show you that the democratic party in this country has not taken sides with Mr. Dorr, I omit entirely the consideration of the meeting of sympathizers "got up" in Boston, New York and Philadelphia. These meetings are very well understood. They are intended only to produce stage effect. They may enable their Presidents and Secretaries to "make something" out of the trouble in which they vent their sympathies. They are intended for no other purpose. They can answer no other purpose. Besides, in the controversy between the friends of law and the apostles of anarchy in Rhode Island, who ever doubted on which side were to be found the sympathies of the "Butt Enders and Barn Burners" of New York and Philadelphia? Who ever doubted that the "Pewter Mug" always frothed and foamed in the cause of the Dorr democracy! Who ever doubted that the "Five Points" went in favor of the "largest liberty?"

Fellow Citizens:—We have examined this topic in one of its aspects. Let us look at it in another. Let me here remind you that the democratic party are in the ascendant in nearly all the twenty six States of the Union. Vermont, New Jersey, Kentucky, and little Delaware, are, I believe, the only States where the Whig party clearly predominates; in Rhode Island the political power being divided equally between the whigs and democrats. Democracy, it would seem, then rules nearly over the whole domain. In how many

States, out of the twenty two subject to its entire and undisputed sway, has a voice been raised in behalf of Mr. Dorr? I answer in only five, and two of these are among the smallest States in the Union. Has Pennsylvania endorsed the attempts which have been made in this State to confound democracy with anarchy? Has the valley of the Mississippi given a responsive echo to the hoarse notes of revolutionary discord which our Rhode Island "Heralds" have given to the breeze? Has the South, always ardent in the support of democracy, felt that this was an occasion in which it became her to come to the rescue of her cherished principles? Has Virginia lifted up her voice, to encourage insurrection in a sister State? No, my fellow citizens, the gigantic West has put forth none of its democratic vigor; and the generous South has expended none of its democratic fervors, in this bad cause.

Virginia has been silent throughout all our troubles. Virginia, the birth place of the patriarchs of democracy—the land of Jefferson and Henry, of Madison and Monroe—has given no countenance to the doctrines which Mr. Dorr broached, when he put the ball of revolution in motion, and which, I beg you to remember, the supporters of Thomas F. Carpenter have never repudiated.

Fellow Citizens:—Dismissing this topic, let us recur to the address number two, which the Dorrite convention number two has recently put forth. In reading this address, you will frequently be puzzled how to construe the language. You will not readily catch the idea intended to be concealed rather than to be conveyed—to be cloaked in ambiguity, rather than in honest English to be made plain. In all such cases of perplexing doubt, it may be well to remember that Dutee J. Pearce, Benjamin Cowell, John R. Waterman, William H. Smith, John A. Brown, John S. Harris, and Samuel H. Wales, were the chief instruments in preparing this address. These are the men who would fain have you think that the great object of their lives is "the cherishment of the people!" These are the disinterested patriots who claim your confidence—unambitious citizens—who never had an office, and never sought one—tutelary guardians of law and order—and, more than all this, the pledged supporters of the Algerine constitution, adopted "by a minority only, and in contravention of the will of the people!"

Fellow Citizens :—When such men ask your confidence, you must not be too scrupulous in your estimates of morality—or too severe in your judgments of character. Dutee J. Pearce, to be sure, sought to "make something out of the Bemis case"—and he did make something out of the Newport frauds. But then, in the latter case, Mr. Dorr says, that "Mr. Pearce meant no fraud!" Benjamin Cowell, it is true, wrote a letter to the "late Governor King," to vindicate the cause of rebellion, but he voted at last for the Algerine constitution! John R. Waterman has declared, that the same Algerine constitution has no binding moral force upon his conscience—but John R. Waterman is an honorable man, and, coming "fresh from the people," he now says, that his petty conscientious scruples must yield to the main object—"the cherishment of the people!" John A. Brown has been furious for "Dorr and liberty." The association of which he is the President, on the 27th of December, denounced the Algerine constitution "as intended to be imposed upon the people without their consent, and against their will, and as entitled to no respect or allegiance whatsoever."

Never mind, fellow citizens, Doctor Brown has likewise come "fresh from the people," with a contrite heart—and you all know how devoted he is to the "cherishment of the people!" As to Harris, and Smith, and Wales, they are patriots of whom the world is not worthy. Harris is fresh from the Morton festival. Wales is fresh from the presence chamber of the "rightful Governor" at Concord—and Smith wears, with modest dignity, the crown of martyrdom. Some of his compeers have surrendered their consciences, in order to maintain the Algerine Constitution. For him a nobler sacrifice was reserved—to Dexter Randall he has surrendered his office! Well may it be said—"the Secretary stands alone—modern degeneracy has not reached him!"

Fellow Citizens:—These are the men who aim to persuade you that they are the friends of the legal constitution; that they may be safely trusted with the political power of the State; that you ought to elect as your Governor, Thomas F. Carpenter, who last April voted for Thomas Wilson Dorr, as Governor! Surely, "the net is spread in vain in the sight of any bird!" Surely, the people of Rhode Island must be most easily deceived, if they can place the slightest confidence in men who, within the short space of six weeks, come before the world, in a grave matter, with two sets of principles—not only different, but directly contradictory.

OLD NARRAGANSETT.

PROVIDENCE JOURNAL, FEBRUARY 21, 1843.

THE CRISIS.

ITS DANGERS AND ITS DUTIES.—NO. XVI.

THE SECOND DORRITE CONVENTION AND ITS DOINGS.

TO THE PEOPLE OF RHODE ISLAND:—

FELLOW CITIZENS:—Keep in mind that the Dorrite convention number one and the Dorrite convention number two, were held in secret, and that the leading spirits of the one were the leading spirits of the other! Keep, also, in mind that a committee of the convention number one was instructed to publish only such portions of the proceedings as it should be thought safe to lay before the people. What secret engagements were entered into by the first convention, for the purpose of establishing the people's constitution "with the least delay," we are, therefore, left to conjecture. The resolutions which they adopted and published were, upon some points, however, sufficiently explicit. They left no doubt upon the mind of any reasonable man, not blinded by passion or by party, that the legal constitution had every thing to fear from its enemies, if its enemies should ever be clothed with political power. These resolutions have been published again and again. Remember, fellow citizens, that they have neither been retracted nor expunged. They still stand upon the record as the explicit and authentic declaration of the sentiments and the purposes of the men who, having failed to intimidate, are now attempting to ensnare you.

Fellow Citizens:—What portion of the records of the Dorrite convention number two has been suppressed, we know not. Enough, however, has been disclosed, to quicken to increased vigilance and activity every friend to the legal constitution, and to kindle in the breast of every honorable man a sentiment of indignation towards men who, by their own records, are proved to be destitute not only of virtue but of shame. The resolutions appended to the jesuitical address of the Dorrite convention number two, are marked by that insipid neutrality in which cunning men, when they seek to decline an issue made upon great principles, instinctively take refuge. These resolutions are intended to blind you to the true issue which has been made up, and which alone you are to try, at the ballot box, on the first Wednesday in April next. In one of them, these men who, for the year past, have been deep in traitorous counsels, and some of whom are not unstained by actual participation in scenes of revolutionary violence, affect to feel aggrieved, because they have been "charged with entertaining revolutionary and insurrectionary designs!" They would have you look upon them as honest and gentle souls, whom the rascally Algerines have pursued, in all this matter, with a "hunt of obloquy."

Have you forgotten, fellow citizens, the Jacobin clubs which assembled weekly at the Town House, and into which Dorr, and Parmenter and Simmons sought to engraft, and did engraft the licentious theories, and the distempered energies of jacobinism? Have you forgotten the elaborate opinion which Thomas W. Dorr, Thomas F. Carpenter, Samuel Y. Atwell, Benjamin Cowell and others—"nine learned lawyers" in all—put forth in order to drug with an opiate the consciences of the ignorant and violent men who were bent on establishing the people's constitution "by all necessary means?" Have you forgotten, and can you ever forget, the night of the attack upon the State's arsenal? Have you forgotten, and can you ever forget, the array, at Acote's Hill, of hundreds of ruffians, Mr. Dorr called them "brave men!" whom he and men like him having, all the while, naught in view but "the cherishment of the people!" had exasperated to the wildest excess of revolutionary fanaticism? No, fellow citizens, these are deep wrongs which cannot and ought not soon to be forgotten. Especially ought they to be recalled to your remembrance, at this crisis, when the very men who, behind the scenes, were the prime agents in all this fearful public mischief, come before you, and in the blandest accents ask you to vote for them—to install them in high places—to welcome them as the predestined restorers of peace, and harmony, and prosperity, to our long agitated and much injured State!

Fellow Citizens:—Annexed is one of the resolutions passed at the late convention, and the only one which seems to deserve farther comment:

"Resolved, That in the capacities, abilities and integrity of the candidates recommended to fill the places of general officers, we have the fullest confidence and the surest guarantee that, if elected, they will promptly adopt all needful measures to put the government into operation and carry out our cherished principles."

Omitting, for the present, all investigation into "the capacity, abilities and integrity" of the candidates nominated by the Dorrites, we may be permitted to draw your attention to "the glorious uncertainty" which hangs over the meaning of this resolution. What are "the cherished principles" of these men, I, for one, should like to know? Do they mean that we shall take the address and the resolutions of the convention number one, or the address and resolutions of the convention number two, as the true exponent of "their cherished principles?" Are the principles avowed in November, or the principles avowed in February, the "cherished principles?" Which of the two sets of principles is to be received as genuine?

Again, in this connexion, I feel a little shy of the adverb "promptly"—apprehending that it may mean "the least possible delay." Again, the phrase "all needful measures"—so like is it to the consecrated phrase "all necessary means," that every friend of "the rightful Governor" and of the people's constitution will feel that it is meant to comfort them! Lastly, what are we to understand by "the government," which General Carpenter and Mr. Atwell are to put in operation? Within the last year, we have been blessed with two governors, two general assemblies, two constitutions, and, in the judgment of some folks, with two governments! Now, we have a right to know, before we vote for General Carpenter and Mr. Atwell, which is the government they are to put into operation. Is it the government under the Algerine constitution, or the government under the people's constitution? Is it the government which Mr. Atwell introduced a bill into the Legislature to vacate in favor of that constitution, or is it the government which his friends, in November last, declared was established by "a minority only," and "in contravention of the sovereign power" of the people?

Let us, fellow citizens, before we clothe these men with political power, ascertain, if possible, what are their "cherished principles," and what is "the government" which they would put into operation.

OLD NARRAGANSETT.

PROVIDENCE JOURNAL, FEBRUARY 25, 1843.

THE CRISIS.

ITS DANGERS AND ITS DUTIES.—NO. XVII.

THE SECOND DORRITE CONVENTION AND ITS DOINGS.

TO THE PEOPLE OF RHODE ISLAND:—

FELLOW CITIZENS:—If the address of the last Dorrite Convention can deceive a single man in Rhode Island, the schoolmaster has been abroad in vain. So diverse, nay, so utterly irreconcilable, are the principles and purposes avowed in the address number one, from the principles and purposes avowed in the address number two, that the contrariety between them presents a curious and somewhat puzzling philosophical problem. How can you account for the phenomenon? Have these men become the victims of a temporary hallucination, or have they been seduced, by the love of fanciful analogies, into a course which exposes their integrity to grave suspicion? Have they concluded that, because we have had, within the year past, two governors, two general assemblies, and two constitutions, it is all right for them to have two consciences—a conscience marked number one, and a conscience marked number two; a December conscience, and a February conscience; a Dorrite conscience, and a democratic conscience!

Leaving you, my fellow citizens, to adopt either solution of this extraordinary problem, or to frame another more satisfactory to yourselves, suffer me to pass to a further examination of the last address which the Dorrites have put forth, in order to secure their main object, namely, "the cherishment of the people!" This examination need not be very extended. It would imply an insult upon your understandings, to suppose that you cannot see the net which is laid for your feet; that you cannot pierce the disguise which the authors of this address have been compelled to adopt; that you cannot detect the double meaning under which they seek to hide from you a dishonest and most mischievous purpose. For the sake, however, of deepening the impression which this address cannot fail to make upon your minds, and of exhibiting the true characters of its authors, it may not be amiss to direct your attention to a few of its most significant passages.

The address opens in a tone of self gratulation, positively amusing. These friends and coadjutors of the "brave men" who attacked the State's arsenal, and who assembled at Acote's hill, for no other purpose than to overthrow, by military force, the existing government of Rhode Island, now have the matchless effrontery to commend themselves to "the wise and good of the whole Union," for "the patriotism and the devotion to republican principles" with which they "united to preserve the public peace! and to defend and maintain constitutional freedom and popular government!" That there may be no mistake, fellow citizens, I give you their very words. They unite to preserve the public peace! They, who so exasperated the passions and so misled the understandings of a portion of our people, that we hardly escaped the worst horrors of a civil war! They defend popular government and constitutional freedom! They who did all that they dared to do, in order to subject the people of this State, their lives, liberties, and properties, to the rule of a ferocious and insolent military domination!

These men proceed to say—"By this union and determination of the people, all apprehensions of any actual or constructive violence—all fears of anarchy, of civil commotion, of revolution, or of insubordination, are at once entirely dissipated and banished." Verily, here is a full and complete catalogue of the offences which these men have themselves committed, and which, with a gravity truly inimitable, they seem to charge upon the friends of law and order? By their "union and determination" have insubordination, violence, and revolution been put down! What say you to this, gallant citizens of Providence, who had resolved to go to the death in defence of your firesides? And what say you, brave men of Kent, and you no less brave men, who, from Warren and Bristol, Rhode Island and Old Narragansett, rushed to this city, to save her from the horrors of ruffian violence, and to put forth a soldier's might in defence of liberty and law?

Fellow Citizens:—Let me next invite your attention to the following passage of the address:—"Two prominent evils [a restricted suffrage, and unequal representation] have been partially redressed, though not to that extent which a more perfect equality would require!" Here, fellow citizens, is a very significant intimation that the work of political reform has not, in the judgment of the Dorrites, been perfected. None of their "cherished principles" have they abandoned. Free as suffrage has been made under the legal constitution, it is not free enough for the Dorrites. Nothing, in this matter, will content them but the provision in the "people's constitution," which would, in effect, confer upon our foreign population and upon the floating masses in Providence and the factory villages the whole political power of the State, and confer it upon them, without any effective check, and for all time. If the farmers of Rhode Island; if, indeed, any portion of the conservative classes are not ready thus to sacrifice their rights and their truest welfare, they will take good care to withhold their votes from General Carpenter and his Dorrite associates. These candidates are pledged to carry out the "cherished principles" of the party which nominated them; and no principle is more cherished by them than the principle of universal suffrage. That such is the fact, you cannot doubt, if you will read the following resolution, adopted by "a mass meeting" of Dorrites, held at Cranston, February 15th, several days after the publication of the address—at the identical mass meeting which was enlivened by "the Dorr quick step":

"Resolved, That we hereby reiterate and reaffirm the doctrine that all political powers are vested in the people, and that by the people we mean the whole people, not that portion of them to whom powers may at any time be delegated for the purposes of government, but the whole people in the State, represented by all the male population of the age of twenty one years and upwards, who are not mentally disqualified to a rational participation in the affairs of the government."

Fellow Citizens:—This resolution surely needs no elaborate comment. Should the cherished principle in respect to suffrage, which it embodies, once be carried out, the farmers of Rhode Island, and in truth all other quiet citizens, might as well stay away from town meeting. Under such a system of unrestricted suffrage, they would, without any power to defend themselves, inevitably be left to the tender mercies of a majority, swayed by the worst demagogues in the State. A consummation so disastrous can be averted only by electing to office men who are in favor of maintaining the legal constitution, and not men who stand pledged to overthrow it, and to establish with the least delay, the people's constitution upon its ruins!

Fellow Citizens:—The Dorrites, should they ever

obtain political power, would also reform the present constitution of the Senate, in order to accommodate it to their notions of "more perfect equality." They would assign to Providence, Smithfield, Cumberland, Warwick, and other manufacturing towns, a much larger proportion of power in that branch of the General Assembly. Not only would this organic change prove to be a calamity to those towns, but it would take from the small agricultural towns, the only effective means by which, hereafter, they can hope to protect their rights and interests against aggression. Most inimical to the influence of the conservative classes throughout the State, would be any alteration in the present organization of the Senate, which, either by diminishing the number of Senators, or by changing the manner in which they are elected, would impair its value as an effective check upon the House of Representatives, whenever that House may, from any cause, be tempted to abuse its power. Break down the salutary restriction under which foreigners are now permitted to exercise the right of suffrage, and conform the Senate to a standard of theoretic perfection, and the demagogues of the day will carry out their "cherished principles" with a vengeance!

Fellow Citizens:—To another important provision of the legal constitution "the cherished principles" of the Dorrites are not less strongly opposed. I refer to the subjoined article, relative to "amendments," which indicates the manner, and the only manner, in which the constitution can, without usurpation or without a resort to the revolutionary power, be changed:

"The General Assembly may propose amendments to this constitution by the votes of a majority of all the members elected to each House. Such propositions for amendment shall be published in the newspapers, and printed copies of them shall be sent to the Secretary of State, with the names of all the members who shall have voted thereon, with the yeas and nays, to all the town and city clerks in the State. The said propositions shall be, by said clerks, inserted in the warrants or notices by them issued, for warning the next annual town and ward meetings in April; and the clerks shall read said propositions to the electors when thus assembled, with the names of all the Representatives and Senators who shall have voted thereon, with the yeas and nays, before the election of Senators and Representatives shall be had. If a majority of all the members elected to each House, at said annual meeting, shall approve any proposition thus made, the same shall be published and submitted to the electors in the mode provided in the act of approval; and if then approved by three fifths of the electors of the State present, and voting thereon in town and ward meetings, it shall become a part of the constitution of the State."

This, fellow citizens, you need not be reminded, is one of the most valuable and truly conservative provisions in the legal constitution. A similar provision in the Landholders' Constitution was strongly objected to by the Dorrites, as in violation of "the republican rule that the majority should govern!" Should they now succeed in breaking down this provision, or should they dare, in carrying out their notions of the sovereignty of the people, to violate it, the constitution will not be worth the parchment upon which it is engrossed; the right of suffrage will be extended, at once, to "all the male population of the age of twenty one years and upwards;" and the protection afforded by the present organization of the Senate, to the conservative classes, will be wrested from them forever. Rhode Island would then become a prey to successive factions; our dearest rights and most important interests, no longer protected by a stable government, would then be at the mercy of unprincipled demagogues operating upon the passions of fluctuating majorities.

Fellow Citizens:—The address disclaims all intention on the part of the Dorrites to change the legal constitution, "by usurpation." With an emphasis somewhat suspicious, they affirm and reaffirm their determination to maintain the legal constitution, till, in the language of Washington, it is changed "by an explicit and authentic act of the whole people." This language, you will recollect, forms a part of the first section of the Bill of Rights in the legal constitution. As understood by Washington, and as understood by the framers and the friends of that constitution, these words are endowed with a power to protect us against all change by usurpation. But I apprehend, and there is too much reason to apprehend, that the Dorrites, in this matter, understand, by an explicit and authentic act of the whole people, something more than what Washington understood by it—and something more than we understand by it! Concerning this power to change the constitution, the Dorrites affect to be at great pains to define their "exact position." Most lamentably, however, do they fail in this their professed object. Listen, fellow citizens, to their language. Mark the solicitude which they seem to feel, lest you should distrust their sincerity, and should come, after all, to the conclusion that, instead of explaining their "exact position," they had only obscured it. "This obligation [that of an oath] will exist," says the address, "till the constitution shall have been changed by an explicit and sovereign act of the whole people." Again:

"Such a change [by legislative enactment] would be a usurpation, unless it was expressly commanded and specially directed, by an explicit act of the whole people, clearly and plainly expressed by them in their sovereign capacity!!"

Again: "We are fully aware that the constitution is and must be obligatory, until it shall be changed in the manner and form herein before indicated." After all these repeated and emphatic asseverations, they have left in doubt the very matter which they professed their desire to make plain. Had they declared, explicitly, that the legal constitution is "sacredly obligatory upon all," until it is changed in the manner and form indicated by the article on amendments, there could have been no misconception as to their "exact position." This is what Washington understood, and this is what we understand, by "an explicit and authentic act of the whole people." Any other mode of changing the constitution than that provided by the constitution itself, would be revolutionary in its character, and a gross usurpation of the rights of the people. I marvel that the Dorrites, if they really wished to make this matter plain, did not refer to the article on amendments, pointing out, as that article does in the most explicit manner, the only mode in which the constitution can be changed. With this article on amendments staring them in the face, will they contend that the substitution of the "People's Constitution," by a convention which might assemble, at the request of the General Assembly, would be what Washington meant, and what we mean by "an explicit and authentic act of the whole people?"

This is now the question, and, until this question be settled, it will be all in vain for the Dorrites to pretend that they mean to maintain, in good faith, the legal constitution. Till this question be settled, the people of Rhode Island will be slow to discard the distrust with which they have all along been compelled to regard the professions and the designs of the Dorrites. This distrust is founded in declarations, formally and repeatedly made, and which, be it remembered, have never been revoked. They will be slow, in any event, to trust the administration of the Constitution to its bitterest enemies; to those who have declared their repugnance to it, in every form of reproachful language which either hatred or contempt can suggest. That I may not be thought to deal in unsupported assertions, I here subjoin various resolutions, &c., adopted by the Dorrites, and all of them going to show what, only a few weeks ago, was their "exact position" in regard to the Constitution, the administration of which they now ask you to commit to their hands. I begin with the solemn "Resolutions and Protests" adopted in this city, November 11th, 1842, by "the friends of the People's Constitution:"

"Resolved, That we protest against all the measures of the charter party of this State, since the adoption of the People's Constitution, which are not in conformity with, and which are contrary to, the provisions of said Constitution.

"Because, The people of this State, by a large majority, have already adopted a written Constitution, which has, by no act of theirs, been annulled or repealed, and which we believe now to be of right the paramount law and Constitution of the State.

"Because, The main provisions of the Constitution are unjust and anti American, making odious distinctions among the citizens, and perpetuating a rotten borough system of unequal representation by which a town with three hundred and sixty five inhabitants, and another town with more than twenty three thousand, have each the same representation in the Senate."

The Rhode Island Suffrage Association, in December, adopted a long and elaborate "Address to the friends of equal rights in this State." This address holds the following language: "We, the friends of equal rights, citizens of Rhode Island, do not consider said pretended Constitution as entitled to any respect or allegiance whatsoever."

Resolutions passed at the Dorrite Convention, which met at Providence, November 29, 1842:

"Resolved, That the people of this State, in the exercise of their sovereign right, have, in their sovereign capacity, formed a constitution, which has been adopted by a majority of the people, and of right ought to be the supreme law.

"And whereas, The government de facto of this State have formed another constitution, in contravention of this sovereign power, and have offered the same to the people, which has been voted for by a minority only:

"And whereas, There is reason to apprehend, that said constitution is intended to be imposed upon a majority of the people against their consent. Therefore,

"Resolved, That we do for ourselves and for the people solemnly protest against the same and the manner of its adoption."

Resolution passed at the Dorrite State Convention, December 20, 1842:

"Resolved, That in recommending this course, (to register) and in order to avoid all doubt or misconstruction of our purpose, we explicitly avow our object to be, to accomplish in a satisfactory manner and with the least delay, the establishment in fact, as well as in right, of the People's Constitution."

Resolutions passed at a meeting of Dorrites in the Fifth Ward of this city, December 19th:

"Resolved, That the people of this State, in the free exercise of their inherent and legitimate sovereignty, have formed, for themselves, a constitution of government; but that they have been prevented from carrying it into operation, by a lawless military force.

"Resolved, That we consider the thing termed a constitution, recently adopted by a small though wealthy faction in this State, to be both illegal in its origin and unequal and unjust in its provisions; and that therefore it is not of right the paramount law of the State.

"Resolved, That in organizing a form of government under this constitution, we intend to do no more than to give the people an opportunity to carry out their own will in opposition to that of the unprincipled despots who would control the free exercise of their inalienable rights.

"Resolved, That in qualifying ourselves to act under the Algerine constitution, and in using such means as may be put in our power, through the forms of "law and order," to cast aside this most odious form of government, and to rear upon its ruins the constitution legally made and adopted by the people, we believe we are performing a solemn duty which we owe to our God, to our country and our posterity."

The language of all these resolutions, fellow citizens, is sufficiently explicit. It leaves no doubt as to what was, only a few weeks since, the "exact position" of the men, who now ask you to clothe them with political power, in order that they may carry out their "cherished principles." Is there a tittle of evidence to show that the position taken by these men in December has been abandoned? Is there a tittle of evidence to show that what were their cherished principles then are not their cherished principles now? It is true, these men disclaim all intention to subvert the legal constitution by a legislative act; but they do not disavow the intention to establish the people's constitution, "with the least delay," by means of a convention, whose will in the premises they will regard as "an explicit and authentic act of the whole people!" More than all—their ominous silence in regard to the mode for changing the constitution provided by the constitution itself, and the earnestness with which they press their loose doctrine of popular sovereignty, leave little room to doubt that General

Carpenter and his associates, if elected, would "promptly adopt all needful measures," to change the constitution, by resorting to some mode which, in their judgment, will be regarded as "an authentic and explicit act of the whole people!"

Fellow Citizens:—I have now done with the Dorrite Convention number two and its doings. Ere long, too, I shall take my final leave of "the crisis, its dangers and its duties;" quitting, not unwillingly, the arena of political contention, for more congenial pursuits, and resigning to other and to abler pens the service in which mine has been so long employed.

OLD NARRAGANSETT.

PROVIDENCE JOURNAL, MARCH 2, 1843.

THE CRISIS.

ITS DANGERS AND ITS DUTIES.—NO. XVIII.

TO THE PEOPLE OF RHODE ISLAND:—

Fellow Citizens:—That the Dorrites meditate the overthrow of the legal constitution, can be doubted by no one who is familiar with the spirit which animates them, and with the positive declarations which, from time to time, they have put forth. They very modestly ask you to clothe them with political power, in order that they may carry out their "cherished principles." What their cherished principles are, you very well know. The Dorrites are hostile to the legal constitution; to the mode in which it was framed and adopted, and to some of the most important provisions which it contains. They are avowedly hostile to the very liberal provision which that constitution makes for the extension of the right of suffrage. Liberal though that provision may be, it is not liberal enough for them. They declare themselves to be in favor of "a wholly unrestricted suffrage," (I here quote the words of Mr. Van Buren, uttered several years ago,) "which would render our elections rather a curse than a blessing, and which would drive from the polls all sober minded people." They are for "cheapening this invaluable right," by allowing every man in the State, of the age of twenty one years, to vote for all officers who are elected or may hereafter be made eligible by the people. To the injurious practical operation of this wholly unrestricted suffrage upon the best interests of the State, I have often directed your serious attention. Upon this topic it is perhaps unnecessary to superadd a word of admonition. I cannot, however, dismiss it, without again exhorting you to struggle, with all your might, to avert the multiplied and irretrievable calamities which would inevitably fall upon the State, should the Dorrites succeed in their endeavors to introduce among us their system of universal suffrage! Under such a system, Providence would shadow forth, in some sort, the civic glories of New York, controlled as that metropolis is, and must be, by men who have never yet learned to control themselves! Under such a system, our agricultural towns would be consigned to a hopeless subjection to a class of voters, who are peculiarly liable to the malign influences of the demagogue, and who, for various reasons, can be supposed to feel no strong attachment either to the interests or to the honor of Rhode Island. Those of you, fellow citizens, who deprecate this radical change in relation to suffrage, which the Dorrites are pledged to introduce, will be careful, on the first Wednesday of April, not to vote for the candidates whom they have recommended to your support. Clothe General Carpenter and his associates on the Dorrite prox with the political power of the State, and they will commence, without delay, the work of reform. They will not suffer your Constitution to exist a single year. They will strangle the infant in its very cradle!

Fellow Citizens:—The Dorrites are likewise bitterly opposed to what they term the "rotten borough" Senate, established by the legal constitution. They are, however, somewhat cautious in proclaiming their hostility to the organization of the Senate, because they know that the agricultural towns, and indeed that the whole conservative interest of the State, look to that branch of the government as their only adequate protection against the evils either of hasty or of oppressive legislation. The people's constitution provided for a Senate organized upon very different principles—upon principles which would have left it without the least effective power to withstand the House, should the House, under the temporary dominion of factious impulses, ever trespass upon the sacred principle of "equal rights."

Think not, fellow citizens, that the Dorrite reformers will spare our Senate. Their "cherished principles" could never be reconciled to the interposition of those constitutional checks, without which, as that distinguished democrat, Charles J. Ingersoll, well observes, "democracy is despotism." These men want no constitution which will allow "the sober second thoughts" of the people ultimately to prevail. They want no constitution which will place the political power of the State in the hands of the "sober minded" democracy—in the hands of those who give "sufficient evidence of permanent common interest with, and attachment to the community." They want no constitution which will not give to the floating masses, congregated in the large towns, an uncontrolled dominion over our staid and permanent population. In truth, they want no constitution which will not allow the demagogues of the State to control the legislation of the State—to fill the offices of the State, and to expend, as may best answer their selfish purposes, the money of the State. The "people's constitution" was made for these ends—and it was admirably adapted to these ends; and if you are unwise enough to enable them to work so great a mischief, for yourselves and your children, these men will give you, and in less than one year, too, this identical people's constitution, line for line, word for word, comma for comma. This is the great scheme which they stand pledged to execute. Upon this issue, which they themselves have made up, let every true Rhode Island man be prepared, on the first

Wednesday of April, to meet them. If those of the people who are interested in the preservation and sound administration of the legal constitution, are but true to their cherished principles, the inevitable result will be the election of James Fenner and of his associates—and by a majority, too, so triumphant as to prove "a caution" to all future disturbers of the public peace.

Fellow Citizens:—The excellent provisions in the legal constitution, which indicate the mode, and the only mode, in which that instrument can be rightfully amended, is especially offensive to the Dorrites. Unless they can find some way of escape from the stringent obligations of these provisions, they know full well, that for the "people's constitution" there is no hope. It is evident, however, that above and beyond these provisions, they recognize a mode of effecting their purpose, and to this mode, if they obtain political power, they will not fail promptly to have recourse. Following out their "cherished principles," which recognize the right of the people to do all sorts of things in all sorts of ways, they will summon into action the inherent sovereignty of the people. In other words, disregarding entirely the chapter on "amendments," they will request the people to elect delegates to a convention for the purpose of amending the legal constitution! The result of a convention, assembled under such auspices and for such a purpose, it is easy to predict. It would inevitably be the establishment, with the least delay, of the people's constitution, in fact, though not in right. In their last address, be it remembered, they do not pretend to consider the provisions in the chapter of amendments as indicating the only mode in which the constitution can be changed. On the contrary, they but too plainly intimate, that they would proceed to change it, in spite of those provisions, if such change "was expressly commanded, and specially directed, by an explicit act of the whole people, clearly and plainly expressed by them in their sovereign capacity." What does this language import, if it does not import a convention; and in what other light could such a change, by the fiat of such a convention, be regarded, than as an act of gross usurpation—revolutionary in its character, and tending to provoke a renewal of the fearful commotions which, within the past year, brought us to the verge of civil war?

The fiat of such a convention thus assembled, and for such a purpose, would be regarded by the Dorrites "as an explicit and authentic act of the whole people." Be it remembered, however, fellow citizens, that the people, in "their sovereign capacity," have already determined that there shall be no such convention. The legal constitution, which is the highest expression of the popular will, explicitly declares that no amendments shall be made in the same, unless "approved by three fifths of the electors of the State, present, and voting thereon." This is the compact which the people have made with each other, and this is the compact which, if they obtain the power, the Dorrites will not hesitate to disturb. By such an outrage, the indignation of the people would be aroused—but if the Dorrites were firmly intrenched, behind what they would affect to consider "an explicit and authentic act of the whole people," what would they care for constitutional barriers, or for the righteous indignation of those whose rights they were trampling in the dust?

Fellow Citizens:—It is in your power to avert the calamities with which you are threatened. It is in your power, by your votes, on the first Wednesday of April, to place the legal constitution beyond the reach of those who stand pledged to overthrow it. I have never, for one moment, suspected you of the folly of wishing to entrust power to men who tell you that they seek for power, in order to subvert, by an act of intolerable usurpation, the government which you have just established. I feel no distrust about the issue of this contest. Governor Fenner and his associates on the Rhode Island Prox, were nominated with cordial unanimity. They will command a strong and a cordial support. Most solicitous, however, should we all be, not only to elect our candidates, but to elect them by a commanding majority—by a majority which shall convince other States and our own, that in Rhode Island there exists a fixed and invincible determination to maintain the supremacy of the laws as the only true mode of maintaining the "equal rights" of the people.

OLD NARRAGANSETT.

PROVIDENCE JOURNAL, MARCH 10, 1843.

THE CRISIS.

ITS DANGERS AND ITS DUTIES.—NO. XIX.

To the People of Rhode Island:—

Fellow Citizens:—The Revolutionists seem not only to be directed by two consciences, but to be contending under two banners. On the one banner, as it floats idly upon the breeze, you may behold inscribed words which are intended to captivate those who believe that constitutions of government ought not to be changed "without law and against law." On the other, you may behold the ancient and favorite motto, —"the rightful Governor" and "the people's constitution"—newly painted and varnished for the occasion! By which sign do they hope to conquer? Is it not quite too late for these poor devices to blind the people of Rhode Island to the true issue which has been made up between the parties, and which, on the first Wednesday of April, they will be called upon to decide? That issue was first made, when a portion of the people of this State, representing a minority, upon any principle of computation, voted to assemble in convention for the purpose of establishing, without legal forms, a constitution of government. That issue was maintained, when a portion of the people, also representing a minority, adopted "the people's constitution," and, under its authority, elected a Governor, Lieutenant Governor, Senators and Representatives. That issue was maintained, when the Foundry Governor and the Foundry Legislature attempted, by an armed force, to subject the people of this State to a government founded in fraud and treason. That issue was maintained, when Thomas W. Dorr headed an armed mob, which educated demagogues, by their counsels and harangues, had maddened to desperation, and marched it against the State's Arsenal. That issue was maintained, when the same Thomas W. Dorr collected another mob of armed desperadoes at Acote's hill, for the avowed purpose of reducing the people of this State into subjection to his lawless sway. In effect, that issue has NEVER BEEN CHANGED. On the contrary, it has been affirmed and re-affirmed, to be the true issue, in speeches, in resolutions, and in addresses, by primary assemblies, and by special conventions, "fresh from the people"—and devoted to "the cherishment of the people!"

Fellow Citizens :—On the first Monday of April, the momentous issue which these men have made up, and which they may in vain seek to change, will be decided at the ballot box. Are you prepared to declare, by your votes, that the whole political power of the State shall be placed in the hands of men whose principles allow them to overthrow governments, whenever and however they may please to overthrow them? Are you prepared to confide the constitution which you have, after so many agitations, succeeded in establishing, to the tender mercies of those who tell you that, "with the least delay," they will establish another upon its ruins? Are you prepared to elect as your chief magistrate a man who voted for "Governor Dorr,"—the man, too, who wrote to "General M'Neill, a letter which his own friends are ashamed to republish, which, by no legal sophistries, can be explained away, and about which the honest men of all parties can entertain but one opinion.

I have put these questions to you, fellow citizens, in the full confidence that a vast majority of you, will, on the first Wednesday of April, give an indignant response in the negative. You have suffered too much, and you have perilled too much, in this noble cause of "Law and Order," to commit its future destinies to men who, in the pursuit of their selfish and profligate ambition, have lashed into fury the wild spirit of revolution and anarchy. These men were so impatient for office, that, discarding all slow and cautious measures, they adopted a summary process in order to effect their purposes. The salutary delay with which constitutional reforms ought always to be accomplished, could not be tolerated by these ardent spirits. They precipitated themselves, at once, into the midst of a revolution—trusting that they should be enabled to ride triumphant on its surges, and reckless who might sink beneath them.

Never forget, fellow citizens, that these men resorted to revolution, in the absence of all practical grievance —when oppression, in none of its forms, was either felt or apprehended; and when all needful constitutional reforms might have been accomplished by constitutional means. Our Rhode Island revolutionists are without excuse for their conduct. They cannot shelter themselves even behind a bad precedent. Since the declaration of American Independence, the constitution of every one of the glorious old thirteen, who fought the battles of American freedom, have been changed; and how and by whom have they been changed? In every instance, by the sovereign people, through the forms of law. In North Carolina, the reforms which time and change of circumstances had rendered necessary, were not effected, till after a struggle of more than twenty years. In that respectable and truly democratic State, the friends of reform, although they constituted a majority of eighteen thousand free white citizens, were unable to obtain a convention, till the year 1835. They did not, however, feel themselves justified in resorting to the "revolutionary power"—although their system of representation was very unequal, and although the old constitution provided no mode for amending its provisions! They waited patiently till, in obedience to the demands of popular sentiment, the Legislature of North Carolina passed an act under which a convention of the delegates of the people assembled in convention, and amended the existing constitution in such particulars as were thought to need amendment. Thus peaceful and dignified was the triumph of the genuine people in the old north State, as, with affectionate respect, the Southrons are wont to designate quiet and patriotic North Carolina. How unlike to this successful endeavor to effect a great constitutional change, by constitutional means, are the movements of our Rhode Island revolutionists, marked, as those movements have alternately been, by fraud and by force—and destined, as they are, to end in irretrievable discomfiture and disgrace!

Fellow Citizens:—Every friend of liberty and law ought to be inflamed with a missionary zeal in support of the candidates nominated by the Rhode Island Party. The great principles for which we contend, the important interests involved in the controversy, and the evils which a failure to elect, by a triumphant majority, James Fenner and his associates in the Rhode Island Prox, would inevitably entail upon the State, ought to stir up every man, be he young or old, conspicuous or obscure, to sleepless vigilance and to strenuous exertion. Every man ought to feel it to be his duty to participate in the toils of the struggle. Every man ought to be animated with an honest pride to share the moral honors which await our triumph. It may stimulate our zeal in the good cause to glance at only a few of the mortifying and disastrous consequences which would be visited upon us, should we suffer ourselves to be defeated by antagonists who are thirsting for "the spoils," and whose desire for revenge not even the spoils could appease.

In the first place, fellow citizens, if you confide to the Dorrites the political power of the State, you must prepare yourselves to witness, not only the destruction of the truly liberal and conservative constitution which you have established, and which you are pledged to maintain,—but the establishment upon its ruins of a constitution which would not leave to you a vestige of temperate freedom. Do not deceive yourselves with the hope that the Dorrites would respect the cautious provisions, relative to the mode of amending it, which form a part of our constitution. Do you think that these men would suffer themselves to be fettered by any such provisions, when they come to carry into effect their "cherished principles"—when they come to fulfill their mission in giving full effect to the transcendent sovereignty of the people, as they understand it? They do not deny that they mean to go behind the chapter on amendments. Taking refuge in convenient generalities, they seek so to wrap up their meditated usurpation—their projected revolutionary aggression upon your rights—as, perchance, to divert you from a just contemplation of the dangers with which your peace is menaced. "When there is a mode of amendment prescribed in the constitution of a State, it ought to be followed." So thought and so said Thomas Wilson Dorr, when a member of the convention which framed the people's constitution, in 1841. This is the true doctrine. Conservative as this doctrine is, it suited his purpose then to advance it. To adhere to it, however, will not suit the purposes which his partisans, under his direction, are now seeking to accomplish. They do not even pretend that they shall adhere to it; but they intimate, in very significant terms, that they know, and that, in accordance with their "cherished principles," they will adopt "a more excellent way" of carrying out the will of the people! Let me tell you again, fellow citizens, and for the last time, that, if you commit the political power of the State to these Dorrites, they will, in less than one year, contrive to fasten upon you the people's constitution, "without law and against law!" Listen to the language of the

Express, uttered when the question of registering was first agitated by the Dorrites:—

"A prospect is open now to the friends of equal rights, to vanquish their opponents, and put them down forever; and, that being accomplished, the principles on which the People's Constitution is founded will be the rule of conduct for the party in power, and the Constitution itself may be revived from its state of suspended animation."

The very paper from which I have made this extract, expressly affirms that the Dorrites do not "mean to repudiate the People's Constitution!" Such, all along, has been, and such still is, the settled purpose of the revolutionary party. It becomes every friend to law and order, to put forth all his might, in order to place the State far beyond the reach of these unprincipled men who, under the mask of an extravagant love for the people, have done incalculable injury to the rights and to the interests of the people.

In the second place, the return of Thomas Wilson Dorr to his native State, from which his treasons have compelled him to become an exile, would be another inevitable consequence of the election of his friend and compatriot, Thomas F. Carpenter. Is it too much to say, that Mr. Dorr's return to Rhode Island would be deemed, by those of us who feel that we have had a sufficient taste of his quality, as a somewhat equivocal blessing! He has used his gifts and his acquirements so little to the advantage of his native State; he has wrought so much evil when he might have done so much good—that it ought to be deemed no unkindness, to desire that he may hereafter labor in some other part of the democratic vineyard, at least till exile has softened him into contrition, and allayed the fever of his distempered ambition. His return in triumph to his native State, would not be the whole of our calamity. In August, according to the terms of the compact, he would be supported as a candidate for Congress, and his friends, should they obtain the power, would so arrange the districts as to secure his election. Listen again to the language of the Express:—

"Let it be required as a condition, that he [Mr. Dorr] is to receive a nomination to an honorable office, from a convention of the friends of democracy and equal rights. That such a consideration will be had to his merits, we entertain no doubt, from having heard the expression of opinions of many democrats, and from the obvious circumstance that no other person in the State could obtain so large a number of votes. The friends of Governor Dorr, who will never consent to surrender him to the tender mercies of Algerine laws, enforced by Algerine courts, spurred on by an Algerine war council, may rest assured, that the interests of that distinguished champion of popular rights will not be compromised by a register of their names, but on the contrary, will give them the power to place him on an eminence beyond the reach of the missiles of Algerine malignity."

The import of this language cannot be misunderstood. If General Carpenter is elected, Mr. Dorr will quit New Hampshire for Rhode Island, confident that, under the system of unrestricted suffrage established by the "people's constitution," his election to Congress could not be prevented. Such a consummation of all our toils and sufferings, we ought most earnestly to deprecate, and most vigorously strive to avert.

In the third place, if General Carpenter is elected, and, at present, I shall suggest no other incentive to quicken your patriotic zeal, the upright and learned magistrates who now dignify the highest judicial tribunal of the State, will be thrust out of office, to make way for men in whose integrity the people could repose no confidence, and for whose learning it would be impossible to feel any respect. When it is recollected, what important rights and interests are liable to be affected by the decisions of the Supreme Court, the prospect of seeing upon the bench of that Court, men fresh from traitorous cabals, and moved by vindictive passions, is not, for one moment, to be tolerated. Such a calamity would, indeed, be deplorable—but, be it remembered, such a calamity, if General Carpenter is elected, would inevitably befall us!

Fellow Citizens:—In order to stimulate your zeal in this contest, I have set before you some of the worst consequences of failure. Do not think, however, that failure is by any one apprehended. On the contrary, the events of every day strengthen the confidence that a glorious triumph is in reserve for the cause of liberty regulated by law. I rejoice to say, the right spirit is abroad in the State. The people of Rhode Island are determined so to settle this Rhode Island question, and the mighty principles which it involves—that the people of other States who, with intense solicitude are now looking to the decision of this question as big with their own fate, shall have no cause to reproach them. They are resolved, on the first Wednesday of

April, to visit with an indignant rebuke that spirit of anarchy which has sorely vexed their own peace, and which, if not quelled, will extend far and wide its baleful influences, and doom to swift destruction every bulwark of popular freedom in this land. They are resolved to give to the whole country, a practical exemplification of DEMOCRACY without LICENTIOUSNESS, and of REFORM without REVOLUTION.

OLD NARRAGANSETT.

PROVIDENCE JOURNAL, MARCH 18, 1843.

THE CRISIS.

ITS DANGERS AND ITS DUTIES.—NO. XX.—AND LAST.

TO THE PEOPLE OF RHODE ISLAND:—

FELLOW CITIZENS:—In addressing you, for the last time, in relation to "THE CRISIS—ITS DANGERS AND ITS DUTIES," I cannot avoid repeating once more, my conviction of the paramount importance of the Rhode Island Question, not only to us, but to the whole country. Mistakes in determining what shall be the policy of the State governments and of the general government, may be extensively injurious to the public prosperity; but, under ordinary circumstances, they would not jeopard the public peace—they would not disturb the established securities of law—they would not threaten destruction to the whole social order. The question, however, which we are about to decide, reaches, in effect, far beyond any mere systems of legislative policy which may temporarily affect the general welfare. It takes hold of the very foundations of society. It puts in peril every constitution in this land. It renders insecure the rights of every individual who looks to laws and to constitutions for protection and for repose. Thus should we, and thus, I am well assured, do we regard the Rhode Island Question. Thus, too, is it regarded beyond the borders of our own little State. Throughout the length and breadth of this immense country, thoughtful minds are looking to the decision of this question, with that profound solicitude known only to those who discern, in the cloud no bigger than a man's hand, the sign of that tempest which is destined to blacken all the sky.

If you, fellow citizens, are prepared to sanction the revolutionary doctrines, broached by the Dorr democracy, and never retracted, not only will you cover Rhode Island with ruin and with dishonor, but you will give to the ball of revolution such a fearful momentum that none may be found able to stay its progress. What constitution in this country is free from anomalies? In what constitution, cannot the men who are always gasping for a grievance, discover some principle or some provision which, in their judgment, is so big with injustice, as to demand, in the last resort, the interposition of "the Revolution Power." Virginia, nay, the whole South, is full of elements, which need only the torch of revolutionary fanaticism, to light them up into baleful conflagration. And this is not all. Unless the doctrines of the Dorr democracy are visited with a withering rebuke, they may chance to disturb the peace even of the sympathizing sisters by whom we are surrounded. How long shall the independent judiciary of Massachusetts be tolerated? How long shall the inequality of representation in Connecticut remain unredressed? How long shall odious property qualifications, and offensive violation of the principle of religious freedom, find refuge among the granite hills of New Hampshire? How long will the sovereign people, acting in their primary capacity, allow the constitution of the Union to escape the searching operation of reform? How long will they permit little Rhode Island, with about one hundred and eight thousand people, to exercise in the Senate as much power as is exercised in the same body, by the Empire State, with nearly three millions of people?

That I may not seem to utter the language of unfounded or of exaggerated fear, let me direct your attention to the fact that a portion of the people of New Jersey already threaten to resort to the same experiment of revolution, upon which Mr. Dorr ventured his hopes of political advancement in Rhode Island. Not discouraged by the results, thus far, of Mr. Dorr's experiment, the Jersey men seem resolved to change their constitution, not through the forms of law, but by the "spontaneous exercise" of what they are pleased to term "the first and last of political rights!" This is a most significant fact, which should admonish this whole people of the dangers which threaten every constitution in the land, and which, if not seasonably averted, will prove fatal to the hopes of all temperate and durable freedom.

Fellow Citizens:—Within the last year, we have succeeded in establishing a truly liberal constitution—a constitution which ought to satisfy every suffrage man who does not want to strip the agricultural interest of every vestige of its ancient power. Till the introduction among us of the cotton manufacture and of kindred branches of domestic industry, the landed interest wielded, with undisputed sway, the political destinies of Rhode Island. The investment of large capitals in manufactures has, I regret to say, materially changed this state of things. A numerous foreign population has been attracted to our large towns; and villages, composed, to a considerable extent, of emigrants from other States and from foreign climes, have sprung up, almost like exhalations, in the counties of Providence and Kent. Taking advantage of this change in the social condition of Rhode Island, a few profligate politicians, seeking only their own promotion, got up, and attempted to carry through, a revolution, which, had you not arrested it, would have transferred from the farmers to the large towns and to the factory villages, the whole political power of the State.

Remember, fellow citizens, that this most mischievous project has not been abandoned. The issue made in the beginning, is the issue now! Will you maintain the legal constitution, which, in the organization of the Senate and in the restrictions upon the right of suffrage, leaves to the farmers a relic of their ancient power; or will you suffer the revolutionists to carry out their "cherished principles," by the full and triumphant establishment of the people's constitution? This is the practical question which you are to decide, by your votes, on the first Wednesday of April next. Suffer the Dorr democracy, which fled before you at the Arsenal and at Acote's hill, to prevail over you at the ballot box, and with what indecent haste will they accomplish every object for which they originally contended! With one of the nine learned lawyers as Governor, and another of that illustrious brotherhood as a "convenient Attorney General," what difficulty will they find in restoring to the people's constitution "its suspended animation?" Exemplifying their flexible notions of popular sovereignty, with what professional dexterity will they shelter their revolutionary aggression upon the legal constitution, under what they would proclaim, and affect to consider, as "an explicit and authentic act of the whole people?"

Fellow Citizens:—Are you willing to trust these men with the whole political power of Rhode Island? Are you willing to write with your own hands the epitaph of the constitution which you have just established? Are you willing to forfeit the precious fruits of all your toils, and dangers, and triumphs in this noble cause? I appeal to you as Rhode Island men—will you surrender the interests of the State to the control of men who follow the lead of Pearce and of Dorr? Will you trust the priceless honor of the State to men who court the alliance of Dillingham and Parmenter? Surely it can never be that a destiny so ignominious is in reserve for this gallant State. It can never be that the land of Greene, of Olney, of

Perry, and of other heroic spirits, is to be desecrated by the rule of men whom they would have disdained to set with the dogs of their flock?

Fellow Citizens:—I take my leave of you, oppressed by no solicitude in regard to the result of the approaching election. Not only can you elect Governor Fenner and his associates on the Rhode Island Prox, but you can elect them by a majority so commanding as to terminate forever the unhappy controversy which has so long agitated the State. Remember what momentous issues hang upon the decision of the Rhode Island question. Remember that the peace and the best interests of our beloved State demand that every good citizen should put forth all his might in the coming strife. Remember, last of all, that in the order of Providence, it hath become our solemn duty, to place a mark of signal reprobation upon those principles of insubordination and anarchy from which we have suffered so much; which are hostile to all constitutions and to all laws; and which, if carried out to their results, would banish from this whole land the exhilaration and the security of true CONSTITUTIONAL FREEDOM.

OLD NARRAGANSETT.

PROVIDENCE JOURNAL, JANUARY 27, 1843.

ADDRESS

ADOPTED AT A CONVENTION OF THE RHODE ISLAND PARTY.

To the Electors of Rhode Island:—

Agreeably to the provisions of the constitution adopted by the people of Rhode Island in November last, the choice of Governor, Lieutenant Governor, Senators, Representatives, Secretary of State, Attorney General, and General Treasurer, will be made on the first Wednesday of April next.

Various causes unite to impress upon the mind of every reflecting citizen a conviction of the vast importance of the approaching election to the future peace, prosperity, and honor of the State. In the exercise of their sovereign power, the people have ordained and established a written constitution of government. This constitution provides for a very large extension of the right of suffrage. It redresses the inequality of power existing in the present organization of the House of Representatives. It constitutes the Senate upon principles which will render that branch of the Legislature a salutary check upon the House, whenever, from any temporary inflammation of the popular mind, such salutary check may be required. In providing, moreover, that each town shall be entitled to elect a Senator, the new constitution, in effect, gives to the agricultural interest a preponderance in one branch of the Legislature, which will enable that interest, if need be, to protect itself against aggression; and to exert, in our public counsels, that conservative influence for which, in all past time, it has been distinguished.

These, fellow citizens, are important changes in our political system. Some of them, time and experience had indicated to be necessary. Others have been made, from an honest desire to reconcile conflicting interests; to meet the demands of public opinion; to restore to every section of the State, and to every class of people, that harmony and confidence which are essential to the good of the whole. To a considerable extent, this desirable result has been accomplished. It cannot, however, be disguised, that, in some sections of the State, the public mind continues to be agitated by doctrines and by schemes which we deem to be utterly subversive of all the principles of sober and durable freedom. These doctrines and these schemes, more than once during the past year, shook the State to its very centre; they exasperated almost to frenzy the passions of a portion of our fellow citizens; they well nigh plunged us into the complicated horrors of a CIVIL WAR. Be it your wisdom and your part, fellow citizens, to avert consequences so destructive to the welfare, and so injurious to the fame of Rhode Island. Be it your wisdom and your part, in the exercise of the elective franchise to place, upon all such doctrines and such schemes, the seal of your indignant reprobation!

Fellow Citizens:—We mean not to deal in vague generalities. We are not seeking to awaken groundless apprehensions. The conviction is forced upon our minds, that our freedom and our peace are still in danger. What are the facts in the case? Again and again, have various primary assemblies of the people, and formal conventions professing to utter the voice of the people, avowed their fixed purpose to be the overthrow of the legal constitution, and the establishment, "with the least possible delay," of a constitution voted for without the forms of law; a constitution adopted, too, as we have reason to believe, by a minority of the people, and under which no Rhode Island man, who is worthy of the name, could endure to live. Avowals, thus solemnly made and reiterated under every variety of circumstances which can give them credit and effect, present to the people of Rhode Island a distinct and a most momentous issue; an issue which can neither be changed nor evaded; an issue which is pregnant with weal or with woe for them and for their children. The adverse parties in this matter cannot meet upon the ground of compromise, because the principles for which each contends, admits no compromise. On the first Wednesday of April, the people must try this issue, just as it has been made up; and they must decide it; not as they would decide an ordinary question in party politics, but as they would settle a question which, in effect, reaches the very framework and foundations of society itself. The adversaries of the legal constitution must abide the consequences, however disastrous, which their own declarations will inevitably bring upon their cause.

They have declared, over and over again, that the

insurgent leader, to whose fortunes, in an evil hour, they allowed themselves to be fastened, "is the rightful Governor of the State of Rhode Island." They have declared, over and over again, that the legal constitution has no binding force whatever upon their consciences. They have declared, over and over again, their object to be the establishment, "in fact, as well as in name," of the people's constitution! Can language be plainer than this? With what grace can declarations like these be retracted, or glossed over, or explained away? When, fellow citizens, since the settlement of Rhode Island, have principles more revolutionary in their character been avowed? If permitted to escape a solemn rebuke from the people, what State can long hope to preserve either its peace or its freedom?

Fellow Citizens:—We have, very briefly, presented to you the true issue and the only issue which you are to try, on the first Wednesday of April next. It now remains for us to commend to your support such candidates for the important offices which it will then become your duty to fill, as, in our judgment, are best qualified to maintain the constitution and .the laws of Rhode Island.

Governor King, after a term of service in which he has won for himself lasting honor, has formally announced his wish—a wish known by his friends to have been long entertained—to retire to private life. At a crisis like the present, demanding not only wisdom but firmness—when a new system of government is about to be put into operation, and possibly to be defended against domestic violence, our attention was very naturally directed towards our distinguished and veteran fellow citizen, James Fenner, as the most suitable candidate for the office of Governor. Believing him to be the man for the crisis, we tendered to him a nomination for that high office. This nomination, we rejoice to add, he has, from a strong sense of public duty, been induced to accept. James Fenner has, for more than forty years, occupied a well defined position before the people of Rhode Island. His political principles and his party attachments have been too consistent and too decided to require explanation at our hands. Surrendering none of those principles and attachments to which through every stage of a long political life he has clung, he now comes forward, as the candidate of a party which, animated solely by the Rhode Island spirit, seeks, as an object of paramount concern, to rescue Rhode Island institutions from the disasters of revolution and of anarchy. Reposing the fullest confidence in his political sagacity; in his firm and intrepid spirit; and in his attachment to the best interests of his native State, we anticipate for him an enthusiastic support, and a commanding majority.

Byron Diman, the candidate whom we have nominated for the office of Lieutenant Governor, is well known to you. In past times, you have honored him with important public trusts, and, on all occasions, his intelligence and his erect and manly spirit have been conspicuous.

Joseph M. Blake, whom we propose to you as a candidate for the office of Attorney General, is likewise not unknown to you, he having been, at different times, a distinguished member of the General Assembly. His talents as a lawyer, and his qualities as a man, indicate his fitness for the high and responsible office for which he has been nominated.

Henry Bowen, the candidate for the office of Secretary of State, and Stephen Cahoone, the candidate for the office of General Treasurer, again stand before you, with unforfeited claims upon your confidence and support.

Fellow Citizens:—Before closing this address, suffer us to advert, very briefly, to certain topics, which the events and the discussions of the past year have clothed with more than ordinary importance. It is the fashion of the day to speak lightly of the forms of law, as if they served only to fetter, with cumbrous technicalities, the free exercise of the popular will. Under this plausible disguise there lurks a most dangerous fallacy. Take away the forms of law, and you take away that which protects the very essence which guards the vital principle of popular freedom. Take away the forms of law from the administration of criminal and civil jurisprudence, and what man could feel his rights to be safe? Take away the forms of law in legislative and in executive proceedings, and where would individuals or minorities find protection against injustice and oppression? Take away the forms of law, when constitutions of government are made, and how can the public will be embodied, and where can be found adequate evidence of the fact that constitutions of government are, in fact, what they claim to be, the highest and most solemn expression of the will of the people? The right of revolution is independent of all laws and it tramples upon all laws. To this great remedial right, belonging alike to minorities and majorities, resort should be had, only when oppression becomes insupportable, and when all the ordinary pacific means of obtaining redress have been tried, and been tried in vain.

Fellow Citizens:—It is, likewise, the fashion of the day to broach doctrines relative to democracy and to equal rights, which, however captivating they may appear, are, in our judgment, alike visionary and dangerous—alien to the true spirit of democracy, and hostile to every sound theory of equal rights. Attached as we are to the fundamental principles of a republican government, we feel deep solicitude to preserve them from aristocratic tendencies, on the one side, and from a fatal impulse towards licentiousness and anarchy, on the other. We are opposed to all partial legislation, designed either to exalt or to depress individuals, corporations, particular classes, or political parties. We believe that our law, regulating the descent of intestate estates, is the true Agrarian law. While it prevents the accumulation of wealth in masses which might be dangerous to the rights of individuals, and, perchance, disturb the regular action of the government, it leaves to enterprise and to industry their appropriate and most operative incentive—the liberty to enjoy unmolested the fruits of industry and of enterprise. This, so far as property may be concerned, is the true doctrine of equality. Any other doctrine, if carried out in practice, would violate the rights of property; impair the freedom of individual effort; lessen the comforts of the poor; and retard the progress of general improvement.

Fellow Citizens:—In this State, and, indeed, throughout our country, the democratic principle is firmly established; and its ultimate ascendency in all civilized governments is hardly to be doubted. With us, then, the great problem is, how shall we secure it from perversion; how shall we rescue it from the influence of impracticable and ferocious theories; how shall we render it a more efficient instrument in imparting to this generation and to generations yet unborn, the blessings of a well ordered freedom, and the fruits of a progressive civilization. The democratic principle, as we understand it, can be maintained only by an alliance with virtue, intelligence, and law. It is hostile to none of the superiorities which God has established; it is at variance with none of the principles of his moral government; it seeks to supplant none of the impulses with which he has endowed us. It acknowledges, as a first principle, the equality of all men before the laws, it leaves every man to employ for his own advantage, and for the advantage of his children, his time, his talents, and his skill. When carried out into its just applications, it shields from violation the most insignificant right of the humblest man in the community; it places within his power the means of bettering his condition, of improving his character, of elevating himself and his children in the scale of moral and intellectual happiness. With an equally jealous care, it guards the fruits of honest industry from the rapacity of those whom indolence and vice may have doomed to poverty and to discontent. it abhors all tyranny,—the tyranny of the majority, no less than the tyranny of the king. Finally, it recognizes the necessity of checks and balances in the organization of every political system which is intended to give full effect to the will of the people, and to protect from violation the rights of the people.

Fellow citizens:—As the friends of the new constitution, we have presented for your suffrages a Prox of general officers, composed of men who will maintain and defend that constitution as "sacredly obligatory upon all, till changed by an explicit and authentic act of the whole people." We have likewise presented to you the issue which, at the approaching election, you are to try and to decide. We look to the result, with a cheering confidence that you will render a verdict in favor of liberty and law. Surely, it can never be that, here in Rhode Island, licentiousness is destined to achieve a disastrous ascendency! It can never be, that democracy is to be wounded and dishonored in the house of its friends! It can never be, that, from the land of Roger Williams, a spirit is destined to go forth which, if left unchecked, would subvert all popular rights; lay waste the monuments of social refinement; turn back the tide of modern civilization; and quench in blood the guiding star of freedom to the nations.

PROVIDENCE JOURNAL, APRIL 1, 1843.

ADDRESS TO THE ELECTORS OF PROVIDENCE,

ADOPTED AT A CITY CONVENTION OF THE RHODE ISLAND PARTY.

FELLOW CITIZENS:—On Wednesday next, you will be required to exercise the elective franchise, according to the provisions of that new constitution of government which the people of Rhode Island, in their sovereign capacity, have ordained and established. This constitution, it will be recollected, provides that the Senate shall consist of the Governor, Lieutenant Governor, and of one Senator from each town in the State. It likewise provides that the House of Representatives shall be constituted on the basis of population—always allowing one Representative for a fraction exceeding half the ratio; that each town shall always be entitled to at least one member; and that no town shall have more than one sixth of the whole number of members to which the House is limited. The Senate and House, it will be seen, are constituted upon principles somewhat dissimilar; and to this very dissimilarity do they owe all the practical value of their organization. In the formation of the legislative department, the constitution wisely establishes such a balance of power between different sections and different interests of the State, as may furnish each section and each interest with efficient means of protecting itself against oppression.

Constituted as the House is, we have no reason to fear that a factious and interested majority, should such ever be found in the Senate, will be able to resist the legitimate and healthful action of public opinion. The city of Providence consented, cheerfully, to the organization of the Senate upon a principle, which, in respect to political power, places her, in that branch of the Legislature, upon an exact equality with all other towns in the State. Thus did she give incontestible evidence that her highest ambition is to obtain for herself and for the State the blessings of a stable and well ordered government. Her people, little covetous of political honors, have never sought, and they seek not now, to exert any undue influence in the government of the State. Orderly, industrious, enterprising, and frugal, they have, during the past year, suffered serious injuries in their regular business, and have been agitated by well founded alarms for the security of their property, and for the comfort and peace of their firesides.

The recurrence of calamities, fellow citizens, so injurious to all our interests—and so hostile to all our social and domestic enjoyments, can, in our judgment, be averted only by confiding the political power of the State to the sincere friends of the Constitution—to the men who made it, and not to the men who stand pledged to overthrow it; to the men who will not suffer it to be changed, except in the mode which itself provides—and not to the men who would dignify an act of revolutionary violence as "an explicit and authentic act of the whole people."

Elected from the several wards of this city to compose a convention for the purpose of recommending to your suffrages a candidate for the office of Senator, and candidates for the House of Representatives, we have endeavored, faithfully, to discharge the responsible trust confided to our discretion. In presenting to you Albert C. Greene, the present Attorney General of Rhode Island, as a candidate for the Senate, we have responded, with entire unanimity ourselves, to what we are confident is the unanimous and most cordial wish of the Rhode Island party in the city of Providence. On his eminent qualifications for this high and honorable office, it is quite unnecessary to enlarge. It remains only that we exhort you to give to the man of your choice a support corresponding to your sense of his merits.

In selecting candidates for the House of Representatives, under circumstances somewhat novel, the number to which the city is entitled, having been increased from four to twelve, we experienced no difficulty which did not readily yield to the spirit of harmony and conciliation which marked all our deliberations and all our votes. Disregarding all former or existing party lines, we sought only to find twelve good men and true, who would faithfully and impartially represent the various interests of our city in the General Assembly, and who would maintain, with zeal, and energy, and effective talent, the great principles of regulated freedom which the Rhode Island party was formed to uphold. Most of these candidates, fellow citizens, are well known to you—they having discharged, to your entire satisfaction, various important public trusts. For those of them who are less extensively known, we bespeak that confidence, in advance, which is due to their substantial worth, and to their active exertions in the cause of "Law and Order."

Fellow Citizens:—The crisis is full of solemn interest. The constitution which we have established is in danger—the peace of this city is in danger—the peace of the whole State is in danger. The advocates of the people's constitution have lost none of their zeal in its favor. They have retracted none of the violent resolutions in which they pledged themselves to overthrow the legal constitution, and, "with the least delay," to establish their own upon its ruins. They are the same men still, moved by the same spirit—following the same leaders—bent upon the same end. Most disastrous to this city would be the triumph of this revolutionary party. Not a year of their rule would elapse, before every man among us, twenty one years old and over, would be admitted to the right of suffrage. Need you be told what would be the inevitable consequences of thus prostrating all qualifications for the exercise of this important political right? The city of Providence would pass, and, it may be, would pass forever, from under the dominion of the conservative classes—the merchants, traders, mechanics, and industrious working men—into the hands of a class of voters, composed to a considerable extent of persons having no common interest with us—and who, lazy and profligate themselves, would follow the lead of demagogues not less lazy and profligate. These, fellow citizens, are not imaginary alarms. The fearful evils which we have predicted, will inevitably come upon us, if we suffer the partisans of Thomas W. Dorr and of Thomas F. Carpenter, to achieve a victory at the ballot box on Wednesday next. Remember, how much depends upon Providence, and how much is rightfully expected from Providence, by those gallant men who, a few months since, rushed hither from every part of the State, to defend our firesides, and to maintain the sovereignty of the laws. The right spirit animates the ranks of the Rhode Island Party—and if every man among us, laying aside, for a few days, the common cares and occupations of common life, devote all his energies to the great cause in which we are engaged, we may confidently anticipate for that cause a glorious and a final triumph.

PROVIDENCE JOURNAL, MARCH 28, 1843.

LETTER TO THOMAS F. CARPENTER, ESQ.

SIR:—Your position as a candidate and as a man is most unenviable. You complain that the "partisan misrepresentations" of your "opponents" have subjected you to unmerited reproach. Let me tell you,

Sir, that your opponents have dealt very gently with you, and that you have cause to thank them for their forbearance. If, in any case, they have misrepresented you, they are not in fault. You have been at pains to perplex the public judgment in regard to your real opinions and to the course which, if elected Governor, you would pursue. It therefore ill becomes you, Sir, to charge your opponents with misrepresenting you, when you have placed it out of the power either of friend or foe to understand you. Most of the people of Rhode Island are plain, practical men, strangers to the mysteries of special pleading, to the logic of the schools, and to the ingenuities of party politicians. However unskilled they may be to thread their way through the mazes of political chicane, they are quick to discover when those who ask their confidence, are not pursuing an honest purpose by honest means. They have observed somewhat attentively your course, during the whole progress of the revolutionary movement in Rhode Island; and who can wonder that they are left without a particle of confidence in any profession which you may now make to that people whom, all along, you have sought to deceive. I do not mean to trace your course from the beginning of the revolution to the present crisis. I have no relish for ambiguities, either in language or in morals—I see no beauty in crooked lines—I like the palpable and not the obscure—I love the broad and intelligible principles of everlasting justice, and not the narrow, technical and deceptive expedients of political cunning. Allow me, then, Sir, very briefly, to direct your attention and the attention of the people of Rhode Island, to a few only of the "fixed facts" which illustrate, so disastrously for your fame, your political course during the past year.

In the first place, where were you, when Dorr and his aiders and abettors were seeking to inflame the popular mind by all sorts of appeals to the popular passions? Were you then endeavoring to allay the agitations to which profligate men had, by means the most profligate, imparted the fearful violence of a social revolution? Did you come forward to throw oil upon the troubled waters? Did you rebuke, with your voice or with your pen, the madness of the people? Did you place yourself in stern and palpable opposition to the frantic schemes of Dorr and his confederates in mischief? Far from all this is the "fixed fact!" You aided and abetted in all the preliminary iniquities of the revolutionary drama. You shunned not the alliance of Dorr, and of Pearce, and of Atwell. Nay, as one of the illustrious nine, you lent to them the influence of your name as a constitutional lawyer, in putting forth that ever memorable document which was intended to deceive the weaker brethren into the belief that their meditated reform was not revolution! For this act alone, knowing, as you must have known, the effect it was meant to produce, you deserve to forfeit, and to forfeit forever, the confidence of the people of Rhode Island. It might have been in your power to still the tempest; but you chose to invoke it. It might have been in your power to compose, by appropriate sedatives, the popular passions; but you chose to throw into the burning cauldron the elements of a fiercer conflagration!

In the second place, it is likewise an unquestioned fact that you voted for Thomas Wilson Dorr, as Governor under the people's constitution! The moral effect of conduct like this, is too obvious to need illustration. If you did not mean to sport with the elective franchise; if you voted for him in good faith; if you desired to elect him as your Governor under that constitution, you assisted, by this act, in giving another impulse to the ball of revolution. How far the public judgment may be modified in your favor by the fact that you yourself was soon afterwards a candidate for the office of Governor under the charter, I leave the public judgment to decide. Perhaps in voting for candidate Dorr, you sought to obtain some remote and contingent benefit for candidate Carpenter.

In the third place, you were a member of the December Dorrite Convention—which not only solemnly proclaimed its purpose to be "the establishment, with the least delay, of the people's constitution in fact as well as in right," but which denounced the legal constitution as "formed in contravention of the sovereign power of the people," and "intended to be imposed upon a majority of the people without their consent!" You, Sir, it would seem, voted for those resolutions. At any rate, you did not object to their passage. They still stand upon the record as your well considered opinions, when you thought sincerity could do you no harm. If such were, in December, your opinions of the people's constitution and of the legal constitution, what, let me ask, has since occurred to change them? What new facts have been revealed; what new constitutional principles have been discovered,—what deep fountain of patriotism has been unsealed,—that, all at once, you are convinced that the action of that convention was revolutionary? No subsequent convention has ever gone behind these resolutions. You may have been forced, by exigent circumstances, to declare that you do not now believe what you then so solemnly affirmed to be true. If, General, you are so expert in changing your front, do not wonder if the people choose for their commander in chief a man who never needs to change his front—a man, who, when the citadel is in danger, thinks only how he may best defend it.

Passing over your famous letter to General McNeill, which your partisans are ashamed to publish, and which you ought to blush for having written, I come, in the fourth and last place, to your letter to your Richmond friends. This letter has been subjected, by a writer in the Journal, to so searching an analysis, that I am relieved from the necessity of making it the topic of any very extended remarks. As furnishing another development, sir, of your real character, and as an indication of the ulterior designs of your party, this last and expurgated edition of Dorrism ought to be carefully considered. What, Sir, are honest and honorable men, at home and abroad, to think of the intelligence or integrity of a candidate for the office of Governor who, in December, maintains upon a grave matter, one set of political principles, and, in March, without indicating any reasons for change, avows a set of political principles not only opposite but directly contradictory? If, Sir, you are liable to meet with such changes, in the course of only a few weeks, what assurances can you give us, that, should you be elected Governor, you would not in the course of a few weeks change again?

For one, Sir, I want a man for Governor, who takes

his position upon some fixed principles, and who will not suffer the fear of losing votes or the desire to win them, to interfere with the exercise of his judgment, or the decisions of his conscience. You were for Dorr and for Dorr's constitution in December. Where are you now? According to the terms of your Richmond letter, you are now for maintaining that constitution which, then, you declared was "formed in contravention of the sovereign will of the people, and intended to be imposed upon them without their consent!" Let me tell you, Sir, these experiments upon the credulity of the people of Rhode Island will fail of their intended effect. They are not so easily gulled, as you seem to think; they will not hesitate to withhold their confidence from any man who seeks to palter with them, in a double sense. What, let me ask you, Sir, do you mean by an explicit and authentic act of the whole people? Would the adoption of the people's constitution, in lieu of the legal constitution, by a convention of the delegates of the people, assembled at the request of the General Assembly, be in your judgment an explicit and authentic act of the whole people? Would the adoption of the people's constitution by a simple majority of the whole people, voting in town meetings legally assembled, be considered by you as an explicit and authentic act of the whole people? In fine, would you recognize as an explicit and authentic act of the whole people, any mode of altering the legal constitution other than that which is provided in the chapter on amendments? This is the whole question. It lies in a nut shell. Why seek to wrap it up in mystery? If you are of opinion that the constitution can be changed in no other mode, except in that pointed out by itself, why do you not say so at once in language which no plain man can misinterpret? If, on the other hand, you believe that this constitution can be changed, without regard to the chapter on amendments, you are guilty of a base subterfuge; you are assisting in a nefarious scheme to deceive the people of this State; you are doing that which ought to cover you not only with defeat, but with dishonor.

A FRIEND TO THE LEGAL CONSTITUTION.

PROVIDENCE JOURNAL, MARCH 30, 1843.

TO B. B. THURSTON, DEXTER RANDALL, AND SAMUEL Y. ATWELL, ESQUIRES.

GENTLEMEN:—I have read your pathetic appeal to the Electors of Rhode Island, put forth under a paroxysm of nervous fear, on the 27th of March, 1843. Why, verily, gentlemen, the Algerine handbill, headed "Dorr Returned," seems to have frightened you from your propriety! Like the handwriting upon the wall, which "troubled the thoughts" of Belshazzar at his impious feast, and "astonished his lords," this anonymous missive fills you with consternation, as if it foreshadowed your doom. This, your appeal to the Electors, is surcharged with strong assertion. It fairly foams with sensibility, as if you really had some right to feel indignant. After all your flourish, gentlemen, you leave untouched and uncontradicted some of the most important allegations made in this famous handbill. You bluster and you whimper by turns; but you do not, after all, meet fairly and fearlessly the whole case. As to "the private and moral character of Thomas F. Carpenter," I have nothing to say; and I should be among the last men in Rhode Island to refuse him any distinction which he has "justly earned for himself," or to impair, in any degree, the "confidence his fellow citizens place in his integrity as a gentleman, patriot and christian." Upon none of these high relationships shall I venture to intrude. I have to deal with him only as candidate Carpenter—and as such I shall not hesitate to bring him to a decisive test.

The handbill, which you denounce as so "foul, slanderous and libellous," asserts as a fact, that General Carpenter upon the 29th of November last, in a self styled democratic convention, drew up in his own hand, and advocated sundry resolutions, which fully affirmed the legality ot the people's constitution, and no less fully affirmed that the constitution now about to be put in operation, was framed in "contravention of the sovereign power of the people, and is intended to be imposed upon them without their consent." Here, Messrs. Thurston, Atwell and Randall, is a distinct and grave charge—concerning which in your appeal to the Electors of Rhode Island you say—

Nothing! Do not, gentlemen, stand mute in a matter of so much moment to your candidate and to the State. Did General Carpenter draught those resolutions, and support them, as is charged by the handbill, or did he not? This is the question, and let me tell you that, in lieu of an answer to this question, the people will not accept your eloquent testimonies in favor of "the moral worth" and "spotless life of Thomas F. Carpenter."

This "foul, slanderous, and libellous" handbill further charges that, a few months since, General Carpenter denounced the misguided men of whom he is now the acknowledged leader, as "rascally insurgents." Do you deny this charge, gentlemen, in your appeal to the Electors? Dare you deny it any where, under the responsibility of your names? If I mistake not, this charge can be substantiated by testimony hardly less conclusive than that upon which General Carpenter is believed to have stigmatized, as "malicious and cowardly Algerines," those brave men, who, without your aid, were endeavoring to put down, what, in gentle phrase, you call "an alleged conspiracy against the repose and quiet of the State!!"

You deny, somewhat indignantly, the charge made in the handbill that General Carpenter invited Dorr to Rhode Island—and you declare that you had "no knowledge of *Mister* Dorr's intention of visiting the State—that you neither invited his return, nor have you had any communication with or from him, either before or since his residence at Pawtucket—that you are wholly ignorant of the inducements and purposes which brought Mr. Dorr here—that you have no control over his movements," &c. I desire, gentlemen, to give you the full benefit of your disclaimers and your denials—and have therefore quoted the very language of your appeal. You make, gentlemen, pretty heavy draughts upon our faith—but that seems with you to be the fashion of the day. But what, after all, is the amount of these formidable denials and disclaimers? It may be, that General Carpenter never formally invited the return of the man whom he voted for as Governor, and whom, in a resolution, he declared to be "the rightful Governor." It may be that you, Mr. Thurston, and you, Mr. Randall, and you, Mr. Atwell, may have had no direct communication with him, and that you have no control over his movements. You cannot, however, deny that this bad man with whom you have chosen to ally yourselves, is again hanging upon our borders. You cannot deny that his supporters are your supporters—his presses your presses—his orators your orators—his principles your principles—and, let me tell you, you can never persuade the people of Rhode Island, with the records of your conventions staring them in the face, that your cause is not his cause. What need of a formal invitation from General Carpenter to him whom it now suits your purpose to call *Mister* Dorr! This would have been a coarse expedient—rendered quite unnecessary by those ties of subtle and mysterious sympathy which unite the brotherhood whose cherished principles you stand pledged to carry out? You cannot, gentlemen, sever yourselves from Thomas W. Dorr. Without his aid, you would never have taken the field. Let him withdraw from you his support, and you would struggle without even a hope of success to sustain you. With all your professed ignorance of his movements, you know that Thomas Wilson Dorr came to Rhode

Island to infuse new life into the party to which alone you look for success. He came hither, gentlemen, to help General Carpenter and yourselves. His fortunes, disguise it as you may, are your fortunes—his fate will be your fate.

You deal, gentlemen, quite too much in generalities. You do not, and you dare not, meet the grave and specific charges of the handbill. This wholesale method of getting rid of these charges which you have adopted will not avail. It will not do for you any longer to attempt to throw dust in the eyes of the people. Have you abandoned any of the revolutionary doctrines which you broached a few months since? Are you not in full and sympathetic communion with the bosom friends of Dorr? Are not his allies your allies? If you triumph, will not he triumph? These are plain, practical questions, and you need not seek to dodge them, by talking about your disavowal of "all actual or constructive violence."

A few words more, gentlemen, and I have done with you for the present. You appeal to "the good and humane of all classes to come forward and rebuke the calumniators of General Carpenter?" Why, gentlemen, with what grace can you make such an appeal—you who read and sustain the Herald and the Express—you who employ convicted felons to blacken, for your benefit, the good and humane of all classes? Nay, more, with marvellous effrontery, you appeal to James Fenner, and ask him "if he can justify" what you are pleased to consider as libels upon Carpenter! Have you, gentlemen, taken leave of all modesty, that you thus appeal to a man whom your conventions, and presses and orators, have denounced as a "renegade democrat"—as a man who has bartered his principles for the hope of office—a man upon whom your whole pack has been unkennelled—a man, even whose person your libellers of the baser sort have been employed to caricature! Dismiss your itinerant slanderers—reform the manners of your press—and reject, with scorn, all alliance with traitors and with felons—and, then you will not sin against all sense of propriety in appealing to "the wise and good," and in lamenting "the degenerate state of society." How have the wise and good fared at the hands of your friends, during the year that has passed? And if society has become degenerate, ask yourselves, in sober mood, what you have done and what you are doing, to elevate its character!

A Rhode Island Man.

PROVIDENCE JOURNAL, JANUARY 18, 1844.

RESOLUTIONS

PASSED AT A LAW AND ORDER CONVENTION.

Whereas the principles of law and order, which the Rhode Island party was formed to establish, and which it stands pledged to maintain, involve, in the judgment of this Convention, matters of paramount concern to the peace, prosperity, freedom and honor of the people of this State: Therefore,

Resolved, That the principles by which the men of the Rhode Island party have hitherto been governed, and the mighty interests which they have, thus far, successfully struggled to defend against revolutionary doctrines and revolutionary violence, commend themselves anew to our regard—as principles, which ought never to be abandoned or put at hazard—as interests which no subordinate ends, should for one moment suffer us to overlook.

Resolved, That the extraordinary prosperity enjoyed by the people of this State during the past year, is, under the providence of God, mainly owing to the establishment of a liberal constitution, adopted by the people in their sovereign capacity, and administered with exemplary discretion and firmnness, by magistrates who feel that life, liberty, and prosperity are insecure, when they are left without the protection of the law.

Resolved, That, in no single year since the adoption of the National Constitution by Rhode Island, has the legislation of this State evinced a spirit of more comprehensive wisdom, or wrought out for the good of the whole people more important and salutary changes in various departments of the public administration.

Resolved, That a state of things under which so much has already been accomplished for the benefit of Rhode Island institutions, and for the welfare of the Rhode Island people, and which is full of promise for the future, ought, by every practicable means, to be maintained undisturbed.

Resolved, That, in all elections to office, whether by the people or by the General Assembly, no narrow and exclusive test ought to be applied to candidates, but that the men of the Rhode Island party should exact no other title to their confidence than unsuspected fealty to the great principles upon which that party was formed.

Resolved, That the Rhode Island party owes much of its moral power to its generous disregard of all past political differences of opinion among its members, in reference either to measures or to men, and to the unfaltering ardor with which it has clung to the grand principles of social order and constitutional freedom.

Resolved, That, on an inflexible adherence to these grand principles, we place our trust for the future, assured no less by our conviction of their inherent power than by our experience of the past, that they will carry the people of Rhode Island triumphantly through every trial of adverse fortune which they may be called to bear.

Resolved, That, in the opinion of this Convention, the work of agitation is not yet over in Rhode Island; that the language and acts of the opponents of the existing constitution, both in their primary meetings and in their more formal assemblies, force upon our minds the conviction that, whenever the opportunity may present itself, they are determined to overthrow that constitution, in a revolutionary spirit, and by a revolutionary process, and to establish upon its ruins a system of government which, under the delusive pretence of securing equal rights to all, would leave all without adequate protection for any right.

Resolved, That while our opponents continue gravely to affirm that the existing Constitution "was thrust upon the people of this State in violation of their wishes, strongly expressed, by fraud and force," we are admonished of the necessity of vigilance and union, and energy, in order that we may maintain, against every attempt to overthrow it, the Constitution which we have established.

Resolved, That our opponents, who profess to be advocates of State rights, have, in a question purely domestic, invoked the interposition of the National Democratic Convention, a tribunal unknown to the constitution and laws of the land; that all such appeals are of most dangerous tendency, not only to the rights of the States, but to every bulwark of constitutional freedom which the fathers of this republic, in their wisdom, have provided.

Resolved, That, while we commit our cause to that superintending Providence which has thus far shielded it from harm, we will keep ourselves prepared to defend it with true hearts and vigorous arms against all assaults, whenever and by whomsoever they may be made.

PROVIDENCE JOURNAL, FEBRUARY 19, 1844.

RESOLUTIONS

PASSED AT A LAW AND ORDER MEETING.

WHEREAS, in the opinion of this meeting, the great interests of the State of Rhode Island demand the election of Henry Clay to the Presidentship of these United States; and likewise demand the election of James Fenner, and his associates in the Rhode Island Prox, to the high and responsible trusts, which, during the past year, they have, with such exemplary fidelity, discharged.

1. Therefore, resolved, That, recognizing in Henry Clay, the able and fearless champion of measures and of principles, which are vital to the peace, prosperity, and honor of Rhode Island, we cannot hesitate, as Rhode Island men, to extend to him, in the approaching political contest, a cordial, earnest, and efficient support.

2. Resolved, That Henry Clay commends himself to the confidence and support of the people of Rhode Island, as the advocate of a just and equal distribution of the proceeds of the sales of the public lands, and as a Statesman, who, on all occasions, has put forth the

resources of his extraordinary mind in the establishment of a system of public policy, which protects American industry against the injurious effects of foreign competition.

3. Resolved, That, while Mr. Clay has exerted all his powers of eloquence and of logic in defence of these great measures of public policy,—measures which have not hitherto divided the opinions of parties in Rhode Island,—he stands before us, and before the country, with another, and a still higher title to gratitude and support, as the intrepid defender, in an hour of peril, of those mighty principles of Law and Order which lie at the foundation of all our political institutions, and which, in their ultimate issues, must affect the cause of popular right, and constitutional freedom, in every civilized land.

4. Resolved, That, although the spirit of revolutionary violence has been signally rebuked within the borders of this State, yet the Rhode Island question cannot be considered as settled, while an organized party aver, in the most solemn manner, that the existing constitution was "thrust upon the people of this State by fraud and force;" while they declare, that, in registering their names, and acting under the existing constitution, they have "not intended to withdraw the objections which have been stated, against its origin, character, and provisions; and that they look forward, with just confidence, to the ultimate prevalence of their principles, and to the adoption of them, as the constitutional law of the State; while, above all, the same organized party are about to invoke, in behalf of their revolutionary projects, the sympathy, if not the active co-operation of the Baltimore Van Buren

Convention,—a body unknown to our laws, and whose interference in our domestic concerns, ought to be repelled as an insult upon the people of Rhode Island, and as a most dangerous infraction of the rights of the States.

5. Resolved, That, in the opinion of this meeting, the Rhode Island question has lost none of its importance: that, touching, as it does, the foundations of all our constitutions, it must be regarded, not as a subordinate question, but as a question which deeply and vitally affects both this State and the Union.

6. Resolved, That, under the circumstances in which Rhode Island is placed, we respond, most cordially, to the recent declaration, formally put forth by the law and order members of the Legislature, that "this is no time to weaken the bonds of the glorious union of the Law and Order party of Rhode Island, but that this union should be strengthened by wise, firm, and temperate counsels, and by that patriotism, which shall sacrifice all personal considerations to the safety, honor, and happiness of the State."

7. Resolved, That we entertain undiminished confidence in the integrity, talents, and genuine Rhode Island spirit of the gentlemen nominated by the law and order convention to compose the Rhode Island Prox; that we respond, with one heart and one mind, to a nomination, which commends to our suffrages men who were determined to maintain the constitution and the laws of this State, against all revolutionary attempts to overthrow them; and that we now pledge our united and strenuous endeavors to obtain, on the first Wednesday in April next, for these tried and

trusty agents of the people, a commanding majority of the votes of the people.

8. Resolved, That, as the friends of Henry Clay in this city, we will, one and all, be diligent and earnest and decided in supporting that true champion of regulated liberty, and of a protective tariff, that we will seek, by calm appeals to the reason and good sense of the people, to enlighten the public mind, in relation to all the important questions at issue between the two great antagonist parties of the country: that it shall be our main object to obtain, at the electoral election in November next, an immense majority of the people of Rhode Island in favor of a statesman, who, if elected to the Chief Magistracy of these United States, would illustrate his administration, by a course of policy, wise, comprehensive, and just; true to the constitution and the laws, most beneficent, in its operation, in the business of the country, and most auspicious to the cause of popular freedom throughout the world.

PROVIDENCE DAILY TRANSCRIPT, MARCH 16, 1844.

PRESERVE THE LAW AND ORDER PARTY.

NO. I.

WHAT is the best mode of advancing the cause of Henry Clay, and of maintaining the existing political institutions of Rhode Island? This is a most important question which ought, therefore, to be very thoughtfully considered, and to be decided by every man among us, under a sense of solemn responsibility to the State and the Union.

It would seem to be very plain that, if we would maintain the Constitution which we have established, and which is still threatened with distraction, we must preserve unbroken the union and organization of the Law and Order party. That party has been tried, and it has been found adequate to any crisis, through which we have hitherto been called to pass. That party has won glorious triumphs in the cause of liberty and law. Should new troubles come upon us, and for new troubles we ought to be prepared, on what party can we so safely rely as upon the Law and Order party—composed of the best men, united for the noblest purposes—moved by the most disinterested and patriotic spirit. What is to be gained by destroying this party, or by weakening the bonds of union which now unite its members? It may be unmanageably large for the politicians. Surely it is not too large for the good of the people. Can we substitute for the existing organization of the Law and Order party, any political organization on which, in a crisis of danger, we could more securely rely? Should those who are anxious that our Constitution should not be overthrown, prefer an alliance with Dorrite Whigs who have rebelled against the government, to an alliance with Law and Order Democrats, who have stood up manfully in defence of the government?

Equally plain does it seem that the best mode of advancing the cause of Henry Clay, especially in Rhode Island, is to preserve the Law and Order party. The members of that party can vote for no other candidate for the Presidency than for the great champion of their own principles. One and all, they avow their repugnance to Mr. Van Buren, and he is and will be the only antagonist of Mr. Clay.

As to the next election of Senator, there will be and there can be no difficulty. It being well understood that Governor Francis will not consent to be a candidate for re-election, it is conceded and desired, on all hands, that whoever may succeed him in the post which he occupies, with so much credit to himself, and with so much advantage to the State, shall be a decided friend to Mr. Clay, and to all his measures. There is, therefore, no need of breaking up the Law and Order party, in order to secure the election of a Clay Senator.

Some of the friends of Law and Order are reproached,

as if they had forced the Rhode Island Question upon the people of the Union, as a new issue, which, because it is not well understood, might prove injurious to Mr. Clay. This reproach is most unjust. This issue was made by the enemies of Mr. Clay, in the desperate hope of injuring his popularity. His Rhode Island friends have not sought to introduce it. They are, however, not afraid of it, either for themselves, or for him. They are ready to meet it manfully, here and everywhere. Some of the warmest of those friends, regard the Rhode Island Question, not as a local or a subordinate Question, but as a question which deeply affects every State in the Union, and which transcends in importance every other question which can be presented to the consideration of the American people. Politicians in other States may seek to dodge this question, but the men of Rhode Island do not want to dodge it. The people of Rhode Island, moreover, do not care that politicians, whether at home or abroad shall dictate to them, on what principles they shall stand, when all that is dear to freemen is at stake.

I do not believe that Mr. Van Buren can be elected. Common prudence, however, demands that the people of Rhode Island should act as if such a calamity were possible. Suppose he should be elected. In what condition should we be to resist the Dorrites, if the organization of the law and order party were broken up? Would the Dorrite Whigs help us in such a crisis? Or could we look for aid to the law and order democrats,—after we had driven them from our ranks—under circumstances which would forever preclude them from joining those ranks again?

A Law and Order Man.

PROVIDENCE DAILY TRANSCRIPT, MARCH 18, 1844.

PRESERVE THE LAW AND ORDER PARTY.

NO. II.

It will be time enough to break up the Law and Order party, when the Rhode Island Question is settled. Can any reasonable man be found to assert that that question, vitally important as it is to all of us, is SETTLED? Look at the proceedings of Congress. In the House of Representatives is now pending a memorial, from the Dorrite members of the Rhode Island Legislature, which, among other extraordinary requests, asks that the Congress of the United States should execute to this State the guaranty, in the National Constitution, of a republican form of government, in favor of "the People's Constitution!" Look at the debate which is now going on in that House, upon a motion growing out of the presentation of this memorial. Mark how the Van Buren orators "go the whole figure," for Dorr, for Dorr's Constitution, and, what is worse still, for the mode in which it was formed, and for the fraud and force by which it was sought to be established. Let any thinking man ponder these plain and indubitable facts, and then say, whether or not the Rhode Island Question is settled!

The Rhode Island Question is now before Congress, and before the whole people of these United States. The friends of law and order have appealed to no such tribunal, and, if they are true to themselves, neither Congress, nor the people of other States will dare to interfere with our domestic concerns, upon principles, too, which would be destructive to State Rights, and which would render insecure every Constitution in the land. Let us meet this meditated and formidable aggression upon our State Rights, in a spirit which shall not dishonor ourselves and encourage our unprincipled assailants. Away with the tone of timid deprecation about new issues, as if we feared to do battle, even to the last, in defence of our own principles! Away with the fallacious talk about the Rhode Island Question being a local and subordinate question, or "a particular and partial subject!" This is indeed dainty language to be applied to a matter which comes home to the bosom and business of every man in Rhode Island! The friends of law and order in this State believe with Henry Clay, that there is "no mode by which an existing government can be overthrown or set aside, and a new one erected in its place, but by the consent and authority of that government, expressed or implied, or by forcible resistance, that is revolution." This is good law and order doctrine, expressed in the very words that fell from the lips of the great orator of the West. Does a doctrine, of such momentous import to the whole country, deserve to be excluded from the public consideration—as a "local issue"—as "a particular and partial subject?"

It is a great mistake to suppose that there can be, in

this State, two separate and independent political organizations, composed, to a considerable extent, of the same men. When, in the history of political parties, was such an anomaly known? If we, the Law and Order Whigs, combine our efforts with those of the law and order democrats, for the purpose of preserving from destruction our State government, both honor and policy demand, that the union should be formed and should be maintained upon principles the most generous and comprehensive. Thus far the most important benefits to the State have attended our union.

Let, then, no "selfish policy," the poor wisdom of selfish politicians, be permitted to break this union, to which, in the hour of danger we firmly clung, and which, whatever assaults may be made upon us from within or without, will enable us triumphantly to repel them. For one, I am not tired of my old democratic associates; at any rate, I wish not to change them for new recruits—for mere soldiers of fortune—who, weary of fighting under the bleared banner of Dorrism, are solicitous to desert it—who, though not at all sorry for their sins, are quite willing to escape the consequences which have rendered hard the way of the transgressor. Come what may, let us not suffer our enemies to trample our precious banner under their feet. Above all, let us who have thus far followed it to victory, beware how we desert it—and come to look upon it as we would look upon a faded memorial of the glorious recollections of the past!

In respect to the election of a United States Senator, which is to be made by the next Legislature, no apprehension need be felt. It is morally certain that, whoever he may be, he will be a decided friend to Mr. Clay and to all his measures—an "out and outer" Clay man—to adopt the expressive language in which some orators are accustomed to captivate the popular ear. For one, I want no doubtful or untrue man, to fill the place which will be vacated by the expiration of Mr. Francis's term of service. No honest and intelligent man believes that any other than a "true and thorough friend" to Mr. Clay is thought of for that post, or that any other than a true and thorough friend to him, could be elected. Under these circumstances, as a Rhode Island man, I was pained and mortified, that one of our late orators should have been betrayed into the use of language, which implied the slightest doubt as to the unwavering fidelity of ·Rhode Island to Mr. Clay, and to the great principles of public policy of which he is the representative. Rhode Island, above all other States, ought to be protected from insinuations which convey a doubt of her friendship for Mr. Clay. Rhode Island scorns to desert her principles or the men who uphold them. She gave to him her vote, when his cause was known to be hopeless. Is it then to be expected that she will be guilty both of ingratitude and folly, by withholding from him a thorough support, when the country is about to reward him, with her selectest honor, for a life devoted to her service?

A Law and Order Man.

PROVIDENCE DAILY TRANSCRIPT, MARCH 21, 1844.

PRESERVE THE LAW AND ORDER PARTY.

NO. III.—AND LAST.

I AM in favor of maintaining the existing organization of the Law and Order Party against every attempt to destroy it, for the following, among other substantial reasons:

1. If the Law and Order Party should now be dissolved it will be dissolved under circumstances which will leave no hope of a re-union. It would be dissolved, too, in the face of a powerful and united party, which stands pledged to overthrow, at the very first opportunity, the Constitution, which we have established. That party would not be slow to take advantage of our divisions, to push an object which they have not abandoned and which they never will abandon. In the event of another struggle, it would be quite too much to expect the Law and Order democrats to combine their efforts with our own. If we deal treacherously with them, we must take the consequences. If we show no confidence in them, they will show no confidence in us.

2. The dissolution of the Law and Order Party will lessen, by at least several hundreds, the majority

for Mr. Clay in November next. It will almost compel Law and Order Democrats, to remain neutral, because a sentiment of self respect will not permit them to offer their aid. They will do nothing derogatory to their principles—nothing to the injury of the cause of Law and Order, but, knowing that the cause of Mr. Clay in Rhode Island is safe without them, they will follow a very natural instinct in shunning all association with men, who are willing to open their doors to the Dorrites while they shut them in the faces of well tried friends. It may not be amiss for those gentlemen, who put themselves before the country as the "out and out friends" of Mr. Clay, to consider whether or not they will gain aught for his cause, by turning their backs upon any of his principles, and upon principles which were once their own.

3. The dissolution of the Law and Order Party will create in our State politics a confusion, from which none but ambitious and interested politicians can hope to profit. Its immediate effect will be to withdraw power and influence from the many, and to concentrate them in the hands of the few. Whether the people will be the gainers by this change, I leave the people to decide!

Another mischievous effect of the rupture of the ties of our political brotherhood, will be the organization of a third party in the State. Our constitution gives to third parties a fearful power, in as much as it requires, in all elections of members to the General Assembly, that a majority and not a plurality shall be necessary to a choice. Of third parties we have had some experience, and we must be dull pupils indeed, if that experience has taught us no wisdom. Dissolve the Law and Order Party, and you prepare the way for the ultimate and no distant triumph of Dorrism. The State will be rent with factions. With one of these factions the Dorrites will unite. A sacrifice of some one of the conservative provisions of the constitution, will be the basis of the union. The overthrow of the whole constitution will be the final result.

4. If Mr. Van Buren should be elected, and that calamity must be considered as possible, every United States officer in this State whose appointment can be controlled by the President, will be a genuine Dorrite. To the influence of such an official corps, backed as they will be by a powerful party at home, and by the whole democracy of the free States, what can we oppose, but shattered forces and distracted counsels? Shall a few politicians be permitted to sow this wind, from which the people can hope to reap nothing but the whirlwind?

5. As things now are, it is next to certain, that the friends of Henry Clay will have the power to elect, in January next, a Senator friendly to him and to his measures. Reverse, however, this state of things, in other words, dissolve the Law and Order Party, and the election of a Clay Senator in the place of Governor Francis, who declines a re-election, is rendered extremely precarious. A seething political cauldron, full of repulsive ingredients, is not subject to well ascertained laws! No man can tell how much will evaporate—or what will sink to the bottom, or what rise to the top. Why not let well alone?

6. Lastly—I am in favor of the continuance of the

Law and Order Party—because faith solemnly plighted demands it. With me, this is, of itself, a conclusive reason—transcending all other reasons—and disposing, at once, of every objection, however ingenious, which may be advanced on the other side. Never should the interests of a clique—or the advancement of an individual, however meritorious he may be, be preferred to the great interests of the people! Never should we do aught or leave aught undone which may expose us even to the suspicion of treachery. Let us adhere firmly to our principles—and let us in good faith redeem all our pledges, whether expressed or implied. We shall then stand before the world with unforfeited honor; we shall deserve success; and, under such auspices, we can hardly fail to command it.

A LAW AND ORDER MAN.

PROVIDENCE DAILY TRANSCRIPT, MARCH 27, 1844.

OUR STATE RIGHTS INVADED!

THE apathy of the people of Rhode Island in relation to the action of Congress upon the Rhode Island Question, is somewhat remarkable. The press is silent, or it utters only the treacherous cry—there is no danger. No public meetings are held to protest against the flagrant usurpation of which the House of Representatives has already been guilty, in a matter involving the very existence of our State Government. The public mind wears the aspect of tame and spiritless acquiescence in a course of action which ought to arouse the indignation of every Law and Order man in Rhode Island.

What is the present position of the Rhode Island Question? Twenty seven men, styling themselves democratic members of the General Assembly of Rhode Island, who are willing that the reproach of the baldest perjury should, for all time, dishonor their names, petition the national House of Representatives, in effect, to destroy our Constitution, and to establish the People's Constitution upon its ruins! How is the Memorial of these perjured and traitorous men received? Is it dismissed with scorn for their unparalleled turpitude and with indignation that Congress should be asked to perpetrate so infamous an outrage upon the rights of an independent sovereign State? No such thing!

This Memorial is most graciously entertained. It is referred to a select Committee, headed by one of the dirty politicians of New Hampshire, who disgraces the name of Edmund Burke! A motion is subsequently made to discharge the Committee from the farther consideration of the Memorial, and this motion is supported on the ground that to entertain the Memorial is a gross violation of the most sacred rights of this State. Does Congress, for this conclusive reason, discharge the Committee, and thus put an end to the whole matter? No such thing. They reject this motion, urged by a constitutional lawyer upon constitutional grounds—and they proceed to consummate their meditated outrage upon the rights of Rhode Island, by giving this select Committee, unlimited power to send for papers and persons!

What this Committee will do in the premises, it would not be difficult to predict. They will present to the House, and cause to be circulated, a Report surcharged with the grossest misrepresentations of the Rhode Island Question—and fitted and intended to mislead the popular judgment, and to influence the popular passions throughout the land. In a country where opinion is sovereign, what mischief such a Report may work, no man can calculate.

What this Committee may say, is comparatively very immaterial. They cannot, in any event, easily fright the people of Rhode Island from their propriety. What I object to, and what, in my judgment, ought to stir to its very depths the spirit of Rhode Island—is the fact—the incontrovertible, the alarming fact—that the popular branch of the general government, in flagrant violation of the constitution of the United States, has by assuming jurisdiction in this matter, established a precedent most dangerous to the reserved rights of the States, and against which every State government ought most solemnly to protest. It matters not how mean, or how profligate, or how shameless, are our Rhode Island Memorialists. It matters not, to what practical extent Congress may dare to push its usurpation. It matters not, in this stage of the proceeding, whether the whole affair may end in words or in deeds, in smoke or in fire. It is enough for us to know, that Congress has already trespassed upon our rights—that Congress has begun, in our case, the march of usurpation—that Congress has already assumed the power to inquire into the validity of the constitution which we have rightfully established, and which we are pledged to maintain! I take issue, not upon the extent of the encroachment, but upon the fact that Congress has encroached at all! I take issue upon the great principle, that the general government has no business, directly or indirectly, to interfere with our domestic government. I wish to make this distinct and palpable issue, and to try it before the whole country. In any struggle which we may be called to maintain, in defence of our State constitution, it is upon ourselves, upon the people of Rhode Island, that we must chiefly rely.

As to politicians, whether at home or abroad, northern or southern, God forbid that we should commit to their custody, either our rights or our honor! We know at what they look. We know that the clearest convictions of duty and that all sensibility to reproach, lose their power over politicians, when they come to think that in consequence of a particular course, votes are to be either lost or won, that the cause of a favorite candidate for the Presidency is to be either injured or advanced. How did "the chivalry" the rampant asserters of State Rights demean themselves, when the House of Representatives was about to invade the rights of Rhode Island? Some of them stood manfully upon their principles, and some, to their shame, be it recorded skulked! What confidence can be placed in the fidelity of such politicians? If, for the ignoble purpose of "coining political capital," as the phrase is, they will, in one stage of the proceeding, abandon their cherished principles, what assurance can we have that they will come to the rescue, if, in the end, it should be found necessary to sacrifice Rhode Island, in order to obtain votes for Mr. Clay, or Mr. Van Buren, or Mr. Calhoun!

It is high time that the Rhode Island Question was settled—not merely in the judgment of the people of Rhode Island—but in the judgment of the American people. It is high time, that unprincipled politicians, at home and abroad had dismissed it as an unavailable topic of agitation. The people of Rhode Island will resist, even unto blood, any and every attempt, come when and whence it may, to fasten upon them the People's Constitution! On this point I have no misgivings. But, in common with the great mass of the people of Rhode Island, I am weary of agitation. I long to repose under the protection of a Government, which, is acknowledged by every man among us to be the only rightful government. Hence my earnest desire, that we should, in the present crisis, show a bold front, and, without timidly pausing to calculate what political capital may be coined out of us or for us, that we should, in the most solemn and authoritative manner, protest against the jurisdiction which the National House of Representatives has assumed, as a most dangerous and flagrant usurpation of the reserved rights of Rhode Island—a usurpation, pregnant with the worst evils of consolidation—a usurpation, which this State and every State, is bound to resist and to repel—by every means within their power, a usurpation, which it specially concerns Rhode Island to protest against, at the outset—a usurpation, which, if not rebuked and disavowed, will constitute a precedent fatal to the rights of the States and to the liberties of the People.

A Law and Order Man.

PROVIDENCE JOURNAL, JULY 6, 1844.

RESOLUTIONS

PASSED AT A MASS MEETING.

Whereas, the friends of Henry Clay and of Theodore Frelinghuysen, from every part of the State of Rhode Island, have assembled in Mass Meeting, on this anniversary of the birth day of American Independence, for the purpose of giving a renewed expression of their attachment to the great principles which those eminent statesmen have steadfastly maintained, and to that course of public policy which, in the event of their election, they stand pledged to pursue—

Therefore, resolved, That the rich blessings of freedom and independence which the men of '76 purchased with their blood, can be preserved only by keeping alive, in the hearts of the present generation, the spirit of '76.

Resolved, That the highest interests of the American people—the preservation of life, liberty, and property—the blessings, if not the continuance of the Union between these States, demand, on the part of both government and people, a profound reverence for the obligations of the Constitution and laws of the land; that the law is the great safeguard of popular freedom; and that "the Constitution which at any time exists, is sacredly obligatory upon all, till changed by an explicit and authentic act of the whole people."

Resolved, That the multiplied and flagrant abuses and usurpations of power, on the part of the acting President of these United States, should admonish the people, that, if they would maintain their constitutional rights, and secure from ruinous vicissitudes the business of the country, they must confide the supreme Executive Power to a man who will illustrate his high station by the exercise of that wisdom, moderation and patriotism which marked the earlier and better days of the Republic.

Resolved, That the principles which the Whig party of '76 perilled life, liberty and property to establish, can be maintained, in their original vigor and purity, only by giving effect, through the medium of the ballot box, to the sound, conservative, constitutional principles of the Whig party of eighteen hundred and forty four.

Resolved, That, at a crisis in our national affairs like the present, we will shrink from no duty to which our country may summon us; that here, amid the joyous and patriotic associations of this our national festival, we pledge ourselves, one and all, to buckle on our armor, and, come what may, to do battle fearlessly, for the right.

Resolved, That we are proud to rally, in defence of our principles, under the banner of Henry Clay and Theodore Frelinghuysen, the Whig candidates for the Presidency and Vice Presidency of these United States, assured that, if elected, they will be found true and faithful to the Constitution; that they will maintain, at all hazards, and against all antagonists, the Union of the States; that they will pursue, in the administration of the government, an upright, wise, and conciliatory policy—a policy which will develop the resources of the country—allay sectional jealousies, and cause this nation to stand before other nations with an unsullied reputation for public faith and honor.

Resolved, That Henry Clay needs no eulogy at our hands; that a name, rendered illustrious by a long course of eminent service in the various departments of the government, by a fearless devotion to great principles, and by a generous ardor for the triumph of freedom throughout all lands, is destined in spite of partisan calumnies, to stand among the brightest in that record of honored names to which the men of other times will look for the highest qualities of the statesman and the patriot.

Resolved, That we hail, with cordial enthusiasm, the nomination of Theodore Frelinghuysen for the office of Vice President as a cheering indication that the people of this country are becoming weary and distrustful of noisy and obtrusive politicians; that perceiving how beautiful, in the character of Mr. Frelinghuysen, is the alliance between talent, and patriotism, and piety, they are about to summon him from the shades of academic seclusion, again to put forth, amid the conflicts of opinion in the Senate, the calm might of his pure character, and to enlighten the counsels of our statesmen with the dictates of his ripened wisdom.

Resolved, That, in the coming contest, Rhode Island will do her duty to herself, to her favorite candidates, and to the country—that, unwearied with the strife which she has been forced to maintain within her borders for the preservation of law and order against revolutionary attempts to overthrow them, she will engage, with renovated ardor, in the great cause which now demands her aid; that she will go, heart and hand, for Clay and Frelinghuysen, the exponents of her cherished principles of national policy, and the intrepid advocates of those momentous political doctrines which she upholds, as essential to the peace of society, to the stability of all laws and constitutions, and to the rights and liberties of the people.

PROVIDENCE JOURNAL, SEPTEMBER 17, 1844.

RHODE ISLAND AFFAIRS.

NO. I.

To the People of Rhode Island:—

Fellow Citizens:—We have reached an extraordinary crisis in the history of our republican institutions. For the first time since the foundation of the government, a great political party is endeavoring to array tumultuary masses of the people in fierce hostility to the regular constitutional action of the public will in one of the States of this Union. This end, too, so big with peril to all the defences of temperate freedom, is sought to be accomplished by inflammatory appeals to the passions, by the grossest misrepresentations of facts, by the most perverse application of universally acknowledged truths. You, my fellow citizens, cannot misunderstand me. I refer to the unwarrantable and dangerous violation of the reserved rights of Rhode Island, by portions of the people of some of our sister States—by aliens to her soil—and strangers to the free spirit which has ever pervaded her institutions. Let us look, for a moment, at the facts of the case.

Thomas W. Dorr, who had twice put himself at the head of an armed mob, for the purpose of overthrowing the legal government of his native State, is at last tried, for one of the highest crimes known to the laws, before the Supreme Court of Rhode Island. In the progress of his trial, be it remembered, he makes the most ample confessions of his participation in the revolutionary movement of which he was the soul. Upon evidence the most conclusive he is found guilty by the jury, and is sentenced by the Court to undergo the penalty annexed by the laws to the crime with which he stood charged. This penalty, less severe than his crimes deserved, and less severe than the penalty annexed by the laws of other States to the same offence,* was provided by the Legislature, years before Mr. Dorr had steeped himself to the lips in treason against his native State. The Legislature, therefore, which enacted the law against treason, is obnoxious, in this case, to no suspicion of vindictiveness. Mr. Dorr's confessions, and the testimony even of his own witnesses, left the jury no alternative. Without a flagrant violation of their oaths, they could not have returned a verdict of acquittal. In performing the duty intrusted to them by the law, the Court, as is well known, could exercise no discretion. They could neither aggravate, nor reduce, nor suspend the penalty. That sentence is now in a process of execution.

In all this, what is there so very unusual? Why all this wild uproar of the political elements, at home and abroad, because the State of Rhode Island, in the

* The statute of New Hampshire, a State which has been most offensively officious in Rhode Island affairs, punishes the crime of treason with death.

exercise of her reserved rights, punishes, according to law, a man who has transgressed the law? Has she done aught beside? Has she violated any of those transcendent obligations which she assumed, when she adopted the Constitution of the United States? Has she ever proved false to the Union, or to the principles upon which the Union was established? Has she ever been wanting in fidelity to her sister States? Has she ever been guilty of the grave impertinence of meddling with their internal affairs? When they have executed their laws upon transgressors, has she ever sought by clamor, and reproach, and misrepresentation, to kindle against them the passions of the masses? This will not be pretended, even by those who disguise the revolutionary aggression which they are attempting upon the rights of Rhode Island, under soft and plausible pretexts. "Legal and constitutional means for the liberation of Governor Dorr!" is all that these men intend, when they take an appeal from the grave and deliberate judgments of Courts and juries to a diseased public opinion; in other words, to the perverted sympathies and to the exasperated passions of the mob!

The "Democratic Mass Meeting," held in this city on the 4th instant, furnishes a curious commentary upon the grave declaration that none but "legal and constitutional means" are sought to be adopted for the "liberation of Governor Dorr." The false and perverse men who, under a delusive pretext, got up this meeting, knew of what materials it would be composed, by what spirit it would be animated—in what manner it would be conducted. Open violence, it is true, was not attempted. The government, faithful to its trust, had adopted the most efficient means to preserve the public peace—and the masses who came hither from abroad on the 4th, at the bidding of men who signalized all but their courage in the late rebellion, went home again, doubtless hating Rhode Island the more, for the harangues to which they had listened, but impressed, at the same time, with the conviction, that she is both prepared and resolved to maintain, at all hazards, her rights and her honor. This famous mass meeting, in its inception, and progress, and results—in its means and in its ends—was a flagrant insult to the people and government of the State of Rhode Island. It assembled, ostensibly, for the purpose of adopting "legal and constitutional means for the liberation of Governor Dorr," and yet the whole drift of the speeches and resolutions upon that occasion, implied aught but reverence either for constitutions or for laws. If the grievous oppressions which these speeches and resolutions falsely charge to the account of the Rhode Island "Algerines," have, in fact, been committed, no man, worthy to bear the name of a man, ought to look either to the laws or to the ballot box for redress. Under such a condition of things, the right of insurrection would indeed be a sacred right. Revolution, immediate, avowed, open revolution would then become the rightful remedy! The men, at home and abroad, who in order to coin political capital for Polk and Dallas, are now busily engaged in slandering the institutions of Rhode Island, and in misrepresenting the conduct of her government and people, ought to take shame to themselves for a course, which while it dishonors them, exposes to peril all the established defences of individual and public liberty, throughout the length and breadth of this land. Read, my fellow citizens, and without indignation, if you can, the following language which "the multitude" assembled in this city on the 4th instant, put forth as their voice:

"We, the vast multitude now assembled on this solemn occasion, do here, in the presence of Almighty God, most seriously and solemnly remonstrate and protest, as well against the illegal and unconstitutional trial of said Thomas Wilson Dorr as against his most unjust and cruel imprisonment, and we call upon the authorities of this State to retrace their steps and restore him to that liberty of which he has been so unjustly deprived; and this solemn Remonstrance and Protest we now make, as well in our own name as in the name of the People of the United States, thousands of whom from sister States are now with us. We call upon them to carry home to their respective States a history of our wrongs, and spread it among the people, that the united voice and action of this great nation may be heard in tones of thunder, against the overthrow of popular sovereignty and civil liberty in Rhode Island."

This is most extraordinary language to be held by those who contemplate only "legal and constitutional means for the liberation of Governor Dorr!" A mass meeting, "a vast multitude," assemble in this city, and undertake to set themselves above the Constitution and the laws of this State. They undertake to review the judgments of our highest Court, and to pronounce the trial of Dorr "illegal and unconstitutional"—and his imprisonment "most unjust and cruel"—and yet more, this same "vast multitude," moved, as all vast multitudes are, more by passion than by reason, modestly "call upon the authorities of this State to retrace their steps, and restore him to that liberty of which he has been unjustly deprived." All this, too, is done "in the name of the people of the United States," and the interposition of the whole people of the United States is invoked in behalf of Mr. Dorr, in language, too, which is sufficiently significant as to the nature of that interposition!

It is conceded, my fellow citizens, even by the Dorrites, (with what sincerity the concession is made I leave you to judge) that our existing constitution is the supreme law of the land. Under that Constitution the people have elected a Governor, and Representatives and Senators in the General Assembly. This General Assembly, in pursuance of powers confided to them by the Constitution, have organized judicial tribunals for the administration of civil and criminal justice. In other words, the people of Rhode Island are living under the government of their own laws and magistrates, quietly and honestly pursuing their customary avocations, and faithfully discharging all their obligations to their sister states, and to the government of the Union. Under such circumstances, it smacks somewhat of intimidation, if not of revolutionary violence, for the people of other States to gather within our borders to denounce our institutions, and to invoke the whole people of the United States to pour out upon our heads the "thunder" of their indignation! These appeals from the decisions of the regularly constituted organs of the public will, I deem to be of most dangerous import to the social order of every State in this Union. If such appeals are to be tolerated, of what avail are all the checks and balances provided by our State and National Constitutions? What obedience will the solemn judgments of the law command? With what hope of success can the small States contend for the preservation of their rights? It may suit the ambitious purposes of the empire State to put in motion her "vast multitude," and to send them abroad commissioned to redress grievances in New Jersey, Delaware, Connecticut or Rhode Island—to take, in fine, "united action" against any sister State, who, in the administration of her internal affairs, may chance to provoke popular odium.

The Dorrites avow that their intention is to create in favor of the liberation of Dorr, a public opinion in this country which shall be found irresistible. What do they mean by public opinion? Do they mean the sedate judgments of the public mind, formed after a full and impartial examination of all the facts of the case, and of the principles which those facts involve, or do they mean the conclusions, unavoidably rash and ill supported, which mass meetings may adopt and put forth? Do they hope to exact homage to that sort of public opinion, which is manufactured by the Globe and Madisonian at Washington, and which subordinate partisan presses are commissioned to circulate? Do they expect to frighten Rhode Island men from their propriety, by parading in the journals devoted to their service, resolutions big with denunciations against Algerine cruelty and oppression? Do they suppose that the men of Rhode Island will yield to a public opinion which is formed amid the fumes of Tammany Hall, which has for its oracles the Empire and the Spartan Clubs—and which, on the 4th of

September, discharged upon this peaceful city the feculence and ruffianism of New York?

Fellow Citizens:—We have been both insulted and wronged by these proceedings. If, however, we continue true to ourselves, we have nothing to fear. Never was Rhode Island more tranquil, or more prosperous—never were her people better prepared or more determined to defend their rights, and to stand firmly upon their principles. All we ask is to be let alone by those who have no business to meddle in our affairs.

Never, never, my fellow citizens, suffer an alien host, however mighty, to intimidate you, or to dictate to you in what manner you shall regulate your "internal police and the conduct of your own affairs." Be moderate, but be firm. Heed not the loose libels which are put forth to defame you; they will soon pass away with the men who forge them. Keep, nevertheless, your armor on, and resolve never to make an equivocal concession, or a dishonorable compromise—never to surrender the cause of "Law and Order," while the blood of heroic sires runs warm in your veins.

A Rhode Island Man.

PROVIDENCE JOURNAL, SEPTEMBER 19, 1844.

RHODE ISLAND AFFAIRS.

NO. II.

To the People of Rhode Island :—

Fellow Citizens :—The Rhode Island question is sought to be made, by the partisans of Polk and Dallas, one of the great issues in the momentous political contest which now agitates the whole country. So be it! As a Rhode Island man, I would court rather than shun this new issue. As a friend to the election of Clay and Frelinghuysen, I would court rather than shun it. As an advocate of liberty regulated by law, I would court rather than shun it. The more the Rhode Island question is examined, at home and abroad, the better will it be for the cause of "law and order" at home and abroad. I fear nothing in this matter but the delusions of ignorance, the sophistry of the passions, and the infatuation of party spirit. Let the Rhode Island question be thoroughly understood by the people of this country;—let it be argued by our gifted men in all their addresses to the people, during the progress of the present political canvass, and who can doubt what will be the intelligent, solemn and irrevocable decision of the people? Mr. Clay, on more than one occasion, has taken his stand boldly upon the principles of "law and order." His opponents have adopted for their rallying cry, "Polk, Dallas and Dorr."

So be it, my fellow citizens! If we cannot sustain Mr. Clay upon the high ground where, as the noble champion of constitutional freedom, he has chosen to stand, we can hope to sustain him on no other. I go farther; if a majority of the people of this Union, either from ignorance of the true merits of the case, or from the lust of political power, or from the madness of party spirit, should ever come to lend a sanction, whether express or implied, to the doctrines broached and maintained by Dorr, the days of this republic will have been numbered. Our constitutions, with all their checks and balances to protect minorities against majorities—the weak against the strong—the peaceful against the violent, will not then be worth the parchment upon which they are engrossed. "The beginning of the end" will have come. The strife of successive factions would terminate in fearful anarchy—and fearful anarchy, if all history be not a lie, would be followed by the repose of a sullen, unmitigated, inexorable despotism. Constitutions and laws, made by the people and for the people, would soon become matters of history—and one man, with an iron will, would settle by the logic of the bayonet all questions about the sovereignty of the people!

For one, my fellow citizens, I wish to have the Rhode Island question fully and fairly tried before the great tribunals of the people, in every State of our widely extended Union. I fear not the issue of thorough, calm and intelligent investigation. At any rate, we all want to have this question settled by the clear, deliberate and authoritative judgment of the people. We are not insensible, as Rhode Island men we cannot be insensible, to any of the great issues which are involved in the present contest for the Presidency. Much as we desire and need "Protection," and much as we deprecate and should deplore "Annexation," let us, however, never forget, that these and all other questions and interests are of subordinate importance; that the revolutionary doctrines of Dorr, should they ever become part and parcel of American constitutional law, will prove, in the end, inevitably fatal to all the securities of life, liberty, and property.

The Dorrites, at home and abroad, are at infinite pains to misrepresent the conduct and principles of the government and people of Rhode Island. Are we not culpably remiss, my fellow citizens, in our efforts to counteract the effect of these misrepresentations? Do not many people in distant States yet believe that the old Charter, aye, the veritable royal charter of the naughty Charles the II. is still the fundamental law of Rhode Island, and that Mr. Dorr is imprisoned solely for his efforts to supplant it by a written Constitution emanating from the people? Do not some people in distant States believe, or affect to believe, that suffrage has never been extended in Rhode Island*—that none

* Suffrage, by the Constitution, is extended to every native citizen of the United States, of the age of twenty one years, who has had his residence and home in the State for two years, and in the town or city where he offers to vote, six months next preceding the time of voting, whose name shall be registered in the town where he resides, on or before the last day of December, in the year next preceding the time of his voting, and who has, within such year, paid a tax or taxes assessed against him, in any town or city in the

but landholders and their eldest sons are permitted to vote,—and that Mr. Dorr is persecuted even unto the trials of martyrdom by the "sand and gravel aristocracy," merely because he seeks to obtain for "the masses" their "equal rights?"

One of the resolutions adopted by the late mass meeting in this city, set forth as a fact that Thomas W. Dorr was tried and condemned by "virtue of the Algerine Law," passed by the Legislature of Rhode Island in 1842. This language is deceptive. Mr. Dorr was indicted, tried, convicted and sentenced, for a violation of the old law of treason, enacted in 1838, before he had even began the work of agitation. This act defined the offence of treason to be levying war against the State; and, in accommodation to the merciful spirit of the age, it reduced the penalty from death to imprisonment for life. The trial was had in the county of Newport, by virtue of a provision of the Algerine law, a provision in accordance with well established legal precedents.

It should never be forgotten, that the government of Rhode Island was at no pains to arrest Mr. Dorr. After inflicting upon the people of this State the most grievous wrongs—after violating our laws, and attempting to subvert our institutions by force of arms,—after months of "exile" from the State which he had well nigh drenched in blood, he came at last within her borders. Under such circumstances, how

State, to the amount of one dollar, or has been enrolled in a military company, been equipped, and done duty therein, according to law, at least for one day, during such year. Naturalized citizens are required to have a freehold, as heretofore, to entitle them to vote. And no person can vote to impose a tax or to expend money, in any town or city, unless he shall have paid a tax, within the year next preceding, upon property valued at least at one hundred and thirty four dollars.—[Vide Constitution.]

could the law sleep? He was immediately arrested and imprisoned. He was tried before a Court, composed of men upon whose integrity, independence, and impartiality, calumny will, in vain, essay to fasten a reproach. The trial was conducted by the judges with great dignity—with a truly judicial caution in the determination of all questions touching the rights of the prisoner at the bar—and with a forbearance which, when sentence was pronounced, his insolent address to the Court rather ungratefully repaid.

It is very easy, at mass meetings, to denounce the trial of Dorr as "illegal and unconstitutional." Will any lawyer who is conversant with the facts of the case, and who is not willing to sink the lawyer in the demagogue, undertake to show wherein this trial was "illegal and unconstitutional?" Were any new doctrines introduced into the law of treason? Were any new rules of evidence adopted, or any old ones disregarded? Did the Court rule any of the questions which were raised, differently from what the most eminent jurists had ruled the same or analogous questions? Is there any pretence for the allegation that the jury was a "packed jury?"* Can any man who reveres the sanctity of an oath, contend that Mr. Dorr could have been acquitted, after he had boldy confessed, in open Court, the facts constituting his treason, which were charged in the indictment?

We hear, too, much flippant declamation and much vituperous reproach about "the unjust and cruel imprisonment" of Mr. Dorr. With what propriety can

*In impanelling the jury for the trial of Dorr, the Court adopted the same rules which were adopted by Chief Justice Marshall in the trial of Aaron Burr for treason. One of the Jurors, too, was a member of the Convention which framed the so called People's Constitution.

that imprisonment be denounced as "unjust and cruel," which a standing law of the State provides—a law, too, enacted years ago, under the influence of no political passions—and which falls, with undiscriminating accuracy, upon the heads of all offenders?

Mr. Dorr, let it never be forgotten, repudiates, as emanating from himself, all attempts to procure his release. He is resolved to accept of no liberation but the "unconditional liberation" which mass meetings now exact from the government of Rhode Island. He is treated by all who have any concern with the prison, with no unkindness. No harsh discrimination is made against him—no weak and unjust discrimination is made in his favor.

The people of Rhode Island, wounded and insulted as they have been by Mr. Dorr, entertain towards him no vindictive feelings. They lament the perverse application of his talents and acquirements; they feel for his family the most sincere and respectful sympathy; they would rejoice to see him, under the influences of a better order of moral sentiments, devoting his powers, not to petty schemes of personal aggrandizement—not to factious and revolutionary enterprises—but to plans for the lasting benefit and ornament of society.

No man among us expects that Mr. Dorr's imprisonment will be for life—no man among us wishes it to be for life. The prerogative of pardon belongs, under our Constitution, to the General Assembly—and to their discretion it may safely be left. Never, upon the question of "law and order," was public opinion more sound in Rhode Island. Never was the government more strongly intrenched in the affections and confidence of the people, and never was it better prepared to defend against all aggressions its own honor and the rights of the people. Thus strongly fortified, the government can exercise in Mr. Dorr's case the power of pardon, without subjecting itself even to the suspicion of being intimidated into concessions. By the conviction and imprisonment of Mr. Dorr, the law, the violated law, has been vindicated! This is a vital consideration—this the crowning triumph of all our struggles in the great cause of constitutional freedom!

The General Assembly, I am quite sure, will never permit mass meetings, at home or abroad, to dictate to them when, or upon what conditions, they shall release Mr. Dorr. On the contrary, the clamor and reproaches of tumultuous masses, I am no less sure, will never provoke them into a passionate and rigid determination indefinitely to prolong his imprisonment. They will, I am persuaded, decide his case upon general principles, upon grave considerations of public policy, and with a jealous regard to the rights, safety and honor of the State.

A Rhode Island Man.

PROVIDENCE JOURNAL, SEPTEMBER 26, 1844.

RHODE ISLAND AFFAIRS.

NO. III.

To the People of Rhode Island:—

Fellow Citizens:—Rhode Island, though a small State, is a full State. In any constitutional sense, she is as much an Empire State as New York. All the powers which she has not delegated to the general government, she has reserved to herself. Of her reserved rights, no State can be more jealous—and no aggressions upon them will she ever tolerate, whether they come from the general government or from an alien host in mass meeting assembled. In any contest for the preservation of these reserved rights, she will not be left to do battle alone—and, in any such contest she will never pause to count the cost either of treasure or of blood. This is so well understood by our gentlemen jacobins at home—that, if the gentlemen jacobins abroad, the Bancrofts, the Mortons, the Hubbards, and the Halletts, would but let us alone, Rhode Island would be left to pursue her peaceful course, ambitious of no distinctions but those which follow in the train of liberty regulated by law. This State, too, in all past time, has enjoyed all the benefits and blessings of a "republican form of government"—and these blessings and benefits she still enjoys. Under the liberal Constitution which she has adopted, suffrage is next to universal. In relation, therefore, to this matter, once the pretext for revolutionary movements in this State, there exists, no longer, among our own people, any plausible reasons for discontent. Rhode Island, too, has no unadjusted quarrels with any of her sister States. She has never sought to violate their rights—she has never deemed it her mission to reform their institutions. In respect to the Union and the government of the Union, it is not too much to add, that she has ever been found true and faithful—impelled from her quiet course by none of those centrifugal forces which cause some of her more ambitious sisters to rush from their orbits.

All these things being so, fellow citizens, are we not justified, as Rhode Island men, in being moved to indignation by the crusade which the apostles of mischief and anarchy abroad are preaching up against Rhode Island? They will not pretend to affirm that we have violated our own constitution and laws—and, if we had, what business is that to them? They will not pretend that we have violated either the laws or the Constitution of the United States. They will not pretend that we are without "a republican form of government." But, say they, the "Algerines" of Rhode Island, in other words, the majority of the people of Rhode Island, have disowned "the great principles of American liberty," and have trampled under foot "the doctrines of the Declaration of American Independence," as we understand them! The Bancrofts, the Mortons, the Hubbards, and the Halletts, inflamed, "about these days," with a burning zeal for the principles of American liberty, which they assert have been violated by the trial and imprisonment of Dorr, seem determined that Rhode Island shall dance to their pipe, or that she shall not dance at all! You are intruding, gentlemen, in this matter, into the field of opinion; you are setting up your own notions as the only true and infallible notions; you are seeking to punish a State, not for a violation of her solemn constitutional obligations, but for not understanding, as you understand them, the principles of American liberty—for not applying, as you apply them, the doctrines of the Declaration of American Independence! In the prosecution of your sinister intent, you have ranged yourselves under the banner of "Polk, Dallas and Dorr." By these names, which regarded as exponents of liberty, law and order, are positively amusing, you hope to conquer. Polk is a SLAVEHOLDER, and the favorite candidate of slaveholders because he is a slaveholder! Dallas is a recorded champion of doctrines subversive of all law! Dorr is a felon convicted of an attempt to overturn, by force of arms, the social order of his native State!

If you think it right, by appeals to the passions, to goad the masses to the verge of revolutionary violence in defence of what you allege to be the true doctrines of American liberty, why don't you attempt to get up a crusade against the State of Maryland, because, in the execution of her laws, she keeps in a felon's cell, and loads with a felon's chains, an American citizen, whose only offence, in the judgment of many, is his too great love for "the principles of American liberty?" Upon your own principles, Torry, however wrong or misguided he may have been, is far more worthy of sympathy than Dorr. The latter is imprisoned because he arrayed an armed mob against the people and government of his native State. The former is imprisoned, because he was impelled to a violation of the laws of Maryland by a fanatical ardor in behalf of the principles of American liberty. I allude to the case of Torry, merely as a topic for illustration. I feel no especial sympathy for him, and I would be among the last, either at home or abroad, to say or to do aught to inflame the passions of the masses against the highly respectable State whose laws he is alleged to have transgressed, and by whose laws he is about to be judged.

It will, however, in this connection, readily occur to every reflecting mind, that if, upon the vague and undefined charges of having violated the doctrines of the Declaration of American Independence, the government and people of Rhode Island are to be arraigned, not at the ballot box—and not before regularly constituted judicial tribunals, but before masses of men, following unprincipled leaders—and moved by strong passions—the institutions of every State, whatever may be the protection of constitution and laws, are liable, at any moment, to be overthrown. The people south of Mason and Dixon's line, entertain very different notions of American liberty from those which the people of New England entertain—but, so long as our southern brethren continue true to the bargain which we have made with them; so long as they fulfill towards their sister States and towards the Union, the obligations which the constitution imposes upon them, we, of the north, are bound, in all good conscience, to let them, their speculative notions, and their domestic institutions, entirely alone. Reserving to ourselves, the sacred right to think as we please, in reference to the institution of slavery—and likewise calmly to express our opinions, we disclaim, and we are bound to disclaim, all desire to get up "mass meetings," within or without the borders of slave States,—for the purpose of inflaming the discontent of any portion of their people—or of subverting, by "the united voice and action of this great nation," an institution which the Constitution recognizes, and which it is bound to protect.

Would it not be well for our southern brethren, before they pass any more resolutions in favor of "Polk, Dallas and Dorr," to comprehend the full extent of the principle for which Dorr and his adherents contend? How would that principle, if carried out fully at the South, operate upon the institutions of the South, upon her peace—upon the elements of her political power—upon the value of her staples—and upon all the forms of her social life?

We, fellow citizens of Rhode Island, feel at present no special apprehensions for ourselves, or for our institutions. We are prepared to take good care of both—and we mean to take good care of both! Our little bark is well trimmed and well manned, and under the direction of a veteran pilot, who has weathered many a political storm, she will ride out in safety the angry tempest which false and bad spirits now invoke to destroy her. Looking, however, into the depths of the distant future, we tremble, and well may we tremble, for the ultimate consequences of principles and measures which spring from the spirit of jacobinism, and which can end only in the triumph of the mob. The cloud, at which we now gaze solicitously, may be no bigger than a man's hand, but it portends a tempest which will blacken the whole sky. Unless the principles broached by Dorr, and espoused, to a considerable extent, by the partisans of "Polk, Dallas, and Dorr," are signally rebuked by the people of this country, they may prepare themselves, not for one revolution only—but for a series of revolutions—which, after torrents of fraternal blood are shed, will end in the destruction of every vestige of popular freedom.

A RHODE ISLAND MAN.

PROVIDENCE JOURNAL, OCTOBER 3, 1844.

RHODE ISLAND AFFAIRS.

NO. IV.

TO THE PEOPLE OF RHODE ISLAND:—

FELLOW CITIZENS:—In seasons of sore public calamity, when practical grievances exist, and are felt by all orders of the community, the conservative classes do not require to be admonished of the necessity of vigilance, and effort, and self sacrifice. At such seasons, they seem to act from a common impulse in the support of a common cause. When they feel the State to be in danger, they put far from them all paltry personal considerations; they repel the agency of hackneyed and intrusive politicians; and they repose, with intuitive sagacity and confidence, on the counsels of those who seek for no spoils, and who abhor the strife to which they find themselves summoned. In seasons of comparative repose and of general prosperity, the matter is far otherwise. Then, the conservative classes need to be stimulated to the exercise of that vigilance which is the price of liberty, and to the performance of those duties upon which the welfare of the community is suspended. The general prosperity which the country now enjoys, and her exemption from all pressing dangers from abroad, it is to be feared, may induce the torpor of inexertion, at a crisis in her domestic affairs, which demands the zealous, persevering and concentrated efforts of all good citizens.

The friends of "law and order," however, in Rhode Island, do not need to be reminded of the services and sacrifices in behalf of the State which the times exact. Though weary of strife, they are resolved not to intermit their zeal, and not to lay aside the armor of championship in a great and good cause, till that cause is no longer threatened with danger. The approaching election of President, whatever may be the result, is a matter of deeper interest, of more vital concernment, to the people of Rhode Island, than to the people of any other State. Should Mr. Clay be elected—and my confidence in that auspicious result is unaffected either by the fierce bluster of enemies or by the croaking of timid friends—we may reasonably expect to enjoy a season of refreshing if not prolonged repose. For four years, at least, would the work of agitation be postponed, or, if not postponed, it would be found abortive. For four years, at least, we should escape all practical exhibition of those wild revolutionary doctrines which have so vexed our peace, and we should, moreover, be sheltered from those insolent foreign aggressions upon our rights which have so justly aroused our indignation, and so severely tasked our forbearance. These are considerations of very grave import. They address themselves, with peculiar emphasis, to the good sense and generous patriotism of the people of Rhode Island—to their sagacious and provident concern for her best interests, and to their jealous love of her stainless honor. No man among us, affects to doubt that the electoral vote of Rhode Island will be given to Henry Clay and Theodore Frelinghuysen. All important, however, should it be deemed to obtain for the Clay electoral ticket, not only a decisive, but a commanding majority—a majority so triumphant that the enemies of law and order, whether at home or abroad, should, even in the event of Polk's election, be convinced that vain would be the effort to rear again in Rhode Island the bleared and tattered banner of rebellion against the Constitution and the laws.

I am haunted by no morbid fears of the election of Polk and Dallas. But even should that disaster fall upon the land, why should we quail? Standing firmly upon our principles, and trusting to our arms, if need be, to support them, who can harm us? Massachusetts and Connecticut will suffer, on the part of their people, no invasion of our rights—and even "the unterrified democracy" of New Hampshire will visit us with no blasts but those of calumny and reproach. New York will have enough to do to take care of her own agitators, without lending a helping hand to ours. Her Spartan Band and her Empire Club have been among us, once. They will not be found here, again!

In the midst of this hot strife for political power, one of the great parties hopes to coin some political capital for itself, by manufacturing sympathy for Thomas W. Dorr. Hence the numerous resolutions which denounce his imprisonment as an offence against the principles of American liberty—and which, in a style of most amusing exaggeration, put him forth before the country as an intrepid confessor of interdicted truth—as a persecuted patriot—as a sublime martyr in the cause of the people! In all these resolutions, my fellow citizens, however threatening may be their language, their is neither blood nor thunder! If Mr. Clay should be elected, we shall be sure to hear no more of them. Should Mr. Polk chance to be elected, we shall hear naught beside their echoes in the distance. The confessor, patriot, and martyr, might, for awhile, be cheered by tokens of sympathy—but these tokens would gradually diminish in number; and the demagogues of the day, after having used Dorr, would not hesitate ultimately to abandon him.

I repeat the assertion, that the friends of law and order in Rhode Island feel no desire that Thomas W. Dorr should be imprisoned for life. They entertain towards him no vindictive feelings, and now that the law has been signally vindicated by his conviction and imprisonment, they would sanction, with their approbation, any act of grace and pardon, touching his case, which the General Assembly, at its approaching session, may think proper to adopt. The people and government of Rhode Island have illustrated, in too many ways, their capacity to maintain their own rights, to be at all sensitive to the imputation, from whatever source it may come, that their mercy would be the dictate of their fears. The rabid partisans of Dorr confidently affirmed that the government dared not arrest him, and yet he was arrested by a single constable! They affirmed that the government dared not try, and could not convict him, and yet he was, under every circumstance favorable to impartiality, both tried and convicted! They affirmed, that the court dared not sentence him to the State Prison, and yet sentenced he was! They affirmed, last of all, that the government dared not execute the sentence of the law, and that if Dorr were incarcerated, the walls of our penitentiary would be prostrated, "without law and against law;" and yet, as we all know, the sentence of the law was executed upon the transgressor—and the walls of our penitentiary are yet standing! Upon what terms the Legislature will extend grace and pardon to Thomas W. Dorr, should be left to the Legislature to determine. Quite sure am I, that the General Assembly will yield, in this matter, nothing to clamor, either at home or abroad.

They will do nothing to compromise the safety, the rights, or the dignity of the State of Rhode Island. They will treat Thomas Wilson Dorr just as they would treat any other man who had rendered himself equally obnoxious to the penalty of the laws. They will make no pusillanimous and unjust exceptions in his favor; least of all will they make any severe exceptions which may operate against him. The law of the land pronounces him to be a guilty man, and as a guilty man will they deal with him. His "unconditional liberation," though it has become the watchword of demagogues abroad, and is demanded by mass meetings at home, is hardly to be expected. The General Assembly will not, I am persuaded, do any act, in this matter, which would wear the appearance of unusual severity, or of excessive caution. They will, on the contrary, take no action which would expose them to the charge, that they had sacrificed a great principle, and blasted, forever, the honor of the State, misled by the impulses of a weak compassion, or by the wish to propitiate any "multitude," however "vast!"

It may suit the purposes of unprincipled men to endeavor to create abroad a strong impression in favor of the character of Thomas W. Dorr, and a strong sympathy in the sufferings which he has brought upon himself. The people of Rhode Island, however, are not easily humbugged. They know the man—for they have had long and bitter experience of his propensities and capacities for mischief. They do not deny him the possession of respectable talents and more than respectable acquisitions—but these talents and acquisitions, they have ever lamented to observe, he has uniformly perverted to the purposes of the veriest demagogism. Under the direction of high principle, he might have been a useful and honored citizen—but he chose to become a regular hackney politician, a demagogue of the worst type, and to play a bold game for the spoils. He might have helped to elevate the character and to improve the condition of the masses; but betrayed by his wretched ambition, he has lived only to embitter their passions and to mislead their understandings. All this is known here at home, and the fact will one day be known abroad. He has sinned greatly, and with small temptation—he has suffered much himself from the consequences of his evil deeds, and those evil deeds have brought incalculable suffering upon others. When he comes to emerge from his prison house, it is to be hoped that, chastened by the experience of adversity, he will abandon the trade of a political agitator, and address himself to some occupation which may enable his fellow citizens to connect his name hereafter with some good service which he shall have done his native State.

What, fellow citizens, is now our most imperative duty? Is it not an immediate and effective organization of the friends of Law and Order throughout the State—an organization perfect in its details, and capable of reaching the most limited districts in every one of our towns? On the fourth day of November, only a month hence, the battle is to be fought in Rhode Island. Ought we not to prepare ourselves for the onset which awaits us? We can, if we but will to do it, give a majority of three thousand votes for Clay and Frelinghuysen. What good citizen, who values the peace, dignity and independence of Rhode Island, will shrink from any labor which may be needed, in such a cause, to achieve such a triumph?

A Rhode Island Man.

PROVIDENCE JOURNAL, OCTOBER 8, 1844.

RHODE ISLAND AFFAIRS.

NO. V.

To the People of Rhode Island:—

Fellow Citizens:—The Dorrite faction in this State, I need not tell you, has parted with none of its bitter hostility towards the constitution which you have established for the protection of life, liberty and property. Thomas Wilson Dorr, a convicted traitor, is still the idol of this faction; and the so called "people's constitution" is still its beau ideal of a republican form of government! If, in relation to this matter, any of you have been beguiled into a treacherous confidence, by the hollow professions of men who seek to make you their dupes, in order that you may become their victims, I ask you to read and ponder the memorial to both Houses of Congress adopted on the 28th ult., by "the Democratic Association of Glocester." This is, in truth, a most precious document! Considering where and by whom it was adopted, it may be deemed a pretty significant indication that the revolutionary spirit which has so fearfully disturbed the reign of the law in Rhode Island, needs nothing but a fit opportunity to renew its work of mischief. The hall of General Jedediah Sprague, in the village of Chepachet, and within sight of Acote, where Dorr mustered all his chivalry, was the spot chosen by the Democratic Association of Glocester, (Amasa Eddy, Dorr's Lieutenant Governor, being President, and Clovis H. Bowen, Secretary,) for the perpetration of a memorial, which, considered either as a statement of facts, or as a constitutional argument, challenges all competition. Henceforth, let the Dorrite members of the General Assembly hide their diminished heads! Their memorial to Congress will now sink into oblivion! Let Slocum, too, the venerable Slocum, surrender the claim, which he can no longer maintain, to be considered the last and most illustrious expounder of constitutional law! The Democratic Association of Glocester has surpassed them all!

These Glocester Dorrites place in the very front of their memorial the following clause of section fourth, article fourth, of the Constitution of the United States: "The United States shall guarantee to every State a republican form of government." It did not, however, suit their purposes quite as well to quote the remaining clause of the same section, viz.: "and shall protect each of them, on application of the Legislature, or of the Executive, when the Legislature cannot be convened, against domestic violence!" That I may escape all charge of mutilating a document which deserves no fleeting record, I subjoin the following extracts. They embrace all its essential parts, and they will serve to show you by what spirit the Dorrite faction continues to be animated, and what new aggressions it meditates upon the peace and constitutional rights of the people of Rhode Island:

"The undersigned aver that when the State of Rhode Island adopted the Constitution of the United States, the State had not a Republican form of Government, nor had it ever had, or been governed by, such a form of government, but the charter of Charles the second, one of the profligate Kings of England, emanating, not from the people of Rhode Island, but from the "Royal will and pleasure" of the said Charles the second, has continued to be the form of government of the people of Rhode Island aforesaid, until the adoption of the People's Constitution, in 1841. That soon after the adoption of the People's Constitution, by a majority of the People of Rhode Island, the minority, which had so long governed the State, by restricting the right of suffrage, and many other important rights to landholders, and their oldest sons, finding themselves about to be deprived of their monopoly of the political power of the State, and reduced to a level with their fellow citizens, refused to submit to the People's Constitution, and retaining in their hands the public stations, offices, revenues, and power of the State, declared the People's Constitution null and void;* hired and enlisted troops, procured

* The language of this memorial is adapted to leave on the public mind the false impression that the Charter of Charles II. is still the fundamental law of this State! The memorialists are at pains to abuse the old Charter, and the "minority" who put down the people's constitution, which as they say, was adopted by "fourteen thousand strong!" They take care, however, to withhold from the public the important fact, that the people of Rhode Island, in November, 1842, adopted a constitution which superseded the old Charter. Under this constitution, which equalized representation and made suffrage next to universal, the people of Rhode Island are now living; and this constitution they are resolved to maintain, until it shall be changed according to the mode provided in the chapter on amendments.

arms and ammunition from other States; declared the State under Martial Law; disarmed large portions of the militia of the State; searched and plundered houses, without warrants, dragged innocent men before military tribunals, and filled the prisons with them, took innocent and peaceful women from their domestic employment, insultingly dragged them before the courts, and indicted them for pretended offences; established a system of espionage, and committed other enormities unworthy of the pirates of Algiers, whose name of Algerines, by general consent, even among themselves, they have ever since borne.

"The undersigned further state, that the act declaring the State under Martial Law, although suspended, has not been repealed, but is at any time liable to be revived by the usurpers of the authority of the State; that troops are continually kept under arms and marched to and fro throughout the State, to watch, intimidate and overawe peaceful meetings of men, women and children, assembled to complain of their grievances, and to petition the government to redress them; and that bands of ruffian Carbineers have been hired from abroad, and commissioned to provoke the good people of this State to resentment, in order to afford a pretext for dispersing peaceful assemblies, and for further acts of rapine and brutal violence.

"The undersigned further state, that it would be useless, and worse than useless, to appeal for redress to any of the Courts now existing in this State. That no person, scarcely even a justice of the peace, is permitted to hold an office, unless he belongs to the Algerine party, and in all important trials for alleged crimes, juries are packed from the same party, and the friends of free suffrage are excluded from the panels.

"The undersigned further state, that they have no remedy for these intolerable acts of oppression, but to procure arms, and wrest from their oppressors the power which they so much abuse, at the hazard ot much bloodshed, or to call upon the United States to guarantee to them a Republican form of government, instead of the Despotism under which they now suffer. The former alternative, although it might perhaps afford the most speedy relief, is not in accordance with the peaceful principles which they love, and desire to cherish. They therefore call upon the Congress of the United States, who have had proofs of these grievances, to exert all the power they possess, to put an immediate end to them, and to afford all such means of redress, as may be within the scope of their power.

"Resolved, That this memorial be signed by the officers of this meeting, and published in all the papers of the State friendly to its objects; and that this meeting appeals to the people of the United States, in their individual capacity, and in their State and national organizations, in every branch of their government, and calls upon them to guarantee to the people of the State of Rhode Island the full benefit and protection to which, by the constitution of the United States, they are at all times entitled, and are now so fully justified in demanding.

"Resolved, That copies of this memorial be transmitted to the President of the United States, to both Houses of Congress, at their approaching session, and to the Governors of the several States; and that printed copies thereof be circulated for signatures throughout the State of Rhode Island."

In commenting upon this very remarkable document which comes from the hall (how chivalric the place!) of General Jedediah Sprague, to animate the courage of the faithful to renewed endeavors in behalf of "the people's constitution," it is somewhat difficult to preserve a tone of remark sufficiently grave. Who can read, without a disposition to merriment, not unmingled with contempt, the long list of "abuses and usurpations" which this memorial charges to the account of the Algerines of Rhode Island—coupled as this list is with the cool declaration, on the part of the memorialists, that a resort to arms for redress, "is not in accordance with the peaceful principles which they love and desire to cherish!" Have you, Glocester Dorrites, lost all sense of shame? If but a tithe of the allegations against the Algerines and the "despotism" which they have established be true, you ought to sound forthwith from the heights of Acote, a trumpet blast which would summon every man of the "fourteen thousand strong," to the work of stern and heroic resistance! If but a tithe of your allegations be true, it is no time to talk about your "peaceful principles." Congress, if it can be gulled into a belief of the statements in your memorial, will scorn the craven spirit which, under such circumstances of aggravated oppression, dictates any other appeal than an appeal to arms. If but a tithe of your allegations be true, not only will you provoke the ridicule and contempt of all honorable men but your very women will cry shame upon your manhood, for your twattle about your love for peace, while you complain of "intolerable acts of oppression!" Whence this new born reverence for "peaceful principles" on the part of the Acote chivalry? How long since were these same men assembled in the hall of this same General Jedediah, for a far different purpose—animated with a fierce revolutionary spirit, and ready to shed the blood of those of their fellow citizens who had resorted to arms in defence of the constitution and the laws? After such a development of character, it ill becomes them to prate about "the peaceful principles which they love, and desire to cherish!"

It has been reserved for the Glocester Democratic Association, for Amasa Eddy, Clovis H. Bowen and others of a like calibre, to make the discovery that Rhode Island, when she adopted the Constitution of the United States, "had not a republican form of government!" The old Charter not republican, and yet it was under the old Charter, that Rhode Island adopted the constitution which provides that the United States shall guarantee to every State a republican form of government! If our government was not republican, then, why did not our sister States make the discovery, and why was not the constitutional guarantee then enforced? The old Charter not republican, under which our Senators and Representatives in Congress have for more than fifty years been chosen—and under which, for a term of more than forty years, the democratic party wielded the political power of Rhode Island! The Glocester Democratic Association is wiser in its day, than was Alexander Hamilton in his. This great master in political science asserts that "the essential criteria of a government purely republican, are that the principal organs of the executive and legislative departments shall be elected by the people, and hold their offices by a responsible and temporary or defeasible tenure." Was the old Charter wanting in any one of these essential criteria of a government purely republican? Were not the organs of the executive and legislative departments elected by the people, and responsible to the people? The whole matter is too plain for argument.

What is the true design of the constitutional guarantee of a republican form of government, which the Glocester Democratic Association now supplicates Congress to execute in behalf of the "People's Constitution?" Is it not intended to protect the Union itself from danger, by guaranteeing to all the States the republican form of government under which they entered the Union? Other confederated governments have comprised States differing from each other in the form of their government—some retaining monarchical and some aristocratic elements. This diversity is always a source of discord, and, under our system, would be fatal. Suppose, for example, that "the Empire State," with her central position, and her three millions of people, should adopt a monarchical form of government, her sister States would find it hard to resist her power. The Union itself, and that glorious constitution under which it was perfected, could not contend against so fearful an element of discord. The constitution, therefore, guarantees to every State a republican form of government, not only to preserve, in an essential matter, uniformity and harmony among the States, but likewise to secure the Union itself against the dangers to which the adoption by any of the States of a form of government, in any wise monarchical or aristocratic, would inevitably expose it.

The Glocester Democratic Association is not content with slandering the people and institutions of Rhode Island. It appeals "to the people of the United States in their individual capacity, and in their State and National organizations, in every branch of their government," and calls upon them to interpose their power, for the destruction of the constitution which you, my fellow citizens, have established. This appeal is in harmony with the appeal once made by Dorr himself. It is in harmony too with the appeal made by the "vast multitude" who assembled in this city on Commencement day, for the purpose of overawing you. Such appeals are disorganizing in the extreme. Do not fear, however, that they will be heeded. What right have "the people of the United States in their individual capacity" to interfere with "the internal police and government of Rhode Island?" What right have "the people of the United States in their State and National organizations," to interfere in a matter which Rhode Island, when she joined the Union, expressly reserved to herself? Let these men invoke, if they please, the power of the mob to crush us—for that is, in effect, the purpose of their memorial. We have naught to fear. We have RIGHT on our side—and we shall not, in the hour of trial, be found wanting in courage to maintain the RIGHT. The mob at home, we have, once and again, suppressed. We are prepared, and we mean to keep ourselves prepared, to resist, successfully, the assaults of any MOB which may be summoned to come upon us from ABROAD!

A RHODE ISLAND MAN.

PROVIDENCE JOURNAL, OCTOBER 21, 1844.

RHODE ISLAND AFFAIRS.

NO. VI.

To the People of Rhode Island:—

Fellow Citizens:—On Monday the 4th day of November, only one fortnight from this day, you will decide, at the ballot box, so far as your votes can affect the decision, some of the most momentous public questions which have ever agitated our country. Shall the tariff remain as it is? Shall the proceeds of the sales of the public lands be distributed among the several States? Shall the Union remain as it is, or shall its borders be extended, at the risk of provoking a sanguinary and expensive war, for the purpose of perpetuating the curse of slavery? Shall the Constitutions which, at any time exist, be held "sacredly obligatory upon all, till changed by an explicit and authentic act of the whole people;" or shall they, in accommodation to the revolutionary doctrines of the hour, be overthrown, by "vast multitudes," acting "without law and against law?" These are among the great issues which you, men of Rhode Island, are about to decide for yourselves, and which it deeply concerns your dearest interests to decide aright. The doctrines of the Dorrite faction, in relation to the mode of changing existing constitutions, it would now seem, are not distinctly placed by the partisans of Polk and Dallas, among the great issues which they address to the whole country. The Baltimore Democratic Convention shied these doctrines—knowing that, south of Mason and Dixon's line, such doctrines would find no favor; that, if carried out, they would prove fatal, not only to the constitutions of the Slave States—but to the whole order of society in those States. The Rhode Island question is, therefore, made an issue, where, and only where, it may be expected to gain support for Polk and Dallas. On that question, however, let us not forget, that these candidates are designedly left to occupy a position of convenient ambiguity. Henry Clay and Theodore Frelinghuysen, stand before the country the avowed and decided champions of the true principles of constitutional freedom. Polk and Dallas are the favorite candidates of the Dorrite faction in this State, and of those in other States who openly espouse the cause of that faction. Their election, therefore, would be hailed by the Dorrites, at home and abroad, as a triumph over those principles of Law and Order, which Clay and Frelinghuysen, in common with all conservative statesmen, are pledged to maintain. I do not affect to believe that, even in the event of Mr. Polk's election, the friends of liberty and law in Rhode Island, would be conquered. While they remain true to themselves, and true to their principles—they can never be conquered! Most disastrous, however, to our peace and to our prosperity, would be the election of the favorite candidate of the Dorrites. It would fill them with false hopes—it would encourage them to renew and to continue, with fresh zeal, the work of agitation. It would, in various ways, summon us to the exercise of vigilance, activity and courage—it would demand heavy draughts upon the resources of the State, in order to maintain the public peace—it would, to an extent which cannot well be foreseen, interrupt the business of every class of our citizens, and impair confidence, especially abroad, in the stability of all our institutions. We, then, who are friends of Law and Order in Rhode Island, are, in some sort, compelled to regard the Rhode Island question as among the great political questions of the day. Let us, then, by our votes, on the first Monday of November, give, to each other and to the whole country, another and an unequivocal pledge, that we mean, in any event, to stand firmly upon our principles—in other words, that we are resolved to maintain our existing constitution "until it is changed by an explicit and authentic act of the whole people."

Protection to American labor has become the policy of the government. Rhode Island is deeply interested in the preservation of that policy against the insidious efforts now making to overthrow it. Mr. Polk is avowedly hostile to the tariff as it is. He was nominated, in contempt of all the usages of the Democratic party, through the influence of a faction, which is bent upon the destruction of the protective policy; and which deems slavery to be the great conservative element of our free institutions! Messrs. Clay and Frelinghuysen were nominated, almost by acclamation, by a great party which regards protection to American labor as essential to the prosperity and independence of the whole country. It has hitherto been thus regarded by all parties in Rhode Island, and I cannot perceive upon what principle any Rhode Island Democrat can now be reconciled to the support of a candidate for the Presidency, who is avowedly hostile to the great interests of Rhode Island! Immense evil would result to the country, even from an attempt to modify the tariff. Such an attempt would beget distrust as to the policy of the government; and, if perchance successful, it would be the parent of most disastrous fluctuations in the business of the country.

In a just distribution of the proceeds of the sales of the public lands, no State is more deeply interested than Rhode Island. She has, within a few years, commenced the great work of providing for all, at the public expense, the means of Education. In the prosecution of this great work, she is resolved to persevere. Nothing is needed to secure its triumphant accomplishment, but adequate pecuniary resources. Give us, my fellow citizens, our fair proportion of that magnificent national domain, which our fathers helped to conquer, or which we have been taxed to pay for, and, in a very short time, we can establish in every one of our towns, a system of free school instruction, which, for efficiency, would be without a parallel in New England. This is a matter which comes home to the business and bosom of every man in Rhode Island. Every man among us, whether he have children or whether he have none, is vitally concerned in the improvement and extension of our system of free schools.

We have now got free suffrage—but let us remember that free suffrage, without free schools, will prove a bane, and not a blessing! This is the doctrine—the settled belief—the clear conviction of thinking men of all parties. Would it not be well, therefore, for thinking men of all parties among us to consider how far this great Rhode Island interest may be affected by the votes which they will give, in the choice of Electors, on the first Monday of November next. Clay and Frelinghuysen are in favor of Distribution—Polk and Dallas are against it! Every Rhode Island man who votes for the Dorrite Electors, votes, in effect, to deprive his own children, or the children of his neighbors and fellow citizens, of those "advantages and opportunities of education" which our Constitution makes it the duty of the General Assembly to secure to the people.

You, my fellow citizens, are exhorted by the revolutionary party in this State, to swallow "Polk, Dallas and Dorr"—and to consider them a sweet morsel! But this is not all. The same revolutionary party insists that you shall swallow, at the same time, Texas and Slavery! Can any of you be persuaded, to take, without loathing, these bitter potions? Must you be asked to vote not only for Polk and Dallas, who, upon all questions affecting Rhode Island interests, are adverse to Rhode Island interests—but, in effect, to vote also for Thomas W. Dorr, who, for the gratification of a pitiful personal ambition, has subjected you to such sore trials? How can any Rhode Island man, who loves freedom, and who reveres his ancestors for the heroic sacrifices which they made in the cause of freedom, how can such Rhode Island man give his voice for James K. Polk, selected as he was, mainly because he is in favor of the annexation of Texas, as the great means of extending and perpetuating the curse of Slavery! We hear much, now a days, from the Dorrites, about the "principles of American liberty"—"the doctrines of the Declaration of American Independence," "equal rights," &c.,—and yet these very men, with rare consistency, are straining every nerve in the cause of a man, who, should he chance to be elected, would foster upon millions of his fellow men, guilty of a skin not colored like his own, the fetters of a cruel, ignominious and hopeless servitude?

Looking calmly at the result of the recent State elections, we are justified, my fellow citizens, in entertaining a strong and exhilarating confidence in the triumph of Clay and Frelinghuysen. Let, however, no man who is a friend to these noble champions of the rights and interests of Rhode Island, be betrayed, by this confidence, into supineness and indifference. No one affects to doubt that Rhode Island will give her voice for Clay and Frelinghuysen. With adequate efforts, with a thorough organization—an overwhelming majority may be obtained, on the first Monday of November, for the Clay Electoral ticket. Without adequate effort—without a thorough organization, the result may be—not defeat—for defeat is not anticipated—but a reduced law and order majority! This would be claimed by the Dorrites, at home and abroad, as proof positive that the people of Rhode Island were beginning to look with more favor upon those revolutionary doctrines which have cost them so many sacrifices—and upon which they have, again and again, placed the seal of their indignant reprobation. If every friend to Henry Clay does his duty, the Dorrites will be left without a pretext thus to defame us.

A Rhode Island Man.

PROVIDENCE JOURNAL, NOVEMBER 18, 1844.

RHODE ISLAND AFFAIRS.

NO. VII.

To the People of Rhode Island:—

Fellow Citizens:—The great struggle is over. The spasm has been succeeded by a collapse; and the victors who but yesterday stood upon the field of battle, clad in armor, and full of fight, now repose upon their laurels, and coolly calculate the value of "the spoils!" Contrary to all rational expectations of the result, Henry Clay has been defeated. The true sense of the true people has, most unequivocally and emphatically, declared itself to be in favor of the man, and of the principles and measures which he stood pledged to maintain. To the stupendous, the unparalleled, the undeniable frauds upon the elective franchise, in the States of New York and Pennsylvania, and to the fanatical perversity of political abolitionism, must we look for the efficient causes which have defeated the election of Henry Clay. His political life is ended! The brilliant reward which a decided majority of those of his countrymen, who have a common interest in the welfare and the institutions of the United States, would have conferred upon him, has been intercepted by "interlopers" who are strangers to our soil and to the principles of our government. These interlopers, manufactured into American citizens for the occasion, would have voted for the Siamese twins, as readily as they voted for Polk and Dallas, had the Siamese twins been proclaimed as the nominees of the Baltimore Democratic Convention. What a mockery of the elective franchise! What a commentary upon the virtue and intelligence of the people! What a manifestation of the capacity of man for self government!

The political career of Henry Clay is ended! Amid the shades of Ashland will now be passed the remnant of a life which has been devoted to the service of his country, and which has been illustrated by more brilliant and commanding qualities than have graced the character of any American Statesman, since the days of Alexander Hamilton. The office of President of these United States could not have added a single cubit to the stature of Henry Clay. Patriotism may sorrow that the just reward of illustrious service has been fraudulently snatched from him; but let patriotism console itself by the thought that neither fraud, nor folly, nor calumny can cast an envious shadow upon his fame and character. What Henry Clay has said and done, during a long, eventful and despite of every reverse, brilliant political career, now awaits the impartial judgment of history. From history, what has he to fear? While he lives, however, he can never become obscure. As his life passes on, tributes of grateful and disinterested homage will flow in upon the retired servant of the State. While he lives, too, he can never become unmindful of his country. From the seclusion of Ashland, he will look, with patriotic solicitude, upon strifes of parties in which he is no more to mingle, and upon that Senate, the field of many noble contests for the right, in which he is never again to lift up his eloquent voice. Had Mr. Clay, fellow citizens, been the successful candidate for the Presidency, I should have been among the last to fling this fleeting tribute to the gale. Under existing circumstances, if delicacy would restrain me from saying more, neither gratitude nor justice would permit me to say less.

"Let others hail the rising sun,
I bow to that whose race is run."

Fellow Citizens, the friends of law and order in Rhode Island have no reason to despair of their cause, because Mr. Clay has been defeated. What have we to fear from external pressure? Let facts, stubborn facts, answer the question. What response does Connecticut make to the appeals of our Rhode Island disorganizers? An increased majority in favor of the principles of law and order! And what is the response of glorious old Massachusetts to like appeals? An overwhelming majority for the principles of law and order! In both of these States, the Dorr question was made an issue. In both of these States it has been examined, and the result shows how it is understood. George Bancroft, who demands the unconditional release of Dorr, and who once harangued, in a somewhat ferocious spirit, an indignation Dorr meeting in Boston, has been defeated as a candidate for the office of Governor of Massachusetts, by a large majority! Benjamin F. Hallett, too, one of the busiest and most mischievous meddlers in our affairs, who was a candidate for Congress in Massachusetts, has likewise been defeated by a large majority! Let it likewise be remarked, that, in the adjoining county of Bristol, where the seeds of Dorrism had been sown broadcast, the radical candidate for Congress and the radical candidates for State Senators were defeated! Even in Taunton, the home of ex-Governor Morton, of "Clam Bake and Mass Meeting" memory, where Dorrism had been preached in the highways and by-ways, even there, was it destined to experience an unexpected and most mortifying rebuke!

We have no reason, fellow citizens, to think that, beyond the limits of Rhode Island, Massachusetts and Connecticut, the Rhode Island question was, to any extent, made an issue in the Presidential election; or that it produced, out of these States, any appreciable influence upon the result. In this connexion it may not be amiss to call public attention to the fact, that, in the city of Rochester, N. Y., the Clay electors prevailed by an increased majority over the majority for Harrison in 1840; and yet, very recently, in this very city of Rochester was held an indignation meeting, which in a paroxysm of futile anger, proscribed all the Banks and all the manufactures of Rhode Island!

Mr. Polk, whatever may be his opinions and sympathies, and it remains to be proved that they are with the Dorrites, will be harrassed by too many troubles of his own to mix himself with ours. He will come into office at the head of a party, composed of the most discordant materials—at the head of a party which, quarrels about the spoils and about the succession are inevitably destined to distract. The minority, too, if a minority the Whig party can rightfully be called, are too powerful in numbers, and in talent, not to possess efficient means of modifying, on all great questions, the policy of the national administration. It must however, be confessed, that Mr. Polk's election has wonderfully exhilarated the spirits, and increased the activity of the Dorrites. In every nook and corner of Rhode Island, they are busy in the work of preparation for the April election. More lively are they than the snakes, which, after a frost bound winter, come abroad, under the influence of vernal suns, to take their fitting place in the grass of our meadows and pastures. The comparison ends not here. They combine with the activity of serpents, the cunning of serpents. To the moderate they will preach moderation;—to the violent, they will preach violence;—they will introduce new issues, and they will mask old ones; they will strive to seduce some by professions of peace; some, by hopes of plunder; and some, by promises of revenge. Whatever shape they may put on, it will, after all, be no questionable shape! They are about to contend, with all their might, for the political power of this city, and for the political power of this State. If, however, the friends of Law and Order continue true to themselves and to their principles, the Dorrites can never triumph;—they can never elevate their leader to a high place;—they can never establish the People's Constitution; they can never make the Judges of our Supreme Court the victims of popular vengeance; they can never so far extend suffrage, as to place, in all time to come, the whole political power of this city and of this State in the hands of the worst demagogues of the day!

All these great mischiefs, my fellow citizens, by seasonable and efficient effort it is in your power to avert. The duty of registering, before the close of the present month, the name of every friend to law and order, not already registered, demands immediate attention. Do not neglect this duty for another day. Let not a town, or village, or neighborhood, or shop, or manufactory, or farm house, be overlooked, in the performance of a duty which may be essential to our success at the election in April.

Rhode Island, my fellow citizens, has won, by her manly defence of the principles of Law and Order, a reputation which she may safely commit to the judgment of history. Be it our care, that her just fame is kept unsullied. Be it our care, that the State which we so much love, shall never be dishonored. We have passed through too many seasons of sore trial, to be disheartened by trivial reverses. Once, our nearest neighbors, Massachusetts and Connecticut, were against us. Now, they are with us. Once, we were without confidence in our own ability to repress the violence of the revolutionary spirit. Now, we can trust to the sound heads and to the strong right arms of our people, the defence of the laws and Constitution of the State. Let us, then, with a cheerful spirit, buckle on our armor for the Spring campaign—resolved that, whoever may be President, and whoever may assault us—we will preserve Law and Order in Rhode Island—and, if need be, that we will preserve them at any and at every cost.

A RHODE ISLAND MAN.

PROVIDENCE JOURNAL, JANUARY 14, 1845.

RHODE ISLAND AFFAIRS.

NO. VIII.—AND LAST.

TO THE PEOPLE OF RHODE ISLAND:—

FELLOW CITIZENS:—In terminating this series of remarks upon the political affairs of Rhode Island, I cannot forbear from inviting your attention to a few topics, which, at this time, would seem to deserve some consideration.

The partisans of Thomas W. Dorr are most industrious in their efforts to propagate the belief that popular sympathy in behalf of "the martyr," is daily becoming more active and more widely diffused. To sustain their bold assumptions, they appeal to the result of the Presidential election, as conclusive evidence that the people of the United States have passed upon all the matters involved in the Rhode Island controversy, and have rendered a solemn verdict against both the government and the people of Rhode Island. Is there not in all these assumptions an egregious fallacy? A Convention of Mr. Dorr's partisans formally commended his cause to the Baltimore Democratic Convention. That Convention heeded not what was meant to be a fraternal appeal for sympathy and for succor. That Convention tacitly refused to make the Rhode Island question one of the issues in the contest for the Presidency! What else could be anticipated? How could Virginia, the Carolinas, Georgia, and indeed any slave State, adopt principles which, if practically illustrated within their own borders, would sweep their cities and plantations with the besom of destruction? In New England, if any where, the Rhode Island question is understood. What indication of an increasing sympathy for Mr. Dorr is furnished by the commanding majorities which were given for Mr. Clay by Rhode Island, Massachusetts, Connecticut and Vermont? The vote of New York, and the vote of Pennsylvania decided the great contest in favor of Mr. Polk. No honest and intelligent man affects to believe, that the agitation of the Rhode Island question made any appreciable difference in the votes of those great States. The truth is, the Dorrites are sadly mortified that the election of Mr. Polk has worked no material change in favor of their champion. At the first moment of triumph they seemed to think that torrents of indignation would overwhelm "the Algerines," and that tides of warm and genial sympathy would flow in upon "the martyr," from the hearts and the homes of the wide spread democracy of the land! The fact has proved to be otherwise. Here and there, a spark of sympathy for Mr. Dorr has been kindled. A "barn burner," has introduced into the Legislature of New York a series of resolutions in relation to Dorr and his principles. These resolutions are probably designed to rebuke the ominous silence which Governor Wright, in his message, preserves towards the quondam correspondent and friend of Senator Wright! Illinois, too, who admits unnaturalized foreigners to vote, and who repudiates her honest debts, has been guilty of a grave impertinence in meddling with the domestic affairs of Rhode Island. Is it strange, that Illinois, going as she does for the largest liberty of the "sovereignty," in more respects than one, should come out for Dorr and for Dorrism? In New Hampshire, however, is to be found the only living fountain of Dorrite sympathy. That spaniel State, always true to her instincts, at one moment barks at the heels of Rhode Island, and at another crouches, in wretched servility, at the feet of those of her sister States who can reward her fawning with thrift. Shame upon her! She has stained her ancient renown, and deserves not to be numbered among the free States of New England. To finish this topic, somewhat abruptly; in the language of the New York Evening Post, a paper which has always manifested sympathy for Dorr, "the [Presidential] election has decided that the administration shall be in democratic hands, and it has decided nothing else."

We hear, now-a-days, my fellow citizens, much captivating declamation about "the power of the people," and "the majesty of the people." How are these phrases to be understood? Taken in one sense, they embody great and acknowledged fundamental truths in the science of free government. Taken in another sense, they embody the most mischievous heresies, heresies which, if once carried out into practice, would destroy every vestige of constitutional freedom in the land. I acknowledge and I reverence the majesty of the people when, to secure their rights, the people institute governments, and when, to escape intolerable oppressions, they overthrow them! I acknowledge and I reverence the majesty of the people, when the people speak and act through the regular constitutional organs which they have established—through the ballot box, through the people's Executive, the people's Legislature, and the people's judges and juries! I acknowledge and I reverence "the sovereign law, the State's collected will." This, and this only, is genuine republicanism. The majesty of the people, viewed in any other light, is naught but rank jacobinism—leading directly to the sovereignty of the mob, and the destruction of all those checks and balances which are the boast and the support of our systems of regulated American liberty. A pregnant illustration of the jacobin tendencies of the times is to be found in that resolution appended to Burke's report on the Rhode Island question, which denounces the conduct of John Pitman, Richard W. Greene, and other citizens of Rhode Island, for their noble efforts to sustain the government of Rhode Island against an armed mob of ruffians, headed by Thomas Wilson Dorr. A similar outrage to this upon the most sacred rights of individuals, would not be attempted in our fatherland. It would make the blood of every Englishman tingle in his veins, at an infamous attempt to deprive him of the sacred immunities thrown around him by the great charters of English liberty. What concern has a committee of the House of Representatives with Judge Pitman? What concern has a majority of that House with Judge Pitman, unless they deem him deserving of impeachment? What concern has a committee of that House, or even a majority of that House, with Richard W. Greene, or any other United States officer, appointed by the Executive, and removable at the pleasure of the Executive? If Judge Pitman has done aught worthy of impeachment, why let him be impeached, and tried acccording to the forms which the Constitution provides.

If he has violated any law, let him be held to answer before a Court and jury, competent to try him. If Mr. Greene, as a United States officer, has done aught worthy of removal, it is the duty and it is the exclusive province of the President to remove him. If he has violated any law of the land, why then let him be tried according to the law of the land. This atrocious outrage upon the most sacred rights of individuals is in exact accordance with the modern notions of "the majesty of the people." In the better days of the Republic, no man could have been found, even in New Hampshire, to offer to the American Congress a resolution so replete with the genuine spirit of Jacobinism—a resolution which, should it be adopted, ought, at once to summon every State in this Union to the defence, the indignant defence, of the rights of its citizens against the usurpations of a political majority in Congress, acting in defiance of all constitutions and all law!

In these days of political degeneracy, my fellow citizens, the very genius of our government seems to be misunderstood. The sages who formed the American Constitution established not a Democracy—but a Representative Republic. You may see from the whole structure of the government how solicitous they were to protect the liberties of individuals and the rights of the States against those tendencies to misrule and oppression which are incident to all Democracies—and which, when the unmitigated despotism of king numbers has become intolerable, are sure to develop themselves in the despotism of a single man. Entertaining this salutary jealousy of Democracy and this ardent desire to preserve the rights of the States—they constituted the two Houses of Congress upon different principles; and they assigned to each State, without reference to its population or territorial extent, an equal vote in the Senate. They moreover established an executive department and a judicial department, and clothed them with such powers, as seemed fitted to render them effectual checks upon that branch of the government most alive to democratic impulses, and, therefore, most likely to oppress individuals and minorities.

In the days of Jefferson and Madison, the term Democrat was disowned as a term of reproach, by every intelligent partisan of those distinguished political leaders. From the Constitution of the United States, the words Democrat and Democracy were carefully excluded; and they are not to be found in a single State Constitution, throughout the length and breadth of this confederated Republic. The people of Missouri, with admirable propriety, expressly designate their government as "a free and independent republic." Would it not be well for the people of this country to go back to old fashioned republican doctrines, and to resist even the modern corruptions of the purity of our mother tongue?* Our fathers repudiated democracy, and went for republicanism, and for nothing but republicanism. They were careful of the liberties of the people, but they never dishonored themselves by pandering to the worst passions of the masses!

In the providence of God, my fellow citizens, the sacred cause of Law and Order has been committed to the people of Rhode Island. Thus far, they have well guarded and well defended the sacred deposit. In the contest which awaits us, and which demands our full and our united strength, we shall, I trust, be found to have parted with no portion of our enthusiasm, courage, and firmness, in support of a great and noble cause. We are about to meet the same enemy, and to contend with him for the same issues. Suffer yourselves not to be diverted from the great concern by mixed and subordinate questions. Who is the more illustrious expounder of constitutional law, Treadwell or Slocum? Which is the genuine Dorr Liberation stock? Was Mr. Dorr a good boy or a naughty boy at Cambridge college? Shall he be liberated with conditions or without conditions? These, my fellow citizens, are, comparatively speaking, all frivolous

* The demagogues of the day, in violation of all philological propriety, now speak of the people as "the masses."

issues. They are not the issues which you are to decide at the ballot box on the first Wednesday in April. By your votes on that day, you will determine questions of transcendent importance to yourselves and to your children. By your votes on that day, you will determine whether the constitution which you have established shall be sustained, or whether, by a summary and revolutionary process, it shall be destroyed; in other words, whether or not Dorr and Dorrism shall mount in triumph over the prostrate cause of Law and Order! This is the true and the grand issue; and you will, I trust, never suffer any man or any set of men, under any pretence, to withdraw you from that issue, or to blind you to the disastrous consequences which defeat would inevitably entail upon all the social interests and political institutions of Rhode Island.

Fellow Citizens:—The pen which "a Rhode Island Man" has, for so many years, wielded in the discussion of "Rhode Island affairs," must now be laid aside, perchance forever. I resign it, leaving no personal griefs unredressed, and harboring no private or political resentments. I resign it, too, with a conviction, which no man can take from me, that I have employed it not to flatter the people, not to advance the political fortunes of any individual, or to subserve any transient interests; but, to the best of my humble ability, to maintain those great conservative principles which it concerns equally, and at all times, every man and every political party to uphold and to defend.

A RHODE ISLAND MAN.

PROVIDENCE JOURNAL, NOVEMBER 28, 1844.

TO THE HON. GEORGE M. DALLAS, VICE-PRESIDENT ELECT OF THE UNITED STATES.

SIR:—You inherit a brilliant name, and you have achieved what in the early days of the republic would have been deemed a brilliant destiny. In those early and uncorrupt days, elevation to high place was not purchased at the expense of the noblest distinctions of individual character. It did not expose to peril all that constitutes the true dignity of a statesman and a gentleman. It was reached by none of the poor artifices of the demagogue. It was sought to be maintained by no avowal of the sympathies and the principles of the jacobin. High place, sir, was then the reward of signal ability, of meritorious service, of a generous love for the true glory of the country, of unswerving attachment to principles which change not as the times change. You are too familiar with the past political history of the United States, and with the degraded and degrading politics of the present times, not to perceive, and, in those better moods, which, I trust, sometimes visit you, not to lament, the sad decline of that manly and virtuous statesmanship which distinguished the administrations of Washington and the elder Adams. Your own success as a politician, I fear, may have gone far to reconcile you to the evil times on which we have fallen, and to make you look, in a spirit of gentle toleration, upon those false standards by which the people are now accustomed to try the merits of public men. A single phrase in your letter signifying your acceptance of the nomination tendered to you by the Baltimore Democratic Convention, is quite sufficient to enable your countrymen to gauge your capacity for the higher duties of an American statesman. In this letter, you are at pains to captivate the masses, by assuring them, in a somewhat lover like tone, how tenderly alive you are to "the genial sympathies of democracy!" The genial sympathies of Democracy! What language for a republican statesman to address to a republican people! In the days of Washington and Adams, and even in still later days, what public man would not have blushed to use such twattle? In the days of Washington and Adams, with what scorn would the American people have treated such experiments upon their credulity?

My business, however, is not with your foolish letter, but with that worse than foolish speech, which, after your election was ascertained, you addressed to the crowd which gathered around your splendid mansion in Walnut street, to interchange with you "the genial sympathies of democracy." The Philadelphia Public Ledger states that Mr. Dallas made this speech at "the door way." Will not history add to this record, and with a deep meaning,—Mr. Dallas, in making such a speech, stumbled at the threshold!

Had you, sir, in your address to your political

friends assembled in Walnut street, confined yourself to topics connected with your recent political triumph, I for one would have pardoned to the intoxication of success any violation of good taste, into which, in the presence of such an audience, even so urbane a gentleman as yourself might have been betrayed. You have, however, travelled out of the record to calumniate Rhode Island, and the people of Rhode Island, and to exalt a man who has spent his whole political life in efforts to aggrandize himself, reckless all the while what might be the cost of his selfish triumph to his native State. On the occasion to which I have referred, it is stated by a correspondent of the Republican Herald, that you "went on to speak nearly as follows:"

"Governor Dorr! It gives me great pleasure to be able to speak a word for that good man who has suffered so much in the cause of the people of his country. Since the formation of our government, the present is the first time that any State has disgraced the Union by the imprisonment of a man for his political opinions; and although I will not speak in harsh terms of the general action of the opposing political party, I cannot in this instance withhold from denouncing, in the most emphatic terms, the cruel conduct of the ruling party in Rhode Island, in relation to their treatment of Mr. Dorr. And I hope and trust that the day is near at hand when the mighty voice of universal indignation will be heard in such terms, as will break asunder the bars and bolts of his prison house, and set the noble patriot free."

All this, sir, is clearly gratuitous on your part. You have gone out of your way, to lend the weight of your moral influence as Vice President elect of the United States, to a popular movement in this State, which was, throughout, a revolutionary movement—revolutionary in its impulses and in its principles—revolutionary in means and in ends. Whatever may be the artificial importance which attaches to your opinions, in consequence of your commanding position, you will utterly fail in this profligate attempt to enlist sympathy for the cause of jacobinism in Rhode Island, and to concentrate upon this gallant little State the indignation of a great and victorious party. The South, sir, the South, destined, in all future time, to determine the succession, and to regulate the policy of the government, never will go with you in the support of doctrines which, if carried out, would prostrate in utter ruin her whole social order. Nay, more. The cool, reflecting people of the free States, who know how to distinguish licentiousness from democracy, will never embark with you in a crusade against those well settled principles of constitutional law which lie at the foundation of all constitutional freedom. Pennsylvania herself, drugged as she now is by all the opiates of party, will be slow to recognize any theories, however plausible, which would subject her Constitution to the chances of being altered "without law and against law." She means to maintain her position as the "Keystone State," and she knows full well that, whensoever the doctrines broached by Thomas Wilson Dorr come to be regarded as the true doctrines of popular sovereignty in this country, the broad arch of republican empire, which she is proud to uphold, will fall, at once, in shapeless ruins.

Let me tell you, sir, that you have drawn upon

your imagination for your facts. Mr. Dorr is not imprisoned for his political opinions. He is imprisoned for the highest crime known to the laws, for a crime which seldom fails to involve murder, rape, arson and robbery. He is imprisoned, not for his theories, but for his practice—not for his thoughts, but for his acts. That he was guilty of the offense of which he stood charged, was proved by plenary testimony, and by his own confessions in open Court. After a trial by a Court and Jury, upon which no charge of partiality has been fastened, he was convicted. He is now undergoing the sentence which the law annexes to the crime of which he was proved to be guilty. What evidence of cruelty, sir, do you discover in all this? And as an American statesman, as a constitutional lawyer, upon what principle do you take it upon yourself to denounce as cruel the whole action of the legally constituted tribunals of a free and sovereign State? After your recent experience in Philadelphia, do you think it either wise or safe thus to appeal from the decision of courts and juries to the passions of the mob?

Mr. Dorr, sir, has never suffered the penalty of a single hour's imprisonment, for "his political opinions." This fact you knew, or ought to have known. Admitting, however, that we had punished him for opinions and not for acts—with how ill a grace could you, a citizen of Philadelphia, reproach the people of Rhode Island! The conflagration of Pennsylvania Hall is not forgotten. The sovereign mob could not tolerate the opinions there advanced by the Abolitionists; they applied the torch—and that beautiful structure fell in ruins! This event alone should have admonished you to withhold the unjust reproach which you have cast upon Rhode Island. But this is not all. Philadelphia furnishes a more recent and fearful example of punishment for the sake of opinion. The mob which, under impulses derived in part from the teachings of gentlemen jacobins, recently reigned triumphant in your streets, spared not even the temples of the living God! They were exasperated against the persons of the Roman Catholics—they were stimulated to a hatred of their opinions—and they accordingly burnt down their churches! These vindictive punishments, and all, too, for the sake of opinion, were inflicted by a Philadelphia mob; and yet a Philadelphia lawyer, the Vice President elect of the United States, takes especial pains to magnify the leader of the armed mob which well nigh overturned the government of Rhode Island! and, either ignorantly or perversely, affirms that we the people of Rhode Island have imprisoned Mr. Dorr for "his political opinions!"

A word more, and I have done. Can it be possible that, thus early, you are dreaming of the succession? Do you seek to anticipate your rivals by striking, so long in advance, for the lowest stratum of democracy? If this be your end and aim, your ambition will o'erleap itself. The people of the United States are not yet prepared to open upon the land the floodgates of jacobinism. They are not yet prepared to withdraw their habitual reverence for laws and for constitutions, and to adopt those extreme and dangerous notions of popular sovereignty, which, in effect, would convert our republican government into a wild and licentious democracy—hostile to all temperate freedom—and destined inevitably to end in an iron despotism.

A Rhode Island Man.

PROVIDENCE JOURNAL, FEBRUARY 28, 1845.

CONGRESS.

Another Session of Congress will close in a few days. The fate of the Texas resolutions in the Senate is still doubtful. The Senate won immortal honor by its firm and noble stand against executive power in the person of the Hero of New Orleans. It has now an opportunity to achieve still higher renown, by protecting the Union of the States, the integrity of the Constitution, and the National Honor, against the combined assaults of a clamorous multitude usurping the name of the people, of a weak Executive preferring the applause of the ignorant and foolish in the present, to the approval of the wise and good in coming time, of a Popular Assembly, whose proceedings if not arrested will speedily bring into disgrace the very name of legislation. Even if this is too much to hope, it will be a source of pride to reflect that the Whig Senators almost without exception maintain their conservative and dignified position. From the debates in the House there seems to be some hope that the Postage Bill of the Senate will become a law. Beyond this there does not seem to be any apprehension that the present session of Congress will accomplish any wise or useful object. It seems to be entirely forgotten by these gentlemen that according to the theory of a free government they are selected from among the body of the people, on account of their superior wisdom and virtue, to take care "that the Republic receive no detriment," that they are sent to Washington to make good laws for the government of the people who send them there. On the contrary they seem to be under the impression that their principal business is, to interfere with the negotiations of the Executive department by passing laws for the government of the territory beyond the Rocky Mountains,—to trample on the treaty making power and extend "the patriarchal institutions of Slavery," and "the harmony of Democratic instincts" to the Isthmus of Darien. To furnish the people with a cheap and convenient means of transmitting intelligence from one part of the country to another—to repay to private citizens the money which the government has received from France, and "fraudulently converted to its own use"—to make an appropriation to procure decent furniture for the Presidential mansion, are objects altogether beneath the notice of a set of men, who deem themselves especially commissioned to extend over a continent the brawling radicalism of modern Democracy.

We speak especially of the House of Representatives, where the genius of locofocoism is unrestrained. In the Senate there yet lingers some of the dignity and glory of the early days of the Republic. How long this conservative body will oppose its influence to the evil tendencies of the times remains to be seen.

The complaint about legislation "by men of none or very little judgment in law," is as old as the days of Coke, and the evil has by no means diminished in these modern times. Excessive and hasty legislation is the fault of our State governments, but the immediate supervision of the people checks this tendency and restrains the local assemblies within certain bounds of decency and decorum. This check does not operate upon the popular branch of the National Legislature. A man sent to the lower House in Maine, who should make a mountebank of himself, by supporting some foolish law, to operate directly upon the citizens of his native town, would be detected. A member of Congress from Maine can play the fool in Washington a long time without being found out at home. But the day of reckoning will come at last. The effects of folly and madness cannot be confined to the Capitol. The members of Congress cannot escape with the simple penalty of making themselves ridiculous and contemptible in the eyes of those who watch their proceedings. The evils of misgovernment or of no government will reach at last the homes of the humble, will be felt by the laborer at his daily toil. He will find that the admission of Texas has thrown no new guards around property, liberty, or life. He will find that braggart legislation about Oregon has done nothing to assist him in furnishing his children with education or with bread. He will find that the flattery of demagogues has not made the village in which he lives more prosperous or more happy. Then these demagogues themselves will learn the difference between that voice of the people which a party catch word can make or destroy, and that voice of the people which is indeed the voice of God—that voice which humanity utters when it can bear outrage and insult no longer.

Recent events have shown clearly enough that the people of this country have yet to learn some lessons in the stern school of experience. The race to which we belong has been tried by the oppression of kings and not found wanting. It has yet to pass the more awful ordeal of the tyranny of the multitude, and it will be found equal even to that trial. When the passions of the hour have subsided, and their fatal consequences are felt in the land, the reaction will come. When that day comes, a modern democrat, startled by a voice new and strange, may ask, with the courtier of old, "People! What? the people?" and like him receive for answer, "The people, like the air, is seldom heard but when it speaks in thunder."

PROVIDENCE JOURNAL, MARCH 7, 1845.

RESOLUTIONS

PASSED AT A LAW AND ORDER MEETING.

Resolved, That, in the opinion of this meeting, the elections to be made in this State, on the first Wednesday of April, involve the same cardinal principles which the Law and Order party was originally formed to defend; which that party has, thus far, steadfastly upheld; and which, by continued Union, Vigilance and Effort, it can triumphantly maintain.

Resolved, That, at the present crisis, when a powerful party within our borders—a party which has, again and again, solemnly declared the government of this State to be a flagrant usurpation, and which stands pledged to the overthrow of our excellent constitution, and to the establishment of the miscalled people's constitution upon its ruins, is organizing, with fresh zeal and activity, its forces, in order to obtain possession of the whole political power of this city and this State; when the House of Representatives of the Congress of the United States have, at the instigation of this same party, published a report slandering the government and the people of Rhode Island, and have entertained resolutions in derogation of her reserved rights, and in violation of the sacred rights of several of her citizens, who, at a crisis of imminent peril, took up arms in her defense; when some of the Legislatures of our sister States, disregarding all comity, and trampling upon the well established principles of American constitutional law, presume to determine by what sort of a constitution Rhode Island shall be governed, and in what manner she shall administer her criminal justice;—at such a crisis as this, we deem the duty of Union, Vigilance and Effort to be sacredly obligatory upon all the friends of Law and Order.

Surveying the momentous issues for which we are about to contend at the ballot box;—looking at the evils which defeat would inevitably bring upon all the great interests of the State; and admonished by past experience that upon ourselves and upon ourselves alone must we rely in the hour of danger,

Resolved, That while we are, at no time, indifferent to the policy of the national government, we are now constrained to regard, as matters of paramount concern to the people of this State, those grave domestic questions which continue to agitate us—which touch the very foundations of our whole social order; which jeopard all the securities of life, liberty and property; which come home to our bosoms and our business; to our halls of legislation and to our courts of justice; to the fields, and manufactories, and workshops in which we toil; and to the firesides around which we feel it a blessed privilege to seek repose.

Resolved, That the constitution which the people of this State have established, contains provisions which ought to recommend it to the warm and untiring support of every friend to regulated liberty, that, in arming the weak with some means of protecting themselves against the encroachments of the strong, it has exemplified the true theory of equal rights; and that, by the qualifications which it has annexed to the right of suffrage—qualifications demanded by the peculiar circumstances of Rhode Island, it has provided some security that the legislation of the General Assembly shall reflect, not the capricious impulses and the excited passions of masses connected with Rhode Island by no permanent ties, but the considerate opinions of those of her people who understand her interests—who love her institutions; and who revert, with somewhat of filial reverence, to the deeds and to the men who illustrate her past history.

Resolved, That we regard, with cordial approbation, the course which Governor Fenner, as the Chief Magistrate of this State, has pursued during the late political year; that we repose entire confidence in his sagacity, energy and devoted attachment to the genuine principles of constitutional liberty; and that we should hail his re-election by a commanding majority, not only as a merited reward of honorable and disinterested public service, but as a renewed expression, on the part of the people of Rhode Island, of their unaltered purpose to maintain, against foes from within and foes from without, the laws and the Constitution of Rhode Island.

Resolved, That we can confidently assure our friends in the other towns of Rhode Island, that Providence will, on the first Wednesday in April, do her whole duty in that contest for political power then to be decided, and on the issue of which are suspended consequences the most momentous to the peace, the interests, and honor of the State.

Resolved, That in view of the vitally important consequences depending on the result of the approaching election, we earnestly recommend that our Law and Order fellow citizens in the other towns of the State, commence, without delay, the work of thorough and systematic organization, in order that they may be fully prepared to do battle in the common cause; to contend successfully for principles which are equally dear to them and to ourselves, and to avert the overthrow of a Constitution which they, in a special manner, are interested to maintain.

Resolved, finally, That, while we cannot repress all indignation at the systematic efforts to defame the government and people of Rhode Island, which originate from her recreant sons at home, and are seconded by a profligate press and by profligate politicians abroad, we yet entertain an unfaltering trust that, by no interested clamor and by no ephemeral obloquy, can the judgment of the country and of posterity be betrayed into lasting injustice; that, looking back upon the early history of Rhode Island, we perceive that she commenced, amid a cloud of calumniators, that "lively experiment of full liberty in religious concernments" which is now the praise of all civilized lands; and that, looking forward to the testimony of future times, we repose in the conviction that, when the strifes, and prejudices, and passions of the day shall have passed into oblivion, history will place upon a record destined never to perish, the sacrifices which Rhode Island has made, and the perils she has encountered, and the triumphs she has won, in the sacred cause of American constitutional Freedom.

PROVIDENCE JOURNAL, MARCH 18, 1845.

RESOLUTIONS

PASSED AT A LAW AND ORDER MEETING.

WHEREAS, we are about to contend with our old enemy, on the old grounds,

Resolved, That we will, one and all, continue to stand firmly on the broad and deep foundations of liberty regulated by Law.

Resolved, That, as Rhode Island men, we pledge ourselves to contend manfully to the last, for the rights and for the honor of Rhode Island, against any and all who may seek to violate the one or to betray the other; and that, whereas, in seasons of fearful peril, we have successfully resisted both fraud and force, we are determined, in these more tranquil times, not to be vanquished by treachery.

Resolved, That, as citizens of a State which has ever been proud and jealous of its freedom, we look to wise laws efficiently executed as the only true guardian of freedom; that, anxious as we are to pursue in quiet those various callings in which all of us are engaged, and upon which most of us depend for support, we can never consent to surrender Rhode

Island into the hands of men, who, in carrying out their principles, would rob industry both of stimulus and protection; and that sincerely as we lament all social alienations and hostilities, we would be among the last to purchase a hollow peace by the sacrifice of those great principles of Law and Order, upon which the solid and lasting tranquillity of the community and the fireside can alone depend.

Resolved, That the comparative quiet and the great prosperity which this State has for the last two years enjoyed, owing mainly to the restoration of confidence at home and abroad, in the stability of our institutions, should admonish us all, whether merchants, mechanics, or manufacturers, whether employer or employed, to cling more closely to those grand conservative principles, without which no man of any class in any community can hope to reap the fruits of his skill and industry, or to enjoy the blessings of a tranquil home.

Resolved, That Dorrism, however it may change its front, can never change its nature; that it strives to exasperate prejudices against the rich, while it gives neither employment nor solace to the poor—that it interrupts, by restless machinations, the pursuits of honest labor; relaxes the obligations of law; and scatters wide, among members of the same community, the seeds of animosity and distrust; that it is at war with the essential principles of a republican government, and is, in fact, destructive of all government; that it resorts to revolution, when only reform is needed; and, finally, that it constitutes that "elective despotism" which Mr. Jefferson deprecated as the worst tyranny which could befall a free people.

Resolved, That Mr. Charles Jackson, late a distinguished member of the Law and Order party, but now the Dorrite candidate for the office of Governor, has a right to bargain for himself, but not to bargain for others; that the coalition which he has formed with the Dorrites is designed, under shallow pretences of humanity and conciliation, to elevate himself to place and to power, and to confide every interest in this State, to a party composed of the most dangerous materials, broaching hitherto the most revolutionary doctrines, and moved too by the most revolutionary impulses.

Resolved, That, relying on the practical good sense of the people of Rhode Island, we are persuaded that, on the first Wednesday in April, they will pronounce a right judgment upon Mr. Charles Jackson's course, in abandoning a party which maintains well defined principles, for a party which now professes to be embarassed by no principles at all.

Whereas, the Dorrite Convention of 1844 declared by resolution that the "People's Constitution is the supreme law, which has been unjustly and ungenerously set aside by a monied aristocracy; and that the Algerine Constitution was thrust upon the people of this State by fraud and force, and that it is insufficient, unsatisfactory, indefinite and deceptive in its provisions;" and whereas the Dorrite Convention of 1845 has declared, by resolution, that this same Algerine Constitution, which was thrust upon the people of this State, "by fraud and force," is now a Constitution which the Dorrites are "bound to support, and which they have no desire to change or amend," except in the mode which itself provides:

Therefore, Resolved, That no confidence ought to be placed in the professions or pledges of a party, which, without any change of circumstances, and upon matters of the gravest import, proclaims, within one year, doctrines and determinations not only different from each other, but flagrantly and irreconcilably contradictory.

Resolved, That the Dorrite Convention of 1845, while it professes its desire not to change or amend the existing Constitution, except in a regular mode, said Convention is careful, in this grave concern, to express nothing but its present desire, and that it neglects to affirm the great conservative doctrine that Constitutions cannot rightfully be changed or amended, except in the mode which their own provisions may establish.

Resolved, in the language of the address to the people of the United States, signed by Charles Jackson and others, in October last, that "we hope if there is to be any sympathy among the citizens of other States, in relation to the troubles in Rhode Island, that it will be a sympathy for violated law and a suffering community, and not for those who are receiving the punishment which the law has provided for their offences."

Resolved, That while we love peace and the things which make for peace, we do not believe that this blessing, so dear to us as citizens and as men, can be secured for the people of this State, by those whose chief vocation it has been, year after year, to create distractions within her borders, to defame her character abroad, and to pour forth, upon all those who have struggled to maintain her rights and her dignity, the most bitter reproach, and the most fierce denunciations.

Resolved, That we will strive to keep "the government of this State in a right position before this great Republic," and that, on the first Wednesday in April, we will proclaim to our sister States, that Dorrism, whether it show itself in arms, or whether it hide itself in masquerade, has nothing but defeat to expect in the land which gave it birth.

PROVIDENCE JOURNAL, MARCH 21, 1845.

THE APPROACHING ELECTION.

To the Friends of Law and Order, in Rhode Island:—

Fellow Citizens:—Where are we now? What change has the new phase which Dorrism has assumed —the new mask which it has put on wrought in our principles, purposes and prospects? How are we affected by the strange conjunction of planets to which, within a few days, our gaze has been directed? At all hours of the day, by the wayside, and at the place of concourse, are these questions familiarly asked by men of every age, and of every employment in life. They are asked, too, by men who have dared and done too much in defence of the rights and honor of Rhode Island, to be, in the slightest degree, alarmed at any meteor which may chance to shoot along our troubled sky; in plain words, by men who feel far less surprise than moral indignation at the convenient facility with which Mr. Charles Jackson has consented to become the acknowledged leader of the Dorrites, and the avowed champion of Dorrism! These questions can be readily and satisfactorily answered. We, the friends of Law and Order are just where we were in 1842. With united strength and unabated zeal, we are resolved to contend, foot to foot, and shoulder to shoulder, against the same men over whom we then won a glorious victory. With spirits rather elevated than depressed by the new move which Mr. Jackson has made upon the political chess board, by the harlequin agility with which he has vaulted into a new position, we are panting to do battle for Rhode Island —for her institutions which no foe shall be permitted to trample down—for her priceless honor, which no politician, however cheaply he may value his own, shall be suffered to barter away! This is our position. We took it without fear; we have maintained it without reproach; we can define it without a blush!

What, on the other hand, fellow citizens, is now the position of Mr. Charles Jackson? What are now his purposes and principles? Who are now his political associates and friends?

These questions, too, admit of an answer entirely satisfactory to every Law and Order man, who is resolved not to become a victim to adroit and unchastened ambition, and who disdains to be made its dupe. The members of the Law and Order party do their own thinking; they follow, in political matters, the directions of their own judgments and consciences; and they will take a very practical, common sense view of Mr. Jackson and of the bold experiment he has just made upon their honesty and sagacity. He may transfer himself to the ranks of the Dorrites, upon such terms as may be agreed upon; but let him not cheat himself with the notion that he can recruit, from the ranks which he has deserted, more than a corporal's guard, to follow him into the Dorrite camp, and to fight with him, like soldiers of fortune, under the soiled and tattered banner of Dorrism! Law and Order men will scorn to be a party, in any sense, to a coalition which, viewed in any light, will stand out, in bold relief, as the baldest and most unscrupulous "business transaction," which can be found recorded in the history of the prostitute politics of modern times! This language, however strong, is not too strong for the occasion. It does not violate the public taste; and, what is better still, it does not outrun the public indignation. Honest, independent and thinking men can suppress neither the language nor the feeling of deep moral reprobation, when political leaders, whatever may be their professions, presume, for considerations exclusively selfish, to trifle with great interests, and to compromise, if not to surrender, great principles.

So sudden and so remarkable was Mr. Jackson's conversion to Dorrism, that people, who are inquisitive about strange mental and moral phenomena, are curious to learn exactly when, and where, and how, the new light broke in upon his hitherto darkened intellect. A like prodigy, happening in Paris, would be dramatised, at once, by the brilliant wits of the French metropolis, to gratify that diseased public taste which is captivated by whatsoever is monstrous and startling in life and character.

This sort of ordeal, Mr. Jackson will escape. Neither he, however, nor his copartners in this extraordinary business transaction, must expect to escape a full and fearless discussion of all the principles to which he has lent the sanction of his name; and a no less full and fearless examination of all the evils, the deplorable evils, which his election, and the triumph of the party to which he has allied himself, would inevitably bring and fasten upon the State.

He must not feel himself aggrieved, because I denounce him, as the acknowledged leader of the Dorrites, and as the avowed champion of Dorrism. He has chosen to connect himself, by the ties of political brotherhood, with the men who, first by fraud, and secondly by force, attempted to subvert the government of his native State. Forsaking the sympathies and associations to which he has long been habituated, he has joined himself to Benjamin Cowell, David Parmenter, John S. Harris, Burrington Anthony, Welcome B. Sayles, Walter R. Danforth and other worthies of the same school! This is a "fixed fact"—which no reasoning can nullify—no ingenuity can explain away—and no mask can conceal!

Mr. Jackson may deny that he is about to be supported by the Dorrites upon any principle which ought to render him obnoxious to the imputation of Dorrism. He may claim to be still an "out and outer Clay Whig," one of the straitest of the sect. He may claim to be still a stanch Law and Order man. He may claim that he has not changed his opinion of the invalidity of the people's constitution. But all these claims, however ingeniously set forth, will not help him. His fellow citizens will judge him by the company which he keeps—by the principles on which he now consents to stand as a candidate for the chief magistracy, by the party to which he is now laboring to confide the political power of this State.

The unconditional liberation of Thomas Wilson Dorr is the one issue upon which Mr. Charles Jackson and the Dorr Democracy have formed a coalition, for the purpose of wresting from the Law and Order party the political power of this State. This may be a single issue—but it is an issue which involves, in a concentrated form, all the great principles, which we, my fellow citizens, have thus far struggled to maintain. The unconditional liberation of Thomas Wilson Dorr is demanded by his political friends, at home and abroad. He refuses to accept of liberation, upon the reasonable and lenient conditions which the State has prescribed. He deems any conditions to be incompatible with his honor—to be tantamount to an admission that he has transgressed some law, and that, in this whole matter, he and not the State has done wrong! In other words, he and his partisans contend that he has committed no crime; that he is obnoxious to no reproach, and that he ought to endure no punishment! Thus will it be seen, that unconditional liberation, demanded by such men, for such reasons, and with such a spirit, is an issue which involves every important principle for which the friends of Law and Order have hitherto contended. It will be hard, in this matter, to throw dust in the eyes of the people of Rhode Island. The notion has got abroad, that quite as much care ought to be taken of the honor of the State as of the honor of a State Prison convict—and that, come what may, the sovereignty of the laws must be upheld, and upheld to the very last!

For the result of the approaching election I entertain no fears. Effort, however, systematic and indefatigable effort, will be needed to insure such a majority as will place our cause out of the reach of danger hereafter.

A better spirit never prevailed in this city; and if our friends in the country come up to the work, as the importance of the work demands, the Constitution of this State will be rescued from the hands of men, who, after they had taken a solemn oath to support it, invoked the interposition of the general government, in order to set it aside.

Hereafter I may invite your attention to a deliberate consideration of the consequences which would inevitably result from the success of the Dorr party. At present, I will only observe, that every man who values the prompt, economical, intelligent, and uncorrupt administration of civil and criminal justice, is deeply concerned not to confide the political power of the State to men who will remove from office those Judges who are most worthy of the public confidence and respect. Should the Dorrites prevail on the first Wednesday in April, Chief Justice Durfee and his associates on the Bench of the Supreme Court, would not escape immediate and vindictive proscription. Let the Dorrites achieve their long sought for triumph over the majesty of the law, by the unconditional liberation of their now imprisoned champion, and they would at once consummate their triumph and his, by the sacrifice of the ministers of the law.

A CONSERVATIVE.

PROVIDENCE JOURNAL, MARCH 22, 1845.

THE WONDERS OF THE DAY.

---

1. CHARLES JACKSON, who calls himself "a Whig member of the Law and Order party," has accepted the nomination of "the Democratic Republican Convention," alias Dorrite Convention, alias "Liberation Convention!"

2. Charles Jackson last evening addressed a meeting of Whigs at Masonic Hall, convened at his own invitation, and gave "an exposition of his opinions as a Whig." And yet, the Herald says, his nomination was made without regard to "party politics!"

3. Charles Jackson, the nominee of "the Democratic Republican," alias Dorrite Convention, yester-

day published an address "to the Whigs of Rhode Island!" In this address he insists upon it that he is "a true Whig and a stiff conservative!"

4. Charles Jackson, the nominee of the aforesaid Democratic Republican, alias Dorrite Convention, more than insinuates that Albert C. Greene, who was elected by Whig votes a Whig Senator in Congress, is a compromising politician! This is very rich, and somewhat modest withal!

5. Charles Jackson has associated himself with Parmenter, Harris, Cowell, Danforth, B. Anthony, &c., &c., for the purpose, the palpable purpose of giving political power to the Dorrites, and of breaking down the Law and Order party. And yet Mr. Charles Jackson flies into heroics, because people "begin to suspect" that he "has abandoned the conservative platform of law and order!" Vide his address to the Whigs of Rhode Island.

6. Charles Jackson in effect complains that the action of the Law and Order party has been determined in accordance with the opinions of a majority of that party. He, it seems, cannot consent to be a member of a party, with which, in regard to "State politics" he professes an almost entire agreement; but he can consent to join himself to the Dorrite party, with which, except in one solitary matter, he professes, upon both national and State politics, to have no agreement at all!

7. Charles Jackson affects to be aggrieved, because he is not a member of the Law and Order party, "for the purposes of planning and directing!" Admitting Mr. Jackson's grievance not to be imaginary, how does it justify him, the champion of "the conservative

principle," in leaving the conservative party for the radical? What is thought of a soldier, who, because he is not consulted in "planning and directing" a campaign, forthwith deserts to the enemy's camp? And what ought to be thought of a public man, aspiring to the post of a statesman, for this most paltry apology for the abandonment of a great party? Will Mr. Jackson tear down "the conservative platform of Law and Order," simply because he cannot obtain a high seat upon it? Will he quit the serene heights of Law and Order, and gravitate to the low levels of Dorrism, for the purpose of being engaged in the sublime mysteries of "planning and directing" the policy of a political party? If this be his taste, if this be his ambition, if this be his purpose—why then "let him go,"—he will go to "his own place!"

Charles Jackson, in his address, says, "the olive branch is now tendered to us by the democratic party," alias the Dorrite party. Does he, in his heart, believe that the Dorrites are sincere? Does he hope that any man, or woman or child, in any town where "the schoolmaster is abroad," will be imposed upon by such twattle? "The olive branch" indeed! Upon what terms is it tendered? Confide, say the Dorrites all the political power of the State to us; elect Charles Jackson Governor; liberate Thomas W. Dorr upon such conditions as may be congenial to his sense of honor; allow us to legislate for you; to appoint your Judges; to execute your laws; to administer your constitution, and all shall be well; the tempest which has agitated us will be hushed; the lion will lie down with the lamb; and, under the new dynasty of Dorrism, a day of millennial peace and glory will dawn upon the

State. This is virtually the gentle language of Mr. Charles Jackson and his new confederates. Mr. Jackson deceives himself; he cannot deceive others. It is not for him to govern, and guide, and melt into tenderness and love, the rude and rebellious spirits, with whom he has entered into communion. They may consent to follow him to victory, but, after the victory be won; he must follow them, and to a lower and a yet lower deep. It is not for him, with all his boasted speculative conservatism, to put a hook into the nose of that leviathan. He may nestle under its side, and he may mount upon its back, but it belongs not to him to tame the monster. It will, in spite of him, prove true to the instincts of its own nature.

Charles Jackson puts himself before the electors of this State, as the great apostle of "the pacification of the State." And yet, he allows himself to be used, aye, used—that is the very word—by a party which has made open war upon the government of Rhode Island, and which, till the nomination of the great Pacificator, kept open, by night and by day, in town and in country, in business and in pleasure, the fountains of political and social bitterness.

Charles Jackson addresses "the religious men of the State." He quotes the language of Scripture—and he commends to their observance the command of our Savior—"Love one another." All this is well. Let us love our enemies, and forgive them, too, as we hope to be forgiven. This, however, is no reason why we should love their iniquities—or why, before they have shown a solitary sign of sincere penitence, we should take them to our confidence and to our hearts—or give them the power to oppress us—and that without remedy.

Finally. I am compelled to the belief, by a review of all these "wonders of the day," that Mr. Jackson cannot make out a good case for himself. As a Whig, he was bound not to connect himself with the bitterest opponents of the Whigs. As a Law and Order man, he was bound not to become the leader of the Dorrites, the inveterate antagonists of Law and Order. As the Pacificator of the State, he was bound not to place himself at the head of the only party which ever made war upon the State.

VARNUM.

PROVIDENCE JOURNAL, MARCH 20, 1845.

TO CHARLES JACKSON, ESQ.

NO. I.

SOME four weeks ago, the organs of Dorrism in this State, published a call for a Convention to nominate a ticket for State officers, to be supported by that jacobin party at the ensuing election. Since then, we have been informed through various channels, that the usual party discussions were to be merged in one, and that, the unconditional liberation of Dorr. To accomplish this purpose, it was deemed most expedient to select a candidate for Governor (if he could be found,) among those who had been conspicuous in maintaining the principles of the Law and Order party. It was a novel and a bold proposition, and one which we did not believe could be entertained by any one who regarded the laws of self respect.

Before the Convention assembled, rumor was busy with her thousand tongues, and she designated Charles Jackson, Esq., as the gentleman who would be honored by that august body as the Dorr candidate for Governor. As one of your friends, I regretted that such a slander was in circulation, and thought that it was a duty which you owed yourself, to arrest the charge. I had never learned that Charles Jackson, either by education or by his declared opinions, or by his votes, in or out of the General Assembly, was a Dorrite. I knew that his associations would repel an alliance with treason, and I supposed that he cherished no sympathy for the traitor. Subsequent events, however, have dispelled all doubts, the curtain has been raised, the mystery has been solved, and there stands the name of Charles Jackson ! ! as the Dorr candidate for Governor of Rhode Island.

In all periods of our political history there have occurred most astonishing changes, among great men and among little men; but this last summerset is about the queerest that history has yet revealed. The Dorr rebellion furnished rich materials to bring out the hidden talents of orators, warriors and statesmen. To achieve the purposes of that noble enterprise, were enlisted the constitutional learning of Dorr, and Slocum, and Wales; the heroic devotion of Dispeau and Landers; the statesmanship of Sayles, and Harris, and Cowell, and Parmenter. The deeds accomplished by these distinguished individuals in their several departments will pass on to future generations, and the reader in the next century will look back with mingled feelings of wonder and pride, that so much moral, political and military glory dawned and flourished in the little domain of Rhode Island. And while engaged in this study, he will observe that the chief conspirator against the government in the year 1842, was indicted, tried, found guilty and sentenced to imprisonment for life, for the crime of treason. A most righteous sentence he will exclaim, and honor to all those men who revered the laws and resolved that they should be maintained and vindicated. Fidelity here will command a sentiment of admiration and gratitude, as enduring as the page on which the deeds are written. But how great will be his surprise, when he learns that one of the most prominent against Dorr and his principles, in the year 1845, by some legerdemain, accepted a nomination for Governor from the very party against whom he had for years been directing his batteries. And yet this is none other than Mr. Charles Jackson.

This then is your position, assumed with all deliberation, with a full knowledge of all the consequences flowing from it, and yet embraced with as much self possession and calm confidence as if it were one of the noblest acts which can adorn the political life of the most distinguished statesman.

What has produced this sudden conversion, what

revelations may be anticipated in the future of your political career it is not for me at present to record—these shall be reserved for another day.

Meanwhile, permit me to offer my congratulations as you now stand upon the very pinnacle of political glory—the observed of all observers, inspiring the admiration of your old friends at the successful termination of the bargain, and at the same time calling down a stronger feeling of indignation than has been usually expressed towards any individual even of your acknowledged talent. And is it strange that public opinion is heard uttering in full and withering tones its condemnatory voice? A leader in the councils of the State, intrusted with her secrets, imparting an energy to all her deliberations, prompt to vindicate the majesty of law, and foremost in the purpose to arrest and punish her most determined enemy, his voice, his arm, his vote, each in its turn and in its place asserting the sacred principles of genuine freedom, expressing the most sovereign contempt for Dorr and his followers and spurning all propositions designed to give him succor, this is the man who now courts the smiles of the felon whom he has helped to brand with deserved infamy. If, however, Mr. Jackson is gratified with his present position, I care not to complain, and yet I feel just like showing him up to the admiring gaze of his fellow citizens. It is not just that so rich a subject for dissection should not have the knife inserted, that we may learn, if possible, what peculiar disease is upon him, and how his intellect has become so clouded.

ONE OF THE PEOPLE.

PROVIDENCE JOURNAL, MARCH 25, 1845.

TO CHARLES JACKSON, ESQ.

NO. II.

The curiosity of the public is not a little excited to learn the time, the place, and the company present, when you resolved to commit political suicide. The terms of the bargain must have been very captivating, or else your vanity led you on without regard to the consequences. And this supposition may be more charitable than true, for one can hardly conceive that vanity alone, would impel a man into the very pit of that radicalism which he has so often described as the origin of all the political evils which have visited the State and Nation. But the day and the hour of your conversion, when was it, and whose were the fortunate ears that heard the first sounds of awakening life, Cowell's or Parmenter's! It must have been a most interesting meeting when you doffed the Algerine and put on the Dorr cap, and I know not the man in this community who will wear it with quite so cool a face as Mr. Charles Jackson. It seems to become him and suit him to a charm, and the only wonder is, that it was not put on a year ago, before this

Dorrism had met with so many disasters. Nevertheless, there are symptoms in your letter which convey the impression that you are not satisfied with your position. You say to these agitators, that you have not altered any opinion heretofore entertained upon State or National politics; nor do you feel obliged to abandon those opinions by accepting the nomination.

Let us examine into this matter and then we can the better determine the value of that man's honor who professes to be a Whig and a Law and Order advocate, when he has enlisted in the company of traitors and disorganizers. As I understand the doctrines of the Whig party, their tendency is, to preserve and maintain a conservative influence in politics, and always to revere the majesty of law. It is not possible that elements so adverse, can be cherished within the same bosom. You are not a Whig if you are a Dorrite, nor if a Dorrite, can you be a Whig. The one or the other class of opinions must prevail, and between these, no union can be formed. When, therefore, you choose to call yourself a Whig, permit me to add, that you and I attach a very different meaning to that term. A Whig and yet a Dorrite! Hold him up to the gaze of the gaping multitude and they will exclaim at the facility with which he assumes his chameleon shape, and ask in what region of the globe such a production was reared, and how many years of toil and anxious watchfulness have been expended upon his education.

But you may whisper in the ear of your former political associates, oh! I have not departed and do not mean to depart from a single point of my Whig faith—it is as dear to me now as when I advocated the election of Henry Clay, and not for all the honors or emoluments of office, would I barter those principles. Very well, then these Dorrites are most consummate fools if they vote for you. Just turn over the leaf of our experience in Rhode Island and observe how you were affected in 1842. Take that memorable act, called the Algerine Law. You were a member of the General Assembly when it was passed, and was in favor of its passage, and have sanctioned the proceedings under it. You were in arms against the Dorr rebels, and under similar circumstances, I presume you would enlist again. Every measure recommended and pursued by the party, received, so far as I know, your approbation, and yet, with a full knowledge of all the facts and a most explicit avowal in your letter that your opinions have undergone no change, still you solicit the suffrages of a party to which you have always turned the cold shoulder. Will they be soft enough to swallow such gammon? Ye Dispeaus and the brave warriors of Federal and Acote's Hill—ye Slocums and all ye expounders of Constitutional Law, from Parmenter down to Cowell—ye highway robbers and ye plunderers of cannon and powder, cast your votes for a man who asserts that you have every one of you committed the crime of treason and are amenable to the law, and those of you who have been convicted, have been most justly condemned! And the sainted Dorr too, he the patriot, the martyr, the jewel of democracy, the persecuted and the outraged, he too wasting his life in the companionship of felons, shut out from the free air of Heaven, incarcerated in a dungeon, painting fans and earning something for the State, which he never did for himself—the pure and incorruptible Dorr, I Charles Jackson, in the face of the whole Dorr party, under my own hand, and with all the responsibility which attaches to my name, here proclaim in this my letter to "Ariel Ballou, Esq., President, &c.," that not an act of the party from its inception, through all its progress, up to the hour of its retreat on Acote's Hill, not one of all its follies and its crimes but have received and do now receive my most cordial detestation. And yet gentlemen, with this insulting language, with this stinging rebuke, with this "out and out" declaration of my abhorrence of you and the cause you espouse, I know that you will all give me your votes for Governor. And why—because "a new question is now presented."

And pray what is this new question? If Mr. Jackson had not stated what it was in his letter, most people would have been extremely puzzled to know what the new question is. We should have been tempted to open the door of our library and take from the shelf the immortal work of Slocum on the Constitution, and there we should have read the celebrated question—"if the soveri*n*nity don't reside in the people, pray where does it reside?" This, however, as we all know, is an old question, which has addled the brains of philosophers and statesmen for centuries, and none could solve it but the distinguished Slocum. The new question to which Mr. Jackson refers is of quite a different cast—"the unconditional liberation of Mr. (not Governor) Dorr, and his restoration to the rights of a citizen." We will dispose of this new question in a future number.

ONE OF THE PEOPLE.

PROVIDENCE JOURNAL, MARCH 26, 1845.

TO CHARLES JACKSON ESQ.

NO. III.

On the 21st day of October, 1844, "An Address to the People of the United States" was published, the object of which is, to correct the gross falsehoods circulated in other States against the people and government of Rhode Island. Two paragraphs in this pamphlet deserve your especial consideration:

"Thomas W. Dorr was convicted, not under the 'Algerine Act,' as it has been called, but under the act of 1838, for levying war against the State, he has been sent to the State Prison in pursuance of the same law; and there he remains with no discrimination of treatment from that of the other prisoners."

Again—"When it is considered that the crime of High Treason is the greatest crime which can be committed against society, and that it was committed by the levying of war against Rhode Island, when there was no pretext which could palliate it, and the extension of suffrage had been offered and rejected, and another act of the Legislature was passed with a view to the same object, we hope, if there is to be any sympathy among the citizens of other States in relation to the troubles in Rhode Island, that it will be a sympathy for violated law, and a suffering community, and not for those who are receiving the punishment which the law has provided for their offences."

Among the signatures to this valuable Address is that of Charles Jackson. So then, it seems, as late as October, you deemed it wise to expend sympathy upon violated law and a suffering community, rather than upon him who was receiving that punishment which his offense so richly merits. In other words, Dorr had committed treason, and for one you thought his imprisonment just, and all sympathy in his behalf a false and misplaced sympathy. But this is not all. In your letter, you say that your opinion has undergone no change—that what you subscribed in October, 1844, is still your opinion in March, 1845. Then let me ask you to reconcile these statements, for they are as wide as the poles asunder. If I can comprehend the meaning of your letter, in one portion you distinctly avow that your opinions are the same as expressed in the pamphlet, and in another portion you state just as explicitly that they are not the same. In one or the other you have played false, or perhaps charity, which you know is a cloak covering a multitude of sins, would suggest that it was very convenient to avow the sentiment in October, because nobody would recollect it in March. But we have the name in both instances and you cannot retreat behind that masked battery. Stand up then like a condemned politician, and plead guilty to the fraud—is that term misapplied in this connection?

But the "new question," let us look at that, and if

I am not mistaken, it is worse for you than the other point we have been considering. The unconditional liberation of Dorr and his restoration to the rights, that is your word, of a citizen, this is the "new question" presented to the people of this State. By the use of the term, new question, one must infer that it is just sprung upon us, and for the first time now agitated. But Mr. Jackson, pause for a moment, and reflect how deceptive this language is—a new question! Have not the columns of the Dorr newspapers and the mouths of the Dorr orators, not only in Rhode Island, but in every State in the Union where political capital could be manufactured, have they not one and all, kept up an unceasing cry for the unconditional liberation of Dorr? Have not some of these very orators, and most of the "loafers" been living for the last nine months upon Dorr liberation stock? Have they not at all their public meetings, from the day of his imprisonment to this hour, passed resolutions upon this subject, and circulated statements which, in the pamphlet I have quoted, you denominated "the grossest falsehoods?" And yet, with all these facts, you talk about a "new question," and upon that issue appeal to these Dorr men for their suffrages! If this is not political audacity, where will you find it?

As yet I have alluded only to the first branch of "the new question;" with the unconditional liberation of Dorr you couple his restoration to the rights of a citizen. Educated as a lawyer, I am surprised to see this term in your letter. He is entitled to the same rights, under certain circumstances, as every other citizen, among which are the protection of person and property, but your allusion is of quite a different meaning. The restoration of his oath, of his liberty and the privileges of an elector—these are the "rights" which you demand, and which you have bargained to restore. These are privileges conferred upon every citizen who has not forfeited them by the commission of crime. It is the crime which has taken them from Dorr, because the statute makes such provision as a part of the penalty; if it did not, it would be a very singular omission. He is then deprived of no rights of which all other felons are not deprived, and why not manifest the same sympathy towards them? Besides this you very well know that Dorr can walk out of the prison whenever his dogged obstinacy permits, and so far as his freedom is concerned, he cannot feel much solicitude, or he would have availed himself of the clemency of the government, months ago. It is a new feature in modern philanthropy, that when a man has committed the highest crime against society, and been sentenced to imprisonment for life, that when he is released he must be restored to all the privileges of a citizen before he condescends to ask the boon. If this is the doctrine, why not deal liberally with all other criminals, and by and by abolish every statute against crime because they restrain human liberty. I know the reply you would make to this question, but it seems to me to be a distinction without a difference. A political offense you contend ought to be overlooked, because, after all, it is a mere difference of opinion, and it is punishing one for the sake of opinion. If this be sound doctrine, then there is no security for government, and if so, where is the security of person and property? It may be the opinion of some libertine that he has a right to violate your domestic circle, or apply the torch to your dwelling, but if it be proved that he had always entertained the opinion that such acts could be perpetrated without adequate punishment, he falls back upon his opinion, and society has no redress.

To argue this point at length, would lead me from my present purpose, and I will only beg you to recollect, that when you express so much solicitude for the liberty and "rights" of Dorr, you will also recollect, that the crime of which he is guilty is the fruit of almost every other crime, and it is not his fault that the very worst were not visited upon the State. For one I rejoice that I have none of this mawkish sensibility for Dorr, and I trust that there is yet fortitude and stability enough in the people of Rhode Island to bear up against the external and internal pressure which is now enlisted in his behalf. If there has been a period when we were bound by every consideration of patriotism, and every suggestion of policy, and every sentiment of dignity, to maintain the position which the General Assembly has taken, now is the period. The honor of the State is not yet confided to your counsels, and for one, I pray that it may never fall into such treacherous arms.

One of the People.

PROVIDENCE JOURNAL, MARCH 31, 1845.

TO CHARLES JACKSON, ESQ.

NO. IV.

If your nomination has effected no other object, it has certainly placed you upon an eminence of notoriety such as few men have attained in one short week. A private citizen, enjoying the respect and confidence of his neighbors, you have suddenly emerged from the shades of retirement, and thrown the political cauldron into such a tempest that most of us look on with feelings of mingled wonder and resentment, and are led to exclaim at your rare talent for swallowing the dose which some one more artful than yourself had prepared. When it was first swallowed, it seems not to have produced the effects which subsequent trickery has accomplished. At one time, there were strong indications that the symptoms of the disease were more favorable, and some imagined that you would escape the infliction of that pain which Dorrism and treachery are sure to produce upon the unfortunate subject. Anxious days, and, if reports be true, anxious nights, were passed in a state of suspended animation, and for a time it was doubtful whether the complaint would be firmly seated, or whether you would reject the poison which had been mixed for your political palate. A council of distinguished physicians was summoned, and after feeling your pulse, and promising some sugar plums if you would be persuaded to take the whole dose, your objections were surmounted, and you are now reported as having the Dorr distemper in all its malignity.

Well, if you feel joyous in such an embrace, I know not the man who is jealous of your position. True the digestive organs have had an unusual amount of food to grind, and of a quality too that would create a nausea upon the stomach of most politicians; but some how or other, you have survived it all, and now stand up as the idol of Dorr democracy. The worshippers of that pestilential god, if report be true, do not all accept you as the pure divinity. With averted eye, and determined purpose, they say they will not bow down and worship the unclean thing. It was formed in iniquity and treachery, and none can pay it homage who revere qualities of the martyr Dorr. Among those who rebel, I will mention the name of the virtuous and honored Parmenter. From his patriotic lips have been heard expressions of the most determined hostility, and all the industry and legal acumen of Cowell have been tasked to induce him to take the stump for Jackson. But Parmenter has not yet restrained the utterance of his indignant rebuke—he says that the nomination of Jackson is an outrage upon the party—that when it was first lisped by Cowell, he forewarned his associates of the dangers which beset their path, and that with a renegade as a candidate, in one short month they would look about for the Dorr party and it wouldn't be found. In one of his most eloquent passages, Parmenter exclaimed—"What think you Charles Jackson cares about the liberation of our martyr Governor—didn't he stand among the foremost of persecutors, and have you ever heard his voice raised for liberation, or did you ever learn that he was a subscriber for liberation stock? If you hug him to your bosom he will sting you to the very death." But not Parmenter alone in this formidable opposition; there is Willard, who had his eye upon the Gubernatorial honors, and he has yet to learn why his eminent services to the faction are postponed; although he now stands indicted for treason, he has yet to learn why the name of Charles Jackson is preferred before his.

Surrounded by such difficulties, apprehensive that the perilous voyage upon which you had embarked might terminate in hopeless shipwreck, or that the virtuous crew would turn mutineers before you reach the port of destination, you summoned them on the peaceful Sabbath, to sign new articles. The conditions have been fixed, the bond has been executed, and your sails are once more unfurled to the popular breeze. I am no Yankee if you don't catch a Tartar before the voyage is terminated.

But after all, was ever man who pretended to be a decent man more beautifully hoaxed? What charms has the office of Governor that you have sacrificed so much to obtain it? One can hardly suppose that you have been the pliant instrument in other hands, by which they might wreak their vengeance upon the Law and Order party, and yet circumstances which have transpired since your nomination justify the conclusion. Only think of it—"an out and out Clay man," and be it remembered, he is not alone of that class of politicians, for there is more than one "out and out Clay man" who is combined with you. Only think, I say, of such a man negotiating with the fiercest Dorrites within our borders. Whatever of sincerity there may be in this bold movement, let the parties concerned share the undivided honors and the unmitigated disgrace. In pursuit of such a bawble, and with such daring effrontery, let not Mr. Charles Jackson, or any other of his political associates, arrange themselves as the apostles of the Whig creed. I call for other evidence of apostleship than the passion for official preferment. I have yet to learn that he is imbued with Whig principles, who deserts to the camp of the enemy in the hour of trial or of peril, and treats with that enemy to leap over the bounds which the conservative principle had erected, and thus destroy the muniments of the constitution. If there is one feature above all others distinguishing a true Whig, it is his unflinching devotion to Law ond Order. If he is possessed of the true spirit, he will spurn all alliance with treason and with traitors as he would the sting of an asp. Can there be communion or fellowship, no matter on what sectional object, with such an enemy. Negotiate with him, sink the honor and dignity of the State; erase from the statute book wholesome laws; acknowledge that you have been wrong when you feel conscious that you have done right, in the broad light of day, for an office, a title, a name;—bargain and sell your reputation and keep the company of men whom at heart you despise, —is this what is meant by "an out and out Whig?"

Of that communion I am not a member, and so far as appearances indicate, the Whig party in Rhode Island spurns the alliance. The lion is not yet ready to lie down with the wolf, much less with the woodchuck.

ONE OF THE PEOPLE.

PROVIDENCE JOURNAL, MARCH 31, 1845.

BRIEF QUESTIONS ADDRESSED TO CHARLES JACKSON, ESQ.

---

1. You declare yourself to be "a true Whig." How, then, can you consent, on a mere "local issue," to lend yourself to the Dorrite faction, which embraces within its ranks hardly a single Whig, which goes for principles and for measures to which the great Whig party of the country has always been opposed; and which, for years, has been conspicuous for its fierce hostility to every man who bears the name of Whig?

2. In your address to the Whigs of Rhode Island, you say that "they opposed the election of General Greene to the Senate, because they believed that one of the strongest Whig States in the Union ought to be represented by uncompromising Whigs." How,

then, can you reconcile it to your political conscience, to your "out and out Whiggism," to form a coalition with the Dorrites, the practical and inevitable effect of which coalition will be the triumph of Locofocoism in this "one of the strongest Whig States?" If you think General Greene a compromising politician, for supporting Governor Francis, who, by the by, voted throughout with the Whigs, what sort of a politician must you be thought, for the coalition which you have made with the Dorrites, alias the Locofocos? General Greene compromised upon a gentleman and a man of honor; you have compromised upon Harris, Anthony, Cowell, and Parmenter?

3. When you attempted to explain "your position as a Whig" to the assembly in Masonic Hall, the other evening, did you not find some difficulty in accommodating your speech to your audience? Were you not very soon admonished, by the upturned faces before you, that the Dorrites, and not the Whigs, had come to the feast, and that it would not do for you to let out, in such a presence, the exalted conservatism which you had bottled up for the edification of true and high minded Whigs?

4. You claim to be a true Whig and a stanch Law and Order man. Do you find yourself quite at home in your new position? Are your new companionships suited to your taste? Do you not feel as if some wild centrifugal force had caused you to rush from your proper orbit? Upon what themes do you and your Dorrite confederates hold converse? If you talk with them upon national politics, how can you dwell together in unity? If you talk with them concerning what you are pleased to call "local issues," upon what

topics, save the liberation of Dorr, have you a right to expect responsive sympathy? Are you not made to feel by the costive speech, by the cold and decent civilities of men who have made up their minds to use you, in their need, that you have placed yourself in a position where you may command votes, but not confidence; where there is no cement but the bond of a common selfishness; and where the talk must be, not of great principles which both parties are equally concerned to uphold, but of the spoils of that anticipated victory, which both parties have made such costly sacrifices to achieve?

5. Do you believe, Sir, that the political power of this State may be more safely entrusted to the Dorrites than to the Whigs and conservatives, with whom you have hitherto acted? If you should chance to be chosen Governor, are you so very verdant as to flatter yourself that you could control these Dorrites? If you sow the wind, you must not expect to escape, or that others will escape, the predicted doom. Both you and others will reap the whirlwind. Upon what will you, then, fall back? Will you seek again the confidence of the Whigs? They will repel your advances with indignation and with scorn. Will you endeavor to regain your position upon "the conservative platform of Law and Order?" You will find your place filled with a true man—or you will discover, with humiliation and with shame, that this sacred platform has been swept away by the surges of that radicalism, which, but for you, would have raved themselves to rest! It cannot be that the barren title of Governor would solace you, in a season of public calamity, amid the wreck of conservative principles—the

decay of public virtue—the instability and confusion of all social concerns and interests? No, Sir, this can never be. The world reverences not barren titles, but men fruitful in good deeds. Cause such a season of calamity to come upon your native State, and that native State does not contain a hill which you would not then call upon to cover you—nor a man of unforfeited honor, however humble, with whom you would not rejoice to exchange places.

PROVIDENCE JOURNAL, MARCH 31 1845.

TO THE HON. JAMES F. SIMMONS.

In your letter to Henry B. Anthony, you commend the Dorrites for "magnanimously relinquishing their dangerous doctrine, in order that quiet and security may be restored to the community, and the government consistently set Mr. Dorr at liberty." Upon what principles of human action do you think it safe to trust these men? Have they, in past times, shown either sincerity, or moderation, or good faith? If upon the issue they have made, they succeed, will they not claim, and rightfully claim, that they have triumphed? Will not the majesty of the law be trampled down? Will not the State be dishonored at home and abroad?

How can you consider the question of liberation as "the main question" at the approaching election? The mode in which a State Prison convict shall be liberated the main question! Is it of no practical importance whether the Law and Order party, or the Dorrite party, decide this question? Is it of no practical importance which of these two parties exercises the political power of Rhode Island; makes her laws; appoints her judges and other magistrates; lays and appropriates taxes; takes care of the military establishment and of the interests of public education; and determines what shall, in all matters, be the policy of the State? Upon what principle of common prudence, do you think it safe to trust all these great interests to the Dorrites?

By supporting Charles Jackson, the Dorrite candidate, do you not, in effect, lend the full weight of your moral influence to break down the conservative party, and to elevate to place and to power, the radical party of the State?

You say, you never assented to the organization of the Law and Order party. Could you have ruled the Law and Order party, as you once ruled the Whig party, would you not have been among the last to abandon it?

Suppose you succeed in your efforts to break up the Law and Order party, can you, with all your ingenuity, reconstruct, from the fragments, a party which can stem the onward tide of radicalism in this State?

The Dorrites have not abandoned their principles—but only waived them. They never authorized the late Convention to adopt the resolutions which you and Mr. Jackson seem to think so very "magnanimous" and sincere. The next Convention which comes fresh from the "soverinnity," will rescind those resolutions; and they will, at the same time, re-affirm all the dangerous doctrines, which, to answer a temporary purpose, the late Convention found it convenient to repudiate? You are using the Dorrites, and the Dorrites are using you. Both of you are playing a selfish game. But one of you can win it. What, in the end, becomes of the rights, interest and honor of Rhode Island?

You say that "distinguished men abroad have expressed a desire to you for Mr. Dorr's release upon any terms compatible with our honor." Have you ever been told by any distinguished man, by any good Whig, that the unconditional liberation of Dorr could be accomplished, without dishonor to the State, by a party got up specially for the purpose of breaking down the Law and Order party, and forcing the General Assembly to terms of unconditional liberation? Do you suppose that there is a man of honor in the country, of any political party, who does not condemn the course of Mr. Jackson in accepting a nomination at the hands of the Dorrites, for the purpose of winning a triumph over the Law and Order party? Are you aware how indignant is the reprobation with which the Whigs abroad regard his conduct and yours, in this unparalleled transaction!

You overrate your own power, or you underrate the sagacity of your fellow citizens, if you suppose that you can blind them to the true issue. They take a very practical, common sense view of the whole matter. They know that the Dorrites, aided, I lament to say, by Mr. Jackson, Governor Arnold, Mr. Samuel F. Man, and yourself, are struggling to wrest from the Law and Order party, composed for the most part, of Whigs, the whole political power of the State. They know that Mr. Jackson was nominated in order to effect this purpose. They know of what materials the Dorrite party is composed, and, without a longer probation of its sincerity than you seem to require, they do not wish to trust this party with power. Do you think it strange that your Whig friends feel more confidence in themselves than in the Dorrites, even though Mr. Charles Jackson and Mr James F. Simmons may become their political endorsers? On the other hand, your Whig friends have tried the Law and Order party, year after year, and have no reason to withdraw from it their confidence. They are willing, at any rate, to try this party for another year. Why, Sir, should you, a Senator of the United States, throw yourself into this contest, in opposition to those who, in all past time, have delighted to honor you? Are not the genuine sympathy and confidence of the Law and Order party better than the sympathy and confidence of the Dorrites? Are you ready, for the sake of destroying the organization of the Law and Order party, to arm the Dorrites with the whole political power of the State?

You, sir, may raise the whirlwind, but you may not be able either to direct it or to allay its fury.

PROVIDENCE JOURNAL, APRIL 2, 1845.

LETTER TO THE HON. JAMES F. SIMMONS.

SIR:—I have read the letter which, on Friday last, you addressed ostensibly to Henry B. Anthony, Esq., the editor of that good Law and Order paper, the Providence Journal. Under the shallow pretence of defending yourself against the assault of an humble paragraphist, you, a distinguished Senator of the United States, seize an occasion to throw yourself into the hot strife which now agitates your native State. No man can mistake, in this matter, your real purpose. Availing yourself, somewhat adroitly, of the influence which belongs to the character and position of the editor of the Providence Journal, you seek to reach and to change the minds of the intelligent and true hearted Whigs of Rhode Island. You will fail, Sir, I venture to predict, you will signally fail, in this desperate enterprise to coin political capital for yourself, and to withdraw the Whigs from their hitherto unfaltering allegiance to the principles and to the cause of Law and Order. I can hardly apply to your letter and to your conduct, that style of decorous remark which, even amid political contests the most exasperated, it is my aim to preserve. Could I detect, throughout the whole of this elaborate production, one sign of that "noble rage" which fires noble bosoms—one graceful and fervid expression of high moral sentiment—one flash of thought or of feeling which told that you were striving, not to conceal a crafty intent, but to suppress strong passions, I should well know how to pardon any error into which a generous vehemence had betrayed you. But, when I find your letter to be cold, arid and jesuitical, full of cunning appeals to obsolete prejudices, and of covert thrusts at men whom you choose to denounce, because you cannot govern them,—when I find you laboring, by gentle and sinister plausibilities, to persuade the Whigs that they may, without danger and without dishonor, throw themselves into the embraces of the Dorrites; that the monstrous and meretricious union between Whiggism and Dorrism,—a union founded upon no principle, and cemented by no bond but that of a common selfishness, is better for the State than the sober, legitimate and honorable tie which binds together Law and Order Whigs and Law and Order Democrats, I cannot help sharing in the general, and the virtuous indignation which you have provoked in the bosom of every true and honorable man.

Something of noble grace, Sir, yet lingers around the ruins of our moral nature—something that makes us hate selfishness and despise cunning,—something that reminds us of our relationship to higher beings, and kindles in our hearts sympathy for truth and for right. You seem, Sir, to make no account of this element in our moral being,—the secret of all wide moral influence, the inseparable adjunct of all great and effective intellectual power. You seem to forget that "winding and crooked courses are the goings of the serpent,"—that "clear and round dealing is the honor of a man's nature, and that mixture of falsehood is like alloy, which may make the metal work the better, but it embaseth it."* Conquer, Sir, if it be not too late, this perverse habit of your mind; superinduce upon your moral constitution higher principles of action, or you will miss the loftiest heights of statesmanship; you will be regarded as one who is "good only in canvasses and factions;" you will live in the recollections of those who are to come after you, only as an expert manager of the politics of the day!

Your acknowledged intellectual ability, your sagacity as a party politician, and your commanding position as a Senator in the Congress of the United States, entitle your counsels, in relation to our State politics, to the candid and respectful consideration of your fellow citizens. While I thus cheerfully recognize your claims to be heard with candor and attention by those whom you have so long and so ably served, neither I nor others can yield such implicit deference to your opinions as to adopt them, with passive servility, in preference to the opinions of men not less wise and thoughtful than yourself. Those of your fellow citizens who compose an immense majority of the Law and Order party have stood by you, in sunshine and in storm. In the earlier stages of your political life, they looked to you with a strong hope that you would not disappoint the brilliant destinies which they forsaw were in reserve for you. They hailed your eleva-

* Bacon's Essays.

tion to the Senate of the United States as if your elevation were, in some sort, their triumph. They have watched, with friendly solicitude, your course as a Senator, and they have felt that some portion of the just fame which you have acquired, in counsel and in debate, was reflected upon themselves. In the progress of events, another tie between your political friends and yourself sprang into being. Treason and anarchy menaced the State, and, like other good citizens, you espoused the cause of Law and Order. You participated largely in the formation of our excellent constitution. You put forth your energies in favor of its adoption by the people. You assented, it was always thought till now, to the organization of the Law and Order party. You have hitherto sustained the nominations of that party. This, Sir, was once your position. What is your position now? I ask the question not without sorrow. Your letter to the editor of the Journal furnishes, to this question, a significant and most intelligible reply. Without giving your friends a decent "order of notice,"—without asking their counsel,—without an expression of solitary regret at the severance of old ties of political brotherhood, you have abandoned those who, through evil and through good report, have cherished and sustained you; and, what is more, you have abandoned them for the confidence, the sympathy, and the support of the Dorrites! I look for you in vain, standing side by side with tried political friends, on "the conservative platform," giving to those friends counsel, and lending them aid. I look for you in vain among those true men who still rally around that glorious banner which they reared in a season of sore calamity, which, once and again, they have followed to victory —which, whoever may prove recreant, they will be the last to desert! Where are you now, Sir? Where, and with whom must I expect to find you? Contending, side by side, with the Dorrites, and under whatsoever plausible pretences you may seek to justify your flagrant defection, contending, in effect, to prostrate the Law and Order party in the dust, and to achieve for Dorrism its long sought for triumph over the dignity and the laws of the State! This, Sir, is your position. It needs no labored definition—by no flimsy apology can it be rescued from dishonor!

You no longer attempt to shelter yourself behind convenient ambiguities of language, which convey to different minds very different and sometimes opposite meanings. You no longer give forth those dark, unintelligible intimations about your course, which, like the famed responses of the ancient oracles, are designed to be obscure. You stand forth, at last, the declared champion of Charles Jackson, the Dorrite candidate for the office of Governor, and the avowed, aye, the vituperous opponent of James Fenner, the Law and Order candidate for Governor! You are exerting all your skill in party tactics to help Mr. Jackson and to harm Governor Fenner. In highways and in byways, in the shop and in the manufactory, in town and in country, in the farmhouse and in the hamlet, you devote yourself to the work of persuading people that "the pacification of the State" can be secured only by the election of Charles Jackson, and by the consequent triumph of Dorr and of Dorrism! I mourn, Sir, sincerely do I mourn, that, fresh as you are from the associations of gentlemen and of men of honor in the Senate of the United States, you have returned to Rhode Island, not to help her in an hour of trial—not to tread in the good old ways—not to stand firmly upon the good old platform—not to fight bravely under the glorious old banner—but to abandon tried friends—to renounce past professions—to violate plighted faith! The fact, Sir, is known that you assented, cordially as it was thought, to the nomination of Governor Fenner. The fact also is known, and you cannot deny it, that, only a few months since, you volunteered, in the presence of a confidential friend, the most solemn protestations that you would "vote for Governor Fenner as long as he lived." Are not these, Sir, your very words?

Governor Fenner was unanimously, and with singular cordiality, nominated for re-election by the Convention of the Law and Order party. In that Convention you were represented; to that party you belonged—nay, more, you professed yourself to be in favor of maintaining the original organization of that party, as understood and expounded by Mr. Charles Jackson. What, then, has wrought this sudden and extraordinary change in your principles, purposes and conduct? How can you, Sir, as a consistent politician, as an honorable man, support Charles Jackson, the Dorrite candidate, in opposition to James Fenner, the Law and Order candidate?

Let me tell you, Sir, the history of this transaction will not be confined to Rhode Island. The record of your defection will follow you to Washington. Senators, high minded Senators, whose eyes beam bright with honor, and who "feel a stain like a wound," will look askance at you for quitting the path of open dealing and of elevated principle to hatch treacherous plots with treacherous men—to brood in secret conclave, with the enemies of Law and Order, over schemes intended to fix the seal of popular reprobation upon the principles of Law and Order!

I lament, Sir, that you have descended from the heights of true civic renown, to stir this Dorrite cauldron, and, by your potent incantations, to make it bubble. I lament that, forgetting your true position as a statesman, you stand before the country upon a false and paltry issue, as the ally of the Dorrites, their "guide, philosopher and friend!"

Your friends, Sir, will not follow you. No man of an erect and manly spirit, no man who acknowledges the validity of party ties, no man who obeys the instincts of nice personal honor, can follow you!

It is asked, on all sides, by right minded and honorable men, why, on your return from Washington, you did not seek to accomplish, through the agency of your friends, your views as to the true policy of Rhode Island in reference to Dorr? Why seclude yourself, by night and by day, in secular seasons, and in sacred seasons, with the confederates of the Dorrites? Why lend yourself to the Dorrites, upon an issue which they have made in order to obtain possession of the political power of the State? Have they changed their nature? Can they abandon their principles? Is it safe to trust their professions—to place any confidence in the resolutions and pledges of men whom, as past experience proves, not even solemn oaths can bind? Is it a time to intrust political power to those who demand as a right, the unconditional liberation of Dorr, and who would hail it as a triumph over Algerine cruelty and injustice? Is the mode in which a convict shall be liberated from the State Prison, an issue which ought to be agitated by the people of Rhode Island in their primary capacity? Finally, is it wise, or right, or safe, to give the Dorrites the power to liberate Dorr; and can "the pacification of the State" be secured by placing the purse and the sword of the State in the hands of a party which has once arrayed itself in arms against her government and people? These, Sir, are plain practical questions, asked by plain practical men—and to which, with all your ingenuity, you will find it hard to give a satisfactory answer.

I have not attempted an answer to your letter—an abler pen than mine has undertaken that task. I have aimed merely to describe its drift—and to indicate the true position in which you have placed yourself. A few words more, and I have done. I like old friends, Sir, as much as you seem to like new issues. I have confidence in the integrity and genuine Rhode Island spirit of the Law and Order democrats who, foot to foot, and shoulder to shoulder, stood by us in the hour of our utmost peril. For one, I would scorn to cast off these men—or to exchange them for new and untried friends. With them I am willing to sink or to swim. With them I am willing to share whatever of prosperity or of adversity may be in reserve for those of us who have made common cause in defence of the constitution of Rhode Island, and in the maintenance of the principles of Law and Order. If you prefer an alliance with the Dorrites, you must be left to follow your own taste, and to be governed by your own convictions of duty. Your old friends,

Sir, will part from you, not without some natural regrets. They will travel back, in memory, to the triumphs which, in years gone by, they and you won for conservative doctrines and for conservative men. As Whigs, they will mourn that, in a season of trial to the grand distinctive principle of the Whig party, "their own familiar friend, in whom they trusted, who did eat of their bread, hath lifted up his heel against them." They sorrow, however, most of all, that, weary of the noble strife for Law and Order, you have joined yourself, in disastrous and ignoble fellowship, to the men who have only waived their radical principles, that, under circumstances more favorable, they may re-assert and establish them. They tried to save you, but in vain. You would have none of their counsel—you despised all their reproof. To your new friends and to yourself they are therefore compelled to leave you. Upon what a poor device, Sir, have you staked your character and fortunes as an American statesman! Whatsoever temporary advantage it may promise to win for you, be assured, it cannot, in the end, achieve that true fame and that abiding popular favor, which are reserved only for unshaken constancy to Principle, to Honor, and to Truth.

A Rhode Island Conservative.

PROVIDENCE JOURNAL, APRIL 10, 1845.

GOVERNOR FENNER.

MR. EDITOR:—Thousands of the true hearted Whigs of Rhode Island respond, most cordially, to the brief but just and eloquent tribute, which, on Tuesday last, you paid to the merits of this veteran servant of the State. You are right, Sir, in your estimate of his "firm yet prudent administration." You are right, also, in your anticipations that, when the history of our noble struggle in the cause of regulated liberty comes to be written, his name will stand out clear and bright upon the record. How full of startling contrasts will that history be! How attractive will be some of its "political portraits"—how repulsive will be others! On one page, will be found the story of men who stood ready to peril every thing to save a noble cause; on another, will be chronicled the acts and the sayings of a few politicians who treacherously perilled a noble cause, in order to save themselves!

As Governor Fenner is about to retire, and to retire forever, to the shades of private life, it may not be amiss to recall to the public memory a few illustrations of the good service which, in a season of imminent peril, he rendered to his native State. In April,

1842, when treason was abroad in our streets, and when many hearts trembled for the issue of the doubtful struggle, James Fenner never quailed. When timid politicians were careful in what position they placed themselves, he, with uncalculating generosity, threw himself, his name, and influence and character, into the midst of a contest, which he at once saw was, in very truth, a contest for the fundamental principles, not only of constitutional freedom, but of social order. Upon the most broad, and patriotic basis, was the Law and Order party formed. The State was in danger;—and good men and true, Whigs and Democrats, came to the rescue! They united in a noble effort to save the State. At an hour like that, no paltry stipulations about the division of offices, could either have arrested or accelerated such a union! The politicians, it is quite probable, might, even then, have been concerned about the future disposal of offices and honors, but the mass of the people, to their honor be it recorded, looked only to the safety of the State, to the maintenance of her constitution and laws, against a most desperate effort to overthrow them. In April, 1842, Governor Fenner was solicited to take the post of first Senator in the Legislature of Rhode Island. He unhesitatingly consented. He had, it is true, been a Senator in the Congress of the United States, and, in past times, he had filled, for many years, the office of Governor of his native State. By no false notions of dignity, however, was he withheld from taking, at a crisis of great public emergency, any post, subordinate though it might be, in which his talents or influence could be most efficiently exerted for the benefit of his fellow citizens.

During the whole of that eventful year, Governor Fenner was fearless and indefatigable in the support of the great cause to which he had pledged his efforts. When the Legislature was in session, no Senator was more punctual or constant in his attendance; and none, it is not too much to say, was more wise in counsel, more firm in purpose, more vigorous in action.

In the course of the same year, Governor King requested the General Assembly to appoint a council to advise him in relation to the duties of his office, rendered, by fearful political agitations, not only arduous, but peculiarly delicate and responsible. Of that council, Governor Fenner was chosen a member. It were needless to add, that, in this new position, he exhibited his characteristic firmness, a far reaching political sagacity, and a generous devotion to Rhode Island, which, when her rights and honor were drawn into peril, made him disdain all compromise. The sittings of the council were frequent, and at times protracted. Governor Fenner, at the sacrifice of that ease and quiet which are demanded by advanced years, never failed to be present; and never was he present, without putting forth the powers of his clear and strong intellect in favor of the wisest measures to protect the government and people against the dangers which threatened them. He remained an active and influential member of Governor King's council, till, at the close of the political year, that body became extinct —the repeated failure of the insurgents to establish, by force, their revolutionary government, having rendered its functions entirely unnecessary.

During the same eventful year, was held a Convention of Delegates, for the purpose of forming a Constitution to be submitted to the people of Rhode Island for their ratification or rejection. Of this Convention, Governor Fenner was a member—spontaneously chosen by his fellow citizens of Providence, in consideration of his ripe experience in political affairs, and of his eminent fitness for the emergent crisis on which the State had been precipitated. He was unanimously elected to preside over that assembly, and he mingled freely in its counsels. Upon the question of suffrage, he favored, in accordance with his previous and well known opinions, the largest extension which seemed compatible with the greatest good of the greatest number.

In January, 1843, Governor King having signified his desire to retire to private life, Governor Fenner was urged by gentlemen of both political parties to become a candidate for the office of Chief Magistrate. At a crisis happily without a parallel in our political history, he did not feel himself at liberty to withhold from his fellow citizens any service, which in their judgment, he could render to the State. The nomination of Governor Fenner by the Law and Order convention was made with genuine cordiality—and, in this connexion, it ought to be added, that among those who most strenuously supported his nomination were certain of the ultra Whigs, who, on the first Wednesday of the present month, successfully strove to defeat his election! James F. Simmons and Lemuel H. Arnold, it is admitted, did not assent cordially to the nomination of Governor Fenner. He was not of their clique, and they well knew that he was a man whom they could not use for their purposes. The counsels of these politicians, however, did not prevail. Governor Fenner was nominated, and, in April, was elected by a majority so overwhelming as to be without a precedent in the history of our contested elections.

The administration of Governor Fenner was cordially approved by a large majority of his fellow citizens. In January, 1844, he was again nominated for the office of Governor, without, as is believed, a dissenting voice ; and, in April, he was again elected, by a commanding majority. During the second year of his administration, no persons, except the Dorrites, complained that James Fenner was other than a firm, discreet and intrepid Governor of Rhode Island—careful in providing for her safety—watchful over her various interests—jealous of her priceless honor!

In January, 1845, he was again nominated for re-election, and as it then appeared, with entire and cordial unanimity. What followed is too well known to require more than a passing remark. A few discontented politicians were resolved to break up the Law and Order party—and to re-establish their ancient rule over the Whig party. Availing themselves of a false issue, and seducing many right minded Whigs into the belief, that they had no other object in view than "the pacification of the State!" they have succeeded, by an alliance with the Dorrites, in defeating the election of James Fenner, the able and unswerving representative of those great conservative principles which the people of Rhode Island have, for years, struggled to maintain. What is to follow, what fresh dishonor is in reserve for Rhode Island, time will disclose!

The tirade which Mr. Senator Simmons, in very bad taste, recently pronounced upon the Chief Magistrate of this State, will not soon be forgotten. He denounced Governor Fenner as a "hard hearted tyrant, incapable of feeling, and destitute of principle—a democrat in private life, and a Bourbon when in power!" These historical parallels are sometimes unfortunate. It is difficult to be reminded of the Bourbons, and to lose all memory of the jesuitical politician, who now swore allegiance to them, and now betrayed them—who one day leagued with the revolutionary party, and the next deserted it; and who, amid all the changes of French politics, was true only to himself!

Governor Fenner, as you well observe, Mr. Editor, "will carry with him into his retirement the respect of thousands of his fellow citizens, which he would not exchange for all the honors of office." The memory of his eminent services in the cause of "Law and Order" will survive the abuse of ephemeral politicians. History will bear witness to his unfaltering devotion to that cause, and, if true to its office, it will place upon an imperishable record, the names of the men who betrayed it!

A Rhode Island Conservative.

PROVIDENCE JOURNAL, MAY 6, 1845.

LETTER TO THE HON. HENRY B. ANTHONY.

To the Editor of the Providence Journal:—

Sir:—The Hon. James F. Simmons, in a long letter addressed to yourself, and published in the Journal of Friday last, is at great pains to persuade the public that I am "governed by a rancorous hostility" towards him; that I have "continually assailed him," that I seem "determined to pursue him as an enemy," &c. In proof of these grave charges, which it suits the purpose of Mr. Simmons to make in terms transcending the license even of rhetorical exaggeration, he asserts that I have written "many, if not all the articles which have appeared against him in the Law and Order papers for the last fifteen months," and some of the first of which, he has been told, "you refused to publish." Can any man gifted with ordinary discernment mistake the drift of these allegations? They are not intended to wound me or to depress me in the estimation of my fellow citizens. Very far from it. Mr. Simmons, however profuse he may be in his charges of "bitterness" and "malignity," is too vain a man, and too shrewd and calculating a politician, to nurse much wrath towards an individual who, without intending it, has, on more than one occasion, gratified his vanity, and who, he well knows, has never sought, for a single moment, to frustrate his schemes of personal ambition. Why should I be the enemy of James F. Simmons? Till his formal renunciation of all allegiance to the Law and Order party, I had always considered him as a political friend and ally, and as such I had treated him. From some of his opinions, it is true, I have been compelled to dissent, but that dissent I have always expressed in terms the most courteous, and with an honest desire, while maintaining what seemed to me to be important truth, to inflict upon Mr. Simmons no unnecessary wound.

Why, Mr. Editor, should I be the enemy of James F. Simmons? As a Rhode Island man, I have felt a just pride, if, indeed, any pride can be just, in his fame and character as a Rhode Island Senator; and yet more, up to the very hour of his defection from the Law and Order party, it is known that I frankly and repeatedly expressed my preference for Mr. Simmons as a candidate for re-election to the Senate of the United States! Widely different have always been our spheres of action and enjoyment. He is, and from his youth has been, a shrewd, a very shrewd politician; he has given himself, with all his might, to the trade and mystery of partisan politics; he has exerted in this State a commanding political influence; he has bewildered himself with the fascinations of political power, and the captivating pageantries of elevated official rank. Surely, it were needless to carry out a contrast between this veteran politician, this favorite of the people, this applauded Senator, and an humble individual, who has been forced, by a most extraordinary pressure, to emerge from still life into the arena of political contention, and who, I must be pardoned for adding, has not, for a single hour, repented of a purpose, early formed, never to chase the phantoms of political ambition. All this Mr. Simmons well knows. His object, however, is to create sympathy, to represent himself as a persecuted man, as a victim which "a corps of men eminent for their acquirements" have selected for destruction! Considering the exigencies of his case, something perhaps should be pardoned to Mr. Simmons, if, in his attempts to defend himself, he do not very scrupulously adhere to the truth which belongs to history; and if, in drawing political portraits, he deals somewhat largely in caricature.

After all, Mr. Editor, is Mr. Simmons a persecuted man? Is he a servant of the State who has generously risked all, or sacrificed all, that he might save the State? Is he entitled to the sympathy which, by devices the most ingenious, he seeks to create? Has he not inflicted upon the Law and Order party a deep, but I trust not an incurable wound? Has he not forsaken the counsels of that party—repudiated its candidates, and wrought confusion in its ranks? Did he not first sleep upon his post, and, at last, desert to the enemy? And what has been the result? The Dorrites have elected their candidate for the office of Governor; and every radical herald from Maine to Georgia, makes itself hoarse in proclaiming this preliminary triumph of Dorrism. A triumph so disastrous for the peace and honor of Rhode Island, it was, be it remembered, in the power of James F. Simmons to avert! Misled, however, by a diseased vanity, or betrayed by his vaulting ambition, he abandoned, in their hour of trial, the friends who had crowned him with the selectest honor, and whom naught but his unwarrantable aggression upon the Law and Order party would ever have repelled from his side. And this, Mr. Editor, is not all. So desperate has he become in his efforts to avert the consequences which his defection may chance to entail upon himself, that, in more instances than one he has, either by an artful insinuation or by a bold declaration, invoked the aid of jacobinism itself, and sought to stir up, for his own benefit, and against good men and true, the fires of its inextinguishable hate! Surely, then, sir, it becomes not him to turn and rend those whom his own acts have forced into an antagonist position—whom he has so deeply wronged—whose confidence he has forfeited —for whose sympathy he has no right to plead!

Mr. Simmons alleges that I am the "author of many if not of all of the publications which have appeared against him in the Law and Order papers of Providence for the last fifteen months." And now, sir, what is the truth in this matter? For the Transcript, to the best of my knowledge and belief, I have never written a line against him. Nay, more, I interested myself to suppress the paragraph in the Transcript extra, which formed the text of Mr. Simmons's first exculpatory address to the public, suggesting to the Editor of that paper that Mr. Simmons had not yet placed himself in an attitude of open and avowed hostility to the Law and Order party.

After taxing my memory, and searching the columns of the Journal, I can discover only four publications, of which I am the author, and which, in any manner, relate to Mr. Simmons. They were all demanded for the defence of the cause of law and order, and all of them appeared after Mr. Simmons had distinctly defined his position—after he had come out boldly in opposition to the Law and Order party, and in favor of the Dorrite candidate for the office of Governor! Thenceforward, it is most true, I no longer treated him as a political ally and friend. He, be it remembered, provoked the war. Why, then, should he complain that he has not escaped the fortune of war?

Mr. Simmons takes occasion to refer to "some" articles written by me, and as he intimates in opposition to him, which you "refused to publish." Now, Sir, what is the truth in this matter? In March, 1844, Mr. Simmons made, in the Town House, a speech before the Providence Clay Club, which I am not alone in thinking, was adapted to throw into the shade the grand conservative principles of the Law and Order party. Deprecating the effect of this speech upon the public mind, I handed you for publication the following letter, addressed to Mr. Simmons, which you, in the most courteous and friendly terms, declined to publish. As I am determined that Mr. Simmons shall not profit from any of my secret sins against him, from any of my suppressed publications, I now ask of you the favor to give this letter a place in the columns of the Journal. The public will perceive that it is entirely free from "malignity" or "bitterness"—that its aim is not to "destroy" Mr. Simmons, but to prevent Mr. Simmons, from destroying, by insidious appeals, the Law and Order party!

I lament, Sir, most sincerely do I lament, the position in which Mr. Simmons has placed himself in relation to old and faithful friends; and happy shall I be, if he be not reserved to illustrate, yet more fully, the remark of a philosophical writer, that "falseness of position naturally leads to falseness of character!" His present course, it is certain, can end well, neither for himself, nor for the State. He may, it is true, achieve success; he may catch the plaudits of the multitude; he may win a selfish political triumph; but the hour awaits him, when every illusion will be dissipated, and when he will learn, perhaps too late to profit from the lesson, that the lasting sympathies of an intelligent and virtuous people are with honor and with truth.

Reserving to myself the privilege of noticing, very briefly, and at no very distant day after the adjournment of the approaching session of the General Assembly, the reply of Mr. Simmons to the interrogatories of "One of the People," I subscribe myself, your friend and fellow citizen,

WILLIAM G. GODDARD.

PROVIDENCE, May 5, 1845.

TO THE HON. JAMES F. SIMMONS.

SIR:—Will you pardon in me a common artifice of humble authors? I seek to attract attention to my thoughts, by addressing them to the public under the auspices of a popular and distinguished name. [Your acknowledged intellectual ability, your sagacity as a party politician, and your commanding position as a member of the Senate of the United States, entitle your counsels in relation to our State politics, to the most respectful consideration of your fellow citizens. While I thus cheerfully recognize your claims to be heard with candor and attention by those whom you have so long and so ably served, I cannot yield such implicit deference to your opinions as to adopt them all, with passive servility, in preference to the opinions of men not less wise and thoughtful than yourself.*] Fresh as you are from the conclaves of the Capitol, and animated as you are by a generous zeal in behalf of that great Statesman, whom we all delight to honor, it would be strange, indeed, if your sympathies were not somewhat exclusive—it would be strange, indeed, if your associations at Washington had not caused you to feel somewhat less strongly than you once felt, the transcendent importance of the Rhode Island Question, and, consequently, the vast importance of maintaining, in unbroken strength and spirit, the Rhode Island Party. All this is very natural—and whatever of wrong in the matter there may be, it ought, in the judgment of charity, to be ascribed to the fallibility of all human judgments.

I respond, most cordially, to the language and sentiments of most of your recent address to the Clay Club in this city. I agree with you that vitally important to Rhode Island and to the country are the great questions which now divide political parties, and which are so soon to be decided, for good or for evil. I sympathize with you in your admiration for the character of Mr. Clay—and in your generous and

*NOTE.—Although the passages enclosed in brackets were incorporated into a letter to Mr. Simmons, published in the Journal, April 2, 1845, under the signature of "a Rhode Island Conservative," yet, to prevent all cavil, I have deemed it advisable not to retrench them.—*W. G. G.*

honest zeal in behalf of him and of the great cause with which he is identified. I look to him as to The People's Last Hope! I look to him as the representative of the true principles of national policy. More than all, I look to him as the fast friend and the intrepid defender of that sacred cause of regulated liberty—which the men of Rhode Island have perilled their lives and fortunes to maintain. Here, perhaps, you may suppose lies the ultimate point of agreement between us. Not so. I am happy to be able to add, in all sincerity, that I desire no less than you do, that this State should elect to the Senate of the United States none but "thorough and true men." I want no "doubtful man" for that or for any other place. I agree with you, Sir, "we want true men;" I agree with you, that "true men are much needed." I agree with you, also, that "they are not always to be found!"

I have, Sir, been thus particular in enumerating the topics of your speech, concerning which there can be no difference of opinion among the law and order men of Rhode Island, because I am compelled to express my irreconcilable dissent from some of your views, and to protest, in the most decided terms, against your estimate of the importance of the Rhode Island question. To tell you the truth, Sir, I was mortified and disheartened at your whole treatment of this question. You brushed it, with most unceremonious hand, into a side pocket, as if it were an incumbrance to be removed, or rubbish which should be kept out of sight. I was mortified and disheartened, Sir, that you, a Rhode Island Senator, and a statesman of no mean repute, should allude to the

Rhode Island question as a "local issue," as a particular and partial subject! The Rhode Island question a local issue! a particular and partial subject! A vast majority of your fellow citizens do not so regard this matter. They believe, with Henry Clay, that there is "no mode by which an existing government can be overthrown and put aside, and a new one erected in its place, but by the consent or authority of that government, express or implied; or by forcible resistance, that is, revolution!" This is the language, and this the doctrine of Henry Clay. This was and still is the doctrine of the Law and Order party in Rhode Island. They are not disposed to repudiate it, or to banish it into seclusion as an obsolete idea, or as a "local issue;" they contend, that unless this doctrine can be maintained in this country, constitutions are of no value to the people, and that whoever is President, no State and no interest would be for a moment secure against revolutionary aggression.

You seem to be apprehensive lest "any new issues should be presented by any Clay Club in this State to the people, here or elsewhere." I do not affect to misunderstand this language. You mean, Sir, to admonish us, not to introduce the Rhode Island question among the great issues which are to be tried before the people in the coming contest. The friends of Law and Order have not sought to introduce the Rhode Island question into the issues of the day, nor have they sought to exclude it. Our opponents, the Dorrites, have already introduced it into Congress, and they intend to bring it before the Baltimore Van Buren Convention. Under such circumstances, how fruitless, how worse than fruitless the tone of deprecation which you have adopted! Come what may, the Rhode Island question will be made an issue, before the country. For one, I am prepared to meet it—" here and elsewhere," now and hereafter—assured that, the more it is discussed, the better it will be understood—and that the great principles for which we in Rhode Island have contended, will commend themselves to a vast majority of the American people as the only true principles of popular freedom.

You exhort us, Sir, in the close of your speech, to " cherish kind feelings towards the reasonable portion of the Dorrite party,"—towards those who are satisfied with the salutary changes which have been introduced into the civil government of Rhode Island. All this may be well—and perhaps in accordance with Scripture you might have extended your kindness yet further. Kindness it may be right to show towards all men. But kindness and confidence are very different things. Confidence is of slow growth, and should not be placed prematurely in those who may abuse it. [I like, Sir, old friends, as much as you seem to like new issues. I want to form no new alliances, " here or elsewhere." I have unlimited confidence in the integrity and true Rhode Island spirit of the Law and Order democrats, who, foot to foot and shoulder to shoulder, stood by us in the hour of our utmost peril. For one, I would scorn to cast off these men, or to exchange them for new and untried friends. With them, I am willing to sink or to swim. With them, I am willing to share whatever of prosperity or of adversity may be in reserve for those of us who have made common cause in defence of the institutions of Rhode Island, and in the maintenance of the principles of law and order.*] These principles, far from being local in their application, extend throughout the length and breadth of this whole land. So far from being subordinate, they transcend immeasurably in importance ANY OTHER QUESTION AND ALL OTHER QUESTIONS which the people of this country are now about to decide.

A RHODE ISLAND MAN.

PROVIDENCE, March 9, 1844.

PROVIDENCE JOURNAL, MAY 19, 1845.

LETTER TO THE HON. HENRY B. ANTHONY.

TO THE EDITOR OF THE PROVIDENCE JOURNAL:—

SIR:—I offer no apology for again addressing you, in reply to Mr. Senator Simmons. Disregarding the immunities of the press, and the rules of controversy, that gentleman has summoned me, by name, into the arena. Although I court no contest with him or with any other antagonist, yet I seek to shun no responsibilities to which a calm, and manly, and fearless defence of the cause of Law and Order may chance to expose me. The mode in which, for the last two

*See Note, page 491.—*Ed.*

months, the war has been carried on against the men and the principles of the conservative party in this State, ought, perhaps to admonish me that I am behind the age, in attempting to set up any claim in behalf of the press, or of those courtesies which, in other times, were established to save controversy from sinking into the rudeness and violence of gladiatorial strife. At the risk, however, of being charged with entertaining somewhat antiquated and dainty notions of personal honor, I desire, on this occasion, to protest, indignantly to protest, against the use, for any political purposes whatsoever, of the unreserved disclosures of opinion in private conversation, and of the contents of the private letters, which public men may address to personal or to political friends. If these things can be done, without meeting from the community a scorching rebuke;—if the sacred confidence of unstudied epistolary correspondence is to be recklessly violated;—if every thought to which utterance is given under the genial influences of the social principle, is to be perverted by cold and crafty politicians, to the purposes of grave public accusation and reproach, men will come to dread society as a snare;—they will stifle their generous sympathies;—they will keep back their honest opinions;—they will, in short, be compelled to find refuge, from this species of treachery, either in timid silence or in suspicious diplomatic reserve. What political advantage, let me ask you, Sir, can compensate the loss of "the free thought of the free soul?" Under a government founded upon opinion, how unwise, too, not to say how wicked, to restrain, by any sort of inquisitorial penalty, the full and fearless expression of opinion!

Mr. Simmons is fond of involution, both in conduct and in style. Into his ingenious and elaborate reply to the interrogatories of "One of the People," he has, for effect, introduced several topics not at all pertinent to the main issues. From the true and original grounds of the controversy, I shall not, however, suffer myself to be diverted, for the purpose either of retorting personalities, or of discussing unimportant and irrelevant questions. Let me, therefore, recall public attention to the questions propounded by "One of the People." They have served Mr. Simmons as a peg whereon to hang a long letter—a letter, too, which fully sustains his reputation for political tact, and for skillful special pleading!

"One of the People" asks,

"Were the Resolutions of the General Assembly of Rhode Island, in reply to the impertinent and abusive Resolutions of the Legislature of New Hampshire, ever presented to the Senate of the United States?"

Mr. Simmons, in his reply to this question, admits that the Resolutions in question were not presented to the Senate.

"There was," says he, "neither direction nor request by our Assembly that they should be laid before the Senate, and upon consultation with my colleague it was thought that they contained expressions calculated to produce an unprofitable discussion, if presented."

As to the matter here stated as fact by Mr. Simmons, he is clearly in the wrong. Our Assembly, as may be seen from its records, did "request our Senators and Representatives to lay these Resolutions before their respective Houses of Congress." This error,

I have no question, was, on the part of Mr. Simmons, entirely inadvertent—and, regarding it as such, I desire not to magnify, but simply to correct it.* The reasons for withholding these Resolutions from the Senate, do not, upon general principles, seem to me to be satisfactory. Not only were the New Hampshire Resolutions grossly affrontive to the government and people of Rhode Island, but they were transmitted by Governor Steele to Governor Fenner, in a manner deliberately and studiously insulting. Hence the somewhat piquant style with which Rhode Island rebuked the impertinence of New Hampshire. Besides, these New Hampshire resolutions, inasmuch as they assumed the right to interfere in the internal government and police of a sister State, become matters of grave concernment to every man who regards the qualified sovereignty of the States as a check upon that popular absolutism which threatens to destroy, throughout the length and breadth of this land, every vestige of sober constitutional freedom. It would seem to me that, in this and in all similar cases, Senators are invested with no discretionary power. It belongs not to them to decide in what language a State shall repel aggressions upon its sovereignty. It was, however, apprehended, that these resolutions would produce an "unprofitable discussion." Has Mr. Simmons, since he electrified the Senate of the United States by his noble speech upon Rhode Island affairs in May, 1842, ever found a single occasion, in the Senate or out of it, on which he has not shied, as "unprofitable," the Rhode Island Ques-

* Since the above was written, Mr. Simmons, in a note to H. B. Anthony, Esq., has himself corrected this error.

tion? And yet, he is challenged to select, from the history of State or of national politics, a more important, or vital, or far reaching question. "One of the People," however, did not make this neglect to present the resolutions of our Legislature, in reply to those of New Hampshire, a matter of very grave reproach against Mr. Simmons;—and I have no desire to press the topic beyond its legitimate claims to attention.

After affirming that "Senator Simmons, during the late canvass in this State, coined for himself no little political capital, by alleging that Governor Fenner withheld the anti Texas resolutions passed by the General Assembly of Rhode Island," "One of the People" asks, "were these resolutions, which it is admitted reached Washington before the question was taken, ever presented to the Senate?" How does Mr. Simmons meet this question? In the first place, availing himself of a verbal distinction, he denies, with some indignation, that he "charged Governor Fenner with withholding the anti Texas resolutions." Unless he intended to produce an impression upon the public mind unfavorable to Governor Fenner, in reference to the transmission of the anti Texas resolutions, why, in his first letter to you, did he introduce the topic at all? Why assert that if the "delay in the transmission of these resolutions was caused by his hostility to the resolutions, he (Governor Fenner) has assumed a great responsibility by refusing fairly to execute the duties of his office?" These are the very words of the honorable Senator. He lacked the courage and the manliness to make against Governor Fenner a distinct and direct charge of malefeasance in office. By an insinuation, however, which is utterly unworthy of him as a man and as a Senator, he seeks to accomplish his object—to beget in the public mind the belief that Governor Fenner delayed to transmit the anti Texas resolutions, because he was hostile to those resolutions! To harm Governor Fenner, he resorts to a paltry insinuation which he knows will produce all the effect that could be wrought by a charge against him in explicit words. And then, after having done the very mischief which he sought to do, he interposes a pitiful salvo in order to protect himself. He intimates that "the delay may have been accidental—that he does not wish to be unkind or to make any charges of intentional neglect!" The exact measure of Senator Simmons's kindness towards Governor Fenner, I leave to be determined by the few Whigs who listened to his speech, which won such loud plaudits from the Dorrites in Masonic Hall!

It is painful, however, to dwell longer upon the poor expedients to which an able man is driven, when he once deserts the path of plain dealing. I therefore pass to the consideration of other topics. And here, to prevent all misconception, it may not be amiss to let the honorable Senator define, in his own words, his own position in reference to the anti Texas resolutions of our General Assembly. I quote from his last letter addressed to yourself:

"The anti Texas resolutions did not contain any direction or request that we should present them. When I addressed the Senate upon that question, I read the resolutions, to show the opinion entertained by the General Assembly, and that our State had made a proper distinction between this question and the one presented in the acquisition of Louisiana. I did not present them formally to the Senate because I had reason to believe that whatever opinions my colleague might entertain, his vote would be in accordance with the wishes of the Assembly. Doubts had been expressed by others as to his course, and it appeared to me that if he desired to have the resolutions appear as the ground of the vote he intended to give, he would introduce them himself; and if he did not, it might appear indelicate for me to do it, as no one had expressed any doubt as to my vote, and I had none about his."

Delicacy, it seems, towards John Brown Francis, prevented James F. Simmons from formally presenting these resolutions to the Senate! How engaging is this considerate tenderness towards his colleague! What gentle care, too, does Mr. Simmons take of his colleague, when he suggests that, upon the Texas question, Governor Francis was regarded as a doubtful man, while no one had expressed any doubt as to his vote! Upon this portion of the honorable Senator's explanation, I cheerfully leave the people of Rhode Island to make their own commentary.

Mr. Simmons's extraordinary explanation in regard to the manner in which the anti Texas resolutions of our General Assembly were disposed of in the Senate of the United States, can hardly be deemed satisfactory by any true anti Texas man. Owing, undoubtedly, to a casual omission on the part of the Legislature, the resolutions, it is true, contained no explicit direction or request that our Senators should present them. The Governor, however, was requested to send a copy of them to each of our Senators and Representatives in Congress, and to the Governors of the several States. For what purpose should he send them? That the Senators and Representatives might lay them before their respective Houses, and that the Governors might lay them before their respective State Legislatures. Besides, in one of these resolutions, the State of Rhode Island "does most solemnly protest against the annexation of Texas or any other foreign State or territory to this Union, unless the same shall be accomplished by an independent expression of the sovereign will of the free people of all and each of these United States." For what purpose was this solemn protest made? Was it intended for our Senators and Representatives alone? Clearly not. It was intended to reach both Houses of Congress; and to operate on the decision at which both Houses of Congress might arrive upon this great national question.

And yet, after all, these resolutions were never, in any formal and constitutional sense, presented to the Senate. The solemn protest of the State of Rhode Island against the annexation of Texas cannot now be found among the records of the Senate! Mr. Simmons, when he made his Texas speech, read the resolutions in question! For what purpose did he read them? Informally to make known to the assembled Representatives of the sovereign States in the confederacy, that Rhode Island solemnly protested against the annexation of Texas to the Union, and to show that "our State made a proper distinction between this question and the one presented in the acquisition of Louisiana!" Specially incumbent upon Mr. Simmons was the duty to present, in the most formal and authentic manner, these anti Texas resolutions. In his published letters and speeches during the late canvass, he complained bitterly of the course which, as he says, Governor Fenner pursued in regard to the Texas question. If, as Mr. Simmons asserts "a letter from Governor Fenner urging the annexation of Texas was, last year, shown, and the fact urged upon Southern Senators to prove that not all of the old thirteen, and not all even of the New England States were opposed to annexation," why did he not present the resolutions of our Legislature, in order to counteract the malign influence which he ascribes to Governor Fenner's letter? Why did he not furnish Southern Senators with the highest and most incontestible evidence that Rhode Island, a New England State, and "one of the old thirteen," was opposed to annexation?

Let me now examine Mr. Simmons's course in relation to the very able and spirited Protest of the General Assembly of Rhode Island against the attempted interference of the General Government in our internal affairs. This Protest, it will be recollected, was adopted at a special session of the Legislature, March 29, 1844. It was accompanied by a resolution requesting our Senators and Representatives "to urge this our Protest and Declaration upon the attention of the respective Houses of Congress." On the 16th of April it was presented to the House, but, much to the surprise and regret of the people of Rhode Island, it was never presented to the Senate till April 24th, nearly a month after the time of its adoption! And, then, the presentation of this document was accompanied by a motion to lay it upon the table! and there, for aught that appears to the contrary, this solemn and indignant protest of a sovereign State against a most dangerous aggression upon her reserved rights, has been permitted to remain undisturbed! Of this, the Legislature and people of Rhode Island have a right to complain. The Protest deserved, on every ground, to be "urged upon the attention" of both Houses of Congress, and more especially upon the attention of the Senate, composed, as that body is, of the immediate representatives of the States, and intrusted, in some sort, with the guardianship of the residuary sovereignty of the States. Inasmuch as the motion to lay the Protest upon the table excludes debate, why was that motion made? Besides, this motion disposes of a proposition only for the present. The Protest might have been taken up, upon motion and vote, at any time when the Senate pleased. Upon such motion, debate would not have been excluded. Why was not such motion made? Mr. Simmons stood mute during every stage of this transaction, and thus standing mute he was false to his trust as a Rhode Island Senator. It is known that he speaks often, and that he can speak well. Upon the very day when the Protest was presented, and put to sleep upon the table of the Senate, he engaged in a debate upon the details of the Post Office bill. Upon every question affecting the interests and the rights of his constituents, except the Rhode Island Question, which more deeply than any other concerns their interests and their rights, he has lifted up his voice. That question, he has systematically shunned in the Senate and out of the Senate. In his famous Clay Club speech, delivered in March, 1844, in the Town House, he treated it as "a local issue, as a partial and particular subject!" During the late canvass for the Presidentship, he addressed mass meetings in Pennsylvania, where the Locofoco orators dwelt mainly, and, as is believed, with mischievous effect, upon the conduct of this State in relation to Dorr and to Dorrism. I have yet to learn that, on any occasion, in Pennsylvania, or elsewhere, he ever sought to vindicate the character of his native State from the calumnies heaped upon it by the sympathizing friends of Dorr, or that he ever improved an opportunity to discuss before the people of any State the true merits of the Rhode Island Question. At the memorable mass meeting held in Taunton, September 10, 1844, Mr. Simmons was introduced to the people by Daniel Webster, in the most eloquent manner, as "the Representative of a State which has recently occupied a distinguished and remarkable position before the whole country—which has maintained her institutions against those who have raised the standard of insurrection within her borders, and against those who, under the influence of miserable and misdirected sympathizers, have gone there from abroad." How did Mr. Simmons respond to the fervid and eloquent remarks of Mr. Webster, which were obviously intended to draw him out upon the great principles involved in the Rhode Island Question? In a cold and costive manner, he acknowledged the tribute paid by Mr. Webster to his native State, and "then proceeded to discuss the questions of policy upon which the two parties are divided!" On this occasion, surely, Mr. Simmons was excluded by no stringent parliamentary rule from discussing the affairs of Rhode Island; and he will not deny that every man upon the ground expected that he would discuss them. Taunton, as is well known, was the centre of an "infected district;" it was the home of an illustrious clam bake apostle of Dorrism, and when Mr. Simmons, amid the deafening shouts of the multitude, rose to speak, every man strained his ear to catch, from the lips of a Rhode Island Senator, a burning rebuke of the sympathizers who had vexed our peace, and a spirit stirring and lofty vindication of the great principles which Rhode Island had struggled to maintain. But, alas! the voice of the Senator was raised only to discuss, at such a time and in such a presence, the policy of antagonist parties!*

How does Mr. Simmons reply to the charge that he stood mute in the Senate, although the radical orators at the other end of the capitol were pouring forth upon the government and people of Rhode Island the

* In this connexion, it may not be amiss to present to the public the following extracts from an account of the enthusiastic Mass Meeting at Taunton, on the 10th of September last. It may be found in the Providence Journal of September 11th:

"Mr. Webster then rose and said: It gives me great pleasure to introduce to you another member of the United States Senate, who represents a State which has recently occupied a distinguished and remarkable position before the whole country. In my deliberate judgment, the course pursued by the Whigs of Rhode Island, during the recent contest in that State, has entitled them to the grateful respect and remembrance of every American citizen. She has maintained her institutions against those who have raised the standard of insurrection within her borders, and against those who, under the influence of miserable and misdirected sympathizers, have gone thence from abroad. She deserves the support of every man who values constitutional liberty and the permanence of principles of law and order in society. I have the honor to introduce to you, gentlemen, Mr. Simmons, of the United States Senate, from Rhode Island. (Here nine enthusiastic cheers were given for Rhode Island.)

"Mr. Simmons said, I wish it was in my power to reply in a suitable manner to the compliment of your distinguished chairman, to the State in which I was born. We of Rhode Island have been educated in the principles of civil liberty from the earliest times, and we think we know how to maintain them. Mr. Simmons then proceeded, in his usual able manner, to discuss the questions of policy upon which the two parties of the country are divided."—*W. G. G.*

most bitter invectives and the most injurious calumnies? Does he deny the fact? No—for it is undeniable. He pleads, in the first place, that the motion to lay the protest upon the table precluded debate; and, in the next place, that it would be out of order to "answer or allude to the proceedings or speeches in the House of Representatives." All this is very true. Mr. Simmons was not expected to answer these radical orators, but he was expected, while they were occupied in vilifying us, to seek an occasion, nay to make an occasion, to raise his voice in defence of the character and institutions of his native State. This duty he neglected to discharge. Had he been anxious to discharge it, the occasion would not have been wanting. Parliamentary rules were not made to preclude debate upon great questions. Had the protest been "urged" upon the attention of the Senate, as it ought to have been, the whole matter would have been opened for discussion, and neither Mr. Simmons nor the people of Rhode Island would now be left to make the humbling confession, that the Rhode Island question is not well understood by the people of other States! Had Virginia, or Kentucky, or South Carolina, protested, in a like solemn manner, against the interference of the general government in their internal affairs, does any man believe that the indignant eloquence of Rives, of Crittenden, and of M'Duffie, could have been restrained by any cold, parliamentary rules? Does any man doubt that, at such a crisis, those chivalric Senators would have raised, in defence of "State Rights" and Regulated Liberty, voices which would have thrilled the bosoms of the masses in every city along our Atlantic border, and woke to new life the lone dweller in every log house beyond the mountains?

It was asked, by "One of the People," "did they (the Rhode Island Senators) embrace the opportunity to support the doctrines of the protest, and to defend their native State against the slanders contained in Burke's Report?" In a tone of triumph not warranted by an error quite immaterial to the main issue, into which I was betrayed, Mr. Simmons affirms that, at the time this protest was presented, Mr. Burke's Report had not been made! This, I admit, is very true; but what does Mr. Simmons gain by the admission? The slanders upon this State, contained in that report, had been uttered in the House, by Rathbun, of New York, Kennedy, of Indiana, and M'Clernand, of Illinois, before the protest was even adopted! Will Mr. Simmons pretend that, in a discussion upon the facts and doctrines set forth in the protest, it would not have been in his power, in spite of any technical parliamentary rule, to vindicate, and triumphantly to vindicate, the government and people of Rhode Island against every slander which had been uttered against them?

I have no desire to place myself in an antagonist position to Mr. Simmons. I lament that he should have said or done aught to shake the public confidence in him as a public man. I should rejoice to see him regain, by a course of manly and elevated conduct, befitting the character of an American Senator, any portion of that favor and respect which, through an unwise trust in the shifts of a hackney politician, he seems to have forfeited. I should not have dwelt thus long upon the charges which "One ot the People" has made against him, had he not, in the most confident manner, pronounced them to be "utterly groundless." No candid and intelligent man, I am persuaded, can resist the conviction that these charges are all substantially true. They were made with no design to "destroy" Mr. Simmons, but to neutralize, as far as may be practicable, the influence which he was exerting to break down and to destroy the Law and Order party.

Mr. Simmons has introduced into his letter sundry topics, somewhat personal, upon which, from a reluctance to obtrude myself upon the public, no less than from an honest desire to avoid all further controversy, I shall forbear to remark. I may, however, be pardoned for adding, that he has caricatured, with what propriety I leave gentlemen of all parties to determine, some opinions which, in the easy confidence of social intercourse, I have expressed to him; and that he has ascribed to me others, which I have never either expressed or entertained!

A few words in relation to the expediency of continuing the organization of the Law and Order party, and I have done. Mr. Benjamin Aborn, Mr. Samuel F. Man and Mr. James F. Simmons, in their printed address to the Whigs of Rhode Island, while they speak of themselves, with quite as much truth as modesty, "as leading members of the Law and Order party," announce, somewhat in the style of an imperial decree, that "its end is accomplished!" The Hon. Lemuel H. Arnold denominates it an "expiring clique;" and the Hon. Richard K. Randolph goes yet farther, in declaring that "the Law and Order party has been broken up!" These gentlemen have renounced, in a formal manner, all allegiance to that party. No man questions their naked right thus to abandon a well tried and honorable political connexion, which has won both blessings and honor for the State. It belongs, however, not to them nor to any leaders of the Law and Order party, to determine when that party has accomplished its end; or when it may be safe and proper to abandon an organization, which, though rightfully deemed to be "paramount" to all other political organizations, never has endangered and never can endanger the ascendency of Whig principles in Rhode Island. This party, as I believe, is yet greatly needed to accomplish ends the most important—to avert calamities the most serious from the government and the people of Rhode Island. I rejoice to perceive that, in spite of every mean and profligate attempt to destroy it, it still gives evidence of vitality in every part. It is strong in the confidence and attachment of an immense majority of its members;—it is strong in the respect and good will of the conservative party throughout the country; it is stronger still in the transcendent importance of the principles which it has hitherto upheld; and which, whatever may be the future destinies of the State, it will inevitably be summoned again to assert and to defend. Let it, then, be maintained, till the many and not the few, the tribes and not the heads of tribes—the people and not the politicians, shall, in their wisdom, decide that for the good of the whole, it ought to be abandoned!

Not intending, under any circumstances of provocation, again to address you, allow me, Mr. Editor, to return you my sincere thanks, for the courtesy which, on all occasions, you have extended to me, and to subscribe myself,

Faithfully, your friend and fellow citizen,

WILLIAM G. GODDARD.

PROVIDENCE, May 15, 1845.

PROVIDENCE JOURNAL, NOVEMBER 19, 1845.

RESOLUTIONS

PASSED AT A CONVENTION OF THE RHODE ISLAND PARTY.

RESOLVED, That, whereas the powers delegated to the general government are few and defined, and those which remain in the State governments are numerous and indefinite, and whereas the former are exercised principally on external objects, as war, peace, negotiation and foreign commerce, and the powers reserved to the States extend to all the objects which, in the ordinary course of affairs, affect the lives, liberties, and properties of the people, and the internal order, improvement, and prosperity of the State, it therefore becomes the paramount concern of the people of the several States to take the first and best care of their domestic governments, organizing them upon sound conservative principles, and confiding the administration of them to sound conservative men.

Resolved, That it is more especially the duty and the interest of the smaller States to take care of themselves, and, as far as practicable, to rely upon themselves, because they are unable either to shape the counsels of the general government or to conciliate its favor; because the influence of the great States is, every year, becoming more effective in. deciding who shall govern the country, and what shall be its course of legislation; and because, moreover, the extension of our borders and the rapid increase of population in the West have quickened into life a gigantic power, moved by strong impulses and passions; intent upon projects of sectional aggrandizement; ambitious, even at the expense of war, to extend, still farther, "the area of freedom," and destined, ere long, to control, either for good or for evil, the whole policy of the general government.

Resolved, That, while we call to remembrance the fact that, during a season of trial, unexampled in our political history, the House of Representatives of the Congress of the United States prostituted its powers to the ignoble purpose of placing upon record an elaborate libel upon the government and people of Rhode Island, and that the Senate of the United States silently laid upon its table, and suffered it to sleep there, the indignant protest which Rhode Island felt herself bound to make against the unconstitutional interference of the general government with her internal affairs, we cling more closely than ever to the conviction that it is the sacred duty of Rhode Island, while she faithfully discharges all her constitutional obligations to the Union and to her sister States, to rely upon herself for the maintenance of her rights, and for the vindication of her honor.

Resolved, That this conviction is strengthened by the "fixed fact" that the present Executive of the United States has appointed to offices of trust and honor several individuals who signalized themselves in the late attempt to overthrow by force the legal government of this State; and some of whom, when they received their commissions from the President, were actually under indictment for grave offences against the sovereign power of the State.

Resolved, That, inasmuch as the State of Rhode Island contains, within her narrow limits, a dense and somewhat fluctuating population, a large portion of which is concentrated within the limits of a single town, she is specially interested to uphold her Constitution, with its existing provisions for the distribution and exercise of political power, and to maintain the wholesome vigor of the laws, to the end that the lives, liberties and happiness of all her people may be secure.

Resolved, That the prosperity of those various important interests and employments which now afford such ample remuneration to the skill and industry of all classes of people in Rhode Island, depends essentially upon the confidence which is felt, at home and abroad, in the stability of our present Constitution; in our continued disposition and ability to uphold an enlightened and upright administration of civil and criminal justice, and in our unalterable determination to continue the political power of the State in the hands of men, who, on all occasions, have proved themselves true to the conservative cause—in the hour of peril intrepidly defending it—in the hour of peace scorning every temptation either to desert or to betray it.

Resolved, That whereas the administration of justice is the chief end of government, and whereas every citizen of Rhode Island who values his constitutional rights has a deep interest in the permanence of our judicial system, as at present organized and administered, it becomes every such citizen to beware how, either by his neutrality or his succor, he gives to our political opponents the power to prostrate those upright judges whom they were never able to intimidate, and whom they have never ceased to defame.

Resolved, That the tone of violence and acrimony which, in primary meetings, in legislative halls, and through the press, our political opponents still maintain towards the conservative party, should be regarded as a sure indication that, however they may change their tactics, they have changed neither their temper nor their purposes; and that, in the event of their success on the first Wednesday in April next, they will commence a series of measures which will work the ultimate overthrow of our present Constitution, and perpetuate, in hands which have been uplifted to break down all social order, the political power of the State.

Resolved, That no sophistry can expel from our minds the conviction, that the principles for which we have so long done battle are still in danger; that these principles immeasurably transcend in importance to this State and nation any of the fugitive triumphs of policy, or the shifting interests of party; and that the great issue to be decided at the election in April next is, whether the people shall intrust political power to those who are in favor of maintaining the existing order of things in Rhode Island, or to those who will seize the first opportunity to overthrow it.

Resolved, That, in our judgment, the election to be held on the first Wednesday in April next ought to summon to most vigorous and united efforts every man who values the great principles of constitutional freedom, inasmuch as upon the issues of that election the fate of those principles is believed to be suspended.

Resolved, That Byron Diman, of Bristol, be nominated a candidate for the office of Governor, and that Isaac P. Hazard, of South Kingstown, be nominated a candidate for the office of Lieutenant Governor; and that we cordially recommend these gentlemen to the support of the electors of Rhode Island, at the election to be held in this State on the first Wednesday in April next.

Resolved, That with equal cordiality we recommend to the electors of Rhode Island the re-election of Henry Bowen, the present Secretary of State, of Joseph M. Blake, the present Attorney General, and of Stephen Cahoone, the present General Treasurer.

Resolved, That, while we rest the claims of these candidates to general confidence, most of all upon their eminent ability to discharge the duties of the offices to which they are respectively nominated, and to maintain the rights and the honor of the State, we recognize, as fresh titles to popular favor in this State, their known attachment to a conservative administration of the general government, and to that protective policy which so deeply affects the labor of the country, and which, let it not be forgotten, our political opponents are striving to overthrow.

Resolved, That we exhort the friends of a protective tariff and of conservative government not to sacrifice realities to names—not to value men more than they value principles—above all, not to blind themselves to the disastrous consequences of lending, directly or indirectly, to our political opponents, any aid which may enable them to achieve even a partial triumph.

Resolved, finally, that, about to engage as we are, with our old enemy upon the old grounds, we are cheered by the responsive sympathies of the conservative men of all parties throughout the Union, and that we are determined to meet him as we have met him in times past, with the tranquil confidence that a battle which is waged in defence of true men and right principles, cannot be lost!

Resolved, That we will put forth our most zealous efforts to secure the election, by a triumphant majority, of the candidates nominated to compose the Rhode Island Prox.

REPORT

ADOPTED IN THE GENERAL ASSEMBLY, JUNE SESSION, 1845.

THE Select Committee to whom, at the session of this General Assembly in May last, were referred sundry resolutions of the State of Maine, respectfully report,

That they have attended to the duty confided to them by the House of Representatives, and that they recommend the adoption, by this Legislature, of the accompanying preamble and resolutions. Your committee have deemed it quite unnecessary to attempt any vindication of the Supreme Court of this State from the grossly calumnious charge of the Legislature of Maine; but in the progress of their inquiry upon the matter committed to them, they have had recourse to sundry opinions delivered by said court during the trial of Thomas W. Dorr, for the crime of treason. These opinions, copies of which are herewith submitted to the House, are not wanted to place far beyond the reach of injury, by the poor demagogues of the day, the reputation of that court for learning and impartiality, and for the intrepid discharge of high constitutional functions, at a season of popular excitement unparalleled in the previous history of this State.

Whereas the Legislature of the State of Maine has passed sundry resolutions reprobating, in terms the most offensive, the government and people of Rhode Island, for their efforts, during the late insurrection, to maintain the supremacy of the Constitution and the laws, protesting against the imprisonment of Thomas W. Dorr, as "unjust, illegal, malignant, and tyrannical," and invoking the interposition of the General Government to procure "his immediate release;" and whereas these Resolutions have been transmitted to His Excellency the Governor, and by him have been communicated to this General Assembly, therefore

Resolved, That this General Assembly does hereby enter its solemn Protest against the interference of the State of Maine with the internal affairs of Rhode Island, as an interference which can plead no constitutional sanction, and which deserves to be rebuked as a dangerous invasion of the most sacred rights of the Government and people of this State.

Resolved, That the obligations of truth, no less than that comity which it is the duty and the interest of sister States to preserve in their intercourse with one another, ought to have restrained the Legislature of Maine from levelling coarse denunciations against the Supreme Court of Rhode Island, for the manner in which, at a memorable crisis in our history, that upright and enlightened tribunal discharged an imperative but painful duty.

Resolved, That the attempt, on the part of the Legislature of Maine, to intermeddle with the administration of criminal justice in this State; to invoke the popular vengeance against the ministers of the law, and to render odious its righteous penalties, furnishes a melancholy illustration of that mad party spirit, which, to accomplish a temporary and selfish purpose, tramples upon all the safeguards of constitutional freedom, and disregards the most impressive admonitions of history.

Resolved, That the appeal which the State of Maine has seen fit to make to the General Government, in behalf of Thomas W. Dorr, by whatsoever plausibilities of language that appeal is sought to be sheltered from reprobation, can be regarded in no other light than as an alarming attempt to concentrate upon a small but sovereign State, the vindictive energies of a government, armed with the whole power of the Union.

Resolved, That the State of Rhode Island, while she faithfully discharges all her Constitutional obligations to her sister States, and to the Government of the Union, can never so far forget her past history—her early struggles in the cause of religious freedom—her toils, and sufferings, and sacrifices, in the war of the Revolution, and her jealous determination, at all times, to secure to the people of Rhode Island the exclusive right to manage their own affairs in their own way, as not to repel, with indignation, every attempt, come when and whence it may, to deprive her of those constitutional safeguards which the fathers of the Republic established, in order to preserve the peace, union and liberty of these confederate States.

Resolved, That his Excellency the Governor be requested to cause a copy of these Resolutions to be transmitted to the President of the United States, to the Governors of the several States, and to each of our Senators and Representatives in Congress.

A DISCOURSE

IN COMMEMORATION OF

THE LIFE AND SERVICES

OF

WILLIAM G. GODDARD, LL. D.,

DELIVERED AT THE REQUEST OF THE FACULTY,

IN THE CHAPEL OF BROWN UNIVERSITY,

MARCH 12, 1846.

BY FRANCIS WAYLAND, D.D., LL.D.,
PRESIDENT OF BROWN UNIVERSITY.

DISCOURSE.*

I RISE, this afternoon, to perform one of the saddest duties to which I have ever been appointed. My colleagues have requested me to deliver a discourse, in commemoration of the life and services of one very dear to us all, but, if I may be allowed to say it, specially dear to me. He was the first officer of this institution with whom I had the honor to become intimately acquainted. Our friendship has continued, without interruption, from its commencement until the day of his death. During the whole period, within which we were associated as officers of instruction, we were in the habit of meeting daily, and many times in the day. The various plans, which, since my knowledge of this institution, have been laid, for the improvement either of its course of education or manner of discipline, have all received the benefit of his wise and thoughtful consideration. The principles on which they depended were developed by mature reflection, and the measures which resulted from them were carried into effect by our mutual labor. And when, in consequence of ill health, he retired from the duties of that chair which he had filled with equal honor to himself and advantage to the University, we all considered his separation from us to be rather in form than in fact. We unanimously invited him to be present at all the meetings of the faculty, assured that his interest remained unabated in the prosperity

* We give the larger portion of this Discourse, as an interesting and fitting termination of these volumes.—*Ed.*

of the institution, on whose reputation his labors had conferred so much additional lustre. We felt that his talents, and labor and fame, were as much as ever the property of the University. For myself, I may truly say, that, for nearly twenty years, I have taken but few important steps the reasons for which I have not discussed in the freest manner with him, and in which, also, I have not been in a great degree either guided by his counsel or encouraged by his approbation. There is scarcely a topic in religion or morals, in literature or social law, on which either of us has reflected, that we have not discussed together. Neither of us was fond of disputation, but both of us loved exceedingly the honest and unstudied interchange of opinions. It so happened, that our views upon most of these subjects were, in an unusual degree, identical. The very last conversation in which we were engaged related to those great truths revealed to us by Jesus Christ, in the belief and love of which all his spiritual disciples are one. A few days previously, I had requested his advice upon a matter of some importance to myself, some of the facts in connection with which I then submitted to him, while the farther consideration of them we deferred to another occasion.

In a moment, and all this interchange of thought, and all this concert of action, have ceased, and, so far as this world is concerned, have ceased forever; and while the living image of our associate and friend seems yet to walk among us, in all its freshness, I am requested to commemorate the services of the dead. You will all, I very well know, sympathize in the emotions with which I undertake this solemn service. It is almost as if he of whom I speak were in the midst of us, to be the hearer of his own eulogy. We have been so long accustomed to his presence on every collegiate occasion; so few days have elapsed since he occupied his wonted seat in this sanctuary; that we are unable to realize the melancholy truth, that we shall see his face no more. And besides this, the deep feeling, which pervades every bosom, leads us instinctively to distrust our own judgments. On the one hand, we fear lest the full utterance of our sentiments should seem like panegyric; and on the other, we are troubled lest eulogy, too much chastened, should do injustice to the memory of the dead. And yet more is this embarrassment increased by the recollection, that the occasion necessarily awakens, of those inimitable delineations of character, which so often flowed from the pen of him whose sudden departure we are now assembled to deplore.

Under such circumstances, I know full well that I must fail to present the portraiture of the late Professor Goddard, as he now reveals himself to your memory, and stands embodied before you in your conceptions. I know, however, that I am surrounded by his friends, who will readily complete the sketch, no matter how imperfectly executed, which I may offer for their contemplation. I know, moreover, that you will all appreciate the difficulty of my task, and pardon the indistinctness with which my thoughts reflect the beauty and the symmetry which you have so frequently admired in the honored and beloved original.

* * * * * * * *

In college, Mr. Goddard was remarkable for his love of classical literature, but especially for his skill in English composition. For the Latin language he retained his fondness through life. At our regular term examinations he frequently discovered a most delicate appreciation of the beauties of Horace, and detected, with instinctive tact, any deviation, in translation, from the meaning of that author, who was his special favorite of all the poets of antiquity. For the mathematics he had no fondness, but rather, I think, a positive dislike. This did not, however, arise from any failure to appreciate the value of the exact sciences, either as an instrument of discovery, or a means of intellectual discipline. He was by far too wise a man to undervalue a branch of knowledge in which it was not his good fortune to excel. I apprehend the fact to have been, that in consequence of some mental idiosyncrasy, he was unable to compare the mathematical relations. He has frequently observed to me, that geometrical figures never conveyed any idea whatever to his mind ; and still more, that he could form no conception of the interior of a building, from any plan of it that was ever presented to him. I have mentioned this little peculiarity, because, as it seems to me, every original feature of minds of a high order deserves to be particularly recorded.

* * * * * * * *

Mr. Goddard had formed very just conceptions of the moral and social obligations devolving upon the conductor of a public press. He believed it to be the duty of an editor not merely to abstain from outraging the moral sentiment of a community; but, still more, by holding forth examples of pre-eminent virtue, and inculcating the principles of everlasting truth, to elevate the standard of public manners, and teach the wayward passions of men obedience to conscience and reverence for law. He believed, that by constantly presenting to the eye of the public, images of beauty, the press might exert a powerful influence in forming and purifying the national taste. He thought it incumbent upon him, on all suitable occasions, to arouse the spirit of the State, to combine together good men of every name, in the promotion of every enterprise by which the ignorant might be enlightened, or the vicious reclaimed; by which vice might be deprived of its means of fascination, or virtue endowed with new elements of attractiveness; by which the intelligent and the wealthy might be excited to beneficence, and the poor and uncultivated be encouraged to self dependence.

In conformity with these views, the press, under Mr. Goddard's superintendence, was ever conducted. The columns of his paper were always enriched with the choicest gems of English literature. His editorial writings were remarkable for the high spirit of individual and social morality, which breathed in every line, no less than for the pure, yet sparkling and epigrammatic English, in which every sentiment was clothed. Though he espoused with youthful ardor the political opinions he ever afterwards professed, yet, as I have been informed, he never in a single instance forfeited the personal respect of his warmest opponents. To every judicious effort to promote the welfare of his fellow citizens, he gave his willing and earnest support; and some of our most valuable public charities owe their origin to the editorial labors of this portion of his life. Of this number is the Providence Institution for Savings, the objects and advantages of which he first laid before the public in this city, and to the establishment of which, his efforts contributed more than those of any other individual.

While Mr. Goddard was employed in conducting a public press, he yet found leisure for extensive and varied literary acquisitions. The remark made respecting the late Lord Holland, that "you could never call upon him without finding him with a good book in his hand," might, with singular truth, be applied to our lamented friend. Though emphatically a literary man, there are few men whose reading was selected with more severe discrimination. For ordinary fictitious literature he seemed to me to have scarcely any fondness. The lighter forms of poetry had but few attractions for him, while of the gems of verse he was a fervent yet discriminating admirer. He most delighted in the classical English authors on religion and morals, on general politics, social order, and the progress of civilization. On the latter subject he was accustomed to reflect with enthusiastic pleasure. Among political authors, I think that his favorites were Burke, Hamilton, and Madison. His chosen divines were Barrow, South, and, in later years, Whately. Of the metaphysicians he preferred Dugald Stewart, and derived great pleasure from contemplating the vigorous thought, and tracing the masterly generalizations of that accomplished philosopher. At the time of his death he had commenced the reperusal of Lord Bacon.

* * * * * * * *

It became the duty of Professor Goddard, immediately after his appointment,* to conduct the studies of the senior and junior classes in moral and intellectual philosophy, and in some portions of our usual course in rhetoric and belles lettres. For the former of these departments he felt that he had no peculiar aptitude, and very soon, by mutual arrangement with his colleagues, he was relieved from the labor of this branch of instruction. He was thus enabled, with great advantage to the University, to devote himself to those studies to which he was ardently attached, and for the instruction in which he possessed peculiar and acknowledged ability. It hence happened, that during the greater portion of his connexion with the University, he gave instruction mainly in the principles and practice of rhetoric, the evidences of natural and revealed religion, and the constitution of the United States.

The success, to which Professor Goddard attained as an instructor, did not result from rigid analysis of a science, or minute and critical acquaintance with an author. His mind rather reluctated from those forms of intellectual labor on which such knowledge depends. He excelled rather in unfolding such general views as illustrate the prin-

* The Professorship of Moral and Intellectual Philosophy in Brown University.—*Ed.*

ciples of a science, by tracing their effects upon the condition and changes of society, and by exhibiting their influence in the formation of individual character. He labored to enkindle in the bosoms of his pupils a love of truth, of virtue, and of goodness. He was also pre-eminently successful in creating in the minds of the undergraduates a just appreciation of the beauties of English composition. His correction of their class papers was elaborate almost beyond belief; so that every dissertation, as it was returned from his hands, presented to the student a model of finished excellence with which his own rude and imperfect attempt could be plainly and visibly contrasted. Whatever be the improvements which our undergraduates of the present day may have made upon the attainments of their predecessors, let it never be forgotten that this improvement was commenced, and for many years carried forward, solely by the labors of Professor Goddard. Perhaps, however, in no department did he so much excel, as in his prelections upon the constitution of the United States. With the history of the formation and adoption of this instrument he was minutely familiar. Each one of its provisions had, at various times, been the object of his careful examination and laborious thought. His pursuits had rendered him accurately acquainted with the political history of our country, from the adoption of the constitution to the present moment. His recitations thus assumed the form of an extemporaneous lecture, or commentary upon the text, in which a marvellous acuteness of discrimination was illustrated by the results of extensive and accurate research; while both were rendered attractive by rare felicity of diction, and the charms of an animating eloquence.

When Professor Goddard relinquished his connexion with the duties of instruction, he by no means intended to wear out his life in indolent leisure. He encouraged himself in the hope that he should be enabled to devote himself to the composition of some work of permanent value to the cause of morals and good learning. The opportunity, however, was never granted to him. His fellow citizens, as though it were a matter of course, seemed to expect his assistance, whenever any good design required that an appeal should be made to the public, or whenever the management of an important trust demanded the skill of a cultivated intellect, and the impulses of a benevolent heart. There is scarcely an institution among us, devoted to the promotion of general intelligence, or the relief of suffering humanity, which has not enjoyed the benefit of his counsel and advice. * * * * It is, moreover, deserving of special remark, that he always refused to hold an office as a matter of form. It was his rule to decline an appointment, whenever he found himself unable to perform the duties which it imposed. I presume that his associates in the several boards of which he was a member will testify, that they rarely embarked in any important undertaking without seeking his advice; and that, from the advice which he gave, they very rarely found it wise to dissent. Such was certainly the case in all the instances in which I had the honor to be associated with him.

* * * * * * * *

If I have correctly estimated the character of Mr. Goddard, its most remarkable feature was delicate and discriminating sensibility. I have already remarked that he possessed neither taste for the mathematics nor aptitude for tracing the relations which they discover. This observation might with truth be more widely extended. He had no fondness for abstruse reasoning of any kind; and I presume rarely followed the successive steps of an intricate metaphysical argument to its conclusion. But it was equally true, that by a sort of instinctive sensibility, he seemed to arrive at precisely the same result which minds differently endowed apprehended only by the slower process of ratiocination. His critical perceptions were more exquisitely delicate than those of any man whom I have ever known. His friends never cased to admire his unsurpassed power of discerning the most microscopic want of adjustment between a thought and the language in which it was clothed. He saw intuitively the precise form which an idea should assume, in any portion of a discourse, and the very tinge and junction of words which would most clearly and happily develop it. He frequently could not give the reason for his choice of an expression, and he might sometimes ask the reason of others; but the reason always existed, and bore testimony to the accuracy of his judgment. Hence the study of the science of rhetoric produced but little effect upon his style. It seemed not to teach him to write, in any respect, either with greater accuracy or elegance, but only to give him firmer confidence in the decisions of his own sensibility. He learned from the study of rules to write with less anxiety, and to correct with greater rapidity, inasmuch as he thus knew that he was right, when before he had only felt it.

The oration which he pronounced before the Rhode Island Society of the Phi Beta Kappa, at the commencement in 1836, furnishes a favorable specimen of Mr. Goddard's literary ability. The reader will immediately perceive that no labor has been expended, either upon the general plan of the discourse, or upon the separate arrangement of its parts. The course of thought is not confined by the pressure of any general and all pervading idea. The several paragraphs, like handfuls of pearls, are rather grouped together by feeling, than marshalled by the understanding. And yet it seems to me that few tracts are to be found in our language, in which so much manly and "large round about sense" is clothed in a style at once so negatively faultless, and so positively beautiful. Every sentence seems a maxim of unquestioned authority ; and yet there is nothing either startling, labored, or out of keeping. It all seems the spontaneous effusion of a mind of which such things were the ordinary product. I have read this discourse lately, and was struck with the similarity of its thoughts to those of Lord Bacon's Essays, a book which I had but just laid down ; while the exquisite finish of the style sometimes reminded me of the vigor of Johnson, and, at others, of the splendor of Burke.

But it was not in the department of literature alone, that this delicate and discriminating sensibility predominated. The same peculiarity might be observed in Mr. Goddard's studies, when they partook of a severer character. He was, as I have said, a diligent and profound thinker upon all subjects of religion, morals, general politics, and human civilization. But even here, he appeared to arrive at the result in which he rested, rather by a moral intuition than by any process of reasoning. His spiritual discernment seemed to indicate to him what the law should be, and, upon investigation, he found his opinions confirmed by the highest authorities. Hence, in his reading, he rather sought for the truths which our great teachers have discovered, than for the processes by which their discoveries have been effected. To theological controversy he paid but little attention ; but of sermons, or other religious writings, which lay bare the human heart, or reveal to us the precepts of duty, or present the scriptural motives for well doing, he was a diligent and earnest student. * * * *

As a specimen of Mr. Goddard's habits of thought on the grave questions of social right, I would refer to his discourse on the occasion of the change of the civil government of Rhode Island. In this address, after glancing at some of the more prominent facts in the early history of his native State, he proceeds to explain and illustrate the principles involved in the constitution under which she was henceforth to be governed. His style becomes at once grave, simple and earnest; abjuring all ornament, and appealing directly to the reason and the conscience of his hearers. The whole discourse, replete with the most important maxims on the science of government, clearly indicates a mind in which a knowledge of the theoretical and practical is happily blended; a mind accustomed to contemplate truth, both in its widest generalizations, and in its minutest applications; that could discover the unchangeable principles on which social law is founded, and at the same time acknowledge the modifications which that law must assume, when it is brought into contact with the passions and selfishness of our imperfect nature. I do not remember any commentary upon the nature of our free institutions, which, in so few pages, contains so much that is of permanent value.

It might seem the result of a studied reserve, were I, in this connexion, to make no reference to the writings of Professor Goddard, during the political agitations of this State, a few years since. It is well known, that as soon as any serious danger to our institutions was apprehended, he stood forth the unwavering advocate of justice and truth, of liberty and law. His essays for the daily press, during this period alone, would fill a moderately sized volume. Day after day, he explained to his fellow citizens the principles of rational liberty; he laid bare, with a masterly hand, the distinction between liberty and licentiousness; and when at last the crisis arrived—with an eloquence that fired the soul of every true hearted man, he urged us all to unite in defence of that heritage of civil and religious liberty which God had bestowed upon our fathers. In this cause he labored on, amid sickness and infirmity, through good report and through evil report, until the efforts of patriotism were crowned with triumphant success. And he labored, as every one of you knows, from the pure love of right. All the ends he aimed at, were his country's, his God's, and truth's. He desired nothing, either for himself or his friends, which he did not equally desire for the humblest citizen amongst us. He labored to sustain a government which should secure to every citizen the rights conferred upon him by his Creator, and which should guard those rights with equal vigilance, both against the oppressions of the many, and the tyranny of the few. It is in no small degree owing to his labors, that the success of these principles in our little State may be attributed.

The manners of Professor Goddard were courteous and refined. His personal habits, without being painfully exact, were scrupulously neat, and in perfect harmony with the character of a literary citizen. His conversation, sometimes playful, never frivolous, was always instructive, and at times singularly forcible, captivating and eloquent. His tastes were simple and easily gratified ; and I think that he preferred a book in his study, or a conversation at the fireside with a friend, to any form of more exciting and outdoor enjoyment. He was, both from nature and principle, eminently, but with discrimination, charitable. To the judiciously benevolent institutions of our city he was a liberal and frequently an unsolicited contributor. Nor did his charity exhaust itself in making others the almoners of his bounty. He sought out the poor and infirm, the disconsolate and the forgotten, and specially those who in age were suffering from the mutability of fortune ; and, while he relieved their wants by pecuniary aid, soothed their sorrows by his sympathy, and animated their hopes by his cheerful encouragement. One of his last visits, only a few days before his death, was made to an aged widow, who has since followed him into eternity, to whom he communicated alms ; while, as she herself told me, he consoled her sinking spirit by the humble piety of his conversation.

The religious opinions of Professor Goddard were those of the divines of the English reformation. He believed most fully in those doctrines which teach the moral corruption of the human heart, the necessity of the influences of the Spirit to our moral transformation, and that our only hope of salvation rests upon the atonement by Jesus Christ. He was conscientiously attached to the Episcopal Church ; but, making a wise distinction between spiritual religion and the various modes in which it may be manifested, he loved true piety, wherever he discovered it, " with a pure heart fervently." He carried into daily practice the sentiment which he uttered only a few days before his death. " The longer I live," said he, " the more dearly do I prize being a Christian ; and the more signally unimportant seem to me the differences by which true Christians are separated from each other." I do not remember to have known a person who, with so ardent an attachment to the truths which he believed, combined so fervent and comprehensive a charity for all that loved the Lord Jesus Christ in sincerity.

* * * * * * * *

From this time, his friends observed that religious truth was gradually obtaining a more controlling influence over his opinions, his affections and his practice. As he grew older, his love for piety, simple, obscure, unadorned piety, became more ardent and reverential. His charity was more earnestly directed to the spiritual wants of man. His conversation, especially of late years, seemed to me to move in constant parallelism with religious ideas ; and it spontaneously turned towards them, as if his mind dwelt in habitual contemplation of the vanities of time and the realities of eternity. He became more prompt in avowing his religious sentiments on all occasions, and in their relation to every subject. His reading became more exclusively religious. Sermons of the English divines, especially those of a practical character, became his constant study. He more frequently made religion the subject of conversation in the domestic circle. On Sunday, the day before his death—his family having been detained from public worship in consequence of a violent storm—after family prayers were concluded, he read for their instruction some interesting passages which he had selected from the sermons of Archbishop Whately ; interspersing them with impressive remarks of his own, on the subject of the importance of religion. These were his dying counsel. It is by such precept and example that " he being dead, yet speaketh."

* * * * * * * *

The death of such a man, at any time, is always felt to be an irreparable loss. I, however, remember no instance, since my residence in this city, in which this sentiment has been so deep and universal.

The sphere of eminent usefulness, which Mr. Goddard filled, was peculiar and uncommon. It rarely happens that affluence is granted to men of so varied learning, so cultivated taste, and so elevated moral principle. Still more rarely are these advantages combined with the leisure and the will to use them with disinterested zeal for the benefit of the community. But it was while thus employing his varied talents, that Mr. Goddard was so suddenly removed from the midst of us. At no time of his life had his influence been so widely acknowledged and so beneficially felt, as at the very moment when it all ceased forever. When we think of the intellectual and moral light which he diffused, of the trusts which he held, of the courses of thought and action which he directed, we seem to look in vain, I do not say for the man, but for the men, by whom his place is to be supplied. Our only hope is in God. "Help, Lord, for the godly man ceaseth ; for the faithful fail from among the children of men."

But what, let us inquire, are the sentiments which it is becoming in us to cherish on the occasion of so mournful a bereavement? In the first place, let us bow in submission before the face of our Father in heaven, who, in inscrutable wisdom, and yet parental goodness, has inflicted upon us this sore calamity. He endowed our departed associate and friend with the intellectual powers and the spiritual graces which made him, for many years, a burning and a shining light. At the time which he had chosen, and in the manner that He himself had selected, He has removed him from this world of trial, and raised him to his sanctuary of rest. "The Lord gave, and the Lord hath taken away ; blessed be the name of the Lord."

A high minded and public spirited citizen, who has, for many years, devoted a large portion of his eminent ability to the promotion of every design by which we and our children could be rendered wiser and better, has ceased from his labors. A more solemn and urgent responsibility is devolved upon every one of us who remains. Let us cheerfully assume those public burdens which our associate and friend laid down only with his life. Let his example teach us that the cause of truth and justice, the cause of liberty and law, of charity and piety, are well worth living for. Highly as we esteem the various gifts of our lamented friend, it is for the use which he made of them, that now we chiefly venerate him. Though we may not be able to supply the loss which the community has sustained in this calamity, yet if each one of us labors with an honest and earnest spirit, our humble offering will be acceptable to the Master.

And lastly, how solemn an admonition does this event bring home to the bosom of each one of us. We are most impressively reminded, that no pre-eminence of usefulness, no ties of affection, no gifts of nature or advantages of fortune, can offer to us the least assurance of length of days. The sun of Mr. Goddard went down while it was yet high noon. Nay more ; how solemnly are we taught, that every one of us is walking upon the borders of eternity, and that the very next footstep may be planted within the limits of the world unseen. We commence a week in health, but where shall we be at the end of it? We rise in the morning, buoyant with hope, but God only knows who of us shall look upon the shadows of the evening. We arrange our plans for the hour, but ere they are half completed, we are numbered with the dead. We commence a conversation, but while the words yet linger on our lips, we are in eternity. Can there be one among us who mistakes the lesson which these conditions of our being are intended to inculcate? They surely teach us that we can only live wisely as we live in habitual preparation for death. Let us then give all diligence to make our calling and election sure, for so an entrance shall be abundantly ministered to us, into the everlasting kingdom of our Lord and Saviour Jesus Christ.

THE END.

www.ingramcontent.com/pod-product-compliance
Lightning Source LLC
LaVergne TN
LVHW021301110826
845150LV00003B/448

* 9 7 8 1 4 2 5 5 6 0 4 6 1 *